Keywords for Disability Studies

D0907445

Keywords for Disability Studies

Edited by Rachel Adams, Benjamin Reiss, and David Serlin

NEW YORK UNIVERSITY PRESS New York *and* London

NEW YORK UNIVERSITY PRESS
New York and London
www.nyupress.org

© 2015 by New York University
All rights reserved

References to Internet websites (URLs) were accurate at the time
of writing. Neither the author nor New York University Press is
responsible for URLs that may have expired or changed since the
manuscript was prepared.

Library of Congress Cataloging-in-Publication Data
Keywords for disability studies / edited by Rachel Adams,
Benjamin Reiss, and David Serlin.
pages cm   Includes bibliographical references.
ISBN 978-1-4798-4115-8 (cl: alk. paper) —
ISBN 978-1-4798-3952-0 (pb: alk. paper)
1. Sociology of disability. 2. Disability studies.
I. Adams, Rachel, 1968– II. Reiss, Benjamin. III. Serlin, David.
HV1568.K49 2015
 305.9'08—dc23   2015002092

New York University Press books are printed on acid-free paper, and
their binding materials are chosen for strength and durability. We
strive to use environmentally responsible suppliers and materials to
the greatest extent possible in publishing our books.

Manufactured in the United States of America

10 9 8 7 6 5 4 3 2 1

Also available as an ebook

In memory of Adrienne Asch (1946–2013) and Tobin Siebers (1953–2015)

Contents

Introduction Rachel Adams, Benjamin Reiss, and
    David Serlin 1

1 Disability Rachel Adams, Benjamin Reiss, and
    David Serlin 5

2 Ability Fiona Kumari Campbell 12

3 Access Bess Williamson 14

4 Accident Jill C. Anderson 17

5 Accommodation Elizabeth F. Emens 18

6 Activism Denise M. Nepveux 21

7 Aesthetics Michael Davidson 26

8 Affect Lisa Cartwright 30

9 Aging Kathleen Woodward 33

10 Blindness D. A. Caeton 34

11 Citizenship Allison Carey 37

12 Cognition Ralph James Savarese 40

13 Communication Carol Padden 43

14 Crip Victoria Ann Lewis 46

15 Deafness Douglas C. Baynton 48

16 Deformity Helen Deutsch 52

17 Dependency Eva Feder Kittay 54

18 Design Christina Cogdell 59

19 Diversity Lennard J. Davis 61

20 Education Margaret Price 64

21 Embodiment Abby Wilkerson 67

22 Ethics Rebecca Garden 70

23 Eugenics Rosemarie Garland-Thomson 74

24 Euthanasia Harold Braswell 79

25 Family Faye Ginsburg and Rayna Rapp 81

26 Fat Kathleen LeBesco 84

27 Freak Leonard Cassuto 85

28 Gender Kim Q. Hall 89

29 Genetics David Wasserman 92

30 History Susan Burch and Kim E. Nielsen 95

31 Human D. Christopher Gabbard 98

32 Identity Julia Miele Rodas 103

33 Illness G. Thomas Couser 105

34 Impairment Michael Ralph 107

35 Institutions Licia Carlson 109

36 Invisibility Susannah B. Mintz 113

37 Madness Sander L. Gilman 114

38 Medicalization Sayantani DasGupta 120

39 Minority Jeffrey A. Brune 122

40 Modernity Janet Lyon 124

41 Narrative David Mitchell and Sharon Snyder 126

42 Normal Tanya Titchkosky 130

43 Pain Martha Stoddard Holmes 133

44 Passing Ellen Samuels 135

45 Performance Petra Kuppers 137

46 Prosthetics Katherine Ott 140

47 Queer Tim Dean 143

48 Race Nirmala Erevelles 145

49 Rehabilitation Gary L. Albrecht 148

50 Representation Michael Bérubé 151

51 Reproduction Adrienne Asch 155

52 Rights Maya Sabatello 158

53 Senses Kathryn Linn Geurts 161

54 Sex Margrit Shildrick 164

55 Sexuality Robert McRuer 167

56 Space Rob Imrie 170

57 Stigma Heather Love 173

58 Technology Mara Mills 176

59 Trauma James Berger 180

60 Visuality Georgina Kleege 182

61 Vulnerability Ani B. Satz 185

62 Work Sarah F. Rose 187

Works Cited 191

About the Contributors 215

Introduction

Rachel Adams, Benjamin Reiss, and David Serlin

In 2005, Gallaudet University—the premier research and teaching institution for Deaf and hearing-impaired students in the world—began designing a new building, the James Lee Sorenson Sign Language and Communication Center. Instead of simply commissioning an architectural firm to do its work, administrators invited faculty and graduate students in the social sciences and humanities to help design the building, which was eventually completed in 2008. To this end, Dirksen Bauman, a Gallaudet faculty member who studies linguistics and critical theory, held a graduate seminar in 2006 entitled "Deaf Space."

Bauman worked with students to think about the political and experiential ramifications of Deaf space rather than simply giving administrators or architects of the new building a laundry list of "needs" that could be incorporated or added on to an existing design. Would a building designed entirely by and for Deaf people look, feel, and be experienced differently from other buildings—and, if so, how might it work? Alternately, because Deaf people already live in the world without specially designated spaces, could there be something fundamentally problematic and even essentialist about creating an identifiable "Deaf" space? Does designing a building for "the Deaf" undermine the goals of the universal design movement, which is intended to provide accommodations and access for all users rather than for a singular population?

By the end of the course, the students had raised these and dozens of other questions about how to construct a new vocabulary for thinking in concrete and useful ways about this seemingly abstract thing called "Deaf space" (Byrd 2013). Such a project, ultimately, was intended to question the results-oriented goals of architects for whom compliance with the law—via the installation of a wheelchair ramp or a chirping elevator—often represents the full extent of their critical vocabulary concerning disability. And many of the lessons learned could be applied to other projects beyond Deaf space.

The questions undergirding Bauman's course have much in common with the project we have undertaken in *Keywords for Disability Studies*. At the most basic level, both are collaborative, interdisciplinary attempts to revisit the categories, concepts, and assumptions that define disability and the experiences of people with disabilities more broadly. Both also question fundamental terms and concepts that may seem settled in order to understand how and why they were used in the first place and how they might evolve in the future. But while Bauman taught his students to think about architecture as a kind of language that resonates with Deaf linguistics and experience, the medium for this book is language itself.

As the editors of this book, we worked with a group of more than sixty authors to produce a collection of essays that explore the conceptual vocabulary of disability studies as it is understood, practiced, and taught in the early twenty-first century. For newcomers seeking a very basic definition of this area of scholarship and research, disability studies explores the social, cultural, and political dimensions of the concept of disability and what it means to be disabled. It grew out of a quest for civil rights, equal access, and inclusion for people with disabilities that began in the 1960s and 1970s. This "first wave" of disability rights activism sought to affirm basic human rights of dignity and respect by tying them to concrete goals like access to education, employment, housing, and transportation. Such activism has led to landmark legislation such as the passage of Section 504 of the Rehabilitation Act of 1973 in the United States, the Declaration of Rights of Disabled Persons in the United Kingdom (1975), the Americans with Disabilities Act (1990), the British Disability Discrimination Act (1995), and the United Nations Convention on the Rights of Persons with Disabilities (2008). Spurred by these developments in the legal and political realm, scholars in the humanities and social sciences began to conceive of disability as a form of embodied difference that could be studied similarly to race, gender, ethnicity, and sexuality. They viewed disability not just as a legal designation but as an arena of social contestation and an identity category in need of analysis across time, geographies, and cultures.

One core tenet shared by scholars of disability studies is opposition to the "medical model" of disability, which sees disability in terms of individual impairments to be corrected and cured. As an alternative, scholars and activists define disability as a social and environmental phenomenon. In the "social model," one is disabled because of the body's interaction with the social and physical environment rather than because of individual pathology or "lack." The social model asks how certain kinds of bodies are disabled by physical barriers,

social stigma, lack of legal recognition, adaptive technologies, and economic resources.

Many of our entries—especially Sayantani Das-Gupta's "Medicalization"—expand upon and even challenge this neat distinction between medical and social models. Not all aspects of disability, they argue, can be attributed to social or environmental barriers. Yet despite its limitations, the social model represented a crucial stage in the development of disability theory and activism because it links disability to other major vectors of identity, such as race, class, gender, sexuality, and citizenship, that are understood as socially produced. As a result, some disability studies scholars have shown how identifying the body as *either* disabled *or* nondisabled is fundamental to many forms of social discrimination based on supposedly innate and "natural" forms of bodily difference. For example, hierarchies of race, class, gender, and sexuality proceed in large part from a set of presumptions about "normal" mental and physical capacities. Indeed, the study of disability often shows quite vividly how the dialectical concepts of "normal" and "abnormal" are responsible for structuring basic aspects of society and culture. The study of disability thus engages some of the most pressing debates of our time: about the beginning and end of life; about prenatal genetic testing, abortion, sterilization, euthanasia, and eugenics; about accommodation in public schools, public transportation, housing, and the workplace; about technologies intended to correct and "cure" the nonnormative bodies of infants, children, and adults; and about the complex relationships between wartime injuries, post-traumatic stress, health care, and citizenship. These questions could not be more relevant, given that people with disabilities are the world's largest minority group and that anyone can potentially become disabled.

Over the past three decades, disability studies as an interdisciplinary field has had far-reaching effects, as evident in the formation of interest groups and caucuses within major scholarly organizations, in the growth of disability studies programs at the undergraduate and graduate levels, and in the publication of countless books, articles, and course offerings. As it has moved out of the humanities and social sciences, disability studies has also begun to challenge core assumptions of professional arenas like law, medicine, and economics, which in some ways mark a return to the field's origins among disability rights activists. Yet despite all of this intellectual and institutional activity, the field is at something of an intellectual crossroads. As it has moved into new terrains, disability has become a remarkably heterogeneous category. The diversity of work currently conducted under the rubric of disability represents varied and sometimes competing interests, and different areas of scholarship have not always been in productive dialogue with each other.

Keywords for Disability Studies is intended both to highlight debates and differences within disability studies and to provide a conceptual architecture that holds together the field's sometimes fractious components. Our goal in designing this volume was not simply to define terms but to use them to delineate the field's debates and problems, while also establishing their importance to many other areas of inquiry across the disciplines. We modeled our project after Raymond Williams's classic book *Keywords: A Vocabulary of Culture and Society*, originally published in 1976. Williams viewed his book as "a way of recording, investigating and presenting problems of meaning in the area in which the meanings of *culture* and *society* have formed." While he offered a certain amount of etymology, unlike a dictionary, his book never attempted to get at "original" or "true" meanings. Meaning for Williams was always in flux, always subject to the forces of history. Shifts in linguistic connotation and usage did not simply *reflect* historical change;

rather, given that "some important social and historical processes occur *within* language" (Williams 1985, 15, 22), linguistic shifts might in fact also drive social change.

Like Williams's project, *Keywords for Disability Studies* seeks to view concepts and the language that gives them shape as matters of social contestation and historical change. This framework is especially appropriate in a field that was born out of an attempt to widen the meanings of disability beyond the scope of the medical practitioners who so often laid claim to them. Despite the field's resistance to the medical model, we have avoided a reflexive opposition to approaches grounded in the health sciences and policy out of a belief that it is time to move past such easy oppositions. Recognizing that there is considerable potential for dialogue and collaboration, we hope that readers in those fields will use our book much as the architects at Gallaudet used the ideas of Bauman and his students: as a way to expand their understanding, rather than as a challenge to their expertise.

Many of our entries cover topics that are largely internal to the field of disability studies, such as "Prosthesis," "Deafness," "Crip," and "Deformity." However, we have avoided specialized terms like "neurodiversity," "dismodernism," or "posthumanism," which have gained currency within the field but might be perplexing to newcomers. Such vocabulary is clearly explained where appropriate within the essays themselves. Given the collective and heterogeneous nature of our subject, we have also tried to avoid terms that isolate specific disabilities wherever possible. Sander L. Gilman's entry on "Madness," for instance, references a range of experiences that are now medicalized as mental illnesses or neurological conditions, but it also suggests the elasticity and porousness of stigmatized realms of psychological, emotional, or developmental difference. Gilman shows how homosexuality and epilepsy were once considered forms of madness, and how new categories of psychiatric or mental disability may be called into question as soon as they are identified. The term also suggests intersections with various forms of embodied difference, such as the fact that in the nineteenth century the Deaf were often presumed to be mentally deficient.

We have also included many entries that one might find in a book addressing keywords in the humanities and social sciences more broadly. This is because we believe that a consideration of disability has the potential to transform the critical terms from nearly any discipline. Indeed our book shares several terms with Williams's, including "Aesthetics," "Communication," "Family," "History," "Institution," "Technology," and "Work." However, it would be misleading to suggest that these entries are conceived according to a neat logic of inside/outside the field. Douglas Baynton's entry on "Deafness," for instance, is in direct conversation with Carol Padden's entry on "Communication," which analyzes sign language as one of many alternatives to speech that people who are considered disabled have found or invented in order to communicate linguistically. Entries on topics like "Race" and "Sexuality" show how such concepts have functioned to construct particular disabilities, how imputed disability has been used to stigmatize racial groups and sexual practices, and how historical processes of colonialism, eugenics, and the ascription of sexual "abnormality" have linked ideologies of race and sexuality to disability. Because our book is conceptually driven rather than encyclopedic, it does not offer entries on important historical or social phenomena like universal design or the Americans with Disabilities Act of 1990. Instead, such topics are threaded through relevant entries like "Access," "Space," "Rights," and "Design." By working conceptually rather than categorically, we hope to combat the isolation and

stigmatization so often associated with disability, instead bringing it into a wider realm of social, cultural, and political circulation.

One important difference between our volume and Raymond Williams's foundational work is that each essay is written by a different author—a format that follows Bruce Burgett and Glenn Hendler's *Keywords for American Cultural Studies* (2007). While we encouraged our authors to write broadly for readers from a range of backgrounds, we also wanted them to acknowledge how their respective disciplinary positions informed their critical perspectives on their chosen topics. One of the key assumptions of disability studies is that there is no neutral or objective position from which to regard the human body and its differences, just as the "normal" body is a fantasy belied by the wondrous spectrum of human difference. In fact, disability was often seen as incommensurate with objectivity, which was reserved for those who decided the fate of the disabled. Therefore, a stance of neutrality or false objectivity would only replicate the conception of disability as a problem to be solved or banished, rather than as a perspective worth considering. And yet we also wanted the book to be more than a collection of individual voices. During the process of writing and editing their entries, contributors were encouraged to share drafts via an editorial wiki web page. Our editorial interventions were often more extensive than usual, with the goal of creating complementarity among entries while maintaining the particularities of a given author's voice and perspective. We see this collaborative spirit as a means of combating some of the divisions that have emerged within the field and within the broader community of people with disabilities.

The capaciousness of our terms stems from our belief that disability studies opens a new lens on the full spectrum of human activity. How cultures draw the line between "normal" and "abnormal" has broad consequences for everyone. Accordingly, we hope that the volume will help crystallize debates and problems internal to disability studies, as well as establish their importance to many other areas of inquiry across the disciplines. And we hope that, as with Bauman's project, the structure we have created together will inspire others not only to build new structures but also to think more creatively and more inclusively about the people who will interact with them.

Editors' note: In the time since we first drafted this introduction, the field of disability studies suffered two great losses with the deaths of Adrienne Asch in November 2013 and Tobin Siebers in January 2015. Their work left its mark on so many of the ideas expressed in this volume. If we imagine disability studies as a collaborative design, its structure was immeasurably enhanced by the wisdom, courage, and insight of Adrienne and Tobin. We hope that our future work in the field will be a tribute to their legacies, and we dedicate this volume to their memory.

1

Disability

Rachel Adams, Benjamin Reiss, and David Serlin

In the 2009 documentary film *Monica and David*, Monica, a woman with Down syndrome, is asked to define the word "handicap." She responds, "When someone is in a wheelchair," adding that the term may also apply to people who cannot hear or walk. "It's a sickness," she concludes. When presented with the same question, her husband, David (who also has Down syndrome), says he does not have a handicap. Asked if he has Down syndrome, he answers, "Sometimes." In this brief exchange, Monica and David exemplify the challenges of defining disability as a coherent condition or category of identity. Yet David's assertion that "sometimes" he has Down syndrome suggests that he understands a central tenet of disability studies: that disability is produced as much by environmental and social factors as it is by bodily conditions. While Down syndrome may prevent David from driving a car or managing his own finances, for example, his genetic condition is not a defining feature of his home and family life.

These insights by Monica and David remind us that the meanings we attribute to disability are shifting, elusive, and sometimes contradictory. Disability encompasses a broad range of bodily, cognitive, and sensory differences and capacities. It is more fluid than most other forms of identity in that it can potentially happen to anyone at any time, giving rise to the insiders' acronym for the nondisabled, TAB (for temporarily able-bodied). As David suggests, disability can be situational;

everyone becomes disabled

it can also <u>wax and wane</u> within any particular body. Disability brings together people who may not agree on a common definition or on how the category applies to themselves and others. Yet those same definitional challenges are precisely what make disability such a rich concept for scholars, activists, and artists. Because "disability" is this volume's organizing term, it is important that we explore how it became attached to such diverse experiences and meanings, and produced such a wide range of social, political, and personal consequences.

The word "disability" has been part of the English language since at least the sixteenth century. According to the *Oxford English Dictionary*, the current sense of "a physical or mental condition that limits a person's movements, senses, or activities [or] the fact or state of having such a condition" was first used in 1547. But the term also covered a broad range of "inabilities" or "incapacities" that included inability to pay a debt or to worship God with a full heart, while some conditions currently treated as disabilities were not regarded as such. Some—like autism or chronic fatigue syndrome—had not been discovered (or invented, depending on one's perspective); others, like chronic pain or various disfigurements, were simply considered inevitable facts of life.

For much of its historical run, "disability" has brushed up against words like "infirmity" and "affliction," both of which held connotations usually ascribed to disability today, as well as phenomena like poverty, ugliness, weakness, sickness, or simply subjection to an unfortunate experience (Baynton 2011). Disability also shared ground with the early modern term "monstrosity" and the classical-era term "deformity"—the former having supernatural overtones and the latter representing a falling away from godliness into a particular kind of moral and physical ugliness (see Helen Deutsch's entry on "Deformity" in this volume). By contrast, the word "cripple," which derives from the idea of one who creeps, represented an attempt to characterize various physical impairments that impeded mobility. Similarly, "invalid" was an early medical shading of a broad range of infirmities resulting from injury or illness.

It was in the nineteenth century that disability became firmly linked, through the discourses of statistics, medicine, and law, to words such as "deviance," "abnormality," and "disorder." Lennard Davis (1995) argues that during this time the modern conception of disability emerged as a by-product of the concept of normalcy. Earlier human bodies were measured against idealized and often spiritual standards of perfection and ability that no earthly individual could match. With the development of statistical science and the bell curve, human ability came to be understood as a continuum, with disability and disabled people occupying the extreme and inferior end of the spectrum.

During the late nineteenth and early twentieth centuries, protecting the normal from the abnormal became a broad medical and social imperative undertaken in the name of progress. Vocabulary terms associated with disability reflect these shifts. Just as the eugenics movement attempted to rid the world of many disabilities through sterilization and segregation, disability terminology emphasized backwardness, atavism, and interruption: people with disabilities were said to be "slow," "retarded," or in a state of "arrested development." Hereditary explanations stressed the degenerate threat disability posed to the white race. People with intellectual disabilities (classified under the broad term "feebleminded"), in particular, were said both to exemplify the debilitating effects of modernity and to represent instances of exceptional regression (Valente 2013). At a time when the industrialized world prized speed and efficiency, the temporal lag associated with disability amounted to being "handicapped in the race for life."

Many of these terms remain as residual signifiers for disability in contemporary society. As Douglas Baynton argues, by the early twentieth century, one had only to say "handicapped" to indicate disability, while in France the primary translation for disabled remains *handicappé* (Baynton 2011; Stiker 1999). On a global scale, however, "disability" has now become the preferred term. It began its ascent in the United States during the Civil War, when "disability" measured one's capacity to serve in the armed forces or one's right to compensation from injuries incurred in military service. As the welfare state developed in the twentieth century, the term came to incorporate chronic illnesses and conditions of impairment that impeded one's ability to work (Linker 2013, 503–505). But paradoxically, as "disability" has muscled out older competitors, it has also grown more ambiguous and unstable in its meanings. This is because as the term has expanded to include new categories of experience and perception as well as phenomena once labeled by other terms, those meanings have simultaneously been challenged by scholars and activists (Kudlick 2003).

Although now someone with a visual impairment may recognize "disability" as the structure that links her to a wheelchair user or a person labeled as autistic, it thickens our sense of such alliances to study how people in earlier times understood—or, alternately, did not understand—their connections to each other. The historical record provides glimmers of cross-disability awareness but also of obstacles to finding common ground or shared values. A 1641 law in colonial Massachusetts, for instance, provided exemptions from public service for settlers who could claim "greatness of age, defect in mind, failing of senses, or impotency of Limbs" (Nielsen 2012, 21). Such unfitness for work ultimately led to organized systems of charity—and, by the nineteenth century, institutional quarantining and attempts at medical "correction" for people with a wide range of impairments.

Paradoxically, such quarantining sometimes promoted social cohesiveness within and even across different types of institutions. In nineteenth-century asylums and other specialized "total institutions," blind and deaf people, people defined as mentally ill or deficient, and other disabled people often came into contact with large numbers of other members of their group for the first time. Thomas Gallaudet, the cofounder of the American Asylum for the Deaf, characterized the typical student at his school as "among his countrymen, for [they] use his native language." Occasionally, this fellow feeling extended across categories of impairment. A patient-run literary journal published in a public nineteenth-century asylum for the insane, for example, records a visit by students from a school for the blind; another article in the journal speculates on the increased susceptibility of blind and deaf people to mental illness, showing an appreciation for the shared social vulnerability of all of these groups. Such institutional dispatches suggest a flickering awareness of institutionalization as the grounds for identifying a common set of experiences. Such connections were the grounds for political activism. Early American deaf-rights activist John Jacobus Flournoy, for instance, was one of the first to use the word "disability" in relation to deafness among a range of physical and mental differences when he wrote in 1855: "The old cry about the incapacity of men's minds from physical disabilities, I think it were time, now in this intelligent age, to *explode*!" (Krentz 2007, 155).

As with segregation, colonialism, and apartheid, shared experiences of social separation and political disenfranchisement ultimately galvanized many people with disabilities and their supporters toward a common purpose. However, before the 1960s, politicized protests against the oppressive features of institutionalization and discrimination were scattered and generally did not speak for broad categories of disability. For instance, in the United States during the 1930s, when the League of the Physically Handicapped decried the Works Progress Administration's policy of failing to employ people with physical disabilities, it did not include people with mental or developmental disabilities in its list of those who had suffered discrimination (Nielsen 2012, 132). And when the league approached leaders of the Deaf community to make common cause, they were rebuffed on the grounds that the Deaf were not disabled or unemployable (Burch 2002, 126). (Today, the Deaf community tends to regard deafness as a culture; whether it is also a "disability" is a contentious point.)

In this volume, the entry by Denise Nepveux on "Activism" tells how isolated protest movements cohered into the broad disability rights movement, which, by the late 1960s, was agitating for inclusion and access on many fronts, and which strengthened the sense of disability as a positive identity category rather than a stigmatized designation of inferiority or lack. Political organizing within the incipient disability rights movements of the 1960s and 1970s attempted to shift "disability" from an exclusively medical concern to a broadly social one, an effort that eventually won important battles. Major legislation and policy initiatives in the United States and worldwide reflect this shift, with profound implications for governments, businesses, and citizens—disabled and nondisabled alike. For example, the first two definitional prongs of the Americans with Disabilities Act (ADA; 1990; amended 2008) locate the meanings of disability within the body: "A physical or mental impairment that substantially limits one or more major life activities of such individual; a record of such an impairment." These definitions are surprisingly similar to the long-standing dictionary definition

of "a physical or mental condition that limits a person's movements, senses, or activities" or "the fact or state of having such a condition." However, the third definitional prong of the ADA, which adds "being regarded as having such an impairment," put perceptions and social attitudes squarely in focus (Emens 2013). The UN Convention on the Rights of Persons with Disabilities (2008) goes even further in defining disability's social dimensions. Disability, according to the convention, "results from the interaction between persons with impairments and attitudinal and environmental barriers that hinders their full and effective participation in society on an equal basis with others." Perhaps most expansively, the vision of accessibility propounded by Ron Mace and the universal design movement since the late 1980s was born out of a belief that particular physical or sensory differences only become disabling when the environment creates barriers to access. These recent developments all emphasize meanings of "disability" that are external to the body, encompassing systems of social organization, institutional practices, and environmental structures. Disability studies scholars refer to this approach as the "social model," which challenges the medical understanding of disability as located exclusively in an individual body, requiring treatment, correction, or cure (Shakespeare 2006b).

Although the social model predominates, in much recent scholarship, disability refers to a subjective state, the condition not only of *identifying* as disabled but also of perceiving the world through a particular kind of lens. As Sharon Snyder and David Mitchell (2006) note, narratives of disability history that focus on legislative triumphs, social inclusion, and the breakdown of stigma risk losing sight of the distinct, individual, and subjective experiences that make up disability's history. Disability subjectivity, they argue, does not come either from bodily impairment or from the socially constructed world outside; instead, they argue for a "cultural model" of disability that explores the disabled body's interface with the environments in which the body is situated. While it may be true that to lose one's leg, or to be visually impaired, or to have a chronic illness in the twenty-first-century United States is incommensurate with what those impairments or conditions meant in eighteenth-century Europe or ancient Egypt, disability itself always begins and ends with the subjective impressions of the individual who experiences the world through her body. Despite the lingering popular sense that disability represents deficiency or defect of body or mind, the cultural (or, alternately, biocultural) model of disability as a relationship between body and society is gaining increasing legitimacy in law, policy, and the social environment worldwide.

Part of the transformation of "disability" from stigma and object of medical correction to source of knowledge reflects this new attention to inwardness. Disability becomes a mode of situating one's understanding of self rather than a marker of isolation, what the late disability historian Paul Longmore (2003, 246) called the "social death" sometimes experienced by people with disabilities. Whereas too often the experience of disability entered the historical record only through the words of those who tried to cure, tame, correct, or end it, disability studies scholarship is now focused on building—as well as excavating from the past—a rich and self-conscious record of the perspectives of disabled people themselves. Memoirs, films, journals, performance spaces, and online social networks promoting what is sometimes defiantly referred to as "crip" culture are all regular features of this new landscape of disability; meanwhile, academic conferences, journals, and degree programs have made disability studies a prominent force on many campuses. Such new developments parallel feminist epistemologies—including

what used to be called "women's way of knowing"—as well as postcolonial and critical race theorists' critiques of hybrid identities and psychic displacements, and queer theory's blending of social analysis and subjective expression. Each of these political-cultural-academic movements began with a first wave of identifying and resisting oppressive structures, which was followed by attempts to recover a cultural heritage as a backdrop for individual and collective expression in the present.

Intersectional modes of analysis point to the common interests, struggles, and pleasures these movements can promote. Deaf artist and activist Joseph Grigely (2005) works in this vein when he speaks of a "proactive" disability studies: one that is focused not just on attaining rights and accommodations for people with disabilities but also on developing dynamic, interactive, and collaborative projects that challenge the tyranny of "normal" in all areas of social and political life. To this end, the subjective experiences of people on the wrong side of "normal" can be used, in the words of the Dutch educational philosopher Pieter Verstraete, "to expose the self to the other," rather than merely to "reduce the other to the self" (2007, 63). Vivid examples of this work of mutual "beholding" rather than objectifying "staring" can be found in Rosemarie Garland-Thomson's (2009) discussion of disabled artists who turn the unwanted attention of others into the subject of their own work.

While some scholars and activists claim or assume that disability is a category that cuts across cultures, others have noted that disability studies rests on assumptions derived from and specific to the Western world, and that its histories and archives continue to have a strongly Euro-American orientation. Disability scholarship and activism in Europe and North America have long sought independence for people with disabilities, a demand that arose in reaction against being treated as passive, voiceless, and dependent. In the 1970s, the independent living movement was born in Berkeley, California, and quickly took hold throughout the United States and Europe, with the goal of achieving greater autonomy and inclusion by providing people with disabilities with personal assistants and adaptive technology. However, as Eva Kittay (1999) has noted, largely overlooked in the quest for autonomy is the fact that the independence of disabled consumers is contingent on the labor of personal assistants who are almost always immigrant women, sometimes with unclaimed disabilities of their own. "Independence" and "autonomy" are concepts that are deeply embedded in the Western philosophical and political traditions of liberalism and are not universally desirable goals in all cultural contexts (Nussbaum 2006).

The global ambitions of the universal design movement, which upholds the worthy goal of a barrier-free environment, also sometimes founder on the realities of global inequalities: this approach relies on architectural innovations and the use of technologies that may be too costly to be realistically implemented in many areas of the developing world. Moreover, the technologies that enable people with disabilities in the Western world are often manufactured by workers who cannot afford to use them, and who may themselves be disabled. For example, the smartphones and computer tablets that give students with disabilities in the West tools to learn alongside their nondisabled peers and that supply increasingly ingenious apps to allow blind, deaf, and mobility-impaired people to navigate their environments are likely to have been assembled under harsh and potentially disabling conditions in China. Michael Davidson argues that a more global disability studies must refine the concept of universal design to account for variations in resources and cultural values. In this way, disability studies can prompt us to consider

how "many aspects of modernity are founded upon unequal valuation of some bodies over others" (Davidson 2008, 171).

Some scholars have offered the concept of "debility" as a supplement to disability, which they see as entangled with Western ideas about individuality, autonomy, and bodily integrity. The dictionary meaning of "debility" overlaps with "disability": it is the "condition of being weak or feeble," in either physical or mental capacity. But a secondary meaning—"political, social, or pecuniary weakness"—makes it useful for scholars attuned to populations made vulnerable by political and economic forces globally: For instance, Jasbir Puar uses the term to signify an "aggregate" condition in which some bodies worldwide are made to pay for "progress" that others enjoy. "Debility," she writes, "is profitable for capitalism" (2012, 153). Like Puar, Julie Livingston uses the term "debility" to supplement the concept of disability and its attendant assumptions about a liberal, rights-based understanding of personhood. In Botswana, for instance, AIDS activists have sought the equal participation of persons with disabilities in the public sphere, but Livingston shows how the liberal model of personhood at the heart of their activism is undercut by Botswanan notions of moral sensibility, which include both an ethos of communal care and an intense aversion to certain types of bodily disfigurement or unruliness. While Euro-American versions of disability rights focus on "enabling persons to participate equally in rational-critical discourse in the public sphere regardless of the vagaries of any individual's particular bodily state," such goals collide with cultural systems that shape the circulation of bodies, emotions, and values differently (Livingston 2008, 289).

Obscuring these different constructions of disability and debility, human rights activists and policy makers around the world tend to idealize Western—and often specifically American—attitudes and practices concerning disability, while labeling those in the "developing" world as "backward" (Kim 2011). Certainly, the United States has done much to bring forward disability rights as a concept to be emulated elsewhere, but the social situation of people with disabilities is by no means uniformly secure. In the United States, health and physical beauty are marketed as commodities more aggressively than in any other culture. The rhetoric of the beauty, fashion, diet, and fitness industries, illustrated by the allure of cosmetic surgery, equates falling from these ideals with moral failure. So, too, in times of economic scarcity in the United States and other market-driven societies, people with disabilities and their supporters are often seen as a burden on public resources. Programs for education, transportation, and public services for people with disabilities are often the first to be cut by budget-conscious politicians. A backlash against civil rights accomplishments blames disability legislation for, in effect, "crippling" the economy. And many who claim accommodation or compensation under the law are viewed with suspicion of malingering—especially those whose disabilities are not immediately visible. The mapping of the human genome has also had ambivalent consequences for disability. Research that promises to cure or prevent disease and to bring new understanding of human character and potential often does little more than succeed in producing a new class of people whose genes tell us that they may someday become disabled by diseases like breast cancer, cystic fibrosis, or Huntington's disease—thereby creating a pervasive anxiety about disability as a future risk. So, too, new technologies for prenatal testing seek to eliminate some types of genetic disability through the termination of fetuses. Such tests further stigmatize genetic conditions by making them seem like preventable mistakes. And in the eyes of many disability rights advocates, they augur a new era of eugenics, in which disability is eradicated before it comes into the world.

Our understanding of disability is enhanced by awareness of the term's complex genealogy, as well as by the enormously varied experiences of embodiment across cultures and socioeconomic locations. If history is any indication, the meanings of disability and the words we use to describe its various manifestations will no doubt undergo profound shifts as a category of identity; a social, legal, and medical designation; and an embodied condition. As a way of perceiving the world, it will help us to understand—and to influence—the way that future takes shape.

2

Ability

Fiona Kumari Campbell

Disability studies scholars recognize that the term "ability" shapes our understanding of what it means to have a livable life. Although it is often treated as the antithesis of "disability," ability has been used as a conceptual sledgehammer to determine and shape social status and caste on both an individual and a collective level. In effect, "ability" employs a judgment that establishes standards of body and mind that are actionable in the present or in projected futures.

Today ability and disability are conjoined as a simple binary. In the past, the relationship was more fluid. Aristotle viewed "monstrous" bodies as natural *anomalia* (Greek for "irregularities" or "unevenness"), that represented different types of "ability." Since the late 1300s, "ability" has signified a quality in a person that makes an action possible; in turn, someone who can execute an expected range of actions is able-bodied, a person who can lead a potentially worthy life. "Ability" in the Anglo-Norman world was a legal term tied to capacity to enter into contracts or inherit property. Hence "ability" began to point to an exclusionary matrix in which it belonged only to propertied men. The rest of the population (nonpropertied men, women, people of color, beggars, and changelings) had an invalidated and disabled status to a greater or lesser extent.

Not all representations of the "abnormal" or disabled body are so infused with negativity. In "On the Refusal of a Pension to the Invalid" (402 BCE), Lysias, a speechwriter and Attic orator, argues that physical impairment did not in itself class an individual as *ordunatous*, or unable (Lysias 1957). It is not surprising, then, to read that Marcus Sergius, a Roman general during the Second Punic War (218 BC), returned to battle as a double amputee, fitted with iron hands. Throughout much of premodern Western history, ability and able-bodiedness referred to a person's role in the community rather than to a fixed condition.

The term began to refer to a type of person in the late fourteenth and early fifteenth centuries, when "abled," as an adjective, described a "capable, vigorous and thriving" person or object (the *Oxford English Dictionary* cites the example of an *abled tree*). Still, it had no coupling with an assumed opposite of a disabled subject. That coupling began to emerge during the age of enlightenment (ca. 1700–1800), which ushered in a new spirit of optimism about the rationality and autonomy of man and afforded the attributes of will, authority, and reason new prominence. Such sentiments held out promises of the perfectibility of the body. Mental or bodily ambiguity came to represent anomaly and aberrance, and the dis/abled person was identified with failure, hopelessness, and the necessity for surveillance, repair, and management.

Science and philosophy during this period were concerned with working out which beings were "human" and which were not. Discussions like those of John Locke in *An Essay Concerning Human Understanding* (1955) were related to physical and intellectual capacity, animality, and species ranking (including a discussion of rankings according to notions of gendered characteristics associated with a hierarchy of abilities). In 1727, "able-bodiedness" referred to those who are "fit, and healthy, physically robust, free from physical disability" (*OED*) and thus fit for the army or work. It is not surprising, then, that there was a shift from able-bodiedness as an attribute of character to able-bodied people as an identifiable class capable of selling their labor. The next 200 years saw the expansion of global markets and colonization, the Industrial Revolution, and the rise of manufacturing. Governments, medicine, and the sciences of population management and economic efficiency were concerned with harnessing labor and regulating idleness and capacity. The human body was marked and measured in terms of efficiency. An example of this typification of abledness occurs in Fritz Lang's film *Metropolis* (1927), in which the cyborg Maria becomes a corporeal clock mediating time, pace, and the quality of well-being itself. Ability came into sharp focus during World War I, when bodies were destroyed and maimed on an unprecedented scale (Carden-Coyne 2009). Whereas "ability" had been partially defined by fitness for armed service, now modern war was transforming the meaning of ability, with a new connotation of lives that needed to be rebuilt.

By the second half of the twentieth century, the contested meanings of ability took on new urgency as society contended with the need to reintegrate large numbers of disabled soldiers and to create a productive workforce. From the twentieth century onward, distinctions between abled and disabled bodies have been linked to notions of the productive body within particularized economies, such as agriculture, manufacturing, or technology. In the 1980s, the term "abled" was decisively coupled with disability in a negative relation. According to the *Oxford English Dictionary*, the term now meant a "full range of ordinary physical or mental abilities"—in other words, not disabled. Whatever new meanings attach themselves to "ability," the concept is now firmly paired with an opposite that is deficient, provisional, and nonproductive. The contemporary world is witnessing a new "abled," signifying an unencumbered worker who is a master of economic possibility and available for further corporeal enhancement as the economy or workplace requires it.

Increasingly, ability and abledness assume an independent, unencumbered self. This hyperproductive, gender-neutral employee has replaced the gendered rhetoric of the main (male) breadwinner. This worker is the übercitizen who is mobile, portable, available 24/7, 365 days a year. People with disabilities rarely fit this mold, as they may have bodily or cognitive needs that cannot be mechanically routinized or normalized. Meanwhile, developments in surgery, pharmacology, and other consumer technologies are rapidly transforming notions of "normal ability." Today's "normals" may end up being tomorrow's abnormals, and what seem like hyperabilities can become standards of future ability. Throughout these changes, what Robert McRuer calls "compulsory able-bodiedness" persists. For McRuer (2002), able-bodiedness, like heterosexuality, is an ideal that is constantly to be striven for but impossible to achieve. More broadly, "ableism" refers to the ideological hypervaluation of ableness and the ways in which such norms of abled and disabled identity are given force in law, social policy, and cultural values. Such norms shape and are shaped by claims about the impaired, non-abled body's legitimacy or fraudulency (for instance, in claiming social benefits), legal protections, and social status.

A disability studies critique of "ableism" takes the focus away from disability as a self-contained designation. Ableism denotes the ideology of a healthy body, a normal mind, appropriate speed of thought, and acceptable expressions of emotion. Key to a system of ableism are two elements: the concept of the normative (and the normal individual); and the enforcement of a divide between a "perfected" or developed humanity and the aberrant, unthinkable, underdeveloped, and therefore not really human. The notion of ableism is useful for thinking not just about disability but also about other forms of difference that result in marginality or disadvantage. Interrogating ableism means thinking about what being abled means today in different contexts, and how those meanings intersect with other ideologies of body and mind such as race, gender, sexuality, and coloniality.

3

Access
Bess Williamson

The noun form of the word "access"—meaning "the power, opportunity, permission, or right to come near or into contact with someone or something"—first appears in published texts in English as early as the 1300s. It has been used to characterize the relationship between the disabled body and the physical environment since the middle to late twentieth century. More specifically, it refers to efforts—most prominent in the United States—to reform architecture and technology to address diverse human abilities.

In its most literal form, "access" describes the ability to enter into, move about within, and operate the facilities of a site, and is associated with architectural features and technologies, including wheelchair ramps, widened toilet stalls, lever-shaped door-handles, Braille lettering, and closed-caption video. Figuratively, however, it can suggest a much broader set of meanings linked to a more inclusive society with greater opportunities for social and political participation. Given these technical and metaphoric interpretations, the push for access has yielded some contradictory results. While improved public infrastructure has been a major success of the disability rights movement of the last half century, technical change does not necessarily translate to the deeper goals of openness, inclusion, or opportunity. In fact, in some cases technical compliance can replace and even obscure the movement's broader goals of social, political, and economic integration.

Though "access" and its corresponding adjective "accessible" have distinct meanings in relation to disability rights, both terms convey broader arguments about rights and opportunities. Discussions of social and economic justice often refer to an ideal of access: "access to jobs," "access to housing," "access to health care," and so forth. These expressions convey the importance of recognizing external barriers that prevent disenfranchised persons from gaining access to resources. They exist in contrast to debates over inherent or biological inequality, such as sexist or racist arguments that view women or nonwhites as physically and mentally incapable of equality. A focus on access is a shift away from attempts to fix or cure disability on an individual level, and toward an emphasis on social or legal interventions. Access implies social potential not dependent on correcting the disabled body, but instead made possible through institutional and material change.

In the history of disability rights, the concept of access linked disabled people's material struggles with other civil rights causes. In debates over the U.S. Civil Rights Act of 1964, President Lyndon B. Johnson declared that "all members of the public should have equal access to facilities open to the public" (tenBroek 1966, 849). The disability rights movement emerging in the same period interpreted this language for its own cause. The legal scholar Jacobus tenBroek wrote in 1966 of a "right to be in the world," rooting the rights of the disabled in core principles of citizenship. Barriers to free mobility, tenBroek wrote, violated a "basic sense of the right not to be unjustly or causelessly confined," a right he traced to the Magna Carta and major Western constitutions (848). Legal advocates Marcia and Robert Burgdorf similarly linked "access" to core American rights. "Free access to public buildings and transportation systems," they wrote in 1975, was a key component of disabled persons' rights to equal protection under the law (Burgdorf and Burgdorf 1975, 855–866).

Access holds the curious distinction of being seemingly easy to define and comprehend but difficult to create. As early as the 1960s, for instance, building codes in the United States defined access in clear, specific terms. Local regulations mandated such features as wheelchair ramps of less than 1:12-foot rise; doorways of at least thirty-two inches in width; and grab bars in toilets (*American National Standard Specifications* 1961). The difference between the ideal and the real, however, often proved significant. The first national law that addressed access, the Architectural Barriers Act of 1968, required that architects design or renovate buildings purchased and leased by the U.S. government "to insure whenever possible that physically handicapped persons will have ready access to, and use of, such buildings." The phrase "ready access" suggested the possibility of a site's availability to any given disabled person. In reality, the components of legal compliance were often piecemeal and failed to add up to overall improvements in usability. Early regulations applied to specific buildings, so a courthouse or hospital might be technically accessible, but without sidewalks, curb cuts, or usable public transportation, actually getting to and into the building remained difficult for many. Even in the present day, compliance with the law can be fleeting when building tenants or managers leave elevators or ramps locked, allow accessible features to fall into disrepair, or obstruct spaces and passageways.

The demand for improved access follows the logic of the "social model" of disability, which shifts attention from the impaired body to the surrounding environment. Early advocates used the term in a very literal way, evaluating sites and products in terms of their function for people with physical and sensory limitations. The category "accessible" delineated the reachable from the unreachable: ramped entrances and clear pathways from stairs and cramped passages. In technical guides and government policies, "accessibility" and "usability" often appeared with the related term "barrier-free." If "access" was the outcome of diligent planning, "barriers" were the existing conditions, often characterized as needless or "thoughtless" obstacles. These analyses of "access" and "barriers" pointed to problems and solutions in the physical environment, not fixes for the individual body. Disability activists likewise point to architecture as an external barrier that prevents people otherwise willing and able to participate in society from doing so. In a 1990 transportation protest, a black disabled man taped a sign to the back of his wheelchair stating, "I can't even get to the back of the bus," linking lack of physical access to the history of racial segregation ("Civil Rights, Disability Rights"). In a number of protest actions—including the occasion of a 2004 Supreme Court ruling on disability discrimination lawsuits—wheelchair users left their chairs at the bases of grand staircases to government buildings and crawled up the steps (Shapiro 2004). These actions perform the argument that it is not physical inability but the absence of architectural accommodation that keeps people with disabilities excluded from the public spaces identified with civic life.

While the most extensive requirements for access mandated by law originated in the United States, access has proven a powerful concept in disability rights discourse on a global level. Architectural access is now included in civil rights legislation in Australia, the United Kingdom, South Africa, and the province of Ontario, Canada. The UN Convention on the Rights of Persons with Disabilities, ratified in 2008, requires signatory nations to provide "reasonable accommodation," including technological and architectural access.

Still, the American model of building ramps, expanding doorways, and installing technologies to improve access does not translate immediately to global contexts, particularly for areas without extensive paved roads or centralized transit infrastructure. Furthermore, in a human rights framework accessibility can describe not only the concerns of those considered "disabled" but also those of women, children, migrants, and others who experience constraints of movement and expression (Meekosha and Dowse 1998). Attention to access, therefore, proves most powerful when interpreted broadly, bringing notice to mobility and communication barriers that may not be as tangible as sidewalk curbs and public announcement systems.

Mandates requiring accessibility remain fraught even after decades of legal battles and new legislation governing arenas ranging from private offices to online shopping. At stake in these debates are core American and Western values of individual and social citizenship. Rights discourse often centers on the value of "independence"—that is, being able to move about and do things on one's own, without the assistance of doctors, nurses, parents, or charitable strangers. The ideal of an accessible public environment follows this conception of citizenship as autonomy. And yet, in practice, claiming the rights to autonomy through accommodation can be interpreted as a neoliberal critique of the welfare state, which fosters the notion that individualism and independence are prerequisites for good citizenship. The late historian Paul Longmore details the "ceremonies of social degradation" that accompany social welfare and other entitlements, inculcated in endless paperwork and bureaucratized misdirection (2003, 240). Access, too, comes with its rituals of shame, as in cases when disabled citizens must pursue legal action to demand usable workplaces or accommodating schedules, leading to frequent accusations of fraud, moneygrubbing, or selfishness. Lennard Davis describes the sense, rooted in modern psychological theory, of disability as a form of narcissism, and the demands for accommodation as "self-concern rather than a societal concern" (2002, 124).

In recent years, some scholars and activists have questioned the centrality of access to the mainstream disability rights agenda. While the principle of access seems infinitely expandable, it often narrows to discussions of architectural details such as stairs and ramps. The International Symbol of Access—the white figure in a wheelchair against a blue background—seems to exemplify the problem of representing disability solely in terms of mobility impairments, and access solely in terms of wheelchair access. It centers the ideal of access on overcoming the realities of barriers. While few would question the importance of establishing and enforcing architectural access, these laws also show some of the limitations of technological interventions in a neoliberal political economy. Access can represent a form of outsourcing, as authorities implement technological change without addressing underlying prejudices and misconceptions. As disability advocates shift their rhetoric, they urge a look "beyond ramps" and emphasize those disabilities (including psychological and intellectual concerns) for which accommodation may not take tangible form (Russell 1998).

4

Accident

Jill C. Anderson

"What happened to you?" The question from strangers to people with visible impairments suggests a popular fixation on *accident* as a cause of disability. It is as though the most important thing to know about disability is its genesis (Linton 2005)—perhaps due to anxiety about whether or not "it could happen to me." This narrow meaning of accident as unforeseen bodily trauma (as compared with illness, congenital trait, or aging) highlights one axis of diversity that both enriches and complicates disability studies.

In a broader and more abstract sense, disability is often relegated to the category of *accident*: unintentional, undesirable, marginal deviations from idealized norms of fitness. It was not always so. Early conceptions of disability imbued certain bodily differences with religious meaning, as coded signs of divine intent or judgment. In step with the values of industrialization, nonconforming bodies later came to be equated with accident, much like assembly-line cast-offs. The spectacle of the mid-nineteenth-century to twentieth-century carnival freak show as a refuge for extraordinary bodies exemplified such marginalization, with its sharp boundary between the onlooker and the "freak of nature" (*lusus naturae*) on display. In spite of the freak show's demise, disability is still often associated with defect as opposed to natural variation. Through the scientific lens, the disabled body becomes a medicalized anomaly—"I'm 'that accident,'" (Wade 2010)—which, if not prevented from existing in the first place (as through eugenic interventions), can at best aspire to "overcome" environmental barriers or be rehabilitated to normalcy. Disability studies rejects the assumptions that underlie this view, foremost by affirmatively valuing disability experience and accepting bodily diversity not as accidental but as essential to society.

Like impairment itself, the disadvantage associated with disability is often glossed as unfortunate happenstance. In one of the field's key contributions to cultural studies, the "social model" locates disability not in individual bodies themselves but in their interactions with social practices, institutions, and the built environment. If disability is the disadvantage that flows from these structural relationships (a view that some criticize as erasing aspects of disability experience such as pain and loss of function), then neither disability nor any presumed standard of fitness is truly accidental.

What of specific instances of bias that exclude people with disabilities: Is disability discrimination haphazard and marginal (contrasted as it often is to race and gender discrimination) or systematic and central to social hierarchy? Who or what is responsible (in a causative sense) for it, and who if anyone should be held responsible (in a legal sense) for remedying it? As with gender and race, whether people can claim a legal remedy for disability discrimination depends in part on whether unequal treatment was inadvertent or intentional. Recent studies of unconscious bias, however, show that this dichotomy overlooks predictable patterns of prejudice that further complicate disability discrimination law.

In sum, though *accident* has no specialized meaning within disability discourse, its multiple senses illuminate the contributions of disability studies as well as tensions within the field.

5

Accommodation
Elizabeth F. Emens

"Accommodation" bears a more positive and powerful meaning in disability discourse than its roots in race and religion contexts would predict. In the history of U.S. racial politics, "accommodation" is a dirty word. Accounts of the early civil rights era used accommodation to refer to a brand of gradualism and compromise associated with Booker T. Washington—a position famously critiqued as "conciliation" by W. E. B. DuBois (1994; Myrdal 1944). But while racial accommodation evokes blacks accommodating the white majority, in the disability context accommodation means changing society in response to disability. The term has thus shifted radically in both sense and reference.

Accommodation gained prominence as a keyword in disability politics and theory through legal discourse. In the United States, which introduced the term into our legal vocabulary, accommodation began as a right of religious employees under the Civil Rights Act of 1964. Almost immediately, however, courts emptied it of force. Most important, in *Hardison* (1977) the Supreme Court has interpreted accommodation not to include religious "preferences," such as avoiding work on Saturday, and to require employers to bear no more than a de minimis cost to accommodate an employee's religion.

Accommodation in U.S. disability law, by contrast, is more robust. The Americans with Disabilities Act (ADA) of 1990, which has served as a model for many other nations' laws (Herr 2002), requires "reasonable accommodations" that do not impose an "undue hardship" on employers, including "making existing facilities . . . readily accessible to and usable by individuals with disabilities" and such specific efforts as "job restructuring, part-time or modified work schedules, . . . the provision of qualified readers or interpreters, and other similar accommodations."

Moreover, contrary to its view of religious accommodations, the Supreme Court said in *US Airways, Inc. v. Barnett* that "the [ADA] requires preferences in the form of 'reasonable accommodations' that are needed for those with disabilities to obtain the same workplace opportunities that those without disabilities automatically enjoy. By definition any special 'accommodation' requires the employer to treat an employee with a disability differently, i.e., preferentially." Though the Court has limited this conclusion significantly, the principle of a broader concept of accommodation for disability remains.

One central conceptual debate surrounding accommodation concerns whether accommodation requirements are fundamentally different from, or of a piece with, other responses to discrimination. This issue touches on the broader problem of analogies. In U.S. debates, race typically serves as a starting point for discussions of discrimination; in Europe and elsewhere, sex begins the conversation. As a result, disability advocates and theorists often confront the demand to analogize disability rights to movements based on these other categories. These demands translate into a particular question about accommodation: Within the rights discourse of law, is *accommodation* a form of *antidiscrimination* or something altogether distinct?

The ADA itself provides one answer by defining "discriminate" to include "not making reasonable accommodations." This is significant because many U.S. courts and some scholars understand discrimination to mean, centrally or exclusively, differentiating in favor of or against a group along a protected axis like race. They therefore see accommodation as an entirely different creature, since it involves making affirmative changes to the environment in response to difference (Karlan and Rutherglen 1996). Consistent with a growing scholarly trend (Bagenstos 2003; Jolls 2001), the text of the ADA cuts against this view by treating the failure to accommodate *as falling within the definition of "discrimination" itself*. Recent amendments to the ADA may, however, inspire courts to interpret the law in ways that emphasize differences, rather than similarities, between disability discrimination and discrimination on the basis of race and sex (Emens 2013).

A second debate concerns the costs and benefits of accommodation. To some minds, discussions of disability accommodation evoke Kurt Vonnegut's Handicapper General, who makes everyone "equal" by requiring them to wear masks, heavy weights, and loud headsets to offset any advantages they might have in beauty, strength, or intelligence (Vonnegut 1968). In this dystopian vision, burdensome adjustments in the name of equality drag down the entire society.

Many employers see accommodations as costly endeavors that will hinder productivity. As a result, accommodation requirements may lead to so-called disemployment effects, depressed hiring of disabled people in response to disability laws (see Bagenstos 2004b). But empirical research indicates that such effects are temporary, suggesting that employers may discover after a time that accommodations are less costly, or more beneficial, than anticipated (Jolls and Prescott 2004).

Indeed, most accommodations are not costly, and many impose no direct costs at all (Schartz, Hendricks, and Blanck 2006). Where Vonnegut's story is about leveling down, accommodations should aim to level up, allowing otherwise qualified people to perform jobs successfully. Moreover, the benefits of accommodations have frequently been underestimated. U.S. courts, for example, have portrayed accommodations as costly to employers and to third parties (such as coworkers and customers) but useful only to the individual disabled employee (Emens 2008). But disability accommodations can have broader benefits to coworkers, customers, and the wider society (Stein 2003). For example, ramps and curb cuts benefit not only people in wheelchairs but also people with strollers, suitcases, or bicycles, and disability has inspired technological innovations such as voice-to-text software, closed captioning, and ergonomic furniture design. Accommodation can therefore be understood in either static or dynamic terms (Emens 2008). On a static model, accommodations are small tweaks to the existing baseline to make room for an individual. On a dynamic model, accommodations take disability as the impetus to recalibrate the baseline for everyone. The static model fits neatly with some early meanings of the term "accommodation"—as referring to "a favour" or "concession" (*OED*)—and is probably the most common popular understanding of the term. But the dynamic model captures important elements of the landscape of accommodation. For example, universal design typifies the dynamic model because it tries to create an environment that is always ready for the widest variety of possible users. More broadly, employers often have a choice—commonly overlooked—about whether to design accommodations on a static or a dynamic model. For example, if an employee asks to work from home (telecommute) to accommodate his disability, the employer can either permit a special exception for this employee or use this request to spur the creation of a telecommuting initiative that may please many employees and create cost savings for the company (Emens 2008).

Of course, there may be trade-offs among accommodations, and also among design principles. For instance, curb cuts may be great for wheelchair users but present new challenges for people with vision impairments, and designing workplace accommodations in ways that create the most third-party benefits may not always lead to the best version of particular accommodations for those who requested them. These problems require careful consideration and, some would say, rethinking of concepts such as universal design (Shakespeare 2006a). They raise the question of whether accommodations should be reserved for those deemed to need them most—such as people with disabilities—or whether the right to accommodation should be expanded to create a greater entitlement for all workers. The nonprofit Workplace Flexibility 2010 initiative has proposed a universal accommodation right, aligning the interests of workers who have obvious needs for accommodation, such as disabled people and caretakers, with the interests of the broader workforce in flexible arrangements that may allow them to pursue any number of needs and interests, including spiritual practices, educational pursuits, or volunteer activities. A universal accommodation right sounds utopian until one considers that it could involve as minimal a requirement as a "right to ask" without consequences.

For some scholars, accommodation will always be too limited a model because it is grounded in antidiscrimination principles. These thinkers argue that accommodation can only go so far without a robust human rights approach that brings together negative and positive liberties—that is, an approach that brings freedom *from* interference with one's aims together with freedom *to* access equal goods and opportunities (Stein 2007; see Berlin 1969). A model for this approach is the UN Convention on the Rights of Persons with Disabilities (CRPD; 2008), which embraces civil, political, economic, and social rights, thereby combining a commitment to accommodation with a complementary insistence on social supports like vocational training. Through the CRPD, the concept of accommodation continues to be important to efforts to create equal opportunities and access both for people with disabilities and for the not-yet-disabled, which is to say, everyone.

These legal and conceptual endeavors all take accommodation to mean altering the environment to respond to disability. But Harriet McBryde Johnson (2003) turns this definition on its head in her elegant essay about her surprisingly cordial meeting with Princeton professor Peter Singer, whose brand of utilitarianism implies that people with disabilities like hers should not exist at all. Johnson explains why she disagrees with those who see Singer as a monster. His views, she observes, are simply not so far from those of many people she encounters every day: "The peculiar drama of my life has placed me in a world that by and large thinks it would be better if people like me did not exist. My fight has been for accommodation, the world to me and me to the world" (Johnson 2003, 79). Johnson thus reminds us that accommodation, in the disability context, may be shadowed by what it has meant in terms of race—the marginalized group in some way compromising with the mainstream—and suggests that the two meanings may be, for better or for worse, inseparable.

6

Activism
Denise M. Nepveux

Activism is a practice of, or orientation toward, taking action, often implying the context of a social or political movement. Although activism emphasizes collective action, an individual and his or her actions may be considered "activist" depending on their relationship to larger struggles. Disability activism refers to "collective political action by and for people with disabilities" (Barnes and Mercer 2010, 176), which contributes to "the continuing struggle of disabled people to gain a voice and to shape our destinies" (Longmore 2003, 231). The word "advocacy" is sometimes used interchangeably with activism, since a person may advocate on behalf of others. But although some scholars and activists include advocacy by parents and other nondisabled allies under the category of disability activism, leadership by disabled people in activism is crucial to collective autonomy.

While recognizing a plurality of disability movements, and groups within disability movements, the late Paul Longmore argued that some shared goals and stances predominate. These include the reframing of "disability" as a social and political, rather than simply a medical and rehabilitative, problem; the shift in priorities from correcting individuals to reforming society; the assertion that the necessary means for social participation and integration, whether devices and services or access and accommodations, should be enforceable civil rights rather than dispensations of charity; the contests for power with professionals and bureaucrats; and the quest for both individual and collective empowerment and self-determination (Longmore 2003, 114).

Addressing disabling barriers to political participation and mobilization is another unifying concern (Charlton 1998). For instance, many disabled adults encounter inaccessible voting arrangements or are ineligible to vote (Barnes and Mercer 2010, 158–160). Educational barriers hinder effective organizing. Transportation barriers make it difficult to hold meetings or participate in public gatherings. Community meetings and political events are often held in structurally inaccessible spaces, with poor air quality or use of scented products, and without accommodations for nondominant languages or multimodal forms of communication. These and other forms of disenfranchisement have motivated activists to demand change and also to take steps to ensure accessible spaces, processes, and communication strategies within disability movements.

Disability activism arose in the late nineteenth and early twentieth centuries as some people with disabilities began to organize to resist restrictions on their freedoms and demand economic opportunities within industrial economies. Blind people and other disabled people in the United States, the United Kingdom, and Ireland formed associations to fight for social and economic rights and modeled their aims and tactics on working-class and trade union struggles (Ó Cathain 2006). In the mid-twentieth century, blind, deaf, and physically disabled people engaged in separate struggles for specific policies, with each group seeking to better its educational or economic opportunities. Parents of children with disabilities organized locally and internationally to resist institutionalization and advocate for community living and educational access.

In the 1960s, a confluence of developments enabled a cross-disability political consciousness to emerge in the United States. Observation of and participation in the civil rights movement, the Black Power movement, the women's movement, and other collective struggles of the 1960s and early 1970s exposed men and women with disabilities to tactics of protest and enabled them to begin recognizing and questioning violations of their human and civil rights. The women's health movement, in particular, questioned medical power and supported individual empowerment. Yet people with disabilities often experienced barriers to full participation in these movements.

Other developments opened opportunities for new understandings and increased expectations of freedom from institutionalization and professional domination. In the late 1940s, for instance, disabled veterans of World War II experienced barrier-free mobility in dedicated spaces at the University of Illinois, Galesburg (later relocated to Urbana-Champaign), which encouraged them to challenge institutionalized barriers to their broader social and economic reintegration outside of the university setting (Pelka 2012). Meanwhile, the first generation of physically disabled youth who had attended public schools began demanding access to higher education and developing new models of user-controlled services. In the early 1960s, University of California, Berkeley, undergraduate Ed Roberts and his colleagues—known as the Rolling Quads—were inspired in part by other forms of student activism at Berkeley, including the Free Speech Movement and the women's movement's refusal of imposed passivity. Roberts went on to establish the Disabled Student Program on campus; in 1972, he cofounded the city of Berkeley's Center for Independent Living (Fleischer and Zames 2001, 36–39).

Section 504 of the Rehabilitation Act of 1973, which mandated equal access in federally funded programs and buildings, created a watershed opportunity for disability activists. Yet by the mid-1970s the U.S.

Department of Health, Education, and Welfare (HEW) had delayed enforcement of the new regulations. In 1977, disability activists—led by the group Disabled in Action—responded with sit-ins of federal buildings in New York, Washington, DC, and San Francisco (Barnartt and Scotch 2001). A broad array of nondisabled ally groups supported the twenty-five-day occupation by disabled activists of the HEW regional headquarters in San Francisco. Through these weeks, a number of emergent disability rights activists—some of whom were also active in the Black Power movement—shared stories and came to understand the relatedness of their experiences across different impairment categories (Schweik 2011). This deepened understanding across categories of race, class, gender, and ability enabled protesters to commit to shared political struggle (Longmore 2003).

Simultaneous developments in the United Kingdom reflected parallel shifts in consciousness as well as political strategy. The Union of the Physically Impaired against Segregation (UPIAS) developed what has become recognized as the social model of disability as a way of rejecting professional and charitable dominance and asserting the inherently unjust social and political bases of disability-related inequality and exclusion. This new way of defining disability in terms of exclusion rather than embodiment helped activists across impairment groups to recognize common experiences of exclusion and restricted life chances and to build a shared politics of disability.

These shifts undergirded extensive coalition building across the globe through the latter decades of the twentieth century and galvanized such remarkable organizational and legislative successes as the United Kingdom's Chronically Sick and Disabled Persons Act (1970), France's Declaration of the Rights of Handicapped Persons (1975), Disabled Peoples International (established in 1981), American Disabled for Accessible Public Transit

(ADAPT; established in 1983), the Americans with Disabilities Act (1990), and the UN Convention on the Rights of Persons with Disabilities (2008).

Despite the spread of cross-disability organizing and the growing embrace of the social model of disability among diverse activists, disability rights movements continue to be "a splintered universe" of loosely affiliated groups and shifting coalitions (Shapiro 1994, 126). Factions within disability movements often have overlapping membership and goals, and they reach out to one another for solidarity and costrategizing on specific campaigns. In the United States, some groups have arisen from specific, impairment-related histories of segregation and other forms of institutionalized oppression; these include blind people's activist groups; psychiatric "survivors," "mad activists," and other current or former mental health service users who protest the treatment and social situation of those who are labeled mentally ill; and self-advocacy movements such as People First and the Autistic Self-Advocacy Network.

Other groups have organized in relation to intersectional political identities, including Feminist Response in Disability Activism (FRIDA) and indigenous peoples' disability activist groups. These groups challenge racism and patriarchy within disability groups. Some groups have organized to address specific issues; ADAPT, for example, first organized in the early 1980s to fight for transportation access, now focuses on deinstitutionalization and community living. Other groups include those that resist a liberal, civil rights–based approach and advocate a more radical vision of social justice, for example, the disability justice movement and Occupy Wall Street–related groups. Not Dead Yet fights physician-assisted suicide and related life-ending policies and practices under which persons with physical disabilities and chronic illnesses are disproportionately targeted. And although they have worked in coalition for cross-disability legislation, Deaf Pride movements continue to distance themselves from disability identity, asserting instead a linguistic and cultural minority identity and refusing to associate deafness with impairment.

There is little agreement as to which actions rise to the level of "activism"; a seemingly wide array of tactics may be considered activist. The term "click-tivist," for instance, has recently been used to dismiss Internet-based activism that may be poorly informed and requires little individual effort. Yet the increasing use of information technology and social media has enabled geographically disparate disability groups to organize, and many groups have broadened their communicative and coalition-building capacities. Disability activists in Ontario, for example, may be unable to meet frequently in person across hundreds of miles, but they strategize online. Deaf activists in Ghana and elsewhere communicate largely by e-mail and text. U.S. activists with chronic fatigue and immune dysfunction syndrome and multiple chemical sensitivities, for whom in-person activism is largely inaccessible, engage from home via the Internet. A monthly "Organizers Forum" phone call allows activists from disability groups across the United States and beyond to connect, learn together, and exchange ideas.

Although much social and policy advocacy now takes place online, street protests, disruptive occupations, and performance-oriented street theater remain crucial ways to draw attention to disability issues that might otherwise be rendered invisible. The line between political protest and performance often has been blurry. ADAPT protesters crawled up the steps of the U.S. Capitol in 1990 to protest delays in passage of the Americans with Disabilities Act. Elderly women activists in Syracuse, New York, protested closure of the Ida Benderson Senior Center in 2011 by organizing and participating in a public head shaving. Jerry's Orphans repeatedly disrupted the (now-defunct) annual Muscular Dystrophy Association Telethon in Chicago and documented these efforts on film.

Some activist events take a playful tone and gesture toward alternative social arrangements and definitions. Mad Pride Week in Toronto, for example, utilizes a variety of participatory performances such as the Mad Hatter's Tea and the Bed Push Parade to celebrate mad pride, history, and culture. Such activism does not propose policy; rather, it makes visible the everyday quality of disability oppression while also celebrating disability experience and culture and engaging bystanders in imagining and even coperforming alternatives.

Simi Linton has observed that "disability studies both emanated from and supports the Disability Rights Movement" (qtd. in Fleischer and Zames 2001, 206). Many groundbreaking scholars in disability studies—Ed Roberts, Simi Linton, Paul Longmore, Jim Charlton, and Carol Gill, to name but a few—emerged directly from activist backgrounds and resistance movements. Activism is—in Robin D. G. Kelly's phrase—an "incubator of knowledge" (qtd. in Schweik 2011), and the collective wisdom of disability activism is preserved in oral history interviews with activists as well as from memoirs, activist blogs, zines, photographs, films, and other forms of social documentation. Yet much of how we think about disability has emerged not only through the work of activists but also through theoretical engagements with disability activism by scholars in disciplines including sociology, history, anthropology, and literary and cultural studies.

Although academia and activism are interdependent, they are often, unfortunately, pitted against one another. On the one hand, activists may perceive the work of academics and scholars as theoretically abstract and call for more accessible and relevant disability scholarship (O'Toole 2009). On the other hand, scholars may dismiss activism as naive or excessively concerned with short-term, utilitarian goals. Yet this relationship, however fraught, might be a productive one if reconfigured as symbiotic and collaborative. Activists can keep scholars current, grounded, and aware, while scholars in turn may construct "usable pasts," depictions and theorizations that aid activists in critically understanding the present in order to work toward a different future (Longmore 2003, 9).

With the significant growth of disability studies programs over the past two decades, the accountability of scholars to disability activist communities is an often-debated question. The privilege and security enabled by academic salaries and benefits are rare commodities among disabled people, who are among the most impoverished and disenfranchised groups globally. Yet such privilege also engenders responsibility to facilitate tangible social and political transformation. Disability scholars often engage directly in activism by advocating for governmental and institutional policy changes, joining community-based activist groups, supporting student activism, and working to end exclusionary practices in scholarly associations and the academy itself.

Of course, scholars also address this accountability through their scholarship. Humanities scholars uncover experiences and knowledge of disability that complicate dominant narratives; activists may take up such knowledge in a variety of ways. Some social researchers (Goodley and Lawthom 2005) engage in participatory action research that sheds light on realities of community life while building self-advocacy among participants. Some UK sociologists, such as Michael Oliver, have insisted upon a strict "emancipatory" model, in which disability scholarship is guided and led by disabled activists in a way that supports the disability community's policy agenda. Doing so is not straightforward, however, as disability activists are not unified, and activist agendas

require both scholarly support and critical examination if they are to promote justice. For example, Kelly (2010) warns that when minority model–based activism glosses over the diversity of needs and interests within the disability community, the resulting policies may help some subgroups while neglecting or harming others.

While scholarship can shed a needed critical light on the inner contradictions of movements, it can also help to foster dialogue and alliances among them. Currently, disability activist-scholars are building bridges with prison abolition movements, organizations, and activist groups that promote antiracist and anticapitalist platforms, and those movements that embrace animal rights, food justice, and environmental justice. These emerging dialogues and coalitional politics promise to complicate and deepen our understandings of disability and its multiple intersections.

7

Aesthetics

Michael Davidson

Whether addressing ideas of beauty in nature or works of art, aesthetic judgments implicate disability insofar as they presume a normative standard of perception and an ideal of bodily perfection as the object of affective response. Although theories of taste and beauty have been in existence since Plato and Aristotle, the term "aesthetics" emerges centrally in the eighteenth century as a discourse about perception and feeling. For Immanuel Kant, for instance, an aesthetic judgment is distinct from one involving deductive reasoning or conceptual information concerning the object. He distinguishes between teleological and aesthetic judgments, the former of which concern objects, purposes, and intentions; the latter are disinterested, based on subjective apprehension. Kant implies that disinterested pleasure is distinct from the self-interested pleasure we obtain from satisfying a drive or solving a problem. In a paradoxical move, however, he also claims that my feeling of pleasure is validated by my presumption that others would feel the same way ("when [a man] puts a thing on a pedestal and calls it beautiful he demands the same delight from others" [Kant 1952], 50). This conflation of noncontingent personal pleasure with collective assent is the cornerstone of bourgeois aesthetics, from Karl Marx to Herbert Marcuse. It is also the source of ableism as the ideology of bodily normalcy.

The claim of disinterestedness presents a conundrum for disability studies. It represents an attempt to legitimate judgments of taste by removing the body that makes such responses possible, or more precisely by diverting bodily responses onto objective forms. But judgments of taste are always framed by social attitudes and cultural contexts. Such values constitute forms of cultural capital in the reinforcement of class privilege, and as such restrict competing views of beauty, sensory satisfaction, and human variety. When the seventeenth-century Spanish artist Diego Velázquez places the Infanta at the center of his painting *Las Meninas*, for instance, he includes a court dwarf at her left, as a grotesque contrast to her youthful perfection. An aesthetic of disinterestedness is never far from a formalist desire to project the work of art as a *cordon sanitaire* against bodily variety and corporeal mutability.

Eighteenth-century and early nineteenth-century aesthetic treatises attempt to provide for subjective experience the kind of authority claimed by empirical science. Yet the criteria for judgment often presuppose an ideal of embodiment. Johann Joachim Winckelmann, for instance, sought artistic perfection in classical sculpture based on the perfect Greek body. He argued that "masterpieces [of classical art] show us a skin which is not tightly stretched, but gently drawn over a healthy flesh, which fills it out without distended protuberances and follows all the movements of the flesh parts of the body in a single unified" direction (1985, 37). By contrast, Gottfried Lessing felt that certain emotions—such as pain—can be better expressed in poetry, while bodily infirmity and variety may be the ideal subject for painting, since they create a challenge for the artist's mimetic potentiality. Lessing believed a modern artist would declare, "Be you as misshapen as is possible, I will paint you nevertheless. Though, indeed, no one may wish to see you, people will still wish to see my picture; not in so far as it represents you, but in so far as it is a demonstration of my art, which knows how to make so good a likeness of such a monster" (1985, 63). For Lessing, realistic depiction of a "misshapen" man is less important for its verisimilitude than for its demonstration of artisanal superiority.

In both Winckelmann and Lessing, the ability of aesthetics to define affective and sensory response depends on—and, indeed, is constituted by—bodily difference. In Kant, by contrast, the aesthetics of beauty is only one half of a dialectic between bounded and unbounded sensations. The latter, associated with theories of the sublime, is the inevitable site of cognitive and physical difference in their challenge to our reasoning faculty. Theories of the sublime during the eighteenth century were inspired, to some extent, by the eighteenth century's discoveries in medical science or what Michel Foucault (1984) calls the "politics of health." In Edmund Burke's *Philosophical Enquiry into the Origin of Our Ideas of the Sublime and Beautiful* (1968), the sublime is defined through the author's medical researches into physical pain. For Burke, the sublime is superior to beauty because it leads to further consciousness and action, whereas beauty recedes into lassitude and passivity. The experience of pain is beyond reason and comprehension, a state that challenges ideas of mortality and finitude. Once released from pain, the individual enjoys the "joys of convalescence" whereby we learn to appreciate a health we had previously taken for granted.

A key theater for theories of the sublime can be found in the Gothic tradition. As an antidote to Enlightenment rationalism, Gothicism engages with various forms of bodily difference and psychological otherness. Where Winckelmann vaunts human perfection in health, smoothness, and unity, the Gothic explores the pathological, uncanny, and monstrous. David Punter observes that "the history of . . . the Gothic [is] a history of invasion and resistance, of the enemy within, of bodies torn and tortured, or else rendered miraculously,

or sometimes catastrophically whole" (2000, 40). Gothic fiction offers a catalog of characters who exhibit bodily deformities, mental disability, or psychic distress: from Mary Shelley's Frankenstein to the blind rabbi of Charles Robert Maturin's *Melmoth the Wanderer* to the giant of *The Castle of Otranto*, the *One-Handed Monk* and the narrator in Edgar Allan Poe's "The Fall of the House of Usher." As a camera obscura on Enlightenment aesthetics, the Gothic displays, according to Ruth Anolik, "human difference as monstrous, and then, paradoxically, [it] subverts the categories of exclusion to argue for the humanity of the monster" (2010, 2).

David Mitchell and Sharon Snyder (2000) refer to such images or metaphors as "narrative prostheses," since their appearance in literary works provides a figurative (and, often, a literal) crutch to a redemptive story of bodily renewal. Oedipus's self-blinding is an inaugural moment in Western art's linkage between moral life and bodily deformity. Similarly, Shakespeare's Richard III's hunchback is a physical embodiment of his corrupted sense of power, while Dickens's Tiny Tim's limp facilitates Scrooge's redemptive vision of charity. The function of such narrative prostheses is to provide readers with a model of bodily difference from which they may distance themselves. What the disabled body disturbs in the moral universe, the redeemed, healthy body recuperates, just as the death of the monster or the villain restores the health of court and state. As Mitchell and Snyder summarize, "While an actual prosthesis is always somewhat discomforting, a textual prosthesis alleviates discomfort by removing the unsightly from view" (2000, 8). The rhetorical trope of pathos, the appeal to an audience's emotions, is often purchased by an identificatory logic that turns aesthetics into pedagogy. Pity and fear, those qualities Aristotle ascribed to tragedy, may be aesthetic criteria for mimesis, but they are embodied in a blind and crippled Oedipus.

Since the late nineteenth century, modernist art has had recourse to deformed or grotesque bodies to metaphorize the condition of what Matthew Arnold called "this strange disease of modern life" (2004, 1093). The canon of high modernism is replete with representations of physical and mental disability—from aestheticism's convalescents to Expressionist portraits of demented urban denizens, to the blind and neurasthenic figures in T. S. Eliot's poem *The Waste Land*, to Andre Breton's cognitively disabled heroine in *Nadja*, to Henry James's invalids Ralph Touchett and Milly Theale, to William Faulkner's cognitively disabled Benjy Compson, to the consumptive heroines of opera, to the incarcerated narrator of Charlotte Perkins Gilman's "The Yellow Wallpaper." Nazi *Entartete Kunst* ("degenerate art") exhibitions of the late 1930s used modernism's depiction of "defective" or dysgenic persons in Expressionism or Surrealism as a sign of Western culture's decline, in contrast to the idealized Aryan bodies in rural settings depicted in the "Great German Art Exhibitions" endorsed by Hitler. If the salient feature of modernist art and literature was its emphasis on the materiality of the medium and the defamiliarization of everyday life, its thematic focus was embodied in a blind soothsayer, a child with Down syndrome, a tubercular artist, and a hysteric woman (Davidson 2008).

The turn in modern aesthetics' dependence on a discourse of disability is powerfully evident in art's reliance on a disabled person to symbolize moral flaws or frame the able-bodied hero's moral recovery. In the late nineteenth century, for instance, convalescence became a key trope for philosophical acuity and aestheticism. Literary figures such as Edgar Allan Poe's narrator of "The Man of the Crowd," des Esseintes in Joris-Karl Huysman's *Au Rebors*, or the title character in Friedrich Nietzsche's *Zarathustra* are only three of many convalescents whose return to avidity from illness inaugurates a new intense, passionate interest in the world. Modern aesthetic theories also have a taxonomic function insofar as they attempt to organize and rationalize sensory experience. For Jacques Rancière, "the practices and forms of visibility of art . . . intervene in the distribution of the sensible and its reconfiguration" (2009, 29). This distributive or categorical function parallels in many ways the biopolitical rationalizing of bodies and cognitive registers that emerged in medical science during the eighteenth and nineteenth centuries but was refined and perfected in the twentieth.

Modernist aesthetics is also dominated by the idea that literature "lays bare the device" of language through formal rupture and non sequitur (Shlovsky 1965). Twentieth-century Russian formalists such as Viktor Shlovsky, Boris Eichenbaumm, and Roman Jakobson have theorized that literary devices such as metaphor, patterned rhyme, and narrative frames "make strange" the everyday and quotidian so that it can be experienced anew. Disability theorists have come to similar conclusions about the ways that disability unseats ideas of bodily normalcy and averageness. Ato Quayson (2007) calls the discomfort that disability occasions among able-bodied persons "aesthetic nervousness," a recognition of bodily contingency that arises in the presence of the nontraditional body. Lennard Davis (2002) argues that disability, because it crosses all identity categories, "dis-modernizes" biopolitical regimes that attempt to fix and categorize bodies through medical technologies and population control. Aesthetic defamiliarization and disability deconstruction are joined by their critique of mimesis—the idea that there is a putatively "real," "given" world that must be represented and cited. When art foregrounds its own operations, when disability unsettles the normative body, mimetic criteria are shattered and the means of aesthetic and social reproduction exposed.

The attempt to differentiate the "normal body" in modernity was aided by a number of developments in visual culture that made the nontraditional body more visible. Photography was enlisted by eugenics and race theorists to catalog aberrant or dysgenic "types," while films such as *The Black Stork* (1917) provided documentary evidence justifying fetal euthanasia, sterilization, and incarceration. Antivagrant laws or "ugly laws" were instituted in a variety of U.S. cities to prevent "unsightly" or disabled persons from appearing on the street (Schweik 2009). As Martin Pernick (1996) observes of such developments, aesthetic values were often used to define those "lives not worth living" and remove them from public view. Modern reform movements in favor of suffragism, birth control, women's health, workplace improvements, and settlement houses were often fueled by eugenicist ideas about health, genetic purity, and ability. In Lennard Davis's terms, "enforcing normalcy" becomes a preoccupation of modern social and medical sciences for which both high art and mass culture provide prosthetic reinforcement.

The twin legacies of an aesthetics of disinterestedness and a biopolitics of health and genetic improvement have helped to shape what Tobin Siebers calls "an aesthetics of human disqualification," a "symbolic process [that] removes individuals from the ranks of quality human beings, putting them at risk of unequal treatment, bodily harm, and death" (2010, 23). Fitter family contests, "ugly laws," and freak shows of the modernist era provided individuals with an opportunity, during a period of social fluidity and change, to imagine themselves as not "ethnic," not "feebleminded," and not disabled. Mass cultural spectacles and modernist art both contributed to such an aesthetics by making visible bodies with which one would not want to be associated while validating sensory responses to bodies that confirmed one's own integrity and vitality.

Siebers (2010) uses the phrase "disability aesthetics" to draw attention both to the formative role of disability *in* aesthetics and the aesthetic practices of disabled artists whose work engages in a critique of ableist attitudes. In 1990, for instance, when disability activists from American Disabled for Accessible Public Transit (ADAPT) left their wheelchairs to crawl up the steps of the U.S. Capitol building in support of the Americans with Disabilities Act, it was an act of civil disobedience. But it was also—vividly—a form of disability performance art. Such theatrical gestures blur the boundary between art and activism that has characterized much disability aesthetics in the recent period. The performance artist Mary Duffy, born without arms, poses nude while adopting the position of classical sculpture. She uses her posture as a nude Venus de Milo (who also lacks arms) to address her audience and rearticulate feminine beauty from a disabled and gendered perspective. The deaf artist Joseph Grigley makes installations out of the "conversation slips" (matchbooks, bar napkins, Post-its) he exchanges with his hearing interlocutors. The neurodiversity activist and autistic artist Amanda Baggs uses a software interface to transcribe her written text into an electronic voice that urges her audience to learn "her" language of repetitions, scratchings, and monotone humming. The blind photographer Evgen Bavcar photographs classical sculpture and archaeological sites, often intruding his hand into the image to instantiate his reliance on a tactile rather than retinal relationship to objects.

The situation of deaf poets and performers presents a specific challenge to traditional aesthetic ideals based on printed or verbal representation. Many deaf persons think of themselves not as disabled but as a linguistic minority who compose their poems and performances through sign language. Many of the themes of d/Deaf performances involve the history of oralist pedagogy that emerged in the mid-nineteenth century and that dominated attitudes toward the assimilation of deaf people into hearing culture (Baynton 1996). Poets such as Clayton Valli, Debbie Rennie, Patrick Graybill, and Ella Mae Lentz create works in American Sign Language (ASL), most often repudiating voice-over translation in order to "speak" directly to a nonhearing audience (Brueggemann 1999). Deaf artists' interest in differentiating themselves from disability illustrates the difficulty of defining disability aesthetics within a single category with a common history. Furthermore, it forces us to rethink the largely ocularcentric character of aesthetic discourse and configure it around other sensory avenues and cognitive registers.

"There is no exquisite beauty, without some strangeness in the proportion." Edgar Allan Poe's quotation of Francis Bacon in "The Philosophy of Composition," summarizes the crucial link between art and otherness, between the aesthetic and the different bodies that constitute it. In an essay that advocates the most extreme example of artisanal control, Poe's belief in poetry's need for "strangeness" exemplifies the aesthetic's uncanny dependence on difference. What Terry Eagleton calls "that humble prosthesis to reason," the aesthetic depends on a body that reason refuses to recognize. One must remember that the ideal forms that the humanities vaunt as epitomes of proportion and grace—the Venus de Milo, *La Victoire de Samothrace*, Leonardo's Vitruvian man—are, respectively, armless, headless, and possessed of multiple arms and legs. The aesthetic discourse that creates disinterested appreciation of the beautiful is also the one that has historically relegated the hunchback to the dungeon, the fat lady to the freak show, and the deaf person to the asylum. The close proximity of aesthetic judgment to carceral isolation and rationalized euthanasia is the darker side of Enlightenment knowledge, even as the increased visibility of the disabled body creates the occasion for its liberation.

8

Affect

Lisa Cartwright

"Affect," a term understood by some to be synonymous with "feelings" and "emotion," is associated with a set of theories that are useful for understanding somatic experiences that generate meaning outside the limits of signification and critical interpretation. The turn to theories of affect among writers including Eve Kosofsky Sedgwick and Adam Frank (1995b) and Brian Massumi (1995) was provoked by a sense that cultural theory had not adequately come to terms with forms of embodied feeling experienced outside the registers of speech, signification, communication, and meaning. A major catalyst of the "affective turn" (Clough 2007) was the publication, in 1995, of two essays: Sedgwick and Frank's "Shame in the Cybernetic Fold," a work that introduced the writings of American experimental psychologist Silvan Tomkins to readers in literary, feminist, and queer theory; and "The Autonomy of Affect," an essay in which Massumi expanded upon French philosophers Gilles Deleuze and Félix Guattari's use of the term "affect" in *A Thousand Plateaus* (1987).

Tomkins's method of understanding affect, articulated in work collected between 1962 and 1991 in four volumes of his lifework, titled *Affect, Imagery, Consciousness* (reprinted as Tomkins 2008), was to observe embodied expression, spontaneous gesture, and comportment as factors through which we might come to understand affect, the motivating force or response system that supports and modulates human drives. Rather than focusing on what people say (as Freud did in his "talking cure"), or on communication, knowledge, and meaning production, Tomkins focused on embodied expressions and interactions to decipher the circuit of emotions through a system of nine categories of affect. Tomkins's writings on shame, the subject of a volume of excerpts from his work edited by Sedgwick and Frank (1995a), have become especially important for disability studies scholars interested in how feelings of shame can be generated, expressed, shared, hidden, or amplified—often outside the realm of language. Sedgwick and Frank (1995b) introduced the writings of Tomkins on shame as a corrective to politically engaged critical theory that—in their view—focused too narrowly on language and disembodied meaning in the critical interpretation of social and political life, missing the variable, sometimes delicate and fleeting but important place of affect in political and social experience. Rather than seeing shame as a sentiment that should be overcome to achieve pride, they propose, with Tomkins, that shame holds a transformative potential that can be worked through even in its indirect or subtle forms to enable expression and identity.

The work of Gilles Deleuze on affect, as interpreted by Massumi, also has been influential in exploring the significance of affect as a concept through which to get past the impasse of signification and meaning as the locus of cultural and political theories of opposition, rights, and political transformation. Ann Cvetkovich and Ann Pellegrini (2003) were among the authors who emphasized the importance of understanding the public and political dimensions of affect and sentiment.

A critical interrogation of positive public affect, notably pride, is needed in disability studies in much the way that public shame and pride have gained centrality in queer studies. If pride is the repudiation of shame, how do we approach with respect those who feel shame without assuming a patronizing educative stance or a sense of pity? A critical interrogation of the affective dynamics of pride may allow disability studies to work through the problematic of humanitarian patronization that is rightfully disparaged in the field. Sally Munt (2000) and Elspeth Probyn (2000) offer insight about the ways in which shame, rather than being something that must be overcome and replaced with pride, offers the potential for queer political affinity and empathy.

One of the core contributions of affect theory is to change the way that influence and power are understood. In the most general sense, to affect someone is to influence or change his or her mental or emotional state. This seems to imply that the object or person that elicits feeling wields power over the person who is "made to feel." But the relationship that makes up affect, if we are to draw from either Tomkins or Deleuze, is far more complicated. Most often, agency is reversed in ways of describing this relationship. We rarely state with absolute certainty, "I moved her," though we are likely to feel some certainty about feelings when we admit, "I was moved by her." Often we attribute our affective response to something we have strongly felt emanating from the other person's outward affect. We may even feel as if our own feelings were directly drawn out of us by that person's emission of *inner* feeling—this is what we call "being affected" by someone: "I was touched [affected] by her [tragic, stunning] life story," or "I was struck [affected] by the change in his behavior." A humanist spin on these formulations is that they describe positive empathetic relationships. What, after all, could be wrong with the idea of one person picking up directly, intimately, on the inner feelings of another? Isn't that what it means to be human?

From a disability studies perspective, however, such a seemingly simple idea is inherently troubling, especially when we consider the historical evidence of those who have exploited empathy—in the form of charity, pity, or awe—to describe perceived physical, cognitive, or mental differences in the other, from the standpoint of a presumed social norm. The person whose life story is perceived as tragic may not believe it is tragic at all, for example, and may feel disgusted that someone has "felt their pain" when in fact he or she does not feel pain at all, or in the imagined way.

Not all affective relationships are misrouted and patronizing, of course. But often when we notice affect, it is precisely through relationships like these that entail considerable projection on the part of the perceiver, and that are weighted on the side of the perceiver's feeling some "direct" connection that is in fact projective (see Cartwright and Benin 2006). Affect is thus subject to a complicated intersubjective dynamic that is not generally in the control of the person whose affect is being "felt," interpreted, or narrated by another. This imbalanced relationship can easily default to a system where normative judgments creep in, on the part of the one feeling and the one whose feelings are "felt" by another. Pity expressed toward one with a disability may generate shame, anger, or disgust in the person who was intended to be the beneficiary of pity as largesse.

Affect thus can bear a close relationship to stigma. This is evident in the use of "affect" to imply that someone's behavior is not natural or genuinely felt—as in the disdainful suggestion that someone is behaving pretentiously or with conceit: "She spoke with an affected manner." We use this phrase to condemn the person in question for performing his or her affect "unnaturally" or in a charade, as if we all shared a template for normative or natural ways of acting in public. But because all mannerisms are modeled after or against normative ways of speaking, gesturing, and interacting, labeling anyone as "affected" can be problematic. Think of how often gay men are said to exhibit a gay "affect" for mannerisms that may be common among gay men but are atypical of straight male behavior. To label one category

of behavior as affected and leave the other (straight male) affective behaviors unmarked is to make the notion of affect itself stigmatic. If I have a cognitive, motor, or sensory difference that keeps me from expressing my feelings through presumed normative (natural) gestures and cadence of voice, then I might gesture and speak deliberately in a performed, "affected" way. For example, I might overcome the social stigma of having "flat affect" in my interactions by scripting my interactions and re-performing them "with feeling" in social settings, taking on a manner of speaking or relating that may seem to my interlocutors to be unnatural or a pretense, but which I have carefully learned in order to pass as neurotypical. To label my mannerisms as "affected" and someone else's similar affect as normal is an irony of the affective social domain, which presumes that "natural behaviors" are spontaneously performed and not consciously learned or assumed.

For some scholars, the structure of affect and empathy is tied historically to the emergence of aesthetics. One classic notion is that nature's "harmonious" lines and colors are the inspiration for architectural form—as if nature "speaks" directly to our feelings through its forms. As Susan Schweik (2009) has argued, aesthetics and affect are intimately tied to the history of mandating normative or ideal-driven models of physical appearance as law. Schweik shows how public outrage against the appearance of "freaks of nature," for example, or aversion toward "ugly" people comes from the undesirability of feeling affective states such as disgust and shame. Affect, in the sense of feeling, is thus powerfully tied to the troubling fate of bodies perceived to violate norms of aesthetic expression in public space. The "ugly laws" that banished people with visible disabilities from public spaces through much of the twentieth century laid blame for this generation of feelings of shame projected as disgrace on the outcasts themselves.

9

Aging

Kathleen Woodward

The biological process of growing older, human aging is almost always accompanied by limitations in physical capacities and, in many cases, diminution of mental acuity. In addition, aging is, like disability, both a biological and a cultural phenomenon that is inflected decisively by the social, legal, medical, statistical, and experiential meanings given to it. For example, old age may be defined by a society in chronological terms (in the United States, ages sixty-two and sixty-five mark eligibility for Social Security) and individually in psychological terms (someone may be seventy-five years old and "feel" fifty). In the United States and many other industrialized nations, aging, as Susan Wendell (1999, 133) has written, is disabling. Aging is invoked rhetorically—at times ominously—as a pressing reason why disability should be of crucial interest to all of us (we are all getting older, we will all be disabled eventually), thereby inadvertently reinforcing the damaging and dominant stereotype of aging as solely an experience of decline and deterioration (Davis 2002; Garland-Thomson 2005; Stiker 1999). But little sustained attention has been given to the imbrication of aging and disability (for exceptions to this rule, see Wendell 1996; Silvers 1999; Kontos 2003). Aging is not—yet—a keyword in disability studies.

Nor have the insights of disability studies been taken up in any depth in age studies, a relatively small field that for the most part, unlike disability studies, has not been entwined with identity politics. In 1969, the gerontologist and psychiatrist Robert N. Butler coined the term "ageism" in analogy with other social prejudices based on biocultural categories, such as sexism and racism. But the cultural study of age, with attention directed to older age understood to be part of the normative American youth–old age system, did not emerge in the United States until the 1980s. As cultural studies scholar Margaret Gullette has memorably put it, we are aged by culture. Gender has been fundamental to the analysis; as lesbian writer and activist Barbara Macdonald wrote in 1983, "Youth is bonded with patriarchy in the enslavement of the older woman. There would, in fact, be no youth culture without the powerless older woman" (39). Also fundamental to analysis has been the spectacle of the aging body. The "decline" associated with aging is largely detected in a visual register, while passing and masquerading as young—aided by a plethora of antiaging products and practices—serve as strategies for evading exposure as old (Katz 2005). At the same time, if disabled bodies can be understood as anomalous and extraordinary, visibly marked aged bodies are typically considered so ordinary that they recede from view, becoming invisible (Woodward 1991, 2006). The able body is the norm; so too is the healthy youthful and middle-aged body.

What are the biopolitical dimensions of aging today in neoliberal economies? As with most biopolitical queries, scale matters. Around the world, many national populations are aging. For centuries in the West, old age was considered part of the spiritual journey of a life (Cole 1992). Beginning in the twentieth century, however, as life expectancy increased enormously and in some cases almost doubled, aging became a medical problem to be solved, with an accelerating search in the twentieth-first century for scientific keys to slow down and stop the process. Aging populations present an enormous economic contradiction: on the one hand, aging populations constitute a huge market; on the other hand, political leaders, economists, policy makers, and others often regard an aging population as a potentially catastrophic impediment to the vitality of their national economies, as insufficiently productive. At the same time, in anticipation of old age, retirement accounts grow globally, which even in times of economic downturn can make enormous sums for investment available; unsurprisingly and ironically, a good portion of those investments are in antiaging research.

Aging is a process; disability is typically understood as a condition, as something one has. Temporally, aging and disability converge in the case of frailty, a syndrome often associated with advanced old age. As such, frailty—and to a certain extent aging itself—is conceptualized simultaneously as a disability in the present and as a risk factor for developing a disability in the future.

10

Blindness
D. A. Caeton

Blindness is a condition of the flesh as well as a signifying operation. William R. Paulson maintains that blindness "means very different things, and moreover it *is* very different things, at different times, different places, and in different kinds of writing" (1987, 4). Such a critical stance can lead the field of disability studies to analyze disability in a manner that reckons with both the ways that bodies are made accessible through language and the ways that bodies exceed language. The state of visual impairment long ago assumed a metaphoric plasticity, making literal blindness serve as a figurative marker for other diminished capacities. This interplay permeates, for example, one of the West's foundational texts, Sophocles's version of the story of Oedipus. It is evident in the confrontation between Tiresias, the blind prophet, and the figuratively blind Oedipus, as well as in the ghastly scene where Oedipus literally blinds himself upon gaining his figurative sight (Stiker 1999).

Perhaps the earliest English-language example of blindness's physical/metaphysical conflation occurs in the tenth-century *Blickling Homilies*. The narrator of the second quire, *Quinquagesima Sunday*, observes of the blind beggar of Jericho, "Right was it that the blind man sat by the way begging, because the Lord himself hath said, 'I am the way of truth,' and he who knows not the brightness of the eternal light is blind; and he liveth and believeth who sitteth by the way begging, and prays for the eternal light, and ceaseth not" (Morris 1880, 16). This exegesis clearly demonstrates a transformation of the physically blind beggar into a surrogate for the intransigent spiritual blindness of all sinners. By taking care of the blind beggar, sinners can move closer to Christ and therefore erase their own metaphoric blindness. In his examination of l'Hospice des Quinze-Vingts, the institution founded in Paris by Louis IX in 1256, Edward Wheatley (2002) argues that the church treated physical blindness as evidence of sin, which could be ministered to in order to imitate Christ's role as protector and healer.

During the European Enlightenment, blindness became fetishized in debates among both rationalists and sensualists. As in the Middle Ages, though, it was not really visual impairment itself that was central to such debates; rather, blindness became a form of "narrative prosthesis" (Mitchell and Snyder 2000; Davidson 2008). Blindness aroused the thoughts of several Enlightenment philosophers because of an intellectual quandary posed by William Molyneux, a Dublin lawyer, to John Locke in 1688. Molyneux asked whether a man born blind who had tactually learned to tell a globe from a cube would be able, upon having his sight restored, to immediately distinguish through vision one object from the other. In later printings of *An Essay Concerning Human Understanding* (1955), Locke answered Molyneux's epistemological problem by arguing that such a man would be incapable of distinguishing the objects by sight alone. Inclusion of the query and Locke's response in Locke's seminal text brought the hypothetical scenario to the attention of eminent philosophers such as Berkeley, Condillac, Leibniz, and Voltaire, who regarded blindness as a mere intellectual puzzle that held no social value by itself. By contrast, it formed the impetus for Diderot's *Letter on the Blind for the Use of Those Who See*, which explored blindness as a valid subject unto itself.

Against a backdrop of emerging industrialization and modernization, blindness became not a marker of sin, as it had been during the Middle Ages, but a marker of sloth. James Gall, a pioneering Scottish educator of the blind, for instance, declared that a blind person's "condition is a state of continuous childhood. . . . He can produce for himself neither food nor clothing; and without the unceasing assistance of his friends he would of necessity perish" (1834, 13). Without intervention, it was feared that the blind would wallow in unproductivity and gross dependence. In the nineteenth-century United States, pedagogy for blind students heavily emphasized Protestant Christianity and nationalistic ideals; together they were meant to implant in blind students an ethos of independence, thereby making them capable of performing sighted normalcy. Furthermore, through educational and vocational institutions blind people were disciplined toward industrious participation in the nation. Such disciplinary practices were intended to transform them into facsimiles of the sighted. Additionally, this inculcation was meant to ameliorate the anxiety many sighted people had over blind people's inability to join the imagined community of the nation.

Throughout the nineteenth and twentieth centuries, blindness was increasingly indexed according to complicated metrics of visual acuity, and there were tremendous efforts to achieve complete empirical exactitude. A universal medical definition, however, has proven elusive, and various global institutions have come to employ different quantitative standards. The inability to secure total agreement regarding the measurement of blindness demonstrates how "the evaluation of impairment is . . . full of errors of reification and false precision" (Stone 1984, 116). As such, the failed quest for an absolute metric has given rise to multiple classification schemes, all of which measure degrees of blindness.

This is illustrated by the U.S. Bureau of the Census and the World Health Organization, which use different criteria for diagnosing what constitutes blindness. For both institutions, the logic of categorization is buttressed by ophthalmological measurements of blindness. Such definitions may prove useful in terms of policy decisions and the disbursement of financial benefits, but they also have the effect of dividing the blind community. Kenneth Jernigan, for instance, a long-serving former president of the National Federation of the Blind, observed in an essay originally published in 1962 that "the complex distinctions which are often made between those who have partial sight and those who are totally blind, between those who have been blind from childhood and those who have become blind as adults are largely meaningless" (2005). For Jernigan, as for many activists and scholars in disability studies, organizing around a common identity for social gains has proven more relevant than classificatory nuances.

Perhaps because no universal technical definition of blindness exists, the scale incorporating multiple measures of blindness employed by different medical domains has not significantly influenced sighted culture at large. Sighted culture accepts only a total, plenary blindness, a stark binary of presence/absence. One either sees nothing or one sees everything; there is no allowance for a liminal state of partial blindness or partial sightedness, what Beth Omansky (2011) has termed the "borderland of blindness." This may explain why sighted people still experience both trepidation and wonder at imagining the phenomenological dimensions of blind people's existence, stemming largely from the belief that the blind body has only limited access to the world through a pitiable, incomplete sensorium. Georgina Kleege wryly recognizes how many sighted people go "into raptures" when describing a blind person's "ability to recognize . . . voices, to eat spaghetti, to unlock a door. People sometimes express astonishment when I find the light switch or pick up my coffee cup" (1999,

27). Guided by such erroneous presumptions, sighted culture fashions the blind body into a totem of daily miracles, where even the most quotidian activities seem extraordinary.

Anxiety among the sighted makes it seem that a life of blindness is necessarily devoid of autonomy, agency, or the possibility for any positive affect. Such a broad cultural misconception empowers the dominant nondisabled culture to believe that blindness is existentially incomplete, a stigmatized state of deprivation. As Michalko (1999) has noted, blindness represents a lack that menaces sighted culture; it is an absence not only of sight but also of independence, intellectual acumen, morality, and productivity. Blind people are thus confronted with two options: either succumb to disciplining practices in order to perform normalcy—that is, some version of sightedness—or else face rejection.

One curious aspect of medical discourse is that it opens the definition of blindness to perpetual revision because the clarity and focus of the techno-medical gaze are always becoming sharper. For example, the reductive social binary of being either sighted or nonsighted diverges from medical conceptualizations of blindness, which acknowledge that people experience various forms of blindness in different and uniquely subjective ways. Some experience a mélange of colors; some see eruptions of paramecium-like shapes; and for some photophobia precludes direct exposure to light. Less than 10 percent of people who identify as blind possess no light perception whatsoever.

Medicine's perpetually revised definitions of blindness imply that the sought-after complete description and comprehension of blindness will someday be the precursor of techno-medical mastery. Moreover, it is presumed that such mastery will cross a biological horizon and at some imagined point take the form of absolute cure. This is not new; medicine has conceived of blindness as being an inevitably conquerable condition, a belief that stretches from the second-century AD cataract surgeries by Galen of Pergamon to the first recorded reversal of blindness, performed by English surgeon William Cheselden in 1728, to the exuberant contemporary fantasies of the posthuman in the early twenty-first century.

Such efforts at mastery are problematic because they often displace efforts to improve the social conditions of current blind people. Future inquiries centered on blindness should instead assist in establishing a greater understanding of how human variation is an asset, and not a liability. Several disability studies scholars have created a foundation upon which future inquiries might be built. Robert McRuer's (2006) work, for example, can facilitate an understanding of how blindness "crips" sighted culture. The concept of the "normate," proposed by Rosemarie Garland-Thomson (1997, 2009), challenges ocularcentrism, including the presumptive right to stare at others that saturates sighted culture. In addition, Shelley Tremain's (2001, 2008) application of Foucauldian theories to the ethics of disability demonstrates how poststructuralism can productively influence new conceptualizations of blindness and sightedness. Finally, the study of blindness can lead to fresh insights in fields outside of disability studies. Because so many cultural categories and disciplinary practices are based on sight and the visual inscription of the body, blindness can reveal how sight influences negative constructions of people of color, women, queer people, and disabled people without visual impairments, thereby recasting modernity's problematic foundational assumptions so that a richer inclusivity might be gained.

11

Citizenship
Allison Carey

Although the disability rights movement (DRM) and the field of disability studies (DS) have emerged and blossomed together, the two have developed along slightly different trajectories. While the DRM has demanded the establishment of laws and policies that treat people with disabilities as equal and valued citizens, DS has created the intellectual and creative groundwork to reimagine disability not as a biological defect but as a valued form of human variation that exists within and is deeply affected by its social context. Because the DRM uses rights as its organizing framework, it is not surprising that citizenship and rights are central intellectual concepts in DS as well. For example, the DRM slogan "nothing about us without us" encapsulates an ideology of valued and equal citizenship. Disability studies has taken up this call by examining the meaning, content, and impact of citizenship as well as the ways in which disability is central to systems of citizenship.

Briefly defined, citizenship serves to demarcate who is a member of the national community and to establish the relational expectations among citizens, noncitizens, and the state. Rights constitute a key resource of citizenship, providing a tool to influence others, pursue one's interests, and mark one as a respected member of the state (Carey 2009). Early scholarship on disability and citizenship focused on documenting the exclusion of people with disabilities from the rights and typical opportunities enjoyed by other citizens. According to

Martha Minow (1990), the United States has a dual-track legal system in which individuals deemed competent and rational enjoy the rights of modern citizenship, whereas those deemed incompetent and irrational are placed in positions of subordination where they are "cared" for and "protected" rather than given equal civil rights. This system of paternalism reinforces the dependence of people with disabilities (Hahn 1983, 1988) and in effect creates a "dependent caste" (Funk 1987) of people with disabilities who have access only to "second-class citizenship" (Eisenberg 1982). Often, early DS research concerning rights left citizenship as a vague or undefined background concept. When citizenship was considered, it tended to be included in a package of rights granted by the state to individuals (Marshall 1950). The goals of DS research, then, were to identify the ways in which people with disabilities were provided with inferior "packages" of rights, examine the problematic assumptions behind this inequality, and thereby insist on access to equal rights.

Disability scholars and activists were rarely satisfied, though, with the assumption that equality would flow from obtaining the "same" package of rights. Disability studies brings to light the importance of human variation and reveals the ways in which the policies, standards, and rights based on an able-bodied norm may further reinforce exclusion. Therefore, it was not long before DS scholars began to develop innovative reformulations of citizenship theory. Some of the most important reformulations rely on the concepts of *practice*, *relationality*, and *embodiment*.

A *practice* approach argues that the exercise of citizenship involves a set of dynamic, relational practices, including constructing, claiming, and using rights. For example, analyses of the Americans with Disabilities Act (ADA) emphasize the active negotiation of rights (Campbell 2005; Engle and Munger 2003; Francis and Silvers 2000; O'Brien 2004). Rather than offering firm guarantees, the rights granted by the ADA provide a set of resources that can be potentially harnessed by people with disabilities to shape identity, discourse, and interaction between themselves and others (Bérubé 2003). Thus, it is not enough to have formal rights; rights that are merely on the books cannot solve all matters of inequality because people must be able to claim and use those rights actively in order to participate in society. A practice approach centers on the role of inequality—including unequal access to resources, valued social roles, and cultural/interpersonal respect—in shaping the ways we experience citizenship (Turner 1993).

Disability studies has also expanded the literature on the *relationality* of rights and citizenship. Liberal political philosophy imagines the citizen as a rational independent person. In line with feminist scholarship, disability studies has interrogated ideas about personhood (Kittay and Carlson 2010a; Reindal 1999) and showed the ways in which our identities, actions related to rights, and power to shape our world are all relational phenomena (Beckett 2006; Carey 2009; Mason 2004). Kittay, for example, critiques the traditional emphasis on independence: "In acknowledging dependency we respect the fact that as individuals our dependency relations are constitutive of who are and that as a society we are inextricably dependent on one another" (2001, 570). Thus citizens are not isolated rational individuals; rather, they are interrelated and interdependent actors whose identities and actions are shaped by their relational web and social context. This account transforms not only the way we think about citizens and citizenship but also law and social change. The concept of relationality undergirds the ADA, which sets forth obligations on the part of employers and community members to create accessible conditions in support of the equal participation of people with disabilities (Silvers 1998). It also is fundamental to alternative approaches to liberal political theory, such as the capabilities approach, human rights theory, and care theory, each of which seeks new ways to include all people as respected and valued citizens in society through recognizing our diverse capabilities and our shared vulnerabilities (Beckett 2006; Kittay and Carlson 2010a; Nussbaum 2006).

Disability studies has also been in the forefront of illuminating the concept of embodied citizenship, as scholars have increasingly sought to move beyond conversations solely about how society treats disability to examine how the body affects our experiences within the "body politic" (Siebers 2008b; Wendell 1996). For example, people with autism not only have different experiences because society treats them differently; they also experience the world differently because they process information differently. Hughes, Russell, and Paterson (2005) therefore call for a theory of embodied citizenship that recognizes and problematizes diverse corporeality in a society that expects bodily conformity and uniformity. As with ideals like rationality and autonomy, the "normal body" is illusory, yet it forms the foundation of traditional ideals of citizenship (Russell 2011). The normal body, argues Rosemarie Garland-Thomson, is assumed to be unimpeded by architectural barriers, stares from those who pass by, gangly uncoordinated and shaky movements, or unarticulated patterns of speech. By contrast, the disabled body is assumed to be susceptible to external forces, "property badly managed, a fortress inadequately defended, a self helplessly violated" (1997, 45). Scholars such as Martin Pernick (1996) and Susan Schweik (2009) showcase the ways in which physical difference defined as monstrous or ugly justifies exclusion, segregation, and even death. Broader ideologies centered on safeguarding the "health" of the nation and creating a "fit" population have also legitimatized the denial of rights (Baynton 2001; Mitchell

and Snyder 2001). Moreover, society enforces "compulsory able-bodiedness" and demands the invisibility and/or compliance of people with disabilities (McRuer 2006). Disability collides with sexuality, race, gender, and class in the formation of a stratification system that privileges some and disadvantages others. Robert McRuer further shows the ways in which systems of oppression uphold each other, such that homosexuality and disability are used in conjunction to reinforce the normativity of heterosexual able-bodiedness.

Disability, therefore, forms a crucial conceptual foundation in the way we experience and justify systems of inequality and membership/exclusion. It does so by producing disability as embodied limitation caused by imposing social barriers and labels that disadvantage particular people. Disability works ideologically to individualize and biologize dependence and "need," treating disabilities as rare individual problems rather than conditions of everyday existence for all people. The assignment of disability thus serves as a broad justification to exclude a range of persons defined as unworthy for national membership and the exercise of rights (Baynton 2001). Consequently, the varied efforts by DS scholars, which began as an attempt to identify and theorize the inferior treatment of people with disabilities as citizens, have transformed the way we conceptualize citizenship for all people. This body of scholarship shows that the dichotomies of normal/abnormal, healthy/unhealthy, fit/unfit, and able/disabled underlie the very foundations of our systems of rights and our valuations of worth and membership (Carey 2009; Mitchell and Snyder 2001; Nielsen 2012).

12

Cognition

Ralph James Savarese

To understand the relationship between cognition and disability, let us appeal to the concept of "situated cognition" in cognitive neuroscience. The field of disability studies attends, after all, to the situatedness, or social construction, of disability. The two branches of situated cognition—*embodied* and *embedded*—can help to illuminate how a different kind of body and a different kind of environment generate a different kind of thought. *Embodied cognition* repairs the traditional mind-body divide, whereas *embedded cognition* reveals the extent to which we all depend on our physical and social environments to think. The former thus blurs the line between "physical" and "mental" disabilities because no condition is strictly one or the other, and the latter points to complex accommodative ecologies that enhance cognition by imaginatively distributing it beyond the individual.

According to Vittorio Gallese and Hannah Chapelle Wojciehowski (2011), "Classic cognitive science heralds a solipsistic account of the mind. . . . The picture . . . is that of a functional system whose processes can be described in terms of manipulations of informational symbols according to a set of formal syntactic rules." (Because sensing, acting, and thinking are not "separate modular domains" but, rather, a kind of dynamic feedback loop, embodied cognition insists that the mind be understood as both serving, and served by, a body. "By having fingers capable of grasping objects and legs capable of walking and climbing walls," write Robert Wilson

and Lucia Foglia, "we sort and categorize stimuli in ways that are radically different from, say, the ways in which they are sorted by butterflies." Sensorimotor experience, to put it simply, "frame[s] the acquisition and development of cognitive structures" (Wilson and Foglia 2011).

By this logic, the sensing and acting associated with congenital deafness or autism or even impaired mobility would spawn a different kind of cognition. Among deaf people, for instance, a study from 2001 reported that "visual attention to the periphery [is] more efficient than in hearing people" (cited in Campbell, MacSweeney, and Waters 2008, 16). As significant, the auditory cortex can be used for sight. In a 2005 study, the movement of visible dot patterns activated "regions that support hearing (and only hearing) in hearing people" (cited in Campbell, MacSweeney, and Waters 2008, 16). Finally, while traditional language areas in the left cerebral hemisphere have been shown to support the use of sign language, the spatial processing demands of grammar in sign language appear to activate the right hemisphere more than processing spoken language does. All of this indicates at least a slightly different sensorimotor foundation or frame for deaf cognition.

And yet, what may seem modest on fMRI scans turns out to be quite significant in reality. That signing occurs in the open field of the hands, as opposed to the closed cave of the mouth, makes of language something truly kinesthetic. With two manual articulators, a face and a body, the signer can exploit simultaneity of expression—indeed, grammatical structures are often expressed nonmanually. Iconicity further distinguishes spoken language from sign language, with the latter containing many more instances of the partial or full onomatopoeia-like union of signifier and signified. This fact makes plain, in a way that the arbitrariness of spoken language does not, that the origin of meaning begins in the body. Any account of deaf cognition must recognize that distinctive sensing and acting have given rise to a distinctive language.

With autism, cognition is conspicuously embodied. Temple Grandin thinks in pictures, whereas Tito Mukhopadhyay thinks in fragmented, synesthetic sound. So significant are his sensory processing, proprioception, and facial recognition challenges that his published writings often seem like a marvel of literary defamiliarization: "Every time I have to hear Mr. Blake's voice, I recognize it by a squished tomato smell. After that, I know that there ought to be Mr. Blake somewhere around carrying his voice with him" (Mukhopadhyay, qtd. in Savarese 2010). In her YouTube video, "In My Language," Amanda Baggs treats what the medical community would call "perseverative behavior" as an attentional virtue. Extolling an autistic preference for detail over category (because the latter masters the world at the cost of seeing it), Baggs remarks, "The way that I move is an ongoing response to what is around me."

Even mobility impairment would produce a different form of cognition, though it might not show up, as it does in autism, on fMRI scans. When Nancy Mairs entitles a book *Waist-High in the World*, she implicitly acknowledges a different form of sensing and acting: namely, that which takes place in a wheelchair.

In contrast to embodied cognition, embedded cognition foregrounds the role of the natural and social environment in thought. Andy Clark and David Chalmers remind us that "our visual systems have evolved to . . . exploit contingent facts about the structure of natural scenes . . . and they take advantage of computational shortcuts afforded by bodily motion and locomotion" (1998, 8). Or, as Wilson and Foglia put it, "Visual experience results from the way we are dynamically hooked up to the world" (Wilson and Foglia, 2011).

Of course, we are also "hooked up" to other people as well as to forms of organized cultural behavior. Lucy Suchman (1987) has shown that workplace activity conditions what we do with our senses and hence how we cognitively operate. Airplane mechanics, for example, engage in a highly particular kind of seeing. We have long known that infants need the environment to shape sensory processing, but they also need other humans to develop intersubjective capacities, not to mention the language that so enhances them.

To capture the symbiotic nature of cognition, Clark and Chalmers deploy a provocative analogy:

The extraordinary efficiency of the fish as a swimming device is partly due . . . to an evolved capacity to couple its swimming behaviors to the pools of external kinetic energy found as swirls, eddies and vortices in its watery environment. These vortices include both naturally occurring ones (e.g., where water hits a rock) and self-induced ones (created by well-timed tail flaps). The fish swims by building these externally occurring processes into the very heart of its locomotion routines. (1998, 9)

By referring to the fish and water as a "device," the authors move us beyond the individual organism to a larger ecology. "In such cases," they write, "the brain . . . complements the external structures, and learns to play its role within a unified, densely coupled system" (8). Edwin Hutchins's seminal essay, "How a Cockpit Remembers Its Speeds" (1995b), provides a version of this ecology, though with a metal bird, the air, and two pilots who make use of sophisticated computers. Cognition in some cases can even become "extended." When "features of an agent's physical, social, and cultural environment . . . do more than distribute cognitive processing, they may well partially constitute that agent's cognitive system" (Wilson and Foglia

2011). Clark and Chalmers (1998, 12) cite the example of a person with Alzheimer's disease who must use a notebook to remember where he is geographically.

"Coupled systems" allow many people with disabilities to function more successfully. Indeed, these systems prove the fundamental point of the social model of disability: that the disabling aspects of physiological distinction are largely manufactured. Stephen Kuusisto captures the machine ensemble of blind man and guide dog when he writes: "Our twin minds go walking, / And I suspect as we enter the subway / on Lexington / That we're a kind of centaur— / Or maybe two owls / Riding the shoulders of Minerva" (2000, 20–21). A more complex coupling—and, in fact, an elaborate ecology—is what enables a young woman with significant cerebral palsy to attend an elite liberal arts college in Iowa. Without a motorized wheelchair, a computer with eye-blinking text-to-voice capabilities, a classroom aide, a personal care assistant, accessible learning spaces and dorms, not to mention her own native intellectual gifts and what might be called external attitudinal energy (those progressive swirls, eddies, and vortices of nondisabled opinion), she would not be able to do it.

The embedded and distributed nature of cognition becomes strangely literal when we consider psychiatric medicines and neuroprostheses such as cochlear implants. The coupling may be internal rather than external, but such couplings are themselves embedded in larger cultural debates about curing disability and medicating purported emotional dysfunction. People with disabilities come to different conclusions about these interventions. Of the decision to treat her own bipolar disorder with Depakote, Suzanne Antonetta remarks, "It's hard to explain how I can believe depakoteering is the right decision for me. . . . I have no use for the 'medical model,' the model of mental difference as straight illness, like a never-ending flu" (2009–2010, 73). Although she believes in "mad gifts" (73), she prefers the "difference in [her] mind" (70) that the drug enables.

While the disabled "device" is potentially emancipatory—and in many ways equivalent to the nondisabled one—it is often coded as lack. In the case of cognitive disability, intense stigma persists. The historical conflation of physical disability with cognitive impairment suggests a perverse reconciliation of mind and body, and the belief that learning is impossible while being cognitively impaired continues to do great damage. At the same time, the neurodiversity movement has begun to attract scientists and doctors—one prominent researcher has referred to autistics as "just of another kind" (Wolman 2008). Embedded and distributed cognition might put pressure on narrow notions of personhood, which have traditionally excluded those deemed "profoundly retarded," encouraging us to see how the shibboleth of rugged individualism does not even apply to the most cognitively competent among us.

13

Communication
Carol Padden

The word "communication" first appeared in 1422, according to the *Oxford English Dictionary*, and was used to refer to "interpersonal contact, social interaction, association." By the sixteenth century, the word had acquired another sense: "the transmission or exchange of information, knowledge or ideas." The plural form, "communications," was introduced in 1907, to refer to transmission by way of machine or technology. Even in this technological sense, however, the notion of communication implies a transmission of information from one biological entity to a similar one. In recent years, technologies and techniques of communication associated with disability are transforming all of these meanings by extending the notion of transmission of information well beyond the circuit of biologically similar speaking bodies. Disability studies and sign language studies have concerned themselves with what have been considered "nontypical" communications, conducted by differently abled bodies, via different appropriations of technology.

All animals communicate, but only humans use language. Bees dance to indicate where pollen is found, but only humans have words and sentences to indicate ideas and concepts, including the dance behavior of bees. Other forms of communication may parallel and at times substitute for speech, but they are not primary linguistic systems.

Sign languages—which are found in all inhabited parts of the world—are similar to spoken languages (Sandler and Lillo-Martin 2006). Sign languages have phonology, as do spoken languages, except instead of vowels and consonants, signs are made up of combinations of movements, locations, and hand shapes. Sentences in natural sign languages display hierarchical organization and exhibit syntactic structure. Young signing children, deaf and hearing (such as those with signing parents), acquire sign language in ways that are not different from children acquiring spoken language (Corina and Singleton 2009). When deaf signers suffer stroke and have damage to the language areas of the brain, they too, like hearing aphasics, can show loss of sign language ability (Hickok and Bellugi 2010). Sign languages may differ from spoken languages in the *modality* of expression, but in terms of their organizational properties, they are fundamentally linguistic. Sign languages of deaf communities may be fully expressive linguistic systems, but they are often viewed as secondary replacements when speech—the default modality in human language—is not possible.

A unimodal view of language, as primarily spoken, ignores contrary examples in human communities of how the body is used for language. Among the Walpiri of western Australia, widows observing a period of mourning do not speak, instead using sign language to communicate with others (Kendon 1988). There are yet more examples of the flexible possibilities of the human body for language. Khoisan languages of southern Africa use clicks as phonemes in addition to the more familiar vowels and consonants of most spoken languages. The existence of clicks is comparatively rare in the world of spoken languages but demonstrates that speech can be molded in diverse ways. In deaf-blind communities, signers communicate by tactile means with each other, holding each other's hands as they sign. It is common to think of these as adaptations, or unusual modifications made to accommodate a special need. "Adaptation" follows from thinking of language as having a basic template, or universal properties, upon which modifications are made. But these examples show that languages are systems that can employ different signaling properties. The body offers multiple communicative resources that are organized differently in different contexts. The ways that language can be built from different parts of the body are surprisingly myriad. If language is viewed as inherently *multimodal*, then humans' ability to move between different modalities in different communities seems less exotic and more indicative of flexibility.

Studies of new sign languages emerging in small villages around the world show that when deaf children are born into a community, hearing residents adapt their gestures to produce longer signed strings in an effort to communicate. As more deaf children enter the community across more than one generation, the community changes from an exclusively speaking community to one where a sign language is a common second language in the community in addition to a spoken language (Meir et al. 2010).

Beyond stretching our notion of how languages transmit information via means other than speech, disability studies can help us to move beyond a transmission view of communication. James W. Carey's "ritual view of communication" focused not on "the act of imparting information but [on] the representation of shared beliefs" (1992, 15). A focus on "ritual" shifts away from the idea of messages and their properties, to performance, activity, and the materiality of communication itself. In this framework, meaning is not so much the definition of a word or sentence but instead is constructed in situ, in social and cultural activity. Human actions are not simply executed but are "situated" in time and place. In this framework, language is not a disembodied, logical system but is perpetually constructed and reconstructed in social and cultural activity. The concept of activity

as a unit of analysis recognizes all levels of expression, from the minute details of discourse—from pitch, emphasis, gesture, head tilts, and eye gaze—to the performative aspects of making meaning within the institutions of the home, school, and the workplace.

The foundation of this communicative ability is "shared intentionality," or the ability to engage with others in a common activity. Humans have a unique predisposition to follow the eye gaze of others and to comprehend others' pointing and indexic reference. A similar construct is "intersubjectivity" (Cole 1996; Wertsch 1991), or the ability of humans to recognize in each other their expressive states, including their emotions, plans, and goals. Understanding the basis of shared intentionality and intersubjectivity necessitates a notion of the mind that encompasses more than the individual and his or her internal space, but is extended through the body and *distributed* in social interaction (Bakhurst and Padden 1991). Communication exists in what Ludwig Wittgenstein referred to as a "web of meaning," an ecologically coherent system that locates human bodies in an interrelated moment.

Such notions from the field of communications as distributed cognition and situated practice overlap conceptually with disability studies' repositioning of the human body. In both fields, human bodies are not simply vessels containing brains but are themselves complicit in human sociality, cognition, language, and social interaction (Rohrer 2007). Bodies interact with and on the world, grasping objects or modeling them abstractly in gesture. A physicist describing the structure of molecules gestures as she speaks in order to show the shape of what is unseen. A young child tries to grasp an object out of reach, and her hand changes into an indexic point producing joint reference (Vygotsky 1978). A group of officers stand around a table and jointly solve the problem of navigating a ship into harbor by moving their hands around a map (Hutchins 1995a). Configuring the mind as an extension of the body leads to a concept of communication as fundamentally *multimodal*, in which all parts of the body are orchestrated together as it interacts with the world.

Multimodality and embodiment together with distributed and situated practice open up ways to conceive of communicative forms and practices in diverse bodies, but disability is not explicitly treated in this work except for a few notable articles. Goodwin (2000) describes an aphasic who, despite a greatly reduced vocabulary and repeated use of gestures, manages to push caregivers into expanding their abilities to interpret his wishes and intentions. A differently abled body does not merely attempt to communicate, but by his realignment of himself with material and communicative resources, he compels new forms of engagement and interaction. In such scenarios, communication is an aspect of human functioning that is always being constructed. For instance, parents of a blind child achieve intersubjectivity and shared intentionality not by shared eye gaze but by coordinating their actions with her hand movements (Bigelow 2003). Autistic children are said to lack shared intentionality because they do not track the eye movement of others, but as recent research has shown, their sociality and interest in others are simply achieved by other means, such as physical proximity and verbal engagement (Akhtar and Gernsbacher 2007).

Disability studies can also shed light on the centrality of technology to notions of communication. In the broad sense of the word, technology is about material objects, the fund of knowledge about their use, and the institutionalization of the technology in cultural life. Technology refers to material and cognitive tools that are extensions of minds and bodies. Counting by use of an abacus is both a technology and a cognitive tool for computation. In such a view of technology, the relationship between the material and the cognitive is continuous, that is, antidualist, and not defined strictly by materiality. Ideas about mind, body, and technology have consequences for communication and disability. If technology is described as an appendage, then it can seem "secondary," "supplemental," "compensatory," or "ventriloquist," all terms which suggest that it adds to or amplifies human behavior. But if technology is seen as extensions of the body and mind, then technology is one part of an activity within which the human body operates rather than a supplement to that activity.

The rapid expansion of technologies of the body—particularly as tools of accommodation for people with disabilities—has led to changing notions of personhood. One recent case involves individuals with "locked-in syndrome" (LIS), who experience minimal outward body movement resulting from trauma that affects their motor behavior, making it difficult if not impossible to ascertain their communicative intentions. One such individual successfully petitioned the Spanish courts to restore his legal rights, namely, the ability to vote and to manage his financial affairs. The Spanish Supreme Court agreed that his use of a digital voice demonstrated that he can "materially carry out his decisions" (Domínguez Rubio and Lezaun 2012, 69). Domínguez Rubio and Lezaun argue that "those capacities and processes that have customarily defined the person—agency, intentionality, speech—need not be performed within the confines of the biological body, but may be enacted through extended systems of care and knowledge" (74). It is such cases of disability, of "extended systems" that stretch beyond the normal speaking body that have redefined communication and language for the present century.

14

Crip

Victoria Ann Lewis

"Crip" is the shortened, informal form of the word "cripple." One finds it in slang usage by the early twentieth century, often in the underworld language associated with begging—such as "he was a phony crip." The word also occurs as a nickname based on a defining physical characteristic, such as the novelist Owen Wister's 1893 reference to a lame character shot in the leg as Crip Jones ("Crip" 1994, 522). During the 1920s, "crip" became a slang synonym for "easy," both in sports and in collegiate registers: a "baseball crip" was an easy pitch, while a "crip course" was an easy course in school. These usages reflect the low social expectations held for people with disabilities, as in the phrase "to give someone the cripple's inch."

With the emergence of the disability civil rights movement in the 1970s, "crip" gained wide usage as an informal, affectionately ironic, and provocative identification among people with disabilities. The term functions as an alternative to both the old-fashioned and rejected "handicapped person" and the new, more formal terms "disabled person" or "person with a disability," both of which gained official status as the preferred terms for standard usage in the mid-1980s. Within the disability community, it signals in-group status and solidarity and is intended to deflate mainstream labels such as "handi-capable," and "physically challenged," terms many activists find patronizing and politically misleading. "Crip" is most often embraced by educated disabled people who have some understanding of the historical and political significance of their experiences as disabled and who want to reclaim a stigmatized term. Usage of the term in the United Kingdom and Australia follows a similar pattern to that in the United States.

Since the 1980s, "crip" has become increasingly prevalent as an adjective/modifier in phrases such as "crip shots," "crip moves," "crip Zen," and "crip poetry slam" to identify a sensibility, identity, or activity in opposition to mainstream assumptions about disability. It also suggests a relaxed, confident claiming of difference, what the late disability historian Paul Longmore called "disability cool." There also has been some linguistic confusion because the term is more widely associated with one of the most notorious Los Angeles gangs, the Crips. Origin myths for the gang name range from a journalistic error (confusing "crip for "crib") to the common use of canes among some gang members as a fashion accessory. Leroy Moore, whose Krip Hop Nation project seeks to highlight the contributions of disabled artists to the contemporary music scene, spells the word with a "K" instead of a "C" to avoid gang identification.

While the noun forms of both "cripple" and "crip" were reclaimed as terms of empowerment rather than degradation under the aegis of the U.S. disability rights and culture movements, "cripple" remains a taboo term in the United States and is marked as derogatory and substandard in most dictionaries and style guides. However, as with appropriation of the word "queer" by many LGBT activists, some disabled artists and activists have deliberately readopted the term "cripple." In her famous essay "On Being a Cripple" (1986), for instance, Nancy Mairs explains her preference for the term—citing, among other reasons, its Old English roots, its freedom from euphemism, and its ability to disturb. Mairs insists that while *Cripple is the word I use to name myself,* she never uses it to refer to another person. Meanwhile, other disabled artists have embraced the term, including Lorenzo Milam in his memoir, *Cripple Liberation Front Marching Band Blues* (1983), poet Cheryl Marie Wade, and activist and radio host Shawn Casey O'Brien of the 1980s rock band The Cripples. In Germany, since 1978, a large-scale political movement has reclaimed the taboo term the *Krüppelgruppen* (literally the "Cripples' Group"), a phrase that deliberately evokes the eugenic policies of the Nazis, to fight for disability rights.

With the growth of disability studies as an academic discipline in the 1990s, "crip" began to appear in a variety of verb forms. One saw, for example, authors grappling with what it meant to analyze a topic or representation and "crip it," a process through which one subjects a text or an idea to "cripping" or being "cripped." While there are examples of "crip" converted into a verb as far back as the fourteenth century, where we read of "a beeste that was broken and *Cripped*," our contemporary usage seems to have originated in academic discourse as a critical strategy borrowed from queer studies. Carrie Sandahl's influential essay "Queering the Crip or Cripping the Queer? Intersections of Queer and Crip Identities in Solo Autobiographical Performance" (2003) and Robert McRuer's *Crip Theory: Cultural Signs of Queerness and Disability* (2006) were among the first texts to introduce the noun-verb conversion to critical studies. Sandahl notes that the power of claiming either "crip" or "cripple" comes from the "sedimented history of its prior usage," and the capacity of both words to injure. The terms "disabled person" or "person with a disability" continue to be preferred in educational, professional, legal, and civil rights discourse, where "crip" may not be understood as either positive or empowering. Sandahl also notes the two positions share "a radical stance towards concepts of normalcy" (2003, 26), a position that McRuer describes as a shared "resistance to cultural homogenization" (2006, 33).

While both crip theory and queer theory advocate for the collapse of the binary division between abnormal and normal, McRuer cautions against development of a crip theory that would universalize and transcend activism in the streets. He grounds crip theory in a materialist analysis that complicates simple disability identity politics while also depending on it. Both neoliberal capitalism and antiglobalization movements continue to enforce a ideology of compulsory able-bodiedness that, in the case of neoliberalism, valorizes individual exceptionalism or, in the case of progressive/left movements, uses the degraded disabled body as the opposing binary term to the free, empowered citizen. Only by "cripping" the human condition, economically, culturally, and geographically, according to McRuer, will progressive social movements be able to "remake the material world."

Both "cripping" and "queering," as interpretive strategies, spin mainstream representations or practices to reveal dominant assumptions and exclusionary effects. It is important to note that while queer theory originated in the academy, the practice of "cripping" originated in the projects of artists and activists. As Ann M. Fox argues, the process of cripping involves not only making the contribution of disabled people to mainstream culture visible but also revealing how "disability might have been an integral part of how that knowledge was produced," and thus capable of questioning "the privileged position of . . . bodily, cognitive . . . normalcy," in cultural production (2010, 39). Fox's assertion is demonstrated by the fact that, long before crip theory appeared, disabled performers, playwrights, and comedians were "cripping" mainstream cultural institutions. One popular target was the telethon, "cripped" by Susan Nussbaum in her comedic play *Telethon* (which debuted in Chicago in 1995), Bill Trzeciak in his 1998 "Telethon" sketch in the play *P.H. *reaks: the hidden history of people* *with disabilities*, and the Mickee Faust Club's video send-up *The Scary Lewis Yell-a-Thon* (2004).

The popularity of "crip" among certain sectors of the disability community shows no sign of abating. The term thrives alongside the more circumspect "disabled person," "disability," or "person with a disability," expanding a newly minted vocabulary for physical and mental difference begun in the 1970s. The shape and sound of the word, with its quick burst of Anglo-Saxon roughness, forms compound words easily, and, most important, matches the pride and panache of a growing, self-defining disability community.

15

Deafness
Douglas C. Baynton

Deafness is not what it used to be. Nor has it ever been just one thing, but many. Typically it refers to those who cannot understand speech through hearing alone, with or without amplification. Colloquially, it may also refer to any hearing impairment, as when a person is described as "a little deaf." Professionals in education and communication sciences distinguish prelingual from postlingual deafness, in recognition of their different implications for speech and language learning. Within the deaf community, in contrast, the term "deaf," as well as its signed equivalent, usually refers to people who identify culturally as deaf, and is sometimes capitalized ("Deaf") to distinguish the culture from the audiological condition.

In the nineteenth-century United States, culturally deaf people frequently referred to themselves as "mutes," while educators used "semi-deaf" as a synonym for hard of hearing, "semi-mute" for the postlingually deafened who retained intelligible speech, and "deaf-mute" or "deaf and dumb" for the prelingually deaf. Deafness also has long been a common metaphor for a refusal to listen or to learn, as when the French writer Victor Hugo declared that "the one true deafness, the incurable deafness, is that of the mind" (qtd. in Lane 1984, ix).

In 1772, British writer Samuel Johnson called deafness the "most desperate of human calamities," a view expressed more often by hearing than by deaf people. Deafness acquired after early childhood is usually experienced as a loss and a sorrow, at least for a time. Of this experience, we have many accounts. In her essay "Letter to the Deaf" (1836), British author Harriet Martineau confessed that becoming deaf as a young woman had been "almost intolerable," but now, at the age of thirty-four, she realized her suffering had arisen almost entirely from "false shame" (248–249). John Burnet, who became deaf at the age of eight, wrote in *Tales of the Deaf and Dumb* (1835) that while deafness "shuts its unfortunate subject out of the Society of his fellows," this is due not to being "deprived of a single sense," but rather to the circumstance "that *others* hear and speak." Were everyone to use "a language addressed not to the ear, but to the eye," he maintained, "the present inferiority of the deaf would entirely vanish" (47). The poet David Wright, who lost his hearing at age seven, wrote in 1969 that despite its impact on his life's trajectory, "deafness does not seem to me to be a disproportionate element of the predicament in which I find myself; that is to say the predicament in which we are all involved because we live and breathe" (1993, 7).

Acquired deafness begins as hearing loss but becomes something different, a state of being in all its complexity. Deafness from birth or early childhood begins as a state of being. Martineau observed that "nothing can be more different" than the two experiences, for "instead of that false shame, the early deaf entertain themselves with a sort of pride of singularity" (1836, 248–249). Wright maintained that he was "no better placed than a hearing person to imagine what it is like to be born into silence" (1993, 236). Historically the early deaf have been far more likely to form communities and develop a mode of communication better adapted than speech to the visual sense than those who acquire deafness later on.

Hundreds of distinct sign languages are in use around the world today, in which the shape, orientation, position, and movement of the hands, combined with facial expression and movements of the head and body, generate a range of linguistic possibilities as vast as the combinations of sounds used in spoken languages. Yet aside from scattered references, we know little about deaf communities prior to the eighteenth century. The literary scholar Dirksen Bauman has described the search for them as "a bit like tracing the paths of fireflies: the field is mostly dark, except for scattered moments of illumination" (2002, 452). In Plato's *Cratylus* (ca. 360 BCE), for example, Socrates briefly refers to deaf people who "make signs with the hand and head and the rest of the body" but elaborates no further. In seventeenth-century Europe, with the growth of great cities, observations begin to multiply: in London, for instance, the diarist Samuel Pepys recorded an encounter with a "Dumb boy" who communicated fluently in "strange signs" (November 9, 1666), while the physician John Bulwer wrote of "men that are born deafe and dumb, who can argue and dispute rhetorically by signes" (1644, 5). In Paris, the philosopher René Descartes observed that "the deaf and dumb invent particular signs by which they express their thoughts" (1892, 283), while in the Dutch city of Groningen, the physician Anthony Deusing described deaf people who communicated with "gestures and various motions of the body" (1656; qtd. in Van Cleve and Crouch 1989, 16). Isolated communities carrying a recessive gene for deafness have occasionally appeared in which the proportion of deaf people was such that all of their members, hearing and deaf, became fluent in a sign language. The anthropologist Nora Groce (1985) discovered such a community on Martha's Vineyard that lasted from the seventeenth to the early twentieth century.

Deaf communities come into clear view in the eighteenth century due to urbanization and the advent of schools for deaf children. In 1779, the deaf Parisian Pierre Desloges wrote that while the communicative ability of deaf people in the French provinces was "limited to physical things and bodily needs," in Paris they conversed "on all subjects with as much order, precision, and rapidity as if we enjoyed the faculty of speech and hearing" (qtd. in Lane 1984, 36). The Abbé Charles-Michel de l'Épée encountered that community by happenstance, studied its sign language, and founded the National Institution for Deaf-Mutes in Paris in 1776. The school gathered young deaf people from across the country, provided them with an education, and introduced them to the urban deaf community. The school had a profound influence on deaf education globally, with teachers and graduates bringing Parisian sign language to other countries in Europe and the Americas, and later to Asia and Africa.

Schools for deaf students greatly accelerated the process of creating a sense of shared identity and distinct cultures. The existence of deaf communities and their languages became increasingly controversial in the latter half of the nineteenth century, spawning a campaign to exclude sign language from the schools. The movement for "pure oralism" was rooted in a burgeoning nationalism that led many nations to suppress minority languages, as well as interpretations of evolutionary theory that cast sign languages as relics of savagery, and eugenic fears that deaf marriages would lead to the proliferation of "defectives." The movement achieved an important symbolic victory when the Milan Congress of 1880, an international conference of educators of the deaf, affirmed the "incontestable superiority of speech over signs." Deaf people and their organizations rallied against pure oralism, arguing that complete reliance on speech inevitably impaired the educational and linguistic development of many if not most deaf children. Nevertheless, oralism soon became the new orthodoxy in deaf education and remained so until the 1970s.

While childhood disease had long been the most common cause of deafness, its rapid decline in Western countries in the second half of the twentieth century meant that those born deaf became increasingly predominant in the community, a demographic shift with profound implications. Whatever successes supporters of oralism had been able to claim earlier in the century had been based largely on the prevalence of postlingually deafened children. Now, success was increasingly rare and educators began to reconsider long-held assumptions. The character of the deaf community also began to change, as native or early signers became the majority. A confluence of factors—among them movements for minority rights, changing attitudes toward the body, and a growing acceptance of cultural diversity—furthered the development of a deaf rights movement based on pride in sign language and deaf identity.

The academic field of deaf studies arose from this movement. Repudiating the pathological model of deafness, it focused on the study of deaf cultural attributes, among them linguistic practices, literatures, rules of etiquette, values, marriage patterns, and community institutions. Ethnic studies rather than disability studies was its primary model. The term "deafness" came to be used mainly to denote hearing loss, as opposed to "deaf" (or "Deaf") cultural identity. "Deafhood," first proposed by British scholar Paddy Ladd (2003), is sometimes used as an alternative. Recent work in the field, however, has brought considerations of the body and concepts from disability studies into deaf studies. A growing emphasis on the centrality of vision to the deaf experience, and the ways in which deaf people process visual information differently from hearing people, has led some to suggest that deaf people might be better referred to as "visual people." Dirksen Bauman and Joseph Murray (2009) have proposed the concept of "deaf gain" (as opposed to "hearing loss") to suggest that diverse sense experiences can lead to valuable alternative ways of understanding.

Today multiple forces are confounding older conceptions of deafness. University students and scholars now study sign language, a movement begun by William Stokoe's linguistic research at Gallaudet University in the late 1950s. In many areas of the world, the stigma of deafness has been much reduced, while opportunities for higher education and employment have improved. At the same time, the majority of deaf children no longer attend separate schools, disrupting the intergenerational transmission of deaf cultural values and languages. Minority groups generally remain cohesive and distinct commensurate with their exclusion by the majority; like other minority groups that have gained social acceptance, the deaf community has seen many of its organizations, which proliferated in the twentieth century, disappear. An oft-discussed question is whether this signals the end of deaf culture or merely its adaptation to changed circumstances.

When the use of cochlear implants in children became widespread in the 1990s, a National Association of the Deaf (NAD) position paper called it "ethically offensive" (1991), and many deaf people viewed it as "cultural genocide." Today, with implants increasingly common, opposition has diminished. The current NAD position, adopted in 2000, accepts implants as "part of today's reality" and calls for "mutual respect for individual and/or group differences and choices." Deaf people are very aware, however, that advances in implant technology, coupled with genetic and stem cell medicine, may in the foreseeable future mean an end to deafness itself. George Veditz predicted a century ago that "as long as we have deaf people, we will have signs" (qtd. in Padden and Humphries 2005, 77). What if there are no deaf people? Among wealthier countries, where implantation rates now range from 50 to 90 percent of deaf children, the continued existence of viable deaf communities is in doubt (Johnston 2004). Markku Jokinen, the former president of the World Federation of the Deaf, argued in 2001 for a community defined by the use of sign language rather than deafness. But whether a sign language–using community can persist without some critical number of deaf members is an open question. The phenomenon of deaf communities was born of a particular moment in history that may now be coming to an end. It was technological developments in agriculture, industry, and transportation that made modern cities—and thus modern deaf communities—possible. A new phase of technological innovation may soon bracket the other end.

16

Deformity

Helen Deutsch

Before modern conceptions of "disability" and the scientific "norms" that defined it, "deformity" demarcated and degraded physical difference. Defined by the *Oxford English Dictionary* as "the quality or condition of being marred or disfigured in appearance; disfigurement, unsightliness, ugliness," deformity has roots in both the embodied realm of the aesthetic and the figurative realm of the moral. "Deformity" reigned supreme in the eighteenth century, that great age of satire, caricature, and sanctioned laughter at cripples (Dickie 2011; Lund 2005). This was also the age of classification, in which differences of sex and race were invented and delineated. In an age during which the norm was not yet fully materialized, deformity was suspended between the early modern understanding of corporeal difference as divine punishment for sin and the nineteenth-century conception of disability as individual obstacle to be virtuously overcome (Davis 2000a). Deformity encapsulates the paradox of a visible sign of unintelligibility, a fall from form written by God or nature on the body. It is linked conceptually with "monstrosity," which is derived from *monstra*, meaning a warning or a portent of catastrophe to come. "Deformity," like "monstrosity," is at once sign and story.

Every essay on deformity must struggle with Francis Bacon's foundational essay "Of Deformity" (1625). Rather than define deformity, the father of modern scientific inquiry makes it a literary matter especially well suited to the essay's "assaying" or trial of truth.

Beginning with the ambiguous claim that "deformed persons are commonly even with nature," Bacon baffles the reader, adding clauses—"for as nature doth ill by them, so do they by nature"—that further complicate rather than explain matters. Is deformity "even" in the sense of "in balance with" nature, or does it "get even with nature" (Brueggemann and Lupo 2005, 1)? And when Bacon goes on to claim that deformed persons are "void of natural affection," does he mean that they are incapable of offering human sympathy, incapable of receiving it, deprived of it, or all of these? So unfixed is deformity's meaning that Bacon suggests we would do better to consider deformity "not as a sign, which is more deceivable; but as a cause that seldom faileth of the effect." In that shift to "cause," deformity transforms the idea of the body as a transparent index of the mind (a correspondence that informs the sciences of eighteenth-century physiognomy and nineteenth-century phrenology) into an apparently more stable natural law of cause and effect. But "seldom" implies that cause and effect can be interrupted by individual agency. Bacon goes on to observe that, "whosoever hath any thing fixed in his person that doth induce contempt, hath a perpetual spur in himself to rescue and deliver himself from scorn." In response to what would later be termed stigmatization, deformity prompts action "which must be either by virtue or malice." Thus while Bacon's essay is widely acknowledged to have been influenced by Shakespeare's paradigm of deformed malignity, Richard III, it concludes with a list of virtuous exceptions, going as far back as Aesop and that moral paragon and epitome of ugliness, Socrates.

Such embodied ambiguity enabled deformity to function as both definitive stigma and interpretive opportunity. The *Oxford English Dictionary*'s second definition of deformity—"misshapen"—intensifies this ambiguity by pointing to a negligent agency, a body created and abandoned by its author. Deformity could be understood as nature's mistake or its jest (*lusus naturae*), divine order's exception and its most innovative expression. Such ambiguity structured the satirical battle between the poet Alexander Pope and his aristocratic opponent, Lady Mary Wortley Montagu, especially the latter's "Verses Address'd to the Imitator of Horace" (1733). Montagu, incensed by Pope's attacks on her as the diseased and slovenly "Sappho," described the poet's person, bent by a curved spine, as at once "Resemblance and Disgrace" of the properly human form, marked like Cain, by God's own hand. In his final imitation of Horace (1738), Pope rewrote his deformity as moral exemplarity, refuting his patron Lord Bolingbroke's cruel laughter at his appearance with a Socratic revelation of his own moral inconsistencies. Critical of the poet's appearance, yet "careless how ill I with myself agree," Bolingbroke is "kind to my dress, my figure, not to Me." "Is this my Guide, Philosopher, and Friend?" Pope asks of the man who inspired his moral treatise, *An Essay on Man* (1733–1734), thereby rendering his own self-division the source of his moral authority (Deutsch 2005b). Similarly, William Hay, in his *Deformity: An Essay* (1754), in which he vows "by a finished piece to atone for an ill tuned person," argued that his detachment from matters of the body rendered him a paragon of Christian stoicism, while his curved spine echoed his contemporary William Hogarth's famous line of beauty (Hay 2004, 3, 83). These personal variations on Bacon's impersonal theme exemplified how deformity, suspended between sign and cause, the literal and the figurative, fact and fiction, rendered the marginal central; they made physical imperfection the sign of a common and inconstant humanity (Deutsch 2005a). Thomas Hobbes, the early modern philosopher most pessimistic about human nature, observed that, "we laugh at some deformed thing in another by comparison whereof [we]

applaud ourselves" (Hobbes 1991, 3). His predecessor and teacher, Michel de Montaigne, turned Hobbes's observation inward when he wrote, "I have seen nothing more deformed than myself," concluding with the moral of deformity's representativeness that "every example is lame" (Montaigne 1981, 787, 819).

The inescapable interdependence of deformity and form that allowed Pope and Hay to make deformity exemplary was allegorized by the famously beautiful and disabled Romantic poet Lord Byron (whose multiple disabilities have been linked to cerebral palsy) in his play *The Deformed Transformed* (1824; cited in Mitchell and Snyder 2001, 368). In a Faustian bargain, the bullied and misshapen hero, Arnold, on the verge of suicide, is persuaded by a dark stranger to trade his soul for the seemingly perfect body of Achilles (who himself was disabled by his heel, the one part of his body that was vulnerable to death). The stranger shadows the transformed Arnold in his original shape, proving the inseparability of deformity and ideal beauty, and the deceiving nature of physical appearance (Mitchell and Snyder 2001, 368). While modernism embraced deformity for its power of defamiliarization (Siebers 2010), the relentless dialectic of deformity and form that Byron saw as the stuff of tragedy can only be undone, perhaps, by the twentieth-century French visionary George Bataille's antimodernist notion of the *informe* or formless, an ironic resistance to definition, "insulting the very opposition of form and content—which is itself formal, arising as it does from a binary logic—declaring it null and void" (Bois and Krauss 1997, 16).

In its provocative indeterminacy, the concept of deformity reminds us that current work on disability aesthetics that recognizes the semantically productive excess of the disabled body has a provoking history (Siebers 2010; Quayson 2007; Garland-Thomson 2009). The cruel eighteenth century taught us that the word wounds. This is a lesson that disability activism and disability studies have taught us over and over again. When the radical thinker and political activist Randolph Bourne revised his 1911 autobiographical essay "The Handicapped—By One of Them" (1977), he changed "deformed" to "handicapped," bolstering a new understanding of disability as socially constructed (Longmore 2003, 38). In changing the language, he hoped to reinforce the essay's call for sympathetic community with "the horde of the unpresentable and the unemployable, the incompetent and the ugly, the queer and crotchety people who make up so large a proportion of human folk" (79). Deformity provokes response; it will always demand interpretation (Pender 2000, 116).

17

Dependency
Eva Feder Kittay

When the failed 2012 presidential candidate Mitt Romney called 47 percent of the U.S. population "dependent," the remark was widely perceived as an insult significant enough to negatively influence the outcome of his presidential bid. Yet if we step back, we well might ask why humans, who belong to a thoroughly social species, so despise dependence. Dependence on others allows for needed care, knowledge, culture, technology, and political, social, and economic goods—the sine qua non of human life in any era. A reliance on government services counts as a primary advantage of a modern, relatively well-ordered state. We might as well decry our dependence on air. There are historical, ideological, and structural reasons why we so often refuse to acknowledge our dependence (MacIntyre 1997). This refusal is evident with respect to disability.

Writers such as Michael Oliver have maintained that dependency itself is central to the fact that disability is experienced "as a particular kind of social problem" (1989, 8). As such, it has shaped the social life of people with disabilities (Barton 1989). Against this position, other disability scholars have insisted that what undermines the ability of disabled people to flourish is the view that being self-sufficient, self-reliant, and self-determining is the norm, and the only desirable state of persons in a liberal society. On this view an acknowledgment of our dependency makes possible the *re*shaping of our understanding and experience of both ability and disability (Shakespeare 2006a; Kittay 1999, 2003; Weicht 2010).

In the 1990s, philosopher Nancy Fraser and historian Linda Gordon famously traced a "genealogy of dependence," claiming that independence was once a status reserved for elites who could command the services of others (Fraser and Gordon 1994, 310), and only later became a status assumed by the many. With the emergence of wage labor, the spread of political enfranchisement, and the lessened importance of status-based birth, independence came with the ability to earn a living sufficient to support oneself and one's family. Women were precluded from economic independence by laws and conventions; paupers by their inability to become waged laborers; colonials by political constraints. More recently, those who are excluded from independent status are thought to have a moral or psychological flaw. Welfare dependence bespeaks laziness or deficient internalized cultural values; emotional dependence displays weakness; chemical dependence shows the lack of willpower.

Fraser and Gordon's examination of "dependency" as a keyword in the U.S. welfare state revealed that the association of dependence on government support with a characterological flaw emerges in a particular historical moment. Interestingly, disability as a source of dependency does not figure in this account. In identifying four registers of dependency—economic, political, sociolegal, and characterological—Fraser and Gordon overlook situations in which obtaining the necessities for life is tied to inevitable biologically based limitations. It is a fact that humans all have a period of extended dependency at the beginning of life and during recurrent periods, such as when they are injured or ill or too frail to fend for themselves. Thus, a fifth register is *the inevitable human dependence register*. Some inevitability we do dread, such as death. Most inevitable conditions

we accept and meet with resilience. The need for food is inevitable, but we accept it as a condition of our lives. This inevitable need becomes the site of cultural identity, family warmth, artistic creation, and sociality. As an inevitable fact of human existence shared in reality or in potentiality by all, the fact of human dependence may not always be palatable, but neither must it always be undesirable. Yet we find a moral or psychological stigma attached to inevitable dependence, just as it does to other forms of dependence.

Nonetheless, no decent society fails to take some responsibility to meet (even if inadequately) the needs of those who find themselves inevitably dependent. And just as inevitably, in each society there are others who must tend to these needs. These *dependency workers* may be family or paid caregivers or attendants. They may be personally provided or supplied by the state. As their efforts and attention are used in the service of another's needs and wants, especially when they are unpaid family members, they are less able to attend to their own needs and to act as independent agents, becoming derivatively dependent (Fineman 1995; Kittay 1999). We see, then, that the concept of inevitable human dimension—the fifth register—reveals two important aspects of "dependency" that are otherwise missed: dependency is not always socially constructed, and dependency workers become derivatively dependent. Meeting human needs is sufficiently complex that we need a division of labor that issues in dependencies and interdependencies. Some prefer to speak of interdependence rather than dependence (Arneil 2009; Fine and Glendinning 2005). However, we cannot acknowledge our interdependency without first recognizing our dependency. Moreover, in some ways we are simply dependent and unable to respond to the other's needs. And that dependence too is part of a normal human life lived intertwined with others.

The paradigmatic example of the fifth register is the child, and many mistakenly assume that this paradigm applies to all who occupy this register. Thus, not uncommonly the inevitably dependent are treated *as* children: incompetent, asexual, "cute," "entering a second childhood." They are then presumed to be proper objects of paternalistic concern. But children are not alone in their inability to fend for themselves, and adults who share a level of dependence are rightfully offended by such infantilization. In our modern industrial and postindustrial world, where independence is construed as the mark of adulthood, it is difficult for many to acknowledge that dependence is recurrent and that we are universally vulnerable to it. Hence, we cloak it in invisibility or stigmatize it with hypervisibility. The independence of the "hale and hearty" worker comes at a cost. The underside of a society that places supreme value on the fully functioning, independent adult worker is the stigmatized and infantilized disabled individual. Disabled people have rejected the notion of dependence as inherent in disability, preferring instead to redefine independence as including "the vast networks of assistance and provision that make modern life possible" (L. Davis 2007, 4). As literary and disability scholar Lennard Davis argues, "The seeming state of exception of disability turns out to be the unexceptional state of existence" (2007, 4). The refusal to be labeled dependent is based, first, on the refusal to be infantilized objects of paternalistic concern and, second, on the supposition that the source of dependence is internal to the individual. In demanding the means by which to become independent, disability scholars and activists countered the narrative of the *inevitability of dependence for disabled people* with a counternarrative (Hilde 2001). People with impairments were *made dependent*, just as they were *dis*abled, by a social environment that did not accommodate their bodies. With the appropriate accommodations and

personal assistants who would be under their direction, disabled people could live *independently*. Judy Heumann, an early American champion of "independent living" promotes it as "a mind process not contingent upon a normal body" (qtd. in Crewe and Zola, 1983).

The counternarrative depends on a shift from an understanding of independence as self-*sufficiency* to one of independence as self-*determination*. This tactic spurred the independent living movement (ILM) and, in the United States, culminated with the Americans with Disabilities Act (1990; amended 2008) and the Individuals with Disabilities Education Act (2004). The ILM emerged in the late 1960s in the United States in cities like Berkeley, Denver, Seattle, and Urbana-Champaign before spreading to other cities and nations. The early founders were relatively young and physically disabled, and their demands were largely tailored to this population (De Jong 1983). They called for accessibility in transportation, living arrangements, education, employment, and inclusion in social and familial life to allow them control over their circumstances comparable to those without physical disabilities. Sorting out the different senses of independence promoted by ILM is not always easy, even to the disabled individual him- or herself. As medical sociologist and disability rights activist Irving Zola writes: "The important thing was that I got there under my own steam, physically independent and mainstreamed. But the price I paid was a high one . . . I, for far too long, contributed to the demise of my own social and psychological independence" (1988, 24). The independence to which he aspired was, he discovered, "the quality of life that [he] . . . could live with help" (De Jong 1983, cited in Zola 1988, 24).

Whatever the precise valence of "independence" promoted in these first-wave expressions of disability rights activism and memoir, such aspiration led to a frequent analogy with other civil rights movements. In those

DEPENDENCY   EVA FEDER KITTAY

struggles, the privileged gain material advantage by the oppression of the other. In a similar vein, the British Council of Organisations of Disabled People (BCODP), which identified itself as "the UK's national organisation of the worldwide Disabled People's Movement," wrote: "However good passivity and the creation of dependency may be for the careers of service providers, it is bad news for disabled people and the public purse. It is a viewpoint which meets with strong resistance in our organization" (BCODP 1987, sec. 3.1, 5). While the call for independence has promoted the interests and improved the life prospects of people with physical disabilities, and while it has successfully been expanded to include some with other disabilities, there are important limitations.

First, the applicability of "independent living" may be limited. While the BCODP derides the idea that disabled people need to be "looked after," some people with disabilities and frailties do indeed require looking after. Surely we should give all people as much self-determination and control over their lives as possible. But certain types of impairments affect the capacity for self-determination, just as certain types of impairments affect mobility or sensory perception.

A second problem with arguments for independence is that they are often tied to the idea that allowing disabled people to be independent ultimately saves public expenditures because the provisions sought are less costly, and disabled people can become productive members of society, thus repaying the costs of the needed services and contributing materially to society. While these strategic utilitarian arguments counter the image of disabled people as "burdens" on society, they feed the sentiment that the public should not have to be responsible for "dependents" who cannot pay their own way. This view not only disadvantages those who are least able to fend for themselves, shifting the cost and

care to struggling families, but also is liable to hurt those whose ability to be self-determining requires increased, not reduced, expenditures. Relatedly, arguments that bind independence to productivity are useful insofar as most people desire meaningful work. But for some, no amount of accommodation can make this possible. Where the expectation for work is imposed on those for whom it is impossible, meaningless tasks take the place of more fulfilling activity. It is an especially punishing view for those whose capacities for productive labor diminish with age (Morris 2004, 2011).

Finally, the demand for independence for disabled people relies heavily on the availability and compliance of caregivers. But there is a danger in the claim that "independence" is achieved by engaging personal assistants. To what extent does the supposition that the disabled person is "independent" render the assistant invisible and effectively subordinate his (or more often her) status and interests to the disabled person being served (Rivas 2002)?

A consideration of dependency forces the question: Can one still protect the benefits to be gained by disabled people's demands for independence without restigmatizing those who do not benefit? Can we accept the inevitability of dependence without denying the negative effects of an *imposed* dependency on the lives of many disabled people? And can we accept reliance on dependency workers without subordinating their interests to those of the disabled person?

Social organization is at least in part a response to inevitable human dependency. Rather than joining the able on a quixotic quest for a nonexistent independence, we might take the occasion of thinking about disability to suggest better ways to manage dependency. We can be *relatively* independent, but even this independence will be at someone's expense if we do not weave dependency needs into the fabric of society. Yet the fact remains that depending on another (or even on a piece of equipment) can leave one feeling frustrated, angry, and helpless. Dependency, aside from its stigma and from its potential assault on one's sense of self-worth, can be experienced adversely by disabled and nondisabled alike.

In a particularly insightful article on managing dependency in frail old age, renowned psychologist and gerontologist Margret Baltes (1995) distinguishes learned helplessness from what she calls "learned dependency" in the context of supported living environments. People develop "learned helplessness" when their attempts to affect their environment do not produce predictable outcomes. They become passive and stop trying to be effective. With learned dependency, by contrast, an individual's dependent behaviors may help him or her initiate social contact, but the person's independent behavior elicits little response from others. In such environments, striving for "independence" is less rewarding than what Baltes refers to as effective "management of dependency." Some of the elderly in her study allowed themselves to receive assistance in areas where they could meet their own needs, but with great effort. They chose instead to reserve energy for areas of life that provided more satisfaction. Rather than battling the loss of capacities when the exercise of these interfered with more important activities, these elderly were capable of richer and more effective lives. They displayed what philosopher Alisdair MacIntyre (1997) called "the virtue of acknowledged dependency." That is to say, they gave dependency its due. This is reminiscent of the strategy Zola adopted and which he chose to call "independence." But we avoid buying into the myth of independence when we think of it instead as "managed dependence."

If we manage dependence, we acknowledge its presence in our lives, select and optimize the opportunities that such acknowledgment makes possible, and can better detect and protect against the fault lines that are part and parcel of our condition as dependent beings. In its name we can demand a reordering of priorities and an assertion of entitlements that are our due, not because we can be independent and productive but because our value derives from the chain of dependent relations that make all our lives possible. Bringing this understanding into the lifeblood of society can be a precious contribution from the community of disabled people.

18

Design

Christina Cogdell

Disability is an ever-present human condition, an integral part of the continuum of every individual's life. Because everyone will be disabled at some point, disability is not a condition of a minority market (Davis 1995, 2002). Yet designing for disability is often regarded as a specialty area among architects or product designers, who often have to work within legal constraints, such as the building accessibility guidelines set forth in the Americans with Disabilities Act (ADA), in order to accommodate the needs of disabled individuals. Prior to the ADA, the work of very few architects and designers considered sensory impairments or wheelchair access and maneuverability in interior spaces, much less in public ones. By failing to consider and integrate limited perceptual and mobility levels, their designs posed barriers to some users. These barriers, as well as social and economic attitudes and policies that ostracize and exclude, socially construct "disability." In contrast, "inclusive design" is a practice that seeks to avoid such barriers, so that individuals with a diverse range of abilities can function more easily and fluidly within the built environment. The inclusion of curb cuts in sidewalks as a result of disability activism offers a famous early example of a simple change that benefits all users, from wheelchair users to cyclists to people wheeling luggage.

Designers can better serve humanity by integrating human changeability and rangeability into design theory and practice from the outset, rather than isolating less common or less frequent ability ranges within the categories of "disability." This is especially so if designers are serious about a vision of sustainability that not only entails environmental and economic concerns but also strives for social equity (Braungart and McDonough 2002). Spaces and products designed for longevity and usefulness could easily support an individual's transition through a full range of abilities. For example, by designing all buildings with full accessibility features in the form of grouped apartments, the assisted living community Ros Anders Gård in Västerhaninge, Sweden, eliminates the need for disruptive relocations as seniors lose abilities. The apartments open onto common spaces and common kitchens, and they are domestic and homelike rather than institutional, so that residents can come early and live there, as independently as possible, for the duration of their lives (Evans 2009).

Because this type of inclusive design is not yet widespread, consumers accept that they will likely need to buy a new house or cooking tools or clothes as they age or gain some weight. Built-in product limitations, combined with manufacturer's cultivation of planned obsolescence and expendability of goods, which force the purchase of specialty designs for changed abilities, have increased the profitability of mass production. In fact, this unsustainable but profitable design strategy stems from twentieth-century machine-based methods of mass production and standardization. Before the emergence of the industrial processes that made large-scale production possible, clothes were sewn for individual bodies to include the possibility of alterations. The onset of mass-produced clothing arose concurrently with social scientific methods of biometrics, anthropometry, and statistical averaging. Consumers became accustomed to the codification of bodily diversity into a small number of normalized sizes and body types, to the exclusion of others (Banta 1995). This process was carried to an extreme in clothing made for individuals in state institutions offering physical and mental care; not just the working professionals but also those receiving their care were made to wear uniforms. This "institutional" culture and aesthetic has marked design for nonnormative populations throughout the twentieth century, and only recently have wheelchairs, hearing aids, and fashion become much more stylish, decorative, and customizable for individual preference, expression, and need.

Early twentieth-century institutional practices, such as the medical model of rehabilitation that isolated disabled individuals from society, reinforced ideas of disability as difference from an idealized normality (Silvers 1998; Serlin 2004; Linker 2011). Many modernist designs of the 1930s and 1940s furthered this approach, as principles of streamline design mirrored progressive eugenic sociopolitical policies aiming to eliminate "degeneracy" from the modern world, at the same time emphasizing the "ideal" as standard (Cogdell 2004; Gorman 2006). Marking the beginnings of a changing attitude in the mid-twentieth century, the firm of Henry Dreyfuss Associates created the ergonomic templates for "Joe" and "Josephine," statistical representations of imaginary male and female types that each encompassed a *range* of sizes (Dreyfuss 1955). Dreyfuss used Joe and Josephine as the basis for ergonomic design, exemplified by the iconic Bell telephone design in which the handheld portion conformed to size and angle constraints that would be comfortable to human hands.

This new approach, whereby a single design could serve a wide range of sizes and abilities, laid the foundation for the principles of universal design, initially promoted by designer and disability rights advocate Ron Mace in the late 1980s and popularized later by OXO's Good Grips line of cooking utensils. Inclusive design, Europe's counterpart to universal design, identifies how particular designs exclude users and attempts to promote inclusion throughout the design process (Clarkson et al. 2003; Pullin 2009; Williamson 2011; Hopper 2012). As the most widespread approach today, inclusive design inherently recognizes that disability and difference are normal, aiming to affirm human rights and dignity by designing for all without stigma. Promising trends in culture and design—such as the recent revival of handcraft and the local, and greater attention to fostering human diversity and biodiversity—suggest a changing mind-set that facilitates broader factoring of full rangeability into all levels of design ideation and production.

19

Diversity

Lennard J. Davis

What is diversity? Its message is beguilingly simple and effective. Humans come in a variety of formats—with differing genders, skin tones, hair color and types, eye shapes, and sizes in the realm of physical differences, and diverse languages, religions, nationalities, and lifestyles in the realm of social differences. While diversity acknowledges the unique identity of such peoples, it also stresses that despite differences, we are all the same—that is, we are all humans with equal rights and privileges. No one group is better or superior to another.

Disability would seem naturally to fall under the rubric of diversity. Yet much of the time, when one sees lists of those included under the diversity banner, disability is either left off or comes along as the caboose on the diversity train. One could explain this negligence by saying that disability is just not that well known as an identity category; and that, when it is, disability will then take its rightful place along with more familiar identity markers such as race, gender, nationality, ethnicity, sexual orientation, and citizenship. One could say it will just take time and more activism and eventually people will be educated. Or one could say the problem is structural. This entry will explore the latter position.

To understand the concept of diversity and how it fits in with (or does not fit in with) disability, we might want to understand when historically the concept came into play and what preceded it. We might begin with the eugenics movement of the late nineteenth and early twentieth centuries, which stressed not the value of diversity but rather a "scientifically" determined notion of normality. Various groups were statistically aggregated based on their health, intelligence, size, strength, and so forth, in an attempt to determine which groups were normal (and therefore which groups were abnormal). Using a bell curve, statisticians determined where individuals fit into various cohorts and how subdivisions of the population compared with each other. Not surprisingly, white, middle-class European citizens were seen as more normal (or less abnormal) than immigrant groups from eastern and southern Europe, Africa, and Asia, as well as the indigenous working classes.

Thus the key distinguisher of groups during this period was how normal or abnormal they were. The goal of social policy and public health during this period was to reduce the number of abnormal people, often called "degenerate" or "feebleminded," and increase the number of "fit" people. Obviously, there was no ideology of diversity, since diversity was exactly what eugenics tried to eliminate or minimize.

The idea that some groups were normal and others were not began to lose public acceptance in the aftermath of the Nazi use of eugenic theories of normality to eradicate groups like Jews, Gypsies, homosexuals, and disabled and Deaf people. Further, the civil rights movement of the 1960s made it harder for the label of "normal" to be applied to any ethnic or national group as opposed to another group that would be seen as abnormal (although it took a few more years for gay and lesbian citizens to lose the "abnormal" qualifier). During the last half of the twentieth century, cinema, photography, television, popular music, and artworks increasingly argued for a "brotherhood of man" and later, as part of the feminist movement, "sisterhood" as a powerful good. The civil rights movement brought about changes in laws that made discrimination based on differences such as race and ethnicity harder to accomplish. The feminist and sexual rights movements included gender in this schema and, eventually, gay, lesbian, and transgender groups were added as well.

Economic discrimination based on race, however, continued, since human rights did not apply to economic justice and income inequality. One way that economic injustice based on race or gender was envisioned as disappearing was through equal opportunity in education and employment. The concept of affirmative action arose in the mid-1960s as a counter to the former discrimination based on race. At first not controversial, the idea of placing one group over another based on former discrimination eventually became a flash point for a new kind of racial prejudice based on the perception of preferential treatment. As "affirmative action" became a somewhat less acceptable phrase based on the ire it created in nonminority populations who complained of reverse discrimination, the word "diversity" may have arisen as an acceptable substitute. Now we have "diversity officers" at universities and in businesses rather than "affirmative action" officers or "minority affairs" administrators.

The Americans with Disabilities Act, implemented in 1990, may have changed some practices and abuses toward people with disabilities. But it did not change very much the way culture regards people with disabilities in relation to diversity. Our current interest in diversity is laudable, but websites and advertisements touting diversity rarely include disability. It is not that disability is simply excluded from visual and narrative representations of diversity in university materials. More significantly, disability is rarely integrated into the general media or, more pointedly, in K–12 and university courses devoted to diversity. Anthologies in all fields now cover topics like race and gender, but the inclusion of disability rarely happens. In popular media, it is rare to see blind people or people with Parkinson's disease included except in settings that reek of melodrama or sentimentality. Is there ever a depiction in a film or television show of a Deaf couple talking or a group of wheelchair users gathered in a park in which the point is not to highlight their disability? When disability does appear on the Internet, it is generally cloistered on web pages devoted to accommodations and services or as an exotic feature on a YouTube video.

Disability is not just missing from a diversity consciousness; disability could very well be antithetical to the current conception of diversity. It seems clear, as Walter Benn Michaels points out in his book *The Trouble with Diversity*, that current conceptions of diversity nicely suit the beliefs and practices of neoliberal capitalism. Michaels argues that the idea of diversity functions to conceal economic inequality. But one could add that diversity also represses forms of difference that are not included under the better-known categories of race, ethnicity, gender, and sexuality. In other words, diversity may only be able to exist as long as we exclude physical, cognitive, and affective impairments from the diversity checklist. Perhaps these need to be repressed because they are a collective memento mori of human frailty; but more than that, they are narcissistic wounds to the neoliberal belief in the free and autonomous subject. The neoliberal subject's main characteristic is individuality and the ability to craft one's destiny and choose one's fate as a consumer-citizen. But in such a mind-set, disability seems a lot less like a lifestyle choice and a whole lot more like an act of fate and evidence of powerlessness.

Universities are not exempt from this neoliberal way of thinking. College courses on diversity are intended to celebrate and empower underrepresented identities. But disability seems harder for "normals" to celebrate and see as empowering. The idea presented by diversity is that any identity is one we all could imagine having, and all identities are worthy of choosing. But the one identity one cannot (and, given the ethos of diversity, should not) choose is to be disabled. No one should make the choice that their partner be disabled or their child be born with a disability. So how could disability legitimately be part of the diversity paradigm, since it speaks so bluntly against the idea of consumer lifestyle choice and seems so obviously to be about helplessness and powerlessness before the exigencies of fate? If diversity celebrates empowerment, disability seems to be the poster student for disempowerment.

Disability is not the only category eschewed by diversity. One never sees crack addicts, homeless people, obese people, or the very poor in any celebration of diversity. These all fall into the category of what some might call the "abject" and must be forcibly repressed in order for the rainbow of diversity to glimmer and shine. This group of outcasts is excluded from the typical frame of university brochures or course materials, and this exclusion emphasizes how limited and problematic the project of diversity really is. These limits are laid out in diversity's main message: "We are all different—therefore we are all the same." But if difference is equated with sameness, then how can being different mean anything? That contradiction is usually resolved by finding one Other to repress—an Other whose existence is barely acknowledged. That Other is disability. What diversity is really saying, if we read between the lines, is that "we are different and yet all the same precisely because there is a deeper difference that we, the diverse, are not." That peculiar sameness of difference in diversity has as its binary opposite the abject, the abnormal, and the extremely marginal—and that binary opposition gives a problematic meaning to the general concept of diverse sameness.

One of those deeper differences might be thought of as medical difference. Medicine defines a norm of human existence, while diversity superficially seems to reject norms. There is no normal human being anymore, as there was in the period of eugenics. Diversity seems to say that there is no race, gender, or ethnicity that defines the norm—as, for example, the white, middle-class heterosexual European male used to do. Indeed, that is a tenet of diversity studies. But in the realm of medicine, the norm still holds powerful sway. No one wants to celebrate abnormality in the medical sense—no one is calling for valuing high blood pressure or low blood sugar. There is no attempt to celebrate "birth defects" or cancer (although we celebrate those fighting cancer). What people most want to hear from the obstetrician is that their child is "normal."

If diversity rejects the idea of a normal ethnicity, it has no problem with the notion of the normal in a medical sense, which means of course it has no problem with branding some bodies and minds normal and some abnormal. As long as disability is seen in this medical sense, it will therefore be considered abnormal and outside the healthy, energetic bodies routinely depicted in celebrations of diversity. Recall that students of color are referred to as African Americans, Asian Americans, and so forth, but on the medical side of campus students with disabilities are most likely to be referred to as patients.

For a long time, in disability studies, there has been a cherished belief that if we work long and hard enough in the academic arena, we will end up convincing people that disability is a real identity on par with the more recognized ones. That position remains a hope, and activists will help that moment come sooner, if it ever comes. But it may well be that diversity as an ideological paradigm is structurally related to the goals of neoliberalism. As such, diversity must never be allowed to undermine the basic tenets of free choice and the screen of empowerment that conceals the lack of choice and the powerlessness of most people. Why should 15 to 20 percent of the population who are disabled be excluded from the diversity paradigm? Is this exclusion simply neglect, or is there something inherent in the way diversity is considered that will make it impossible to recognize disability as a valid and even desirable human identity?

20

Education
Margaret Price

Scholars of disability studies (DS) who engage the topic of education tend to struggle with its chimerical nature: sometimes "schools" are abusive prisons, sometimes pathways toward greater social justice, and it is not always easy to tell the difference. While contemporary theories of DS education tend to point toward hopeful developments such as inclusivity and participatory design, scholars are also aware that certain features of asylums of the nineteenth century lingered in classrooms of the twentieth and even twenty-first centuries. This history and the wide variety of current educational theories lead DS scholars to conclude that "normality is a shifting social construction comprised of several competing interests" (Rogers and Mancini 2010, 100). Disability studies scholars and activists continue to debate just what those "competing interests" are, how they emerged historically, how their power should be addressed, and how positive change can be effected in educational settings.

In the modern West, disability has predominantly been figured as an individual, usually medical, "problem" that requires intervention and "cure." As such, the classroom is often imagined as an important setting for those interventions and cures to take place. A medical/interventionist model of disability uses institutions of many kinds, including medical clinics, psychiatric hospitals and clinics, prisons, and schools, to effect a "solution" for disability. One strand of DS analysis focuses on the ways that different educational settings use the concept of disability in order to measure attributes such as intelligence, to track and predict performances in order to exploit the differences between "gifted" and "slow" students, and ultimately to achieve a variety of segregationist effects whose aim is to uphold existing power structures. In other words, "schooling operates as a field of application for disciplinary power" (Graham and Slee 2008, 282).

To a large degree, the conflation of school with the site of "cure" has its origins in the asylum. Asylums existed before the 1800s, but it was during that century that these "total institutions" (Goffman 1961) helped shape the modern conception of disability as any human variation beyond the imagined normal. Some asylums were simply punitive, particularly when designated for nonwhite inmates (Burch and Joyner 2007), but many claimed educational aspects. For example, insane asylums during the eighteenth and nineteenth centuries claimed a progressive goal—to "repair those minds that had been broken by the modern world" (Reiss 2008, 3; see also Geller and Harris 1994). This apparently benign goal, however, was attached to a coercive and even violent practice. While methods of "repair" did include schooling and vocational training, they also included painful, humiliating, and at times permanently damaging "treatments" such as physical restraint, forcible drugging (often through the use of laxatives), and—by the mid-twentieth century— sterilization, lobotomies, and electroshock. And the remediation itself was invariably aimed at aspects of human difference that presented some challenge to the status quo: for example, as feminist scholars have pointed out, asylums were often used as a means to incarcerate women who failed to meet accepted standards of "feminine" behavior.

Early asylums for the deaf, like insane asylums, were popularly considered nothing more than pens to house "dumb Animals" (John Bulwer, qtd. in Wrigley 1996, 2). However, one significant difference in the trajectories of institutions for the d/Deaf and institutions for the mad is that in some cases deaf asylums morphed into schools for the d/Deaf. These became among the first institutional spaces in which Deaf and disability culture flourished. This was not a simple transition, however, since both asylums and schools were often places where "interest in cure and in exclusion coincide[d]" (Foucault 1965, 10). For example, while early "deaf and dumb" asylums in nineteenth-century Europe and the United Kingdom promoted sign language, later oralist "schools" for deaf children, established in an attempt to eradicate Deaf culture, were often cruelly abusive, using tactics such as tying students' arms to their sides to prevent them from signing. Through the mid-1800s, however, Deaf culture continued to resist this oppression, and signing schools appeared in countries including France, the United Kingdom, and the United States. Capital-D Deaf schools grew in number and popularity through the early twentieth century and foreshadowed the efforts of early twentieth-century schools to provide cultural and physical space for what would become radical organizing among advocates for disability and Deaf rights. Some of the efforts that emerged from schools included the establishment of the Rolling Quads in 1970 and the Center for Independent Living in 1972, both at the University of California at Berkeley, and the "Deaf President Now" protest at Gallaudet University in 1988.

Although (arguably) less violent than asylums, special education programs for students with a wide range of disability labels, developed through the middle to late twentieth century, were similarly aimed at both physical separation and discipline. In the United States, the emergence of special education as practiced today followed the Rehabilitation Act of 1973 and the Individuals with Disabilities Education Act (IDEA) of 1975.

While these laws, and the programs that arose in response, were genuine attempts to increase accessibility, many problems resulted. Designating some forms of education as "special" meant that in practice schools became preoccupied with "classifying, labeling, and sorting so-called deviant behaviors" (Rogers and Mancini 2010, 90). Unsurprisingly, the deviance of disability overlaps with other categories of difference; for example, black males are vastly overrepresented in certain diagnostic categories, including ADHD and oppositional defiant disorder (Erevelles 2005; Rogers and Mancini 2010; Stubblefield 2009). Whether intentionally or not, programs in special education often uphold the oppression of particular groups of students—those who are perceived to deviate from an illusory norm—by casting their educational challenges as arising from "disability."

In response to problems with the special education model, teachers and scholars began to move toward an "inclusion" model in the 1980s and 1990s. Inclusive education is meant to redress the segregationist qualities of special education. It represents an important philosophical shift, namely, the realization that separate educational experiences are rarely equal, and thus the creation of more flexible programs is needed. In practice, however, this goal is not always successful. One difficulty is that programs claiming to be inclusive may offer only "cosmetic adjustments" that preserve the status quo. (Graham and Slee 2008, 277–278). Another problem is the vagueness of the term itself, which has been used to designate changed policies in settings as specific as classrooms, and as general as the educational system at large (Artiles, Kozleski, and Waitoller 2011, 3). A somewhat more specific approach within inclusive education is "universal instructional design" (UID), sometimes also called "universal design for learning" (UDL) or simply "universal design" (UD). The "universal" part of the term is generally understood to be aspirational rather than descriptive: this approach sets as its ideal a learning environment that is accessible to all learning styles, abilities, and personalities but also acknowledges that such efforts must always be understood as partial and engaged in a process of continual revision.

Contemporary theories of education in DS are moving further away from the "universal" in UDL, even in name; some authors, such as Palmeri (2006), instead are exploring "participatory design" (sometimes referred to as "human-centered" or "inclusive" design). This approach recognizes that the access needs of various users in a single space (whether physical or virtual) cannot be reliably predicted and may indeed conflict with one another; therefore, there can be no "one-size-fits-all" approach to creating accessible infrastructures. For example, scholars including Catherine Kudlick and Jay Dolmage have led efforts at conferences (the Society for Disability Studies and the Conference on College Composition and Communication, respectively) to demonstrate a crowdsourcing model of audio/visual description. In this model, the audience describes an image collaboratively, in real time; then discusses what elements of the image went unmentioned; and, finally, reflects on the political choice to leave some elements of a visual image "invisible" to an audience member who does not see it, or sees it differently from other audience members. The point of such presentations is to demonstrate that access measures such as captioning and image descriptions are not value-neutral but rather political and power-laden choices.

The future of disability education will be increasingly interdisciplinary, as "education" as a field of study incorporates principles from areas including architecture, communication, and human-computer interaction. At the same time, "disability" as an educational concept is broadening to include more emphasis on mental disability (Price 2011; Stubblefield 2009), as well as intersectional concerns including race and class (Artiles, Kozleski, and Waitoller 2011; Erevelles 2005). While the promise of new approaches is always appealing, scholars and practitioners in disability education must also acknowledge the historical legacy of the asylum. Efforts in disability education must continually strive to avoid the oppressive and normalizing tendencies that endanger any institution, moving recursively toward the hope of a more just world.

21

Embodiment
Abby Wilkerson

One of the earliest goals of disability studies was to expose the various methods by which some bodies are marked as different and deviant while others are marked as normal. Disability studies scholarship focused on medicalization, rehabilitation, segregation, institutionalization, sterilization, and genocide demonstrated how such practices were instrumental to ideas of normalization and deviance. More recently, however, disability scholarship and disability culture more broadly have turned away from forces of institutionalization or medicalization to explore the relationship between disability and the concept of "embodiment." Embodiment is a way of thinking about bodily experience that is not engaged solely with recovering the historical mistreatment of disabled people. Rather, it includes pleasures, pain, suffering, sensorial and sensual engagements with the world, vulnerabilities, capabilities, and constraints as they arise within specific times and places.

Although embodiment sometimes serves as a synonym for corporeality—the state of living in/through/ as a body—disability studies scholars have tended to use the term in relation to phenomenology, the philosophical study of conscious experience from an individual person's subjective perspective. This approach to the concept of embodiment is intended to serve as a corrective to Cartesian dualism, the historic Western legacy derived from the French philosopher René Descartes that posits a strict dichotomy between mind and body in which the former assumes rational control over the latter's messiness and irrationality. Thomas Hobbes's *Leviathan*, for instance, affirms the political value of discrete and rational independent subjects who are the authors of their own existence. Hobbes regarded "men as mushrooms," originating out of nothing, born of no woman (Benhabib 1992, 156), thereby implying that by being "self-made" some men could achieve rational control of mind over body. Many disability studies scholars have suggested that Hobbes's definition of personhood is a normative fantasy of the physically and cognitively privileged.

Feminist phenomenology engages with ideas of rationality and body to understand embodiment as a form of gendered experience. This approach to phenomenology, which takes its cues from Edmund Husserl and Simone de Beauvoir, understands embodiment as a form of subjectivity that is manifested bodily, a ground of intentional activity and the means of encountering the world. Feminist phenomenology's version of embodiment reveals how bodily normativity is coded as masculine and constant. Bodily changes—such as aging, menstruation, menopause, or pregnancy—are regarded as forms of risk, disturbance, or breakdown, and irrationality (as in the womb-related derivation of the word "hysteria"). Seen through the lens of disability studies, embodiment frames bodily change as a horizon for self-understanding and self-definition, and the body as an agent interacting with others and with the world more generally (Weiss 1999).

Embodied disability perspectives not only generate incisive critiques of social norms and practices; they are also the basis for understanding and critiquing other areas of philosophical inquiry such as ontology, epistemology, political economy, and aesthetics. Along with feminist, postcolonial, and critical race approaches to embodiment, disability studies offers a distinct departure from Western liberalism's understanding of personhood as rational and disembodied. Taken together, these perspectives produce a radical cultural/material politics of disability while bringing new insights to the phenomenology of embodiment more generally. Indeed, a disability studies approach to embodiment contributes significantly to intersectional critiques of liberal individualism as expressed (or, rather, embodied) historically in the interests and expectations, all normative and invisible, of able-bodied white bourgeois heterosexual men.

Many disability theorists insist on a pluralistic understanding of embodiments as multiple, intersectional, and interdependent. Some clearly convey that individuals experience forms of interdependence that often shift and change over time, rather than strict independence (Panzarino 1994). The survival and well-being of human bodies, they argue, require extensive networks that orchestrate caregiving, personal assistance, and many other forms of labor (Kittay 1999). Witness, for example, the dehumanization of people who rely on feeding tubes or feeding assistance. Bodies that require nonnormative means of taking nourishment risk a socially imposed loss of personhood (Gerber 2007; Wilkerson 2011). Theories of interdependence and collaboration repudiate the concept of autonomy and control over one's body as authentic measures of personhood and expand normative definitions of what constitutes social and political inclusion.

Disability-informed theories of embodiment also provide the basis for rethinking the parameters of selfhood and identity, especially in relation to caregivers and prosthetic devices (Bost 2008, 358). Some Latina feminist narratives, for example, are structured by a critical sensibility of chronic illnesses such as AIDS and diabetes. "Bodily matter" and "its friction against existing material boundaries" demonstrate that "the language of illness provides a metaphor for politics based on wounds and connections rather than universalizing identities" (Bost 2008, 353). While disability itself is not synonymous with illness—a significant insight of disability culture and activism—illnesses and wounds can serve to ground a radical disability politics. Their material presence can unsettle abstract and totalizing identity categories—the idea of "health" and "illness" as diametrically opposite rather than mutually reinforcing—while also fostering solidarity and coalition against ableist and otherwise oppressive social definitions of normalcy.

Disability narratives involving chronic illness often rely on embodiment to establish a sense of identity "predicated on fluid boundaries" (Lindgren 2004, 159). They convey a phenomenological sense of illness as "uncannily both me and not-me," suggesting possibilities for "models of identity that incorporate difference" (159). In addition, disability perspectives significantly advance the phenomenological concept of "intercorporeality," which "emphasizes that the experience of being embodied is never a private affair, but is always already mediated by our continual interactions with other human and nonhuman bodies" (Weiss 1999, 5). Intercorporeality, as a concept, allows scholars to pay close attention to the dynamics of care relations (Kittay 1999), prosthetic relations between bodies and medical devices, and other forms of social and technological interdependence.

Disability intercorporealities also have the capacity to "crip" conventional understandings of kinship. For instance, families with disabled children are "rewriting kinship" and finding routes to collective action through shared resistance to public policies and cultural norms that devalue or marginalize disabled relatives, or that pressure women to abort disabled fetuses (Rapp and Ginsburg 2001). Queer disability narratives also rewrite kinship in new ways, including Latina feminist notions of "queer *familia*" as a condition for survival and connection (Bost 2008, 355; Panzarino 1994). Disability theories of intercorporeality also attend to new forms of "embodied pleasure," such as the "bodily attunement" of a child and occupational therapist who are both engaged in the poetics of autistic speech and movement (Park 2010).

Disabled embodiment provides epistemological resources for working through vexed questions of suffering and impairment. A phenomenologically grounded notion of embodiment can generate knowledge of pain as suffused with social meaning. Indeed, for some scholars, a focus on embodiment entails respect for experiences of suffering (Lindgren 2004, 151). At the same time, focusing on illness and suffering can "expand one's sense of embodiment" (Bost 2008, 350) through, for example, opening up an experience of physical pain as a channel of vital knowledge that can include politically radical possibilities.

In recent years, disability-informed theories of embodiment grounded in political economy have inspired analyses of globalization. In these approaches to embodiment, disability is understood as materially and geographically based, rather than a mere effect of discourse or flaws located within individual bodies or minds, as dominant paradigms of globalization would have it (Davidson 2008, xviii). Embodiment becomes a mode of material/cultural analysis that illuminates "the political economy of difference" (Erevelles 2001, 99) by attending to whose bodies are affected, and how, as capitalist profit imperatives meet changing labor and market structures. Work in this area of disability studies ranges from critiques of "disembodied citizenship" and the global organ trade (Davidson 2008) to analyses of political subjecthood in late capitalism (Erevelles 2001), to examinations of the global agro-industrial food system and claims of an obesity pandemic (Wilkerson 2011), and the neoliberal demand for flexible bodies (McRuer 2006). Such work advances disability studies' imperative to situate embodiment within specific environments and attend closely to material circumstances.

Finally, disability perspectives on embodiment have also produced a generative and critical aesthetics. Disabled embodiment refutes social conceptions of disability as pathology and social norms of productivity by providing "different conceptions of the erotic body" that contest hegemonic notions of beauty and vitality (Siebers 2008a, 302). Thus, thinking critically about embodiment helps facilitate the politically radical potential of a "critical disability aesthetics" to create identifications beyond normative notions of bodies, lives, and persons (Davidson 2008, xvii). As a result, the embodied experiential knowledge of disabled people has become a fundamental resource for disability cultures and modes of disability activism: as the late Latina feminist scholar Gloria Anzaldúa once observed, "'Along with your dreams the body's the royal road to consciousness'" (Bost 2008, 350).

22

Ethics
Rebecca Garden

Ethics is a field of philosophical inquiry that investigates questions of just or right actions and what sort of life is considered good. Ethics addresses individual experiences of goodness in life and individual moral actions, as well as the morality of the collective: questions of social responsibility and justice. Ethical analyses traditionally take place in relation to principles, norms, and standards. In order to establish ethical principles to guide individual behavior, it is necessary to make generalizations about what is good or what is right and what constitutes harm.

As a field of study, however, ethics is made even more ethical when challenged by the perspectives of those who are believed to fall outside of the norms that have shaped it. Disability studies not only deconstructs the norms of mainstream moral philosophy but also has challenged the very conception of the norm and thus the way that many ethical analyses of goodness in life, the life "worth living," and right actions have either excluded or discounted human variation associated with disability.

Disability studies engages with multiple aspects of ethics: the ethics of existence, or the right to exist, as well as the right of inclusion, for those who are not "average" or considered normal but who nonetheless deserve equal access to social processes and social goods. Discussions regarding the "elimination" of disability point out the ways in which the ethical frameworks of medicine and bioethics have failed to encompass the experiences and values of disabled people, resulting not only in inequalities but also in preventing or ending certain kinds of life. Thus, disability ethics historicizes and analyzes the social practices that are based on the mainstream belief held by some philosophers that life with disability is not worth living. Lennard Davis (1995), for example, traces the historical development of norms of ability in relation to the ideology of human perfectibility in order to show how developments in the sciences, such as statistics, intelligence tests, and constructions such as the bell curve, have obscured and marginalized variation in favor of the norm.

Davis demonstrates how nineteenth-century norms in statistics fed into the science of eugenics, which strove to eliminate the abnormal or pathological in order to achieve an ideal society. The science of eugenics, which pursued the ideal of health and normalcy by preventing the birth of those considered abnormal, rationalized the abrogation of basic human rights of "undesirable elements" through the forced sterilization of so-called imbeciles in asylums and prisons, ratified by the U.S. Supreme Court in the 1927 decision *Buck v. Bell*. Decades before the rise of the Third Reich and its Nazi gas chambers, eugenicists in the United States and Great Britain debated the role of "euthanasia" in eliminating "incurable" cases of illness and deviance, discussing measures such as "lethal chambers" of poisonous gas (Stone 2002).

Rosemarie Garland-Thomson argues that attempts to conform anomalous bodies and minds to a standard or norm, through practices such as "curing, repairing, or improving disabled bodies through procedures as diverse as reconstructive and aesthetic surgery, medication, technology, gene therapy, and faith healing" (2004, 779–780), are part of a "cultural logic of euthanasia." Eugenic theories and practices are also imbricated with modern-day genetics, demanding vigilant ethical

analysis. Deaf studies scholars Carol Padden and Tom Humphries (2005), for example, argue that many components of the science of eugenics are still at work in current biomedical genetic practices involving deafness and reproduction.

Shelley Tremain (2005, 2008) has shown that many ethical conversations surrounding disability are linked to institutions, particularly medicine, which exercise authority over those determined to be abnormal or impaired. Drawing on Foucault's formulation of "biopower"—the governing and control of individuals and populations through a combined force of disciplinary knowledge and power—Tremain, like Davis, foregrounds the emergence of technologies of measurement and systems of management that led to the medical management not only of illness and injury but also of anomaly (2008). Bodies (and minds) become the locus of normalization and differences; they are a "'problem' which must be resolved or eliminated" (Tremain 2008, 102).

While not always explicit, disability studies expresses its commitment to ethics through its sustained critique of disability oppression and demand for equal rights and access (Scully 2008, 10). The ethical analysis of disability draws connections between historical and contemporary practices that abrogate the right of disabled people to "live in the world," as the late Adrienne Asch put it (2001). Asch's work charted the entrance of disability rights into the arena of bioethics, which is involved with decisions about the standard medical treatment for infants born with severe impairments whose lives hinge on immediate medical intervention. For instance, in 1982, an infant known as Baby Doe, born with Down syndrome as well as a life-threatening but treatable condition, was allowed to die without receiving surgery. Disability studies scholars and disability rights advocates, including Asch, argued that the medical community, parents, and nondisabled society at large were "unable to imagine having a child with a disability as anything but a tragedy and disaster for themselves and for their nondisabled family members" (Asch 2001, 304). The absence—in health care and in society—of a disability perspective, which represents life with a disability as meaningful rather than tragic, enables this kind of disability discrimination.

Many studies as well as disability ethicists have demonstrated how nondisabled people, including health care providers, consistently imagine life lived with a disability more negatively than the way that disabled people describe their own quality of life (Amundson 2010). Indeed, Asch documented the view of many disability rights advocates, as well as some in mainstream bioethics, that "even a demonstrably loving and involved family may be unable to put aside its own view of how limited life with disability is to imagine such a life from the vantage point of someone with impairment" (2001, 309). Such attitudes have grave implications for ethical decisions that are made in the context of medicine, and influence decisions health care professionals make on behalf of or when advising disabled people. The inability, or unwillingness, to imagine life with disability shapes medical decisions about prenatal testing and selective abortion, as well as the viability of treatments, such as chemotherapy, for people with significant developmental disabilities.

In response to these attitudes, some disability studies scholars who advocate for greater ethicality in decisions made by and for disabled people, particularly in cases of life-and-death decisions, have called for an "expanded imagination" of life lived with disability (Gill 2006). Recognizing the link between this ability to imagine life with disability as a good life—that is, a holistic concept of disability shaped by disabled people as agents of their own social and political power—disability studies scholars have worked toward justice and equality by

examining the ethics of the "representation" of disability. This engagement reflects the understanding, as articulated by W. J. T. Mitchell, that "representation is that by which we make our will known and, simultaneously, that which alienates our will from ourselves in both the aesthetic and political spheres" (1995, 21).

One area of representation that has been a central focus of disability studies' engagement with ethics has been the rejection of the medical model of disability, which is characterized by the reduction of human variation to disorders and syndromes, and of bodily and cognitive differences to pathological or diagnostic categories. In her seminal work *Claiming Disability*, Simi Linton (1998) rejects disability as a category determined and defined by medicine and "claims" it as a "social/political category" (12) with a distinct identity. Focusing on language and its "representation" of disability, she echoes the disability rights movement's rejection of the "need for the medical language of symptoms and diagnostic categories" (8). Further, she unpacks the language of "passivity and victimization" used to describe disabled people, rejecting the idea that people "suffer" from, are "afflicted" with, or are "victims" of various conditions. This rejection of the medicalization of impairment and difference has enabled other "affirmative" models of disability identity (Swain and French 2000). The social model of disability repudiates the medical model and rejects medical care, cures, and rehabilitation in favor of social change that creates access and inclusion and thus reduces or eliminates the social effect of discrimination (Shakespeare 2006b).

Although many disability scholars and activists have embraced the social model, the rejection of the medical model has had the unintended consequence of producing new forms of oppression *within* disability culture. The rejection of medical diagnosis and treatment can result in a hierarchy that diminishes people with chronic illness or other conditions that require medical care or those who claim disability identity and yet seek medical treatment or cure for conditions or diseases. Susan Wendell (2001), for example, highlights this ethical complexity within the movement for disability rights and equality, distinguishing between the "healthy disabled"—such as Eli Clare, who observes that "my CP [cerebral palsy] simply is not a medical condition" (1999, 105)—and the "unhealthy disabled" who "*are* sick, diseased, and ill" (Wendell 2001, 18). Wendell points out that the social model's emphasis on oppressive attitudes, representations, institutions, and policies has the potential to minimize the concerns of disabled people who require medical care (18).

Other disability studies scholars have identified other forms of oppression and marginalization within disability studies. Emily Thornton Savarese and Ralph James Savarese, for example, argue that "the field of disability studies has been slow to take up cognitive disability, and it has done so with some discomfort—in part because notions of social construction, while important, seem inadequate to the task of assessing physiological differences in the very organ of perception, and in part because these differences seem such a threat to what most makes us human" (2010b). Similarly, Mark Osteen (2007) observes a "disciplinary vigilance" in disability studies that reproduces rather than dispels biases and misrepresentations and has led to the neglect of some forms of impairment, suffering, and pain. Osteen argues that by ignoring cognitive, intellectual, and neurological disabilities, disability studies has "excluded the intellectually disabled just as mainstream society has done" (2007, 3) and suggests that an overemphasis on the social model of disability has discouraged considerations of cognitive disability.

Disability studies is now reassessing the ethicality of its theoretical framework through critiques and complications of the social model. While the social model has been effective as a direct rebuttal to the historical legacies of the medicalization and pathologization of the disabled body, it belies the complexity of the issues as well as the field and its various lines of inquiry. In the way that the experiences and theories of autism, for example, have challenged the social model, perspectives from embodied experiences and social practices that were once on the margins of disability culture and identity now challenge norms and majority positions that have dominated disability discourse. Disability studies must encompass not only its predominant focus on physical disability but also embodied identities that are intrinsically linked to disability but often neglected in disability studies scholarship: for example, "fat," "madness" and neurodiversity, Deaf culture, and intersectional identities involving transnational identity and gender and sexual identity. These related fields of inquiry draw on the humanities, the sciences, and social sciences to identify the stigmatization of difference and explore the way that stigma informs and distorts assessments of health and the normal. There are obvious parallels with disability studies' identification of discrimination based on differences in appearance and physiology—fat studies' focus on the medicalization of weight as obesity and the social construction of obesity as an individual moral failing, for instance—and on the legal and social struggle for equal access and accommodation (Rothblum and Solovay 2009).

Ironically, some attempts to reject stigmatization often reproduce it in another form, such as when a member of one identity group rejects another "spoiled" identity: "I use a wheelchair but I'm not *cognitively* disabled," or "I am Deaf but I'm not *disabled*." Disability ethicists regard such negative formulations as essentially constructing a "new normal" that simply reconfigures the abnormal and sustains, rather than demolishes, the binary, and thus prevents alliances between disability studies and other fields of inquiry. Clare (1999) identifies this kind of reproduction of privilege within marginalized groups. His critique, primarily of classism and regionalism within queer and environmental activist cultures (in which the middle-class urban is often privileged over the working-class rural), raises concerns about classism and other forms of discrimination within disability studies. Davis (2005) raises similar questions about the boundary between disability and Deaf cultures, interrogating disability studies scholars' for purportedly embracing Deaf culture while nonetheless isolating themselves from American Sign Language. Similarly, Erevelles (2011) has raised questions about disability studies' adherence to the standards of normative modes of communication and argument that can exclude or marginalize those with cognitive and communication differences, as well as arguing for the need to expand the predominantly Western and Eurocentric field to address disability in a global context.

There are concerns unique to individual embodiment and experiences that cannot be recognized by a category or culture that is too broadly construed. Establishing boundaries may be a way to respect important differences; however, disability studies must be careful of situations where boundaries manifest as hierarchies. This recognition of the potential for oppression within disability studies and of the value of diverse perspectives will enrich and expand disability ethics' analyses of social oppression.

23

Eugenics
Rosemarie Garland-Thomson

"Eugenics" is the modern scientific term that emerged in the late nineteenth-century and early twentieth-century West to name the contemporary rationales and actions with which modern nation-states shaped the membership of their citizenry. The word "eugenics" itself was coined in 1883 by Sir Francis Galton, a prominent English anthropologist and statistician. Derived from the Greek to describe the pursuit of the "well born," eugenics was promoted as the new science of improving the human race through selective breeding. Galton's theories about creating a better future with a better population captivated American scientists in the industrial age. Yet the ideology and practice of controlling who reproduces, how they reproduce, and what they reproduce in the interest of shaping the composition of a particular population group long predate the industrial age.

All communities—from tribal kinship groups to modern nation-states—control the composition of their population through practices that encourage valued members to flourish and discourage less valued members of the group from thriving. Social orders create structures to control which individuals are included in or excluded from group membership, as well as the traits that appear in the individuals who make up the sanctioned population. In this way, a collective social body takes shape through the ways a community distributes resources, manages reproduction and sexuality, structures family units, builds environments, and disseminates cultural narratives. In other words, the borders of every autonomous community are both geographic and physiological.

Traditionally, social groups shape their populations primarily through regulating reproduction or excluding alien members. Such community-making measures always entail some degree of violence. Regulating reproduction through family and gender structures, for instance, requires strict control of female sexuality and male access to women. Most groups also shape their membership through overt violence, such as formal warfare, intertribal raids, rape, or killing. Wars and tribal conquest—for example, the Japanese occupation of Nanjing or the eruption of ethnic violence following the breakup of the former Yugoslavia—control both internal and external group membership. Rape throws into chaos patriarchal lineage and ownership of women and their offspring by interrupting exclusive sexual access to the women of a particular group, allowing the alien forces to literally and figuratively penetrate a community by contaminating its reproductive order. Genocide and ethnic cleansing are correlative traditional killing practices that shape future communities not only by culling present members but also by eliminating the reproducers in the enemy group. While these forms of violent tribalism do not use modern scientific means and rationales for eugenic community shaping, such acts of population control also underlie the modern eugenic logic of purification of the social body. Whatever the formal, functional, sensory, or developmental manifestations, the devalued human variations that eugenic logic targets are understood as disabilities: the flaws, excesses, deficiencies, or pathologies a particular social order disavows at a particular time.

By contrast to these methods of tribal purification, modern eugenics hides the violence of traditional population control practices behind scientific rationalism, technological pragmatism, and the ideology of progress. At the turn of the twentieth century, for instance, the United States was experiencing dramatic social change in the form of mass immigration, predominantly from southern and eastern Europe, as well as the internal migration of blacks from the South to northern cities. Such population shifts introduced an influx of labor, accompanying social changes, and new juxtapositions of ethnic and class groups arising from the increasingly rapid urbanization. By the first decades of the twentieth century, eugenics had become a modern social movement embraced by scientists throughout the modern West as well as by philanthropists such as Andrew Carnegie, politicians such as Theodore Roosevelt, and reproductive rights activists such as Margaret Sanger. The aim of modern eugenics was to rid society of the characteristics that dominant groups consider to be disabilities in the broadest sense and, often by extension, people with disabilities. What counts as disability and who counts as disabled change over time and across cultures, as do the social or governmental initiatives mustered to eliminate them. What we now consider racial and ethnic variations, minority sexual orientation, behavioral deviance, criminality, aspects of gender differences, chronic illness, and even atypical temperaments have all counted as forms of biological inferiority understood as disabilities under the logic of eugenic science.

Under the banner of modern progress, eugenic science became state policies. These policies included compiling records of so-called genetically inferior family lines; developing intellectual categories and measurements such as IQ, hereditary genius, and the elastic label "feebleminded"; passing antimiscegenation laws; encouraging selective reproduction counseling and rewarding supposed good breeding and fitness; and institutionalizing and forcibly sterilizing the supposedly inferior (Trent 1994; Lombardo 2008). The targets of eugenic policy were people with few resources or social capital. Eugenicists employed genetic, racist, and nativist logic to discourage reproduction by the supposedly unfit, whom they blamed for escalating crime and poverty rates. In total, more than 65,000 Americans were sterilized in these scientists' pursuit of an improved American citizenry. Eugenicists in other nations—including Sweden, Brazil, and Germany—launched similar programs, often in consultation with American eugenicists, who conducted international conferences and world tours.

Before World War II, eugenic progress seemed to many a positive and sensible way to shape a modern nation, even though cautions generally placed limits on its practice. Faith in the scientific concept of evolution and its implementation through capitalism, technological development, and secular social progress drove swift modernization in the late nineteenth and early twentieth centuries toward perpetual improvement through controlling the present in order to ensure future outcomes. Such an understanding of the present as a site for investment in a tractable, improved future differs from traditional worldviews based on acceptance or fatalism. The belief that the hand of God is ultimately at work in the world faded toward the end of the nineteenth century into the idea that human beings determine the arc of their own collective and individual history, making way for the concept of a national future intentionally peopled with the best citizens. The science of eugenics and its implementation through technology were the manifestation of this distinctly modern ambition.

The well-documented and familiar story of eugenics in our modern era begins with this now-discredited pseudoscience. Galton's theories of inheritance now seem to us misguided elitism and bad science, even while the related science of evolution pioneered by his cousin Charles Darwin remains foundational to our currently accepted understanding of human development. Our current recoil against this understanding of eugenics as an unfortunate scientific and policy mistake of the past originates from eugenics' most intensive application of social engineering in the twentieth century: Nazi Germany's ambitious project to create a eugenically shaped German citizenry—indeed, a eugenically shaped world. In the desperate and destroyed Germany of the late 1920s and early 1930s, the Third Reich came to power and adapted U.S.-led medical-scientific theories to invent the worthy Aryan citizen and its array of devalued opposites, a wide swath of human variation termed "life unworthy of life" in an influential book by two German professors, Alfred Hoche and Karl Binding, titled *The Authorization for the Destruction of Life Unworthy of Life* (1920). The Nazis fused ancient tribal anti-Semitism with modern eugenics in a reckless and ambitious attempt to shape a German national body that combined racial purity with eugenic elimination of all people—indeed, of all the human traits—they deemed inferior or alien. In doing so, they consolidated nationhood through the older model of ethnic tribal membership based on heritage and the newer model of national population-building based on the eugenic concept of biological superiority or inferiority.

The Nazi totalitarian regime's eugenic nation-building augmented traditional military warfare with modern technologies of control such as bureaucratic profiling, dissemination of racist propaganda, codification of racial difference through law and scientific research, and the implementation of medical measures to kill those who did not fit the Aryan model. Nazi Germany's eugenic project to advance the so-called Aryan race began with mandatory sterilization programs in the mid-1930s followed by a eugenic euthanasia program, beginning in 1939, in which disabled Germans of all ages living in institutions such as orphanages and medical care facilities were rounded up and transferred to extermination facilities. There, the Nazis, in cooperation with medical practitioners, developed the gas chambers and sham medical examinations that were later used in the more ambitious project to exterminate the Jews of Europe and other groups considered to be eugenically inferior (Garland-Thomson 2012). Between 1939 and 1945, several hundred thousand people with disabilities were murdered by the Nazi program of extermination (Burleigh 1995; Friedlander 1995). Thus, what was distinctly modern in the German nation-building project was using eugenic killing in addition to military killing as a way to forge a desired national population. In this sense, one could argue that the Nazi eradication of disability of any kind expanded to include the millions of Jews, Catholics, Gypsies, homosexuals, and others who were targeted in the Holocaust. By fully operationalizing eugenics to create its desired, ostensibly improved population of citizens, the Third Reich thus carried eugenic logic to its final, terrible conclusion.

The horror generated by the Holocaust, along with improved understanding of genetics and long-standing opposition from religious groups and prominent scientists, eventually discredited eugenics as a social movement, and the United States, Germany, and other nations largely abandoned eugenic programs after World War II. The Nuremberg trials, the United Nations, and, indeed, the entire array of civil rights movements and the increased democratization they brought about helped undermine the logic of eugenics. Similar to slavery or public torture, eugenics now seems part of the unenlightened historical past from which we have moved on in our progressive contemporary moment.

Nonetheless, the aspiration to shape future generations of people collectively and individually persists in reproductive practices ranging from genius sperm banks to routine genetic screening. Advanced technologies of genetic engineering, such as euphenics, aim to eliminate disease and introduce reproductive techniques to control the health and appearance of one's children. More broadly, the increasing commodification of normalizing products and processes such as cosmetic surgery has heightened the standardization of people themselves. These developments constitute what Daniel Kevles calls the "new eugenics" (1985, 267). Eliminating disability and disabled people is the primary aim of this new eugenics of enhancement, health, and normalization.

Reproductive technology is now the most robust new eugenic practice. Authorized by science and sanctioned as health care, medical control of reproduction through birth control, sterilization, embryological manipulation, prenatal and genetic testing, and selective abortion shapes populations in developed societies today. Understood as voluntary rather than imposed, the use of reproductive technology to sculpt individuals, families, and larger groups responds to cultural attitudes and ideologies about what kinds of people are valuable and desirable and what kinds are not (Parens and Asch 2007).

Proponents of eliminating disability and disabled people under various rationales and practices such as selective abortion, euthanasia, the right to die, and genetic engineering contend that reproductive technology and euthanasia are not eugenic because they are voluntary and noncoercive, a blend of pragmatism, liberalism, and consumerism (Rose 2007; Cowan 2008). Although some of these proponents of "liberal eugenics" ostensibly resist the intrusion of medical institutions into private life while others welcome it, together they support a velvet eugenics that goes largely uncontested in comparison to the violent eugenics of militarism (Agar 2004). One prominent example of a contemporary disability targeted by the new velvet eugenics is the collection of traits we think of as Down syndrome. This highly stigmatized way of being in the world is understood as medically abnormal and highly undesirable even though it is a regularly occurring, albeit minority, form of embodiment. Prenatal screening and other forms of reproductive technology have enabled the precise targeting of this group for exclusion from our shared community: recent studies suggest that up to 90 percent of fetuses with Down syndrome are selectively aborted (Mansfield, Hopfer, and Marteau 1999). Meanwhile, the shaping of populations in non-Western societies through sex selection abortion to produce culturally valued sons rather than devalued daughters raises alarm (Hvistendahl 2011).

Since the 1970s, counter-eugenic arguments based on civil and human rights, ethics, social justice, and the desire to preserve diversity have come from unlikely allies including scientists, religious conservatives, and disability rights groups such as Not Dead Yet (Hubbard 1990; Johnson 2003; Sandel 2007; Scully 2008; Garland-Thomson 2012). The counter-eugenic initiative arises from the egalitarian value of diversity and a rights-based understanding of disability enacted in policies and legislation such as the Americans with Disabilities Act of 1990 and the UN Convention on the Rights of People with Disabilities of 2008, which mandate accommodation of disability and integration of people with disabilities as full citizens. Yet an uneasy cultural contradiction exists in the United States and across the developed, democratized world between counter-eugenics and liberal eugenics, between inclusion and elimination of people with disabilities. A social and legislative counter-eugenic initiative works to integrate people with disabilities into the public world by creating an accessible, barrier-free material environment. In contrast, the eugenic initiative to eliminate disability and disabled people arises from the liberal ideal that social improvement and freedom of choice authorize shaping individuals, families, and communities of people by eliminating devalued human traits in the interest of reducing suffering, increasing life quality, and building a more desirable citizenry. These contradictory cultural logics are manifest in a wide variety of policies, institutional practices, and individual actions that occur within the particular historical contexts of nations and communities across the modernizing world.

A dynamic tension thus perpetually operates in the United States and the increasingly developed world between eugenic and egalitarian aspirations for shaping a citizenry. In the United States, for example, progressive politics shifted beginning in the 1950s and 1960s from the eugenic project of eliminating stigmatized groups to including a wider variation of people who had previously been excluded by segregation laws, discriminatory attitudes, and structural barriers. The larger civil and human rights movements emerged in various forms at midcentury, creating legislation, changing practices, and demanding the inclusion of previously excluded groups, including women, African Americans, people with disabilities, sexual minorities, and other ethnic and minority groups. The disability rights movement that also emerged in the late 1960s and early 1970s focused on integrating people with disabilities into the public sphere by removing architectural barriers, creating an accessible built environment, desegregating public education and the workplace, and providing antidiscrimination legislation (Scotch 1984; Shapiro 1994). The inclusive built environment that began to appear during and after that time made it possible for people with disabilities, who had previously been the targets of eugenic elimination, to enter into the public sphere—as well as the public spaces on which access to that sphere depends—to exercise the rights and obligations of democratic citizenship.

The contradiction between disability rights and liberal eugenics is manifest in beliefs, practices, and policies that determine who inhabits our shared public world. The counter-eugenic initiative, for instance, enables wheelchair users to inhabit public spaces, transportation, employment, and commercial culture on a scale impossible before the legal mandates of the 1970s began to change the built environment. At the same time, the eugenic initiative increasingly produces medical technologies that identify and eliminate through selective reproductive procedures potential wheelchair users born with traits such as spina bifida. Similarly, people with developmental and cognitive disabilities are now integrated into mainstream educational settings that accommodate their specific needs rather than being segregated in separate and unequal institutions. Simultaneously, medical technology routinely identifies fetuses indicating physical, cognitive, or developmental impairment to be evaluated for termination. This struggle between the new liberal eugenics and the egalitarian principle of full access to the rights and privileges of citizenship in a democratic order is central to the organization of human communities in the twenty-first century. Eugenics, understood in this way, is one of the most urgent and fundamental issues of our current historical time and place.

24

Euthanasia
Harold Braswell

Although *euthanasia* is Greek for "good death," the term's meaning has varied throughout its history. In Western societies, prior to the nineteenth century, euthanasia was a death blessed by God; such a death could be hoped for but was beyond human control. The rise of medical authority in the late nineteenth century led to a redefinition of euthanasia as a medically induced death in response to incurable pain, illness, and/or disability. Euthanasia advocates began to argue for *voluntary* euthanasia for those who desired to die, as well as *involuntary* euthanasia for those who, though not suicidal, were judged to be unworthy of living because of their incurable medical conditions. While this shift enhanced the agency of humans over what had previously been provenance of the divine, the exercise of this agency was shaped by the assumption that life with incurable illness and disability was inherently negative, even unlivable (Lavi 2005).

Like eugenics, euthanasia was a progressive political cause in early twentieth-century Europe and the United States. Euthanasia advocates, such as Killick Millard and Ann Mitchell, considered the incurably ill to be socially costly and argued that eliminating them would promote a more egalitarian distribution of wealth. Such ideas were implemented in American eugenics programs, which became inspirations for the involuntary euthanasia of the disabled in Nazi Germany. The revelation of Nazi euthanasia led U.S. and European euthanasia advocates to lose popular support until the late 1960s.

Then, buoyed by abuses in existing end-of-life care practices, they reframed euthanasia as an act of individual liberty in opposition to paternalistic medical authority. By advocating only voluntary euthanasia, euthanasia supporters distanced themselves from Nazism. In the United States, this strategy led to increasing acceptance of euthanasia, signaled by the California Natural Death Act of 1976 and, from the same year, the case of Karen Ann Quinlan (Dowbiggin 2005).

Since the 1970s, the extent to which voluntary euthanasia should be legalized has been a central question of the field of bioethics. Bioethicists classify voluntary euthanasia according to a threefold typology. In voluntary *active* euthanasia, the medical provider directly administers a life-ending substance. Voluntary *passive* euthanasia entails removing medical technology that had been keeping a patient alive. In the third type, *physician-assisted suicide*, the medical provider supplies—but does not administer—life-ending narcotics to a suicidal patient. In addition, there are also debates—and regional policy differences—regarding which among the terminally ill, the chronically ill, or even the "severely" disabled should be permitted to end their lives. Despite such disagreements over which forms of euthanasia should be approved, bioethical debates have largely been premised on the putative necessity of medically assisted death for consenting persons with "significant" incurable medical conditions (Kuhse and Singer 2006).

Disability studies scholars have criticized this bioethical framing of euthanasia. They argue that the suffering of individuals eligible for euthanasia is due not to a person's biological condition but to social discrimination against the incurably sick and disabled. Desire to die among these populations occurs when patients internalize this discrimination. Rather than seeing euthanasia as the product of free choice, in other words, scholars argue that such a choice is the result of disability

oppression. Transient depression among the ill and disabled should be treated appropriately, as would any other form of suicidal ideation. Yet the fact that so many medical professionals consider suicidal ideation among these populations to be potentially rational is the epitome of the discrimination that creates the individual's suffering to begin with. Thus, euthanasia advocates are complicit in the problem they mean to allay (Braswell 2011; Gill 2010).

While disability studies scholars broadly accept this critique of the euthanasia of the chronically ill and disabled, the field is divided about its applicability to the terminally ill. Some argue that terminal illness is fundamentally different from disability, and that physician-assisted suicide and active euthanasia for the terminally ill promote autonomy (Batavia 1997). Nevertheless, Felicia Ackerman (1998) has argued that an absolute distinction between disability and terminal illness neglects the stigmatization of disability that underpins euthanasia campaigns and devalues life with terminal illness. Though ostensibly protecting the autonomous choice of the terminally ill, this distinction tacitly encourages them to die. The implication of Ackerman's critique is that making euthanasia available to any one group will coerce that group into suicide. Furthermore, libertarian arguments to make euthanasia available to everyone neglect the extent to which the so-called choice to commit suicide is influenced by oppressive power relations.

Disability studies scholars have similarly argued that passive euthanasia—the withholding of life-sustaining treatment, or what is popularly called "pulling the plug"—encourages persons dependent on medical technology to end their lives. While often valid, these critiques neglect the harm caused to terminal patients by many "life-prolonging" treatments (Ouellette 2011). But, rather than accept passive euthanasia—which addresses aggressive treatment by denying treatment—disability studies should work toward conception of end-of-life care that eschews abusive therapeutics by using medicine to promote meaningful life with terminal illness. This conception can be found in hospice, which emerged in the 1960s as an alternative to both euthanasia and the hospital care of the dying. While the relationship between hospice and euthanasia remains contested (Putnam 2002), disability studies scholars can work with hospice professionals to implement end-of-life care that is astute about ableist power dynamics and responsive to the needs of the terminally ill. Such collaboration entails rethinking the bioethical categories that underpin the euthanasia debate.

The framing of euthanasia as an autonomous choice in response to a neutral medical diagnosis neglects the social nature of both medicine and individual identity. The social model of disability can reformulate bioethical categories like "autonomy" and "informed consent" even as a richer engagement with bioethics can produce a disability studies conception of euthanasia. Rejecting individual suicide, this conception would highlight deficiencies in the distribution and practice of end-of-life care. Disability studies can spur the development of care that is more practically effective and widely distributed, providing individuals throughout society with deaths that, if not "good," are at least easier to bear.

25

Family
Faye Ginsburg and Rayna Rapp

The word "family" is highly charged in disability studies. On the one hand, families are seen as the site of nurturance, narrative, and theory building for those with disabilities (Bérubé 1996; Davis 2000a; Grinker 2007; Kittay 1999). On the other, families are recognized as potential sites of repression, rejection, and infantilization. Whether seen positively or negatively, the term "family" is often taken for granted as a preordained, self-sufficient unit in discussions of family life influenced by disability. In the American context, the ideal of family generally involves parent-child relations in a classic heterosexual, nuclear, able-bodied household despite the coexistence of many other forms of family organization that incorporate members with disabilities: single parents, same-sex unions, extended family formations, and "families we choose."

Some of the earliest and much ongoing work on disability and family life builds on this assumed heteronormative Euro-American nuclear form. This writing predominantly comes out of clinical and applied research in the "helping professions" addressing the inclusion of family members with disabilities. It also is evident in memoirs ranging from parental reflections on raising a child with a difference, to first-person chronicles of living with a disability, to activist accounts. More recently, disability studies scholars from different disciplines such as anthropology, philosophy, history, and literary studies have taken more analytic, critical, cross-cultural approaches to understanding how the social categories of "disability" and "family" inform each other.

We have proposed the term "kinship imaginary" as a way to underscore this new analytic perspective, emphasizing that families are both flesh-and-blood collaborations and always acts of cultural imagination (Rapp and Ginsburg 2011). This conception draws on the basic anthropological/historical recognition that families are social constructions that vary across class, culture, time, and geography. To rephrase an insight from Marx, *people make their own families but they do not make them as they please . . . but under circumstances existing already, given and transmitted from the past.* In the process of incorporating disability, family members often find themselves transforming seemingly stable notions of kinship that they themselves may have taken for granted, occasionally becoming "accidental activists" as a result (Silverman 2011).

Through much of the twentieth century, "family life" was an arena in which state policies and public culture defined and pathologized disability. As early as the 1860s, "ugly laws" prohibited citizens with disability from appearing in public space (Schweik 2009). By the early twentieth century, institutionalization of the disabled and eugenic measures both continued to purge disability from public space and "protected" the nuclear family. In the United States, discrimination against disability included the encouragement of passive infanticide and other eugenic ideologies that migrated to Nazi Germany, where murderous prejudice against disability escalated to genocide (Pernick 1996; Longmore and Umansky 2001). In much of the developed West, more mundane forms of bias against disability persisted well after World War II, as families were regularly encouraged to institutionalize their disabled children "for their own good" (Stern 2005).

Toward the end of the twentieth century, a change in the zeitgeist and the law began to favor inclusion of people with disabilities in families, schools, and communities, although discrimination continues to be an enormous problem. This shift in the kinship imaginary emerged from multiple processes: family activism, de-institutionalization, progressive legal and educational reform, and most recently the growth of an international disability rights movement. As the relationship of people with disabilities to their natal families was redefined, kinship imaginaries have required continual reinvention, from the rearrangement of caretaking responsibilities in the household to the production of family narratives embracing rather than excluding the fact of disability (Groce 1985). This sort of "public storytelling" has worked its way into media of all sorts and in many parts of the world, ranging from personal memoirs and television shows to scholarly works that offer compelling perspectives on the "new normal" established by living life with a difference in many parts of the world (e.g., Grinker 2007).

A powerful redefinition of family through the prism of disability has come from feminist philosophers. Eva Kittay attends to "love's labor," the often unrecognized, mostly unremunerated, and deeply gendered work of caring for family members whose disabilities render them profoundly dependent, work inspired by her experiences providing care for a daughter, Sesha, born with severe cognitive impairment. Kittay (1999) develops a sophisticated analysis of the gendered assumptions built into our kinship imaginary via a "dependency critique" of equality as an ideology that hides the overwhelmingly female labor involved in caretaking of people with disabilities across the life span. She champions the recognition of caretaking labor that human dependency requires and the interdependence that characterizes all family life. Martha Nussbaum (2006) also critiques theories of social justice built on ideologies of equal rational autonomous subjects. Instead, she proposes a legal philosophy that accounts for unequal capacity, asking how we can best extend the equal rights of citizenship to those with mental and physical disabilities.

The philosopher Peter Singer (1993, 1995), by contrast, promotes an extreme utilitarian and neo-eugenic position, advocating that families have the choice to euthanize severely disabled newborns based on the hypothetical burden they might place on parents' preferences for happiness. This position has been challenged by disability activists, notably in a widely circulated article by the late Harriet McBryde Johnson, a disability rights lawyer who sketches a primal family drama imagined from Singer's philosophical perspective:

> He simply thinks it would have been better, all things considered, to have given my parents the option of killing the baby I once was, and to let other parents kill similar babies as they come along and thereby avoid the suffering that comes with lives like mine and satisfy the reasonable preferences of parents for a different kind of child. (2003, 50)

Add to Johnson's voice anthropologist Gail Landsman's (2009) empirically grounded critique of Singer in her study of American mothers who were recently given a disability diagnosis for their infants. In analyzing changes in maternal narratives over several years, Landsman shows how these mothers struggled to transform the medical model into an alternative narrative of family life that readily encompasses disability.

New medical technologies have resurrected old questions about the status and stratification of disability in families. Since the 1970s, a burgeoning popular and scholarly literature has responded to the escalating number of genetic tests that are increasingly being used for "quality control" of anomalies present in both parents and fetuses. Feminist disability scholars have raised ethical issues about the cultural values that encourage termination of pregnancies—or not implanting embryos—with genetically diagnosed disabilities (Asch 2007). While the range of conditions available for testing is increasing geometrically, the fund of social knowledge accompanying such decision making—what it might be like to live with a particular disability—is woefully inadequate for a generation of women who face the dilemma of being "moral pioneers" (Rapp 2000).

While there are eugenic echoes in these practices, the "choice" regarding who is admitted to the human community has shifted from the state to the family, assisted by emergent expert professions such as genetic counseling. At the same time, however, the spread of disability consciousness has given greater support to couples with disabilities that choose to create families of their own. Additionally, medical technologies in the developed world have also increasingly provided lifesaving possibilities for compromised infants, those with spinal cord injuries, wounded soldiers, the frail elderly, and other disabled family members who might not otherwise have lived. Their survival brings new challenges to family reframed by the fact of disability.

In parts of the world where such medical technologies are rarely available, kinship imaginaries—as well as the very category of disability itself—have quite different configurations in diverse cultural and economic settings. While models of personhood focused on the individual have guided the scholarship on disability in the United States and other wealthy countries, kinship- and community-based supports in resource-poor and non-Western settings (where an estimated 80 percent of people with disabilities live) often grow out of radically interdependent understandings of personhood in which families—however they are defined—play a profoundly important role (Ingstad and Whyte 2007). In places such as China or India, the presence or absence of disability in familial life is constructed by broader notions of kinship and radically different epistemologies from those used in the West (Kohrman 2005). A condition such as epilepsy may be seen as a divine gift, or else as a rare genetic condition understood as an ancestral curse. Family members with disabilities may be hidden and silenced, integrated as laborers, or encouraged to migrate from villages to cities in search of education, work, or services (Phillips 2011). By turning its attention to such contrastive kinship imaginaries, disability studies can aspire to a more global presence, offering a salutary recognition that people with disabilities everywhere shape and are shaped by family life in all its diversity.

26

Fat
Kathleen LeBesco

Fatness shares with more traditionally recognized forms of disability what Rosemarie Garland-Thomson calls "the attribution of corporeal deviance—not so much a property of bodies as a product of cultural rules about what bodies should be or do" (1997, 6). Conceptually, however, fatness and disability are tense bedfellows: many people with more traditionally recognized forms of disability resist being lumped together with those fat people who they feel could (but don't) control their condition, and most fat people don't recognize themselves as disabled, preferring to maintain a safe distance from perceived illness and stigma.

There are, nonetheless, many points of convergence in fat politics and disability politics: shared goals of access; eradication of prejudice, discrimination, and harassment; open forms of cultural expression; and recognition of dignity and happiness. Politicized fat people tend to resist the same medical model that draws the ire of people with disabilities; they don't see themselves as aberrations from the slim ideal or as something in need of "fixing." Instead, they embrace a mantra of size diversity. They demand access to employment, health care, armless chairs, and airline seats, noting that the built environment actively militates against their successful inclusion in many spaces. In other words, the dominant social attitudes toward fatness are the problem, not fatness itself. Fatness is (controversially) included in the U.S. Rehabilitation Act of 1973 and the Americans with

Disabilities Act of 1990, legally protecting fat Americans from discrimination as long as their condition substantially limits at least one major life activity or is perceived as doing so. But as Vade and Solovay note, to succeed, a claimant must "locate the problem on her own body" (2009, 170) rather than in discriminatory attitudes.

Like disability activists, fat activists are interested in the power of representation and naming. They resist mainstream medicalized or pathologizing labels ("obese" and "overweight," like "invalid," "retarded," "wheelchair-bound") in favor of reclaiming a descriptor that previously has been used explicitly to insult: "fat." Beyond naming, fat activists lobby for change in popular representations as a viable route to transforming public perceptions and consciousness; they critique portrayals of simple villains, victims, and buffoons in favor of more nuanced and complex depictions. In addition, a talented corps of artists helps to deepen and strengthen fat culture by creating examples of politically inflected film, performance, sculpture, painting, dance, and writing.

A growing number of scholars are committed to thinking about the relation between fat politics and disability politics, pointing out that the preoccupation with control and the flight from stigma serve neither particularly well. Huff exhorts fat people and people with disabilities to resist being pitted against one another, "when a coalition would be beneficial to both groups, who share an interest in both the deconstruction of the notion of the normal body and the reallocation of public space" (2009, 184). Scholars and activists including Charlotte Cooper, April Herndon, and Ragen Chastain have made inroads in developing such coalitions, which hold promise for destabilizing notions of normal embodiment and for reimagining the ways our bodies take up space.

27

Freak
Leonard Cassuto

"Freak" labels disability as spectacle. The freak stands as an archetypal "other," a disabled figure on theatrical display before an able-bodied audience that uses the display to define its own sense of belonging.

"Freak" is a prismatic term that refracts the history of disability, including its most sordid past. To track the display of freaks and the history of freak shows over time is to witness some of the most deplorable treatment of people with disabilities—but the close study of freak display also offers a site from which to educe prurient historical attitudes toward disability that might otherwise remain hidden. In contemporary times, the gradual waning of the freak show reflects the medicalization of the freak, but it also parallels the gains made by people with disabilities under the banner of the disability rights movement.

The figure of the freak literally embodies the fundamental opposition that disability studies has aimed first to expose and understand, and then to redefine and redirect: namely, the conflict between an able-bodied "us" and a disabled "them." In disability studies scholarship, the treatment of freaks and freak shows reflects the early emphasis within the field on the development of a strategic opposition between essentialism and constructionism, pursued through analysis of freak display from the perspectives of the exhibitors, their audiences, and the human beings who were exhibited. Freak studies have consequently served as a different kind of prism, refracting the field's agenda in both activism and scholarship.

The contemporary study of freaks and freak shows grows from a fundamental disagreement between two scholars. In *Freaks* (1978), Leslie Fiedler held that the inherent otherness of the freak ("mythic and mysterious," yet also "one of us" [24]) inspires our wonder. Fiedler was less concerned with the material conditions of freak display than with the unconscious allure of what he called the "true freak," a figure to whom we are drawn to satisfy a "psychic need" (27). Fiedler summed up an enormous amount of history and scholarship (without notes, as was his wont), and he carried the understanding of "freak" to its diverse incarnations in 1960s youth culture—and in the process, he provided a link between the freak and the able-bodied that would prove portentous for later work by others.

Robert Bogdan challenged Fiedler's essentialist position in 1990 with a contructionist argument that "'Freak' is a way of thinking, of presenting, a set of practices, an institution—not a characteristic of an individual" (11). While Fiedler parsed even distinctions such as the one between someone with limbs amputated in utero and a "true phocomelic" whose limbs are foreshortened and oddly shaped through a particular birth defect (23), Bogdan rejects such categories. To Fiedler, the phocomelic is a "true freak." To Bogdan, a freak is simply someone who is persuasively presented as one. The display alone, insists Bogdan, is what turns a human being with a peculiarity (such as a disability) into a freak. As its title suggests, Bogdan's *Freak Show* (1990) focuses on the meaning and history of such displays. For Fiedler, the freak is the basis of the performance. For Bogdan, the performance creates the freak.

Bogdan's constructionist position ultimately came to dominate freak studies, providing the conceptual basis for important work by Rosemarie Garland-Thomson (1997, 2009), Rachel Adams (2001), and many others, which appeared during a period when disability studies in the humanities was coalescing as a scholarly field. These works have led to a vital scholarly discourse that has, among other things, recovered the perspectives of the people who were displayed as freaks (e.g., Wu 2012).

Freaks have been displayed since the beginning of recorded history (Huet 1993; Garland-Thomson 1997). Human oddities, whether alive, dead, or stillborn, were confined (often against their will) and categorized through theatrical display, which became more sophisticated and refined over time. As a specific entrepreneurial outgrowth of such displays, the freak show evolved relatively recently, beginning in the eighteenth century. Popular exhibits like Saartjie Baartman quickly set the template. Born a slave, Baartman was imported for display in England and France during the early 1810s, and created a sensation by virtue of the large breasts and buttocks that were typical of the South African tribe into which she was born. As the "Hottentot Venus" she became a notorious symbol of racial inferiority and sexual deviance. Freak shows were particularly popular in the United States, where their heyday extended from around 1835 to 1940, and they proliferated elsewhere as well (Rothfels 1996; Semonin 1996; Durbach 2009). The popularity of freak shows contributed materially to the growth of museums and circuses, two institutions whose proprietors quickly realized the benefits of housing them (Bogdan 1990); they also provided sensational reading material for the popular commercial press.

The show business empire of P. T. Barnum rested from the start on a foundation of canny freak display. Beginning at his New York museum and extending through his days as a circus impresario, Barnum relied on the box-office draw of famous freaks like Tom Thumb, Chang and Eng Bunker (whose ethnicity led to the term "Siamese twins"), and "What Is It?"—the stage name of an African American man named William Henry Johnson who was displayed as an evolutionary missing link.

Freak display works through the theatrical creation of wonder. Bodies in freak shows were arranged and posed, and pamphlet literature was prepared, all to inspire a sense of awesome mystery centered in human anomaly, along with the fear and horror that course darkly below. Freaks were perceived to straddle the unstable boundary of the socially delimited property marked "human"—and as such, freaks physically threatened the integrity of that boundary. The ambiguous body of the freak makes the guardianship of that territory complicated and difficult, a work of constant maintenance. But the effort carries rewards: the staged management of human difference allowed freak show spectators to validate their own citizenship, their race, and even their personhood itself.

The freak does a lot of cultural work, then. Foremost, the freak acts as a living tool to define the normal, an ideological construct that requires an antithesis (Davis 1995). The visible ambiguity of the freakish—whether based on biological anomaly, theatrical simulation, or some combination of the two—embodies the "not normal." Freak shows thus became a destination for viewers who wanted to affirm their own "normal" identities.

Freak shows likewise affirmed what Garland-Thomson (1997), working from a concept developed by Erving Goffman, calls the "normate": an idealized social identity based on dominant identity categories. Normate-based thinking gained power in comparison with unconventional bodies of all kinds. For example, Barnum packaged a spectacularly elderly African American woman, Joice Heth, as George Washington's 161-year-old slave nurse. The explosion of skepticism that resulted from Barnum's claim turned the wheels of his publicity mill, and when Heth died in 1836, Barnum staged a public autopsy that turned the black body into an exhibition of decrepitude at a time of rising white anxiety and resentment over the behavior of younger and more rebellious blacks (Reiss 2001). Thus did Heth affirm the values of whiteness in life and death together.

After the Civil War, freak shows also displayed people from exotic lands against crudely rendered backdrops meant to suggest their so-called natural habitat. These "racial freaks"—whose only "disability" was their traditional culture—were always figured as nonwhite, thus firming up the American racial hierarchy during an era when it underwent torturous national self-examination (Cassuto 1997).

The rise of the medical profession has been widely credited with killing off the freak show (Bogdan 1990; Garland-Thomson 1996). Medicine claimed the same territory of human oddity as the freak show did, but instead of setting up the odd body as an enduring mystery to generate a sense of wonder, the medical establishment proposed rational explanations for human variation. The medical case study operates as a version of a detective story, in which the culprit, disability, is identified and explained. Thus could Johnny the Leopard Boy be reborn as "poor John, a victim of vitiligo," no longer a subject of display, except to doctors. Medicine steadily gained authority in the United States beginning in the late nineteenth century. By the mid-twentieth century, freak display had acquired an aura of bad taste, and the freak show retreated from the public square.

But freak shows have not so much disappeared as dispersed. Just as freak show spectators could once wander from booth to booth in a sideshow tent, viewers may now flip from channel to channel, where they can see grotesquely overweight contestants engaging in weight-loss contests, real-life geek displays on *Fear Factor*, or a reality show about a family of dwarfs. Abigail and Brittany Hensel, conjoined twins who share one body and whose parents struggled for years to shield them from prurient attention, signed in 2012 to do a reality show.

The freak show remains alive and well, then, a still-viable prism for collective anxiety—but with a change. Mass culture would have us believe that freaks now write their own script from their own lives. Surely freaks do write their own stories to a certain extent—just as they did in earlier days, in some cases (Gamson 1999). Chang and Eng Bunker, to name one example, became wealthy and exerted considerable control over their own display. But it remains difficult to imagine the embrace of such display as an uncoerced choice. As David A. Gerber (1996) has suggested, a choice between bad options is not really a free choice at all. Perhaps the sense of unsavoriness that lingers in today's freak displays results from a lurking awareness that freakery remains a different and more disturbing kind of show business.

This conversation about the nature and ethics of freak display has proven instrumental to the larger disability studies objective of balancing the importance of constructionist views of disability (the ways that environment produces zones of "ability" and "disability") opposite what Garland-Thomson calls "strategic" arguments for essentialism—ways that difference "should be claimed, but not cast as lack" (1997, 23).

The study of freaks and freak shows was central to the early development of disability studies in the humanities, but it has receded to the margins of scholarship in the field in recent years. The shift surely stems from the understandable focus of disability studies on the subjectivity of people with disabilities, a perspective that can be difficult to recover from the archives of freak shows from years ago. But people still stare at other people with odd bodies, and that dynamic continues to fuel compelling inquiry. Indeed, we might say that just as the traditional freak show has dispersed, the study of freaks has likewise disseminated outward. Today the insights of freak scholarship within disability studies remain foundational to continuing important work in the field, even if the word "freak" is not always mentioned. Garland-Thomson's (2009) recent work on staring, for example, incorporates insights gained from the study of freak display into an examination of "how we look" at each other and the rules of engagement that prevail on both sides.

James Baldwin wrote that "freaks are called freaks . . . because they are human beings" who evoke "our most profound terrors and desires" (1998, 828). As civilized as humans may claim to be, anomalous bodies retain their powerful effect on perception, belief, and behavior. "We are a part of each other," said Baldwin, and we might say that disability studies is devoted to enshrining that truth within human relations (828). The idea, and the name, and especially the body of the freak will remain a test of our collective ability to stay focused on that goal.

28

Gender

Kim Q. Hall

Gender and disability, along with race, class, nationality, and sexuality, are constitutive features of the ways in which our fully integrated selves—what Margaret Price (2011) calls "bodyminds"—are lived and known. Gender has emerged as a key site of disability critique in four general areas: (1) sex, impairment, and the "realness" of the body; (2) the medicalization of gender; (3) the mutually reinforcing structures of gender and disability oppression; and (4) the reconfiguration of gender through disability experience. Thus, if disability theorists hope to understand and critique norms of bodily appearance and bodymind functioning, as well as offer meaningful alternative conceptions of the world and being, they must attend to how gender structures and is structured by those norms. Similarly, feminist and queer theorists cannot develop adequate accounts of gender without attending to the entanglement of the meaning and materialization of gender and disability.

Just as disability theorists have distinguished between impairment and disability, feminist theorists have distinguished between sex and gender. Sex refers to the chromosomal, anatomical, and physiological characteristics that mark the body as male, female, or intersex. Gender, by contrast, refers to socially, culturally, and historically contingent norms of appearance, bodily comportment, behavior, and desire that define what it means to be masculine, and thus a man, and feminine, and thus a woman. In this picture, those who queer gender norms, such as butches, femmes,

trans-identified people, and other gender-transgressive people, fall along a gender continuum. Feminist and disability theorists have worked diligently to show how gender and disability are socially and culturally produced in order to combat the naturalization and regulation of "woman," nonnormative gender, and disability. In oppressive contexts, naturalized conceptions of gender and disability operate to rationalize and normalize injustice against women, gender-transgressive people, and disabled people.

One consequence of sex-gender and impairment-disability distinctions is the relegation of sex and impairment to the body. Some feminist and disability theorists are concerned about the extent to which those distinctions lead to a devaluation of the material body, in particular purportedly real physical dimensions of gender and disability (Alaimo and Hekman 2008; Siebers 2008a, 2008b). In defense of a "materialist turn" in feminism, Stacy Alaimo and Susan Hekman contend that focusing on ideology or representation alone neglects attention to, among other things, bodily pain and diseases that affect women's "real" bodies (2008, 3–4, 6). For them, understanding the body and nature as produced by interactions between the material and the discursive (7) enables a more constructive critical attention to bodily conditions, like pregnancy, that must be acknowledged as sex-linked to a certain extent in order to understand them and provide access to the best care possible. This recent feminist turn to "the material" has a corollary in some disability discussions about pain and impairment. For example, Tobin Siebers argues for a realism about the disabled body that attends to the body's agency and the "real" embodied lives of disabled people (2008b, 67–68).

Other feminist, queer, and disability theorists question the assumption that sex and impairment are mere facts of bodily materiality (Hall 2005, 2009; Kafer 2013;

Salamon 2010). As Gayle Salamon (2010) and Alison Kafer (2013) point out, it is difficult, if not impossible, to know what impairment and sex mean or how they are inhabited independent of the social and cultural context in which bodies are lived and assigned meaning. In addition, assuming the facticity of sex naturalizes binary understandings of sex and gender, which is often made possible by ignoring the lived bodily experience of gender-transgressive people (Salamon 2010; Spade, "About Purportedly Gendered Body Parts"). Among other negative consequences, naturalizing binary sex and gender often results in pathologizing gender-transgressive people and inhibits their access to health care.

Feminist theorists have rigorously critiqued the heteronormative gender bias that informs the medicalization of gender (Fausto-Sterling 2000; Butler and Weed 2011). As Fausto-Sterling (2000, 3) argues, the medical model relies on a flawed view of nature, and biomedical knowledge about sex difference reveals much more about dominant gender beliefs than about nature. The medical model conceptualizes disability, transgender, and intersex as problems in need of cure/elimination. In the case of intersex, "cure" involves surgical creation of binary sex; in the case of transgender, "cure" has involved sex reassignment surgery to fix gender identity disorder (GID). While trans people who desire sex reassignment surgery and hormone replacement therapy may not perceive these procedures as a cure for "misaligned" sex and gender, they have been forced to submit to a GID diagnosis in order to receive permission to access the medical services they need to exercise gender autonomy. The most recent edition of the *Diagnostic and Statistical Manual of Mental Disorders* (*DSM-5*), published in 2013, replaced GID with a new category, gender dysphoria (Beredjick 2012). The effects of this new diagnosis for gender-transgressive people remain to be seen. While many trans activists welcome the end of characterizing gender transgression as a disorder, they also wonder about the implications for legal advocacy because of the strategic use of the GID diagnosis in fighting discrimination against trans people (Beredjick 2012). Still, the introduction of gender dysphoria into the *DSM-5* does not signal an end to the medical regulation of gender.

In recognition of some degree of overlap between trans and disability experience, one can consider the successful, but fraught, use of state disability statutes in legal advocacy for trans rights. Like disability advocates, trans advocates can and have used state disability discrimination laws to locate the problems of exclusion and discrimination in the built and conceptual environment rather than in the bodies of trans people (Spade 2003, 32–33). Both disabled and trans people are stigmatized, a problem that can be addressed by changing dominant beliefs, attitudes, and environments, not by "curing"/eliminating nonnormative bodyminds.

Identifying the mutually reinforcing structures of gender and disability oppression involves understanding how other axes of identity, such as race, class, and sexuality, inform gender and disability. Spade's use of the Americans with Disabilities Act in legal advocacy for trans rights is often on behalf of poor people and people of color who have no health insurance and are most vulnerable to regulation of myriad state institutions such as prisons and foster care systems. Eugenics and "eugenic logic" (Garland-Thomson 2012) are also sites where gender, race, class, and sexuality oppression converge to the detriment of nonnormative bodyminds. Susan Burch and Hannah Joyner (2007) describe the life of Junius Wilson, an African American deaf man born in North Carolina in 1908 and imprisoned in 1925 in the then-named State Hospital for the Colored Insane, where he was sterilized and castrated. Burch and Joyner explain how white racist mythologies of the black male rapist, along with Wilson's inability to communicate with others because of his deafness (and because others could not comprehend his Raleigh signing), were used by white state authorities to diagnose Wilson as a sexual pervert and prescribe sterilization and castration as a cure (2007, 47). Had Wilson been white, his experience would have been different. Historically, beliefs about gender have informed definitions of and treatments for mental disability. Thus, racialized, classed, and heteronormative gender regulation has been an important function of the diagnosis of mental disability (Carlson 2001, 2010; Price 2011).

In addition to making visible and analyzing the interrelatedness of gender, race, class, disability, sexuality, and other axes of identity, feminist queer disability theorists understand how disability experience can be a site for critical reconfigurations of gender. While some disability theorists argue for recognition of disabled people as "real men" and "real women," others have used disability as a critical resource through which to reimagine gender beyond heteronormative and able-bodied binaries. Embodying "normate" (Garland-Thomson 2011) gender, for example, requires having a body whose appearance and capacity are in conformity with dominant gender norms (Garland-Thomson 2011; James 2011; Mintz 2011; Serlin 2003). Naomi Finkelstein (2003, 311) describes feeling "emasculated" by fibromyalgia–rheumatoid arthritis while also understanding it as an experience that enables reconfiguring what it means to be butch. Being a "crip butch" reconfigures masculinity as openness to vulnerability and simultaneously exposes cracks in narrow gender norms (317). Similarly, Eli Clare (1999) writes about the complex process of trying to reclaim one's gendered disabled body, a process that involves negotiating categories like "woman" and "tomboy" that don't quite fit, as well as urban markers of gender that leave no room for white, working-class, rural gender-transgressive experience.

While feminist insights about gender have been useful for disability theorists, disability studies, especially in its feminist, queer, and crip incarnations, promises to transform understandings of gender. Indeed, in its critique of heteronormative gender, feminist and queer disability studies crips gender (Sandahl 2003; McRuer 2006), creating an opening for the emergence of another world and more capacious, democratic ways of being in it.

29

Genetics

David Wasserman

Genetics has received a great deal of attention from disability studies, but largely confined to one issue: the practice of routinely aborting fetuses found to have a genetic or chromosomal "abnormality." Opposition to this practice has been based on several related themes that are central to disability scholarship. First, an actual or potential person should not be judged by a single characteristic, however salient. Second, a person's biological endowment does not determine how well (or not) his or her life will develop and what criteria are used to make such judgments. Third, social and physical environments play a pervasive role in determining how well a person's life goes (Parens and Asch 2007; Asch and Barlevy, 2012).

Disability scholarship can and should make a broader contribution to ethical and policy issues in human genetics. Beyond raising doubts about prenatal selection, it can also shine a critical light on the growing reliance on postnatal genetic testing to inform personal and institutional decision making.

Since the 1960s, it has been possible to detect non-standard chromosomal patterns associated with some disabilities, such as the one additional chromosome found in people with Down syndrome. In the 1980s and 1990s, it became possible to associate gene regions on a chromosome, then specific gene sequences, with a variety of health conditions such as Huntington's disease, cystic fibrosis, breast cancer, and Alzheimer's disease. In the past fifteen years, genetic variants have been linked with physical and mental characteristics not previously regarded as diseases or disabilities, such as shyness, short stature, and baldness. Most recently, it has become possible to test an individual's entire genome for variants that have a known or suspected connection with an indefinite number of conditions or characteristics. This comprehensive genetic testing is beginning to be introduced into a variety of clinical settings, from reproductive to geriatric. It has the potential to be used in many nonclinical settings as well, such as employment, insurance, and matchmaking (Donley, Hull, and Berkman 2012).

The expanded scope and wider use of genetic testing may substantially increase the number of individuals regarded as diseased or disabled. The identification of genetic variants associated with disfavored characteristics like shyness, short stature, or baldness makes it more likely that those characteristics will be "medicalized"— that is, regarded as diseases or disabilities rather than as ordinary human variations. The identification of genetic variants that raise the probability of a disease or disability makes it more likely that "asymptomatic" individuals with those variants will nonetheless be regarded as diseased or disabled. And for individuals already regarded as diseased or disabled, the identification of genetic causes for their conditions may exacerbate the tendency to see those conditions as essential characteristics that are impervious to treatment.

Disability scholars can respond effectively to these concerns on both a practical and a conceptual level. They can argue for treating genetic discrimination as a form of disability discrimination. They can defend policies for genetic testing that challenge rather than reinforce the dichotomy between abnormal and normal, disabled and nondisabled. They can question both the uncritical deference to, and the wholesale rejection of, norms of human functioning. They can question whether genetic screening is more appropriate and effective in preventing disability than improving public safety—given that the vast majority of disabilities are not congenital but are in fact "acquired." Finally, they can emphasize the critical importance of inclusion in a world where there will always be significant variation in human structure and function.

Although in the United States there is a specific law protecting individuals from genetic discrimination in health insurance (the Genetic Information Nondiscrimination Act [2008]), individuals with genetic predispositions to disease or disability may find broader protection under disability discrimination laws in the United States and other countries. There is some debate about whether the current U.S. law covers genetically predisposed individuals who are not symptomatic (Asch 1996; Eisenberg 2010). If it does not, disability scholars and advocates should seek its further amendment. The attitudes toward genetically predisposed individuals generally involve the same mix of devaluation, distancing, and oversolicitude as the attitudes toward individuals with visible disabilities.

The social model of disability can also serve as a powerful check on the tendency to medicalize disfavored characteristics. The treatment of a condition like alcoholism as a disease or symptom can be a helpful alternative to treating it as a moral defect (Conrad and Schneider 1992). But medicalization may be as inappropriate for restlessness or impulsivity as it was for homosexual orientation as a condition (Phelan 2005). In the case of newly pathologized conditions, a social response may be more respectful and effective than a medical one: acceptance and accommodation rather than treatment.

The uncritical medicalization of human variations is likely to be encouraged by the identification of genetic variants that contribute to such physical and mental differences. Finding that a disfavored characteristic is associated with an atypical genetic variant may lead to a new diagnosis of a disease or disability. This process will be accelerated by the spread of comprehensive genetic testing into routine pre- and postnatal health care, as such testing finds ever more genetic markers associated with variations in physical and mental function. Jo C. Phelan's (2005) research suggests that for deviant behavior, "geneticization" may not be a good bargain: although it does reduce blame, it does not reduce overall stigma and may in fact increase social distancing.

Conditions that are already regarded as chronic diseases may also be further stigmatized by the discovery of predisposing genes. For example, cardiovascular disease, late-onset cancers, and senile dementia all were previously seen as ordinary concomitants of aging due largely to unknown factors. With the identification of genetic predispositions, however, people who acquire such conditions may be seen instead as victims of their own genomes even if the specific predisposing genes are unknown. They may be regarded not simply as unlucky but as constitutionally unhealthy. The discovery of genetic predispositions to some conditions previously attributed to unhealthy lifestyle, like type 2 diabetes, may reduce blame. But people with such physical conditions will gain little if they are stigmatized as disabled rather than as gluttonous, lazy, or reckless.

A genetic association may also reinforce the stigmatization of characteristics already regarded as physical or mental disabilities. Although the large majority of disabilities are caused by injuries and "normal" aging, finding genetic predispositions to some disabilities may increase the tendency to see people with disabilities as fundamentally different from "the rest of us," and to see their disabilities as essential to their identities.

Disability scholars can help to combat the pathologization of difference latent in such developments if they recognize the potential of comprehensive genetic testing to *legitimize* a broader spectrum of functional and structural variation. The increasing proportion of individuals found to be genetically predisposed to *some* disease, disability, or atypical trait should in theory weaken the dichotomy between disabled and nondisabled people. All people have genetic variants that may well put them at a disadvantage in some environments. Awareness of the range of genetic variants we have, and of the extent to which their impact on our well-being depends on interaction with our biological, physical, and social environments, may help us to appreciate the arbitrariness of what counts as "normal."

This awareness, however, may be blunted, as some commentators propose, if genetic testing is restricted to genetic variants associated with more "serious" diseases and disabilities (Botkin 1994). Disability scholars and advocates have reason to oppose *any* line drawing (Asch 2003; Wasserman 2003). Such lines are inevitably highly stigmatizing to those on their far side. An unrestricted testing regime not only would maximize reproductive liberty but also would repudiate the prevailing view of disabilities as conditions uniquely worth testing for and selecting against.

A further challenge to the "tyranny of the normal" comes from what has come to be called genetic enhancement. On the one hand, radical genetic enhancements could nullify many of the practical advantages of typical functioning. If we could be genetically engineered to have jet-powered cushions attached to our torsos instead of legs, "normal" legs might appear disabled by comparison (Boorse 1975). But even more fantastical than the technical feasibility of such radical enhancements is the idea that they could be universally available. Their unequal distribution would greatly increase the functional disparities within society and the challenges for universal design (Wasserman 2012). Disability

scholars can enrich the debate on genetic and other biological enhancement, illuminating both the value and the danger in setting aside standards of normal functioning.

A final way in which the disability critique of genetic testing should be directed beyond the reproductive context is in emphasizing the prevention of disability by safety rather than by selection. Even if prenatal selection against disability were universal, it would have only a slight impact on the overall incidence of disability. As geneticists have long recognized, it is practically impossible for routine selection to eliminate specific disabilities (Paul and Spencer 2000). More important, most disabilities are not caused solely or primarily by genetic or chromosomal variations; their proximate causes are injuries, aging, and common chronic diseases (Pope and Tarlov 1991). Strengthening traffic, residential, and workplace safety laws, for instance, could result in a more dramatic reduction in major disabilities than the most comprehensive program of prenatal genetic screening. An emphasis on safety does not preclude an important role for genetic components in research programs that aim to reduce or mitigate chronic disease and the disabling effects of aging. But research on genetic variation is likely to prove more useful in explaining the etiology of diseases and in customizing prevention and treatment than in providing an ethically or practically sound basis for prenatal selection.

If disability scholars are committed to discouraging the mistaken view of prenatal selection as a panacea and promoting more effective and appropriate prevention measures, they should also stress the limits of *any* form of prevention. Our societies will always have a wide range of physical and mental variation; we will always have injuries and diseases that limit function. It is as critical to learn to live with disability as it is to reduce its incidence.

30

History

Susan Burch and Kim E. Nielsen

Historians grapple with and learn from disability via two distinct but overlapping methods of analyzing change over time. First, they examine the daily and structural lives of those considered disabled and others who interact with them; second, they analyze changing historical conceptualizations of disability, able-bodiedness, and able-mindedness. Many disability historians also explore disability and ableism's relation to other frameworks of power—such as race, class, sexuality, age, gender, and family. Central to disability history is the analytical and archival task of unpacking the largely Western and contemporary cross-impairment category we now call disability.

Historical scholarship differs from other disciplines because of its reliance on evidentiary materials from the past and interest in change and continuities over time. Primary sources vary, but traditionally historians have drawn primarily on "official" text-based resources, such as proclamations and laws, newspapers, memoirs, court proceedings, and church records. Because of a historian's power to select which sources to examine, and because of a society's power to retain and/or rid itself of some evidentiary sources, history also forces questions about knowledge: what counts as knowledge, who is authorized to provide knowledge, who is the intended recipient of knowledge, and how it is preserved and disseminated. These issues are significant for all historical research, but because those in power (particularly medical and institutional experts) have frequently dismissed people with disabilities as unworthy and deficient—unable to accurately document their own lives—these questions are particularly salient to historicizing disability.

The increased engagement of people with disabilities in the production of historical knowledge, the concomitant rise of disability scholarship, and the increased use of disability as an analytical tool have encouraged archivists, librarians, museum curators, and others to expand and redefine their own historical work. There is literally more *history* available because of this. More reflective and inclusive indices, exhibits, libraries and collections, and courses in disability history have changed how the broader discipline "gets done." Part of this change includes reflecting upon and learning from historical terminology used to describe disability, such as "cripple," "abnormal," "retard," "incompetent," "lunatic," "delinquent," "deviant," "feebleminded," and "special"; as well as nondisability status: "normal," "competent," "fit," and "citizen." Providing new data and interpretations contributes to the broader increase of understanding; this movement transcends disciplines as well as cultural and geographic boundaries.

The cultural meanings and lived experience of disability are marked both by continuities and by changes over time. Understandings of epilepsy and epileptics, for example, illustrate both tendencies. Since ancient times and across the globe, epileptics have appeared in historic sources. Considerable interest in the causes of what today is considered epilepsy figured prominently in these stories. According to many cultures, the evil eye, jinn possession, or God's punishment produced "the falling sickness" (Dwyer 1992; Carod-Artal and Vazquez-Cabrera 2007; Wolf 2010; Fadiman 1998). In other communities, "the sacred disease" has denoted positive divine intervention, and those so touched have held exalted status. Other interpretations, also sustained to varying degrees across millennia, have cast epileptics as mentally ill, "unfit," or mentally disabled. Epileptics themselves have offered widely ranging expressions of their experiences, but especially in the past several decades, and in specific geographic contexts, an additional framework has emerged that emphasizes epileptic community as an authentic cultural identity.

Historical study draws attention to dynamic relations and outcomes. Hostility, fear, and wonderment were among the varied responses to epileptics across different times and places. While the experience of epileptics—mirroring the broader history of numerous disability groups—changed sharply in the modern era in the Global North, certain themes remain constant across a broader history. In the nineteenth- and twentieth-century United States, as just one era and location, epileptics often were forcibly institutionalized, subjected to forced sterilizations, and prohibited from marrying or having sexual relations with others. Foreign epileptics were prohibited from entering the country. By the late twentieth century, many of these restrictions had been lifted. At the same time, erroneous and long-standing beliefs that epilepsy was contagious and that epileptics were unfit to parent or to work continue to shape daily experiences of epileptics, their families, and the broader society. Historians of disability assess these diverse interventions across time and place—including exorcisms, trepanning (drilling holes in the skull), homeopathic and pharmaceutical remedies, invitations to serve as shamans, institutionalization, immigration and employment bans, forced sterilizations, and marriage restrictions—to demonstrate wide-ranging and culture-specific understandings of epilepsy. Such historical developments also point to the ways that epileptics have been situated in the overlap of religious and spiritual traditions, magic and science, and legal and economic systems.

Historians' rigorous consideration of context and developments across time is particularly important for the social (relational) model of disability. According to this model, bodily and mental impairments encompass different meanings and experiences depending on the environments in which they exist. For example, the Arab-Islamic world in the early modern period, which emphasized oral dissemination of knowledge, presented unique opportunities for some people who were blind or had low vision. Ottoman sources detail numerous, prominent roles that blind men filled in Muslim society: muezzin (the man who calls other Muslims to prayer), mullahs, Qur'an teachers and reciters, and Hadith scholars (Scalenghe 2014, 47; Weygand 2009; Barasch 2001). Indeed, what blind has meant, and how blind—as a category and a lived experience—has been expressed have varied as widely as its definitions.

A historical approach also makes transparent the ways that people with disabilities have both been shaped by and responded to broader forces in history. Disabled slaves in the United States, like all enslaved peoples, sought to resist slavery and shape their own lives. In 1840, for example, a New Orleans slave named Bob who had an amputated leg stole away from his master with the assistance of a crutch. Similarly, a slave named Peggy was "very much parrot toed and walks badly," but she ran away from her Virginia master in 1798. Although slave owners tended to dismiss disabled slaves as *refuse* or *unsound*, disabled slaves often engaged in significant skilled and unskilled work that included working in the fields, caring for children, and household labor. Sojourner Truth, the noted abolitionist and women's rights activist, had, in her words, "a badly diseased hand, which greatly diminished her usefulness" to her master. But such self-acknowledged impairment did not limit her future political activism or leadership (Gilbert and Truth 1850, 39; Boster 2009).

Similarly, many institutionalized people left abundant evidence of their efforts to shape their own

HISTORY SUSAN BURCH AND KIM E. NIELSEN

surroundings. Young women institutionalized in early twentieth-century Chicago as "feebleminded" and "defective," for example, quickly realized that by responding as expected when they were questioned, they could better and shape their circumstances—in essence, manipulating the institutional experts who determined much of their lives (Rembis 2011). Between 1851 and 1860, residents of the New York State Lunatic Asylum in Utica, New York, created a monthly journal of poetry, editorials, essays, plays, and art. While rigorously supervised, *The Opal* also became a means by which asylum residents criticized medical practices, such as physical restraints and isolation, offered their own political and social commentary on national events, established community, and expressed anger and resistance.

Wars and conflict provide additional and vivid examples of the relationship between historical forces and historical actors shaping the experiences and meanings of disability. The Bolshevik revolution profoundly shaped the course of twentieth-century history, bearing human marks across generations. The ensuing civil war exacerbated the loss of human life, contributing to especially dire economic circumstances of the Soviet regime. Amid this complex, sometimes inspiring, and often harrowing wave of change, deaf citizens experienced unprecedented opportunities. During the previous century, deaf schools, funded exclusively and sporadically by secular and religious philanthropists, privileged only a select few. By the 1920s, however, deaf youth generally had access to primary, secondary, and—to some degree—higher education. As in other nations, sustained residential schools for Soviet deaf students became the touchstones for vibrant cultural communities. Emerging from this increasingly unified world, deaf leaders like Pavel Savel'ev cultivated profitable ties to the Soviet regime based on common interests, particularly employment. Recognizing that deaf people

had long struggled to gain full access to the workplace, Savel'ev's proposal to establish deaf-only factory-educational facilities (*rabfacs*) achieved multiple goals. The state benefited from the influx of engaged, capable laborers who expressed gratitude for the opportunity to work; deaf people, in turn, enjoyed greater social status and concomitant resources: food rations, homes, funding for deaf art exhibits, sports clubs, newspapers, and other community projects. For most of the twentieth century, the state supported deaf cultural oases: towns where members communicated in Russian Sign Language, lived and worked together, and shared richly in deaf cultural traditions (Burch, 2000).

Disability history is inextricably entangled with all other topics of history. For instance, disability rights movements in all of their manifestations share central themes in history: struggle, citizenship, labor, power, violence, health, representation, and community. The rise of disability rights activism in Germany, particularly since the 1960s, points to the powerful role of transnational activism. Early activists in Germany, drawing on examples of African Americans and their antiracist allies in the United States, challenged mainstream discriminatory attitudes and policies. Invoking the civil rights rhetoric of integration and inclusion, these activists demanded a reckoning with their nation's history of violence against people with disabilities. Collective action focused on self-empowerment, dismantling of environmental and attitudinal barriers, and greater access to the workplace. Specifically rejecting patronizing representations in the United Nations Year of the Disabled platform, German disability activists in 1981 challenged philanthropists who relied on the charity model of disability and demanded full and equal citizenship rights. One leader, Franz Christoph, applied unsuccessfully for political asylum, claiming that Germany persecuted disabled people. A "cripple tribunal" (*Krüppeltribunal*) drew public attention to a litany of abuses: under- and unemployment, inaccessible transportation and health care, limited housing options, and other forms of daily marginalization and oppression (Poore 2007, 281; Köbsell 2006; Bosl 2014). The efforts, while uneven in their impact, galvanized the emerging disability cultural community in Germany. As these stories illustrate, disability history can teach much about larger historical questions and themes.

This is partly why historical scholarship is foundational to disability studies. At its core, disability studies is built on the premise that neither disability nor able-bodiedness and able-mindedness are simply and wholly biologically determined. As the examples of disabled American slaves, institutionalized white men and women, and Russian deaf activists illustrate, people with disabilities have in all circumstances sought to shape their daily and structural lives. Simultaneously, larger historical forces and incidents have influenced the options and methods before them. The study of history provides means by which to substantiate this argument and reflect on its implications. When examined historically and across cultures, it is clear that definitions of disability and related terms are variable, culturally shaped, influenced by other power structures, and built in interaction with major historical forces such as (but not limited to) religion, politics, and economic systems. Historical scholarship also provides evidence of the rich lives and activism of people with disabilities, providing lessons and resources for contemporary activists. Knowledge of others' activism and efforts nourishes contemporary communities. The stories and debates of the past invite questions into the present and lend insight into how current positions, relations, and understandings have been shaped by the past. Disability history facilitates a richer imagining of alternatives and structural opportunities for change.

31

Human

D. Christopher Gabbard

The term "human" occupies a central place in disability studies because people living with physical, sensory, intellectual, or psychosocial impairments have so often been deemed to be not fully human or even animals with human faces. However, people with disabilities are hardly alone in this, for members of various groups and populations have been (and, indeed, continue to be) marginalized as the Other at different historical moments. In addition to those who have been labeled deaf, dumb, blind, idiot, mad, and leprous, a list of groups whose humanity has been discounted or denied includes slaves, women, colonized populations, and people of color/nonwhite people.

Literature has proven to be a powerful place to understand how the human has been constructed. Representations often have proceeded by way of negation: those who are not considered fully human define what it is to be so. Literary figures that have served to engage in this paradoxical operation include Shakespeare's Caliban, Swift's Yahoos, Wordsworth's idiot boy, Faulkner's Benjy, and Shelley's monster in *Frankenstein*. Only very recently have scholars begun to perceive these characters as disabled. Once they started to see them as such—as embodiments of a nonhuman Other—it became possible to trace the lineage of disabled characters back to Oedipus. Thus, since the beginning of Western culture, disabled characters have symbolized the crossroads of human and nonhuman. Such characters extensively populate literature if one begins to look.

Once Charlotte Brönte's Jane Eyre is reunited with Mr. Rochester—who has been blinded and maimed—she tells him, "It is time some one undertook to rehumanise you." Moreover, numerous authors ruminate on the human vis-à-vis the concept of impairment. In his essay "Of Deformity," for instance, Francis Bacon posited that deformed human beings were inhuman not by virtue of their deformity but on account of negative social responses that rendered them "void of natural affection." William Hay, a disfigured and hunchbacked British Parliamentarian, vigorously contested Bacon's claim in what would turn out to be the first disability memoir, *Deformity, An Essay* (1754). Hay (2004) used the memoir to assert his humanity.

When the philosopher Emmanuel Kant famously asked, "What is man?" he was posing a question particularly characteristic of the Enlightenment era (1680–1800). The inability to resolve this question since then has had everything to do with its peculiarly self-reflexive nature. There is no objective thing called "human" existing somewhere "out there." Instead, we have a historical record of the discussion of what it means to be human. It is a discussion that only within recent history has begun to include voices from the disabled community.

Understanding this discussion requires briefly reviewing the history of the idea of the human. Plato and Aristotle inaugurated *descriptive* and *prescriptive* definitions. Plato offhandedly referred to man as a featherless biped, which, more seriously, can be interpreted as a descriptive definition in which human status is signified by human morphology and parentage. The counterposing prescriptive definition is attributed to Aristotle: "Man is an *animal rationale*." Early Christian thinkers defined the human by what it was not; that is, it was distinguished from spiritual and animal entities, although it was acknowledged that humans were hybrids composed of both. Augustine of Hippo (354–430), and, later, Albertus Magnus (1206–1280) and Thomas Aquinas (1225–1274) adopted a descriptive definition in which any body of human shape and parentage was considered to have a human essence, to be inhabited by a soul, no matter how deficient the mind or deformed the body. This criterion dominated throughout the Middle Ages and the first part of the early modern period as the primary indicator of human status. Change began to occur in the early seventeenth century when philosophers like René Descartes put forward the concept of mind-body dualism, which made it possible to conceive of a human body without a working (rational) mind and to equate these supposedly mindless human bodies with animals, which Descartes believed to be soulless machines.

At the beginning of the Enlightenment, John Locke was instrumental in bringing about Western culture's transition from a descriptive to a prescriptive definition of the human. Where once birth and shape—resemblance between parents and offspring—determined human status, Locke insisted on *intellectual resemblance*. The chief counterexample he used was the "changeling." C. F. Goodey (2011) argues that the changeling provided Locke with a mechanism to move from a descriptive to a prescriptive definition of the human, and also to establish a lasting distinction between "person" and "man." A person has full human moral standing and significance because he is able to think abstractly, process information swiftly, and retain and quickly recall memories. A person has a continuous identity over time. Once mature, a person can act autonomously and independently of paternal authority. The concept of personhood legitimizes an agent to enter into contracts (such as the social contract), make claims to justice, and participate in the public sphere. The opposite of person was "man," an entity of human shape and parentage but not necessarily capable of reason. Unless a man could prove himself capable of abstract thought and memory, he would remain a nonperson—that is, a changeling forever dependent upon paternal authority. This nonperson changeling enabled Locke to shift the argumentative weight concerning who qualifies as *human* from man to person.

Locke's influence could not have been more profound, for he not only established personhood as the first tier of human status but also propounded both a normative standard of mental ability and a line of social contract theory that eventually would be used to underwrite modern constitutional government. His theories undergird the subject, the person at the center of classical liberalism, whom Locke describes as independent, self-sufficient, entrepreneurial, property owning, and capable of engaging equally with other subjects. By virtue of his humanity, in other words, the liberal subject is entitled to political claims for justice. Over the last several centuries this model of the liberal subject powered by reason has influenced the rise of the Western liberal democracies. Since the second half of the twentieth century, however, such a model has come under attack. Feminist, postcolonial, and queer theorists have pointed out that such a model was presumptively male, white, Anglo-European, and heterosexual. Responses to this critique have been varied: on the one hand, many democracies have sought to extend the prerogatives of liberal personhood to ever-wider segments of the population; on the other hand, poststructuralists and postmodernists have sought to destabilize the subject entirely.

A disability consciousness brings a number of questions relating to the expectations associated with the liberal subject to the conversation about the human. For disabled people, Locke's liberalism is a two-edged sword. On the one hand, it enables them to create their own identities, meanings, and values apart from the expectations of authority and general social trends. More important, liberalism makes it possible to describe the human in terms of rights, freedom, and dignity. It underwrites claims to justice having to do with civil rights, such as those encoded in the Americans with Disabilities Act (ADA) of 1990, a vital piece of legislation for disabled people. In other words, liberalism's rights-based political discourse and history provide a foundational precedent for the demand that people with disabilities be treated equally and with justice.

On the other hand, disability highlights problems with the tradition out of which classical liberalism initially sprang. Locke was writing against patriarchalism (note: not *patriarchy*), an ideology that legitimated the seventeenth-century English absolutist monarchy on the basis of the divine right of kings. Patriarchalism depended on a familial metaphor: as God the Father rules over the earth, so the king rules like a father over his people, who are his children. Locke challenged this metaphor by pointing out its obvious flaw: children eventually grow up and leave their father's house. However, a critic today can point out the obvious flaw in Locke's use of the same metaphor: children do indeed grow up, but the liberal subject Locke postulates does not resemble a mature and experienced adult so much as an adolescent demanding freedom from his parents. And with adolescence comes an adolescent mind-set, namely, the assumption that one will always be strong, vigorous, healthy, whole, and able. Locke's liberal subject is motivated by a sense of invincibility and immortality, as well as of teenage rebellion. To extend the familial metaphor, flawed as it may be, members of the disabled community bring to the discussion of the human the adult realization that the body is vulnerable to age, infirmity, and the unexpected exigencies of life. In sum, disability studies theorists critique Locke's model

HUMAN   D. CHRISTOPHER GABBARD

of the subject on the point of its always being healthy, whole, and able-bodied.

Classical liberalism made sense in the early Enlightenment when the issue at hand was breaking the monarch's grip on power. It makes far less sense in the postmodern age. Scholars of disability charge that classical liberalism's subject is a "one-size-fits-all" teenage expectation that every citizen will be strong, vigorous, whole, healthy, and able. The fact that classical liberalism mandates economic self-sufficiency and autonomy compounds the problem because dependency comes to be viewed with suspicion and contempt. It interprets any form of need either as a lack of maturity or as perpetual reliance upon paternal authority. A disability perspective exposes classical liberalism to be an ideology rife with ableism: the belief that people with impairments are inferior to those with typically functioning bodies and minds. Thus, the ADA's mandate that "reasonable accommodation" be made becomes a point of contention. For some, reasonable accommodation runs against the grain of liberalism's rugged competitive individualism. For others, it means responding to disabled people's claims to justice by implementing access, thereby making it possible for them to exercise their own forms of rugged individualism.

Debates about liberal conceptions of the human are complicated by individuals with intellectual and developmental disabilities. According to Locke and his philosophical heirs, individuals so designated supposedly cannot reason and as such do not qualify as persons. If the primary marker of the human is the ability to reason, then people who appear unable to reason are left out. The consequences of such exclusions can be significant, for a purportedly just society need not honor a nonperson's claims to justice. Georges Canguilhem, Martha Nussbaum, and others have noted that disabled people, especially those with cognitive

disabilities, often maintain the legal status of children. In the first half of the twentieth century, the supposedly equivocal personhood of individuals with intellectual and developmental disabilities provided the rationale for eugenic practices that frequently entailed forced sterilization. Today, the issue surfaces most pointedly in debates about prenatal testing, abortion, and euthanasia. Arguably, prenatal screening—amniocentesis and chorionic villus sampling—has made possible a new eugenics by detecting genetic disorders and eliminating "defective" fetuses through "selective abortion." When told that Down syndrome may be in the offing for their child, prospective parents typically receive little counseling that the life expectations for people with Down syndrome have risen dramatically. Instead, the mechanism of "choice" may be biased toward abortion. Some see the practice of selective abortion as an implicit challenge to the right of disabled people to exist. Those in the disabled community argue that bodily variation, even in the forms that lead to disability, should be acknowledged as part of the diversity of human embodiment.

At the extreme are contemporary philosophers like Peter Singer, who argue that individuals with intellectual and developmental disabilities such as people Down syndrome as well as those with traumatic brain injury, dementia, and Alzheimer's disease should be deemed nonpersons. Hence, while prenatal screening reveals nothing about the humanity of the fetus, in the minds of some it determines personhood. Further, Singer contends that because a distinction between abortion and infanticide is logically indefensible, parents of a newborn with whom they are unsatisfied—for any reason—should have the option of terminating his or her life.

One cannot help but note that Singer and likeminded members of the intellectual elite have succumbed to the narcissistic myth of intellectual supremacy in advocating such appalling positions. In response, philosophers such as Eva Feder Kittay and Licia Carlson have produced systematic and compelling book-length rebuttals from a disability studies perspective (2010b). Kittay, herself the mother of a child with cognitive impairment, forcefully argues that the classical liberal subject to which Singer adheres must, to be viable, presume an opposing category—the "retarded"—as a static, absolute, uniform, unproblematic, and self-evident natural kind. Anyone familiar with people with intellectual and developmental disabilities, Kittay counters, knows no such category exists. By implication, if the category of the "retarded" that buttresses the liberal subject turns out to be insubstantial, the liberal subject likewise becomes unstable.

Denying full human dignity to people with intellectual and developmental disabilities forces the question: Why determine human status by a performance criterion such as reasoning ability? On what grounds are characteristics such as intelligence and rationality so enshrined that they constitute the most essential human traits? Why are they not just as arbitrary a basis for determining human status as the human-shape-and-parents criterion? Michael Bérubé observes that any performance criterion "will leave some mother's child behind. It will create a residuum of the abject, a fraction of the human family that is to be left out of the accounting" (2009, 355). A disability perspective maintains that, if a choice must be made among many competing and equally arbitrary criteria, why not opt for an inclusive definition?

In discussing the human, a disability critique points out that impairment is not what it used to be—at least in the sense that it no longer remains the exclusive property of a profoundly marginalized segment of the population. People who in earlier generations would have died from an injury, ailment, or congenital disability today are surviving on account of medical, technological, and pharmaceutical interventions. They are living on in the millions, and doing so with the aid of devices, drugs, implants, replacements, procedures, and prosthetics. Artificial hearts, baclofen pumps, sex reassignment surgeries, in vitro fertilizations, and prosthetic implants of hips, knees, and vertebrae have altered the way we think about the body. Thus, while the prescriptive "performance criterion" emerges as an arbitrary signifier of the human, so too it turns out is the descriptive "human shape" definition, at least as we have understood it up until now. As Andrew Solomon notes in *Far from the Tree*, "We like categories and clubs as much as we ever have; it's only that the ones we thought were inviolable turn out not to be, and others we never imagined are taking their place" (2012, 668).

More than ever, people with impairments align with Donna Haraway's vision of the cyborg as a posthuman hybrid whose body transgresses the boundaries separating human, animal, and machine (1991). One has only to consider the recent cases of Tammy Duckworth and James Langevin, both serving in the U.S. Congress, the former having lost both of her legs in the Iraq War, the latter injured in an accidental shooting when he was sixteen and now a quadriplegic. Ian Brown posits that a new genre of human being has come into existence—or, perhaps it should be said, new *genres* that undermine the once relatively stable category of the *human*. Given the postmodern critiques launched by feminism, postcolonialism, and queer theory, the human starts to look like little more than a remainder from the Enlightenment, a question Kant posed that could never be answered. It may no longer be possible to fit all that one considers human into the cramped and narrow confines of *the human*. It may be time to imagine a more capacious category.

32

Identity

Julia Miele Rodas

Identity is the idea of the self understood within and against the social context, a means by which the individual is categorized and located as part of, or set apart from, recognized social, political, and cultural groups. As "the means by which the person comes to join a particular social body" (Siebers 2008b, 15), identity is a symbolic performance, an activity that names and aligns the self, by which the individual is composed as socially significant. It cannot exist, therefore, except in social relief—against a backdrop by which the self is made visible to both self and other. Disability identity has a complex and dynamic history. At its core is the disability rights movement, which for the first time asserted disability as a minority identity and as a platform for collective political action. In the entry on "Minority" in this volume, Jeffrey Brune indicates that Louis Anthony Dexter and Erving Goffman laid the groundwork for understanding disability in political terms in the early 1960s. Activists like Ed Roberts, Paul Longmore, Justin Dart, Judith Heumann, and others, however, were instrumental in developing and acting on this foundation. Fighting institutionalized political, social, and economic discrimination, such activists not only impacted public policy but also shifted and helped to shape a disability community, galvanizing a diverse and diffuse population of disabled people and helping to forge what many have come to understand as disability identity. This politicized identity is grounded in the idea that disability is a socially constructed category, an identity that is shaped by cultural and historical forces rather than being determined primarily by the body.

Viewing disability as a social construction has been a crucial political concept, a mode of resistance to the pejorative constructs of the social majority and received forms of knowledge that insist on disability exclusively as a medical condition or fact of the body. Simi Linton advocates strongly for this constructionist position in *Claiming Disability*, observing that people with disabilities are "bound together . . . by the social and political circumstances that have forged us as a group" and referring to group alliance as leading to "civil rights victories and the foundation of a clearly identified disabled community" (1998, 4, 5). Tobin Siebers argues for the centrality of "identity politics . . . to the future of minority peoples and their quest for social justice and inclusion" (2008b, 17). Understanding disability as a social construct and disability identity as politically constituted are foundational for disability theory and culture, baseline concepts upon which all other thinking and writing about disability identity must be measured.

Historically, disability has been passively constructed by clinical, literary, and social discourses that demean, disparage, and pathologize. The long-standing "medical model" of disability locates disability exclusively in the body, seeing the body as deviant, broken, and in need of a cure performed by nondisabled agents. This model likewise categorizes people with disabilities according to impairments, making it hard for a blind or deaf person to imagine common ground with an amputee, or a person with mental illness or an intellectual disability. Likewise, the charity model of disability seeks to "cure" disability through interventions like fund-raising, which often perpetuate negative stereotypes that interfere with self-determination (Kemp

1981). Pursuing a long-standing thread in literary disability studies, David Mitchell and Sharon Snyder's *Narrative Prosthesis* (2000) observes that in literature and other forms of imaginative representation, disability has long been associated with malevolence and corruption. It is essential that the development of the social model, upon which modern concepts of disability identity are constructed, continue to be understood in terms of this preexisting multitude of damaging ableist narratives that continue to inform public discourse about disability identity.

Even as the paradigm of disability identity shifts from the passive construction of disability as "problem" to be fixed to a model in which disabled people increasingly understand themselves and are understood by others as political and social agents, disability theorists and activists have continued to challenge emerging conventions. Some have alleged that disability identity itself is coercive and essentialist, as well as being grounded in narratives of oppression. In response to these critiques, scholars have developed critical perspectives that recognize disability identity as multiple, fragmented, and complex. Indeed, Lennard Davis suggests that "the unstable nature of disability . . . spells the end of many identity groups," including disability itself, and that these shifting boundaries are the hallmark of postmodern identity, creating "a dismodernist approach to disability as a neoidentity" (2002, 26). Mindful of key philosophical discourses of the body, Davis's "dismodernism" is ultimately rooted in Donna Haraway's influential "Cyborg Manifesto" (originally published in 1985), which asserts that "we are all chimeras, theorized and fabricated hybrids of machine and organism," and that we ought to take "pleasure in the confusion of boundaries" (1991, 150). But, while such thinking has had a powerful impact on disability theory, not all scholars are ready to deconstruct disability identity, or identity politics in general. Rosemarie Garland-Thomson, for instance, suggests that while ongoing debates in disability studies are sometimes predicated on the "reductive notion that identity studies are intellectual ghettos limited to a narrow constituency," that is no reason to reject them altogether. She points out that some of the "most sophisticated and nuanced analyses of disability" come "from scholars conversant with feminist theory" (2011, 14), which has a more expansive tradition of "collaborative, interdisciplinary inquiry and a self-conscious cultural critique that interrogates how subjects are multiply interpellated" (15). And while Davis calls attention to the extreme porousness of disability as an identity category, Siebers argues for the importance of "identity politics as crucial to the future of minority peoples." He calls for a theory of "complex embodiment" that recognizes how bodies and bodily experience structure social experience as much as bodies are subject to existing social frameworks (Siebers 2008b, 25).

Looking forward, disability identity is also increasingly interlaced with other ongoing social, political, and academic explorations. Disability scholars and activists, redressing the early limits of disability studies, are working within critical studies of race and ethnicity and global and postcolonial studies frameworks to expand and complicate ideas of disability identity. Mainstream conversations about biopolitics, including debates about prenatal testing, selective abortion, gene therapies, eugenics, and other emerging technologies of the body, are deeply inflected by the presence of disability and are increasingly overlapping and intersecting with issues of disability identity. Thus, what Siebers might recognize as "complex embodiment" is becoming a more central subject of public and academic discourse. Despite more sophisticated approaches and a more significant role in public discourse, however, the complex sense of disability identity outlined here does not yet occupy a secure place in the public imagination. And early work by disability scholars and activists—those who first identified and agitated against the structural inequities of ableist social institutions—continues to play an important role in shaping the future of disability identity.

33

Illness

G. Thomas Couser

Though not particularly difficult to define in everyday usage, "illness" is a highly vexed term in the context of disability studies. "Illness" needs to be distinguished first from "disease," its close counterpart. In academic discourse, "disease" typically refers to a pathological entity in the abstract—disembodied, as it were, rather than as experienced by any particular person. Polio is a disease, as is cancer. In contrast, "illness" refers to a particular person's experience of a disease: its various effects on the person's existence and identity. Thus, progressive clinical practice attends to illness rather than to disease. This approach was pioneered by Arthur Kleinman (1988), a psychiatrist and medical anthropologist. It is significant that other important figures who work in this tradition—including sociologist Arthur Frank (1995) and internist and literary critic Rita Charon (2006)—are not solely medical practitioners or researchers.

In narrative medicine, the clinician elicits, and carefully attends to, a comprehensive account of the patient's illness. The fundamental impulse behind it—to understand the meaning of the patient's experience of his or her body in context—may seem positive with regard to understanding disability as well as illness (Couser 1997), but it does not transcend its clinical origins. Thus, from a disability studies perspective, the terms "illness" and "patient" are problematic. The issue is the common tendency to collapse the distinction between disability and disease. This is not just a matter of connotation, such as the association of disease with contagion. (After all, "disability" has its own negative connotations; this is one of the rationales for "person-first" terminology, which puts syntactic distance between individual and bodily condition.) Rather, "illness" is problematic because sickness is conceptually distinct from disability in ways that are at the heart of disability studies.

Conflating disability with illness necessarily invokes and engages what disability studies scholars have identified as the medical model of disability. It "hails," or interpellates, disabled people as sick; that is, it constructs their condition as requiring medical intervention. It thus obstructs the differentiation, central to disability studies, between "impairment" (a dysfunction in the body, which may be amenable to cure or prosthetic modification) and "disability" (aspects of the environment that exclude or impede those with impairments, which requires altering the context—legal, social, and architectural—in which the body exists). These aspects, which make up what has become known as the social model of disability, help make the distinction between illness and disability palpable. Thus, lumping the disabled with the ill threatens to eclipse the social model and thus to obviate any need for accommodation. While narrative medicine seeks to understand all of the ways in which a condition is experienced by an individual, it remains a variant of the medical model. It may aspire to healing the person, not merely the patient, but it has no designs on the world.

However distinct "illness" and "disability" may be in concept, though, in practice the two often overlap or coexist in the same individuals. Thus, while illness and disability are not the same things, the two populations—"the ill" and "the disabled"—are not seen as separate. Indeed, conceptually and practically speaking, illness and disability have a reciprocal relation: illness may cause disability, and disability may cause

illness. In many instances, blindness, deafness, and paralysis are caused by diseases, and disabling conditions often have complications in the form of illness. Paralysis, for example, can lead to urinary tract infections or bedsores. Moreover, some illnesses—especially chronic or terminal ones such as HIV/AIDS and some forms of cancer—carry powerful stigmas like those assigned to disability.

In any case, the border between disability and illness is not always clear—and what counts as either one is not clear, either. Indeed, for legal purposes, many "physical" illnesses, such as HIV/AIDS, cancer, and diabetes, and "mental" illnesses, such as schizophrenia and bipolar syndrome, count as disabilities. In the United States, the authors of the Americans with Disabilities Act of 1990 (restored to its original intentions by the ADA Amendments Act of 2008) were clear about granting rights to people with illness as well as disability as conventionally understood. The legal definition of disability was intentionally broad and inclusive, and properly so.

Yet recent developments in the field of disability studies explicitly challenge distinctions between illness and disability. The British scholar and activist Tom Shakespeare, for one notable example, has critiqued the social model, which he sees as limited and, indeed, gravely flawed. In *Disability Rights and Wrongs* (2006a), Shakespeare indicts the social model for undermining political organization on the basis of particular impairments and generating unhelpful suspicion of, if not overt hostility to, medical research and development. Having initially advanced the argument that disability is a harmful social construction, akin to race and gender, then, disability studies scholars are now reckoning with ways in which the analogy fails. For one thing—and this is a difficult admission to make, for obvious reasons—there is some sense in which, unlike race and gender, impairment entails limitations that are *not* social or cultural in their basis and which social reform *cannot* ameliorate. Indeed, impairment may cause chronic pain, progressive degeneration, and early death. As a result, the social model alone may fail to produce adequate accounts of the lives of disabled people or remedies for their disadvantages (Shakespeare 2006a, 41).

The point is that although disability and impairment are distinct from disease and illness, disability, like illness, involves real dysfunction in the body. And the failure of the field to acknowledge this in its theorizing has been of more benefit to academic discourse than to many of those living with disabling conditions. Shakespeare does not call for the abandonment of accommodation; rather, he endeavors to point out its insufficiency if it is reflexively opposed to a medical or biological model. Indeed, he argues that intervention must be more aggressive and comprehensive, acknowledging the reality of impairment and seeking to make up for bodily deficits: "Disabled people are among those who need more from others and from their society. . . . Creating a level playing field is not enough: redistribution is required to promote true social inclusion" (2006a, 66–67). The dire economic consequences of disability thus demand new approaches and new remedies. One of these is to acknowledge the kinship and the overlap between two populations, the ill and the disabled.

34

Impairment
Michael Ralph

"Impairment" is often used as a synonym for "disability," as when a person is described as "hearing impaired." In this context, "impairment" is a euphemism, deemed more appropriate than terms like "handicapped" or "deformed," which are now largely defunct. Yet the status of "impairment" as a substitute for different conceptions of debility is complicated by the fact that, both within disability studies and in medical conceptions of the body, "impairment" is frequently distinguished from "disability."

Within the British "social model" of disability, "impairment" signifies physical or biological lack (a missing arm, the experience of blindness), while "disability" refers to the process that converts a perceived deficiency into an obstacle. As the British activist group the Union of the Physically Impaired against Segregation (UPIAS) put it in 1975: "Disability is something imposed on top of our impairments, by the way we are unnecessarily isolated and excluded from full participation in society" (14). As a result, clinicians, scholars, activists, and the lay public alike often construe impairment as more scientific—as somehow more reliable and precise—than disability (Oliver 1996; Oppenheim 2009, 474–475; McRuer 2006, 34).

Yet this concept of impairment has its roots not in the medical profession or in disability activism but in changes in the structure of the U.S. life insurance industry that accompanied the formal abolition of slavery. As a term, it served to condense several different classes of risk—including region, race, family medical history, and national origin—and as a way to avoid language that suddenly conflicted with the imperative to forge an ostensibly free society.

By the beginning of the nineteenth century, insuring slaves was a well-enshrined practice—from seeking protection against the potential loss of human cargo, it had evolved to include protocols for assessing the value of bonded workers. In the decades that followed the legal abolition of slavery, actuaries and underwriters associated with the life insurance industry began to use the concept of "impairment" to uphold a differential hierarchy in the value of a human life.

As early as 1847, the famed scientist Josiah C. Nott had complained that insurance companies were biased against Southern whites because their actuarial tables did not account for regional variation. By the last few decades of the nineteenth century, insurance companies had eliminated this regional bias, yet they charged African Americans higher rates for coverage. Even black-owned life insurance companies penalized African American consumers in line with these same, ostensibly objective, medical assessments (Ralph 2012).

By the 1880s, such blatant discrimination proved unsavory as a routine practice. It was at this moment that insurers began to use the concept of impairment as a proxy for people with weaker vital statistics. When states began to adopt legislation from the 1890s onward prohibiting discrimination by race, underwriters simply reclassified African Americans as low-income wage workers (who could be charged more, since they were statistically prone to industrial accidents) or characterized them as mentally impaired (a category to which African Americans were generally held to belong; Dilts 2012).

The concept of "impairment" thus emerged from the scientific assessments of medical experts, actuaries, and underwriters concerned to fix the monetary value of social difference and debility. Turning their attention to family medical history, blood and urine samples, and emerging physiological indices like blood pressure, scientists established medical impairment as the ground for differentiating between demographics. In the process, the hierarchical calculus of value that was explicit in the context of legalized enslavement now became the basis for private medical assessments. These scientific developments effectively privatized inequality. This genealogy of the term "impairment" thus points to a long entanglement of race and disability as proxies for the value of a human life.

With good reason, the disability rights movement—particularly as it emerged in Great Britain—insisted on emphasizing disability at the expense of impairment. Impairment, with its connotations of limitation, lack, and deficiency, endorses the fantasy of a normative human body. Whereas impairment is often treated as an objective fact of the body, many scholars have by now shown how notions of impairment are historically derived, institutionally fixed, and culturally mediated. Others have argued that it is worth preserving the concept of impairment as a way of describing those aspects of disability that cannot be ascribed to social and environmental factors (Shakespeare 2006b, 197–204; Davis 2002). Without denying the importance of the social model, it is worth recognizing that bodies and minds are never assimilated the same way in any context. While preserving what is useful about the concept of impairment, history teaches us that we should be critical not only of the discourses in which it appears but also of the political and intellectual projects that continue to animate it.

IMPAIRMENT   MICHAEL RALPH

35

Institutions

Licia Carlson

The field of disability studies (DS) is both critical and productive: disability theorists critique definitions and practices that devalue disability, and they are also committed to the development of a positive disability culture, identity, and politics. These two facets of DS can be seen in the complex relationship between disability and institutions. Critical work in the field has been devoted to examining the centuries-long practice of institutionalizing people with disabilities and exposing the dehumanizing consequences of segregation and marginalization. Yet DS has also produced alternative histories, or counter-stories, that reveal forms of resistance to these institutions and trace the development of institutional structures that support disability rights and empower people with disabilities.

Because "institution" is such a broad term, it is helpful to distinguish among its various meanings. The *Oxford English Dictionary* defines an institution as "an establishment, organization, or association, instituted for the promotion of some object, esp. one of public or general utility, religious, charitable, educational, etc., e.g. a church, school, college, hospital, asylum, reformatory, mission, or the like." In the context of disability, institutions can refer both to physical residential structures established *specifically* to house, educate, and/or treat people with various kinds of disabilities; and to structures and organizations that are not formed exclusively for people with disabilities but that have a significant impact on their lives (such as hospitals, almshouses, schools, and prisons).

Disability studies scholars also address *institutionalization* as an active process. The various calls either to institutionalize people with disabilities (thereby removing them from mainstream society) or else to *de*-institutionalize them (with the aims of normalization and integration) reflect complex social goals. Disability studies scholarship aims to expose the underlying economic, political, and ideological forces that define these processes and the effects that they have had cumulatively on people with disabilities. A final use of the term has emerged from social theories that analyze structural forms of oppression like sexism, racism, and homophobia. "Institutionalized ableism" (borrowed from civil rights leader Stokely Carmichael's term "institutional racism") refers to the ways in which discriminatory ideas and assumptions that devalue people with disabilities are entrenched in social structures, theories, and concrete practices.

The history of segregating people with disabilities is much longer than the history of residential institutions specifically built for them. Many different kinds of institutions prefigured the asylums, training schools, rehabilitation hospitals, and other facilities that spread through the nineteenth and twentieth centuries. For example, the efforts to contain leprosy in twelfth-century Europe "represent the first time that institutional, segregated facilities were systematically used in Europe to address the issues presented by people with disabilities" (Braddock and Parish 2001, 20). The Bethlehem Hospital, which opened in 1247 just beyond London's city walls, was originally built to treat the physically ill, but it was transformed into an institution for the mentally ill and eventually became the "longest continuing mental hospital in Europe" (Braddock and Parish 2001, 19).

The seventeenth and eighteenth centuries witnessed a period of what Michel Foucault (2006) has called "the great confinement," where "vast houses of confinement," designed to exclude the poor, criminal, mad, and other undesirables from society, proliferated in Europe. In the United States, the first almshouse opened in Boston in 1662, followed by the first general hospital in Philadelphia in 1752, both of which housed people with disabilities (Braddock and Parish 2001, 23, 26). Accompanying this institutional growth was an equally burgeoning interest—medical, pedagogical, and philosophical—in the nature and treatment of various disabilities. The Enlightenment focus on the relationship among reason, language, and education yielded works on the distinction between idiocy and insanity, the nature of deafness, and the educability of deaf-mutes and produced some of the earliest residential schools for people with disabilities. Each of these inquiries ultimately led to the development of specialized institutions, such as the first school for the deaf in Paris, opened in 1760 by Charles-Michel de l'Épée.

The number of institutions devoted exclusively to people with disabilities rose significantly in the nineteenth century when hundreds of "schools," "training schools," "hospital-schools," "rehabilitation hospitals," and "asylums" were built. In the United States, this included new institutions for epileptics, the deaf and "dumb," the blind, the "mad," the "feebleminded," and the "crippled and deformed." A complex confluence of factors accounted for this institutional explosion: the professionalization of experts who studied and treated disability; a growing interest in education, training, rehabilitation, and new forms of "moral therapies"; economic and social concerns about transforming "the disabled" into productive working members of society (particularly after the Civil War); and the emergence of reformers like Dorothea Dix (1802–1887), who argued that the mentally disabled had been wrongly housed with dangerous criminals and paupers and deserved institutions of their own. Though institutionalization was often justified on charitable grounds, many of the residential facilities that were built upon the hopes of improving the lives of people with disabilities became custodial warehouses, sites of oppression and abuse, and resulted in further marginalization and exclusion.

The sharp rise in institutionalization continued into the early decades of the twentieth century, prompted by the eugenics movement's framing of disability as a positive social danger. New classifications of feeblemindedness, such as the "imbecile" and the "moron," were premised on the belief that these individuals were a menace to society and should be prevented from reproducing. Institutions became sites of involuntary sterilization, overcrowding, and permanent incarceration. By midcentury, these large institutions were coming under scrutiny and even attack. With the emergence of parental advocacy groups, the antipsychiatry movement, and high-profile exposés of the horrifying conditions in the institutions, the tide began to shift, culminating in the deinstitutionalization movement of the 1970s. The closing of large state hospitals and institutions did not improve the lives of all people with disabilities, as many were unable to secure adequate housing and social support. However, the last three decades have marked significant progress in reversing the isolation, marginalization, and dehumanization left in the wake of institutionalization. The disability rights movement has been active on many fronts, yielding the independent living movement, legal victories (such as the Americans with Disabilities Act of 1990) ensuring community-based residential settings, and increased economic and social support for people with disabilities.

One of the significant contributions of DS within these continued efforts has been to problematize facile or linear histories that ignore the multiple aims, contradictory justifications, and unintended consequences inherent in the institutional history of disability. Many historians, for example, divide the history of institutionalization into distinct periods: the optimism of the mid-nineteenth century, the segregation campaigns of the eugenics movement in the early twentieth century, and the period of reform during the years of deinstitutionalization in the last decades of the twentieth century. Yet such neat compartmentalizations often obscure deeper continuities as well as continuing struggles. Philip Ferguson (1994), for instance, argues that while many of the early institutions created in the nineteenth century were intended to be "schools" rather than custodial facilities, this was not true of institutions/facilities for the "severely mentally retarded" who were viewed as chronic cases in need of permanent incarceration. In Deaf history, different institutions were established by manualists and oralists, who are generally considered to represent opposite ideologies; yet, as Douglas Baynton argues, "both created images of deaf people as outsiders" (2006a, 35). Similarly, it is too simplistic to say that deinstitutionalization spelled the end of institutional lives for people with disabilities. Many individuals who could otherwise live independently or in community settings, for example, cannot afford the necessary personal attendant care and are thus confined to nursing homes (Shapiro 1994). And sadly, smaller community settings do not necessarily guarantee safe environments, as reports continue to emerge regarding abuse and dehumanizing treatment in the group homes that have proliferated in the wake of closing or downsizing the larger custodial institutions.

In addition to complicating the history of institutions, DS scholars also examine the mechanisms internal to institutions that *produce* disability. Many of these were "total institutions" in the sense that sociologist Erving Goffman defined them in his book *Asylums*, places where "a large number of like-situated individuals, cut off from the wider society for an appreciable period of time, together lead an enclosed, formally administered round of life" (1961, xiii). Goffman's analysis of what life in a total institution does to its "inmates" has helped to explain how and why people with disabilities have been stripped of their identities, rights, and humanity in various institutional settings. Although Goffman's work predates the emergence of DS as a distinct academic field, his scholarship on institutions and on stigma has been important to many disability theorists.

The work of twentieth-century French philosopher Michel Foucault has also been central in studying the dynamics of institutionalization. His texts on the modern prison system, the birth of the asylum, and the emergence of "biopower" have informed the analysis of what Shelley Tremain (2005) has called the "government of disability." Foucault's definition of the institution as a site of disciplinary power in which the subject is created and defined by experts applies to the institutions for the "feebleminded" that produced new *kinds* and typologies of individuals (Carlson 2010). In addition to defining new forms of "feeblemindedness," these institutions were also self-authenticating and self-perpetuating entities, as they established professional legitimacy for the superintendents in charge and were sustained by the use of inmate labor (Trent 1994; Carlson 2010).

Work in DS also exposes the ableist logic of institutionalization. The many justifications for segregating people with disabilities—ranging from a philanthropic desire to help and protect, to the commitment to educate, to the belief that such individuals must be removed from society—betray the underlying assumptions at the heart of ableism. These include the following ideas: (1) that disability should be defined as an individual trait, a pathology, deficit, or abnormality identified by medical "experts" as in need of correction and/or management; (2) that paternalism is warranted, since people with disabilities are unable to act autonomously and make decisions for themselves; (3) that these individuals are different enough from the "normal" individual, sufficiently *other*, that they warrant separate treatment in a specially designed facility; and (4) that their lives are better managed by professional experts who are granted higher authority than the individuals themselves. Interestingly, some DS scholars have also challenged the discourse of *de*institutionalization, arguing that terms like "inclusion" and "normalization" are neither neutral nor unproblematic (Stiker 1999; Silvers 1999).

Finally, DS broadens the scope of analysis by identifying forms of resistance both within and beyond the walls of institutions, including the voices of people with disabilities, and offering global, cross-cultural perspectives. In his influential book *The History of Sexuality* (1978), Foucault speaks about the many forms of counterdiscourse that come "from below." DS offers an account of institutions "from below" by incorporating, when available, the first-person narratives of people with disabilities and tracing the close connections between institutionalization, deinstitutionalization, and the disability rights movement (Pelka 2012; Traustadottir and Johnson 2008). When one examines the ways people with disabilities have shaped this history, it becomes clear that they cannot be viewed merely as passive victims of an oppressive system. They have been instrumental in challenging institutionalization in multiple ways: through forms of self-advocacy such as the independent living movement and People First, political activism, and important battles on legal and educational fronts. Moreover, in some cases the very creation of institutions inadvertently provided the impetus for organization and resistance. For example, historian Douglas Baynton explains that it was the *creation* of residential schools for the deaf in the nineteenth century that allowed hearing-impaired individuals to become "a cultural and linguistic community" (2006a, 33).

The development of the disability rights movement and a positive disability culture has led to greater self-determination and independence for many people with disabilities. Yet some in DS have argued that independence and autonomy are not the only goals to be celebrated and pursued; in fact, the devaluation of disability can be seen as the consequence of privileging these values above all else. For some individuals, independent living may be neither possible nor a desired end; in finding the most appropriate and just living conditions, it is equally important to acknowledge and value forms of dependency and interdependency (Kittay 1999).

Disability theorists and activists have challenged many of the assumptions underlying institutionalization: that people with disabilities are dependent, incapacitated, and in need of protection and segregation. Multiple forms of advocacy *for, with, and by* people with disabilities have for the most part encouraged society to move beyond a reliance on "total institutions" as a means of quarantining and fixing disability. The more insidious features of institutionalized ableism may be harder to dismantle.

36

Invisibility

Susannah B. Mintz

"Invisibility" refers to the absence of disability from the conversations and activities that establish the way a society functions, encompassing social relationships, intellectual and artistic work, and politics. While recent high-profile celebrity cases like Christopher Reeve and Olympic runner Oscar Pistorius have brought injury and impairment into popular awareness, the problem of people with disabilities as an oppressed social group remains largely undiscussed. Douglas Baynton writes that "disability is everywhere in history, once you begin looking for it, but conspicuously absent in the histories we write" (2001, 52). A similar point has been made about disabled figures in literature, art, and film: they abound, yet until recently they have been ignored by scholars or interpreted for metaphoric import within an otherwise ableist reading. Media stories of "overcoming" disability can obscure the reality of most disabled people's lives, reinforcing desires for rehabilitation or cure and deflecting attention from matters of education, employment, and access to services. That "diversity" dialogues on many American college campuses may include race, class, gender, and sexual orientation but not disability suggests the ongoing invisibility of the needs and concerns of people with disabilities. Similarly, most Americans are likely unaware of the terms of the Americans with Disabilities Act (ADA) or its impact, even though compliance with the ADA structures the work spaces and personnel guidelines of organizations and businesses across the country.

Invisibility, then, can refer to a range of exclusions that reinforce the marginalizing of disability. Invisibility also refers to diseases, conditions, and sensations that cannot be observed externally, such as chronic pain, cognitive or psychiatric impairment, or Deafness. So-called invisible disabilities present unique challenges in a society already prone to suspicion about the reality status of illness and provoked to anxiety by incapacity and pain. "To have pain is to have *certainty*," Elaine Scarry famously declared in *The Body in Pain*, while "to hear about pain is to have *doubt*" (1985, 13); the same is true for conditions that cannot be "verified" by looking. In a visual culture, what cannot be seen cannot be known, and so it is easy to discount or distrust.

If invisibility is thus associated with a lack of political and social agency, becoming *visible* would imply gaining a measure of legitimacy, whether as a result of community effort or by making oneself known through activism, art, or research; many in the disability community have adopted the phrase "coming out" to describe celebrating a sense of disabled selfhood. Such a dynamic, however, with its inherent hierarchy—"visibility" being the positive term, "invisibility" the bad—is not without its own complications. According to the logics of disability's paradoxical social status, visibility is also problematic, since the disabled body is subject to staring and, historically, legislated hiddenness (Garland-Thomson 2009; Schweik 2009).

Moreover, the equation of legitimacy with being "seen" might seem troubling in that it reinforces the symbolism of vision, long entrenched in Western thought, in which knowledge, intelligence, and control are linked to sight. Philosophers from Plato onward have employed visual metaphors to convey intellectual perceptiveness and mastery (such as "vision," "insight," or even "I see" to mean understand), and such metaphors are so embedded in our language that we may use them without registering the inherent bias. From the perspective of Blind identity and activism, the very term "invisibility" thus becomes a locus of conflicts about language and disability, demonstrating the assumptions that infuse the words we use with prejudices perhaps so subtle that even advocates might miss the effects they have on others.

37

Madness

Sander L. Gilman

To attempt to capture the relationship between "madness" and "disability" is to define one ambiguous and constantly shifting term by another. Madness has for centuries had legal and medical meanings, which today are more tangled and subject to political and ideological pressures than ever in light of the framing of madness as a type of disability. For now madness has to figure itself not only in relation to ideas about competency, moral ability, curability, and so forth but also in relation to questions of access, stigma, and advocacy. In recent centuries, the term suggests the medical, social, and cultural categories dealing with all forms of psychic pain that came under the purview of alienists, psychiatrists, and neurologists. But increasingly, madness has also been understood from a patient/client/inmate perspective rather than from a psychiatric practitioner's or clinician's perspective.

A broad understanding of madness therefore must account for medical perspectives (both allopathic and complementary/alternative practices), as well as multiple social, political, and cultural understandings of madness and mad people, all fluid and ever moving across the world. Every society has its own categories and perspectives and experiences of madness—from melancholia in ancient Athens to spirit madness in modern Evangelical churches; from the American medical missionaries in China in the nineteenth century to the botanicas of the Dominicans in New York City today. Across the globe, societies see categories of madness as something that impinges on human activity, for ill or for good. But what constitutes madness in any given society or community or historical moment is constantly shifting: symptoms change, and their meanings seem always in flux.

Even as different etiologies and meanings of madness emerge to explain the somatic, psychological, social, cultural causes of madness, the concept of psychic pain (or anguish or suffering) remains central to all of these categories. This concept has its modern origins in John Locke's view in *An Essay Concerning Human Understanding* (1690) that pain is "sometimes occasioned by disorder in the Body, sometimes by Thoughts of the Mind" (1955, 20). However else madness has been defined, such psychic pain was and remains a litmus test for madness, whether as a reason for intervention or as a perceived source for greater insight into the mad or their creative capacities. Likewise, it may be related to other categories of illness and pain or may be a state that transcends the normal (Gilman 1982; Porter 2003).

Legal and medical meanings of madness are often intertwined. From the forensic definitions of madness created by the Romans, which focused on competency, aging, and property, to the McNaughton rule of Victorian England, which focused on the moral ability to know right from wrong, legal definitions of madness parallel and mimic medical and social definitions, sometimes even recycling older medical definitions. Today one speaks not of madness but rather of psychiatric illness/diagnosis in the world of law. Yet the contemporary functional definition within the law remains inherently one developed by Victorian alienists. The so-called incompetency defense in court often generates a complicated political response, especially in high-profile cases of political assassination (such as in the murder of President James Garfield by Charles Guiteau in 1881) or infanticide (the use of postnatal psychosis in the case of Susan Smith in 1995). In both cases the defense, using a version of the McNaughton rule, was unsuccessful. Several American states have now banned this defense (Millard 2011).

Once we have settled on a particular definition/construct of madness and psychic pain, then we can ask about the consequences of these definitions for those who are affected by them. Central to all definitions of madness is the idea of innate mental or psychological difference. This stereotype may be positive—the association of creativity with madness, for instance, goes back to the ancients—but most have negative consequences. These include physically isolating the mad from society, limiting the rights of the mad, and seeing madness as a diminution of one's humanity.

The Greeks regarded madness as the result of a physical imbalance of the four humors, the bodily fluids that they believed regulated health and temperament. The Chinese at the same time conceived of madness as an imbalance of the primal forces of yin and yang. Jewish beliefs, mirrored in the accounts in the Tanach (Old Testament), stressed moral failing and divine intervention as a primary cause of madness (Daniel 4:31–33). All of these cultures placed the mad in a separate category: for some a higher one of prophecy and illumination, but for most one of marginality and exclusion. All developed therapeutic interventions for the latter, not necessarily for the former.

Roman and medieval medicine made the distinction between the naturally born idiot and the lunatic, terms that overlap with and permeate medieval law and medicine. The former were not seen as treatable, but the latter were. The moral stigma and legal treatment of both, however, were clearly parallel. The question of causation mixed theological, physiological, and mystical etiologies, to varying degrees at different times and places. The means of treatment was similarly mixed:

from spiritual exorcism to the use of somatic interventions such as diet to restore mental balance and physical control to restrain the individual from actions that could harm their estates. This was also the case in Islamic medicine, which had transmitted much of Greco-Roman medical attitudes on madness in the Middle Ages to Europe, but which also was permeated by Christian and Jewish medical practice in Europe and beyond.

As the notion of the hospital evolved in the early Middle Ages, specialized institutions for the mad developed as early as AD 705 in Baghdad. By the late Middle Ages, this tradition had spread into Spain and Western Europe. While a form of medical incarceration appeared for diseases such as leprosy and madness, the mad were rarely permanently housed in such facilities. Unlike lepers, they were usually incarcerated for a limited time, usually because of the costs to local communities. By the Renaissance, madness also became a conceit for the view that one's mad actions are a sign of sanity in a world gone mad, as William Shakespeare has Hamlet say: "I essentially am not in madnesse, / But mad in craft" (3.4.171). This view of madness as a form of sanity would become a commonplace of Romantic views of insanity and, indeed, part of the idea of madness thereafter.

By the nineteenth century in Western Europe, the "moral treatment" of the insane and the separation of idiots seen as inherently incurable from the treatable lunatics were commonplace. Moral treatment aimed at the return of the lunatics to their proper place in the world through the moral and secular correction of the misunderstandings of the world and their inappropriate actions. Thus weekly dances for the inmates were a standard practice in the reformed asylum to reestablish the moral order of their inmates. Originally led by lay directors, such clinical facilities underwent a process of medicalization across Europe and North America throughout the nineteenth century, so that by the close of the century their directors were virtually all medically trained alienists. This development in treatment paralleled the professionalization of psychiatry and neurology and the creation of a systematic set of diagnostic categories and treatments. Most of these were based on physiological principles, though strongly psychological interventions continued through the close of the century.

Even so, the nineteenth century emphasized somatic definitions of madness. In 1868, Wilhelm Griesinger wrote: "The so-called mental illnesses are found in individuals suffering from brain- and nerve illness" (iii). By the 1890s this view seems to have become universal in Western psychiatry. The neurologists of the time, such as the young Sigmund Freud, assumed this as a fact but questioned the relationship between organic sources of madness and the wide range of psychological manifestations of mental illness. Freud began a movement, psychoanalysis, that understood a wide range of mental states as potentially leading to psychic pain yet without any direct organic cause. Indeed, his great insight is that bodily symptoms, such as paralysis, can have purely psychological causes and should be treated by psychological interventions such as talk therapy rather than physical treatments such as electrotherapy (Gilman 1993).

The somaticization of madness increased across the twentieth century, but it came at a cost. More and more symptoms were related to specific neurological deficits such as dementia. Developmental disorders came to be sorted out from illnesses with complex neurological causes—reductively dividing environmental diseases from genetic ones, for example—and thus further separating out those diseases seen as purely illness of the spirit, the psyche, or the mind. Thus the idiot and the lunatic, often housed in the same state institution through the nineteenth century, were by the early twentieth century seen as manifesting quite different social and medical causes. Indeed, biological interventions such as sterilization dealt with such individuals not to aid them but to improve society by eliminating their ability to reproduce. As the U.S. Supreme Court justice Oliver Wendell Holmes Jr. concluded in affirming the Commonwealth of Virginia's eugenic sterilization law in *Buck v. Bell* (1927): "It is better for all the world, if instead of waiting to execute degenerate offspring for crime, or to let them starve for their imbecility, society can prevent those who are manifestly unfit from continuing their kind. . . . Three generations of imbeciles are enough."

Yet with more detailed knowledge of the causes and meanings of madness, the boundaries that defined it began to shift. Thus general paralysis of the insane, the most common diagnosis for psychiatric patients in the nineteenth-century asylum, came to be recognized as the last stages of syphilitic infection after the development of a specific test for the syphilis spirochetes in 1906; it thus became a potentially treatable neurological disease rather than a form of mental illness. After specific treatments for syphilis were developed, it simply vanished from the diagnostic repertoire of most physicians who dealt with madness and entered other medical specialties.

The desire in the twentieth century was to find more and more cases in which madness is the result of specific biological, neurological, or genetic factors. Eugenic interventions, such as sterilization, came to be repudiated after the horrors of the Holocaust and its eugenically inspired mass murder of "inferior" races as well as the disabled. Rather, post–World War II medicine sought specific biomedical interventions (mainly psychotropic drugs) that can have an impact on the symptoms of madness, then defined in terms of psychosis (a lesser or greater loss of the psychic connection to reality) and neurosis (the impairment of rationality that leads to psychic pain; Shorter 1998).

Developmental disorders seem to have been bracketed in the search for a drug to cure madness. Yet the discovery of DNA in 1952 and the subsequent discovery of the specific mutations for Down syndrome in 1959 are more or less simultaneous with the first uses of lithium to treat the symptoms of depression and Thorazine (chlorpromazine hydrochloride) in 1950 to treat the symptoms of schizophrenia. The idea that there could be a genetic intervention to prevent all such developmental disorders is also an artifact of this post–World War II science, paralleling the now seemingly universal use of psychotropic drugs, from mood enhancers (Prozac) to drugs to treat hyperactivity (Ritalin). The expansion of drug treatment was at first heralded by patients and physicians alike but quickly became a target of patient and social discontent given massive side effects as well as the overprescription of many such drugs to ever-widening categories of individuals.

With the expansion of psychotropic drugs the patient self-consciously became the client, whose role in treatment became ever more self-aware. Twenty-first-century patient populations are in effect consumers of medical care who organize and make demands—whether for deinstitutionalization and the closing of large public facilities that housed individuals believed to be unable to function in the world or, more broadly, for the release from the negative stigma of madness. Even the medical treatment of mental states as illness comes into question.

In the 1960s, alternative perspectives on madness began to emerge in the works of Erving Goffman, R. D. Laing, and Thomas Szasz, which offered a reexamination of the social causes of madness. These had a powerful impact on the demedicalization of madness among feminist and gay activists in the 1970s. Where Goffman saw the asylum as a repressive means of social control, Szasz saw madness as invented by the patient as well as society, and Laing saw it as the "healthy" product of sick social or familial structures. The idea of a relativization of madness (now freed of any medical implication) first appeared in sociological literature in France in the work of Georges Canguilhem in the 1940s and that of his student Michel Foucault in the 1960s. Foucault (2006) famously dismissed the antithesis of sanity and madness as the result of medical power. One concrete result was that entire categories of madness such as homosexuality (in 1973) and premenstrual syndrome (in 1987) came to be dismissed from psychiatric diagnosis. More generally, though, the very idea of madness came to be suspect.

Medical discourses of rehabilitation and disability inspired the creation of the category of psychiatric disability. Particularly influential was the World Health Organization's *International Classification of Impairments, Disabilities and Handicaps* (1980), which framed certain disabilities as the result of an illness. A psychiatric disability could be caused by a psychiatric impairment, resulting in the stigma of madness that impinges on the ability of the individual to function in the community. Different from other disabilities such as developmental disabilities, psychiatric disabilities are seen as episodic and intermittent. But here the acknowledgment of the causality of the stigma of madness does not touch the underlying medical assumptions about the meaning of madness.

One reaction to this medicalized model of disability within the disability rights movement (and its allied academic field of disability studies) is to see all forms of mental ability and emotional stability as ranged on a spectrum of human psychological/mental diversity. Harvey Blume coined the term "neurodiversity" in 1998 as a defining quality of being human: "Neurodiversity may be every bit as crucial for the human race as

biodiversity is for life in general. . . . Cybernetics and computer culture, for example, may favor a somewhat autistic cast of mind." This followed from work in disability studies that spoke of the "extraordinary" body (Garland-Thomson 1997), the "rejected" body (Wendell, 1996) or the "recovering" body (Couser 1997), or, more recently, the "problem" body (Chivers and Markotic 2010). Disability thus dealt with the "reception or construction of [the] difference" presented by a "physical or mental impairment" (Davis 2000a, 56). Here one suddenly has the idea of the "extraordinary," "rejected," "recovering," or "problem" mind rather than the pathological one.

Such ideas of madness and disability develop parallel to the growth of popular interest in autism, which came to be the litmus test for madness within disability studies (Hellker and Yergeau 2011). Medically, autism has been defined as a psychiatric category since the early twentieth century. It is now seen as a developmental disorder with genetic or environmental causes. Certainly the flawed claims about measles-mumps-rubella vaccination as the cause of autism colored its reevaluation at the end of the twentieth century, as such claims stressed autism's potential elimination through social action rather than through genetic or medical intervention.

Today autism is seen more and more as an alternative, even a preferred, mental state rather than a deficit. It is the answer to Erich Fromm's (1955) view that madness in modern society is a sign of humanity's fall from a sense of relatedness, rootedness, and orientation. Autism has come to be a sign that individual autonomy challenges and often trumps notions of social isolation. The fascination with idiot savants in the late twentieth-century public sphere (such as the autistic Raymond in Barry Levinson's film *Rain Man* [1988]) gives way to a new focus on the autistic individual as a representative of

MADNESS   SANDER L. GILMAN

neurodiversity (exemplified by the film *Temple Grandin* [2010], Mick Jackson's biopic that describes the youth of Temple Grandin, the iconic autist who is a professor at Colorado State University; and Max Mayer's *Adam* [2009], the account of a young man with Asperger's syndrome). This framing of autism draws on debates from the 1960s about the autonomy of the client/patient and the recent notion of a broader spectrum of mental health held by disability studies scholars. It rejects any sense of the autist as being severely impaired and in need of special facilities. Indeed, both activists and scholars of disability have promoted the growing sense that autists are often better enabled in a world that does not recognize their abilities. This is the theme of a bestselling novel by Mark Haddon, *The Curious Incident of the Dog in the Night-Time* (2003). (See the various positions in the special issue of the *Disability Studies Quarterly* on neurodiversity devoted to autism [Savarese 2010].)

The need for public facilities for severely impacted autistic people has diminished as quickly in the twenty-first century as it did for the "mad" in general in the 1960s. The source of this decline is the sense that autistic individuals must function as part of a newly redefined public sphere that, according to law and custom, is now open to them, no matter how severe their individual state. In practice, though, the model for this is Asperger's syndrome rather than severe, debilitating autism. Thus the politics of madness-as-disability can be clearly seen in the debates about autism in the twenty-first century. The Americans with Disabilities Act (1990) defines disabling madness as "any mental or psychological disorder, such as mental retardation, organic brain syndrome, emotional or mental illness, and specific learning disabilities," that "substantially limits one or more major life activities of an individual" or that causes one to be "regarded as having such an impairment." Both aspects of this definition assume a psychiatric diagnosis.

The British Disability Discrimination Act (1995) follows the standard handbooks of psychiatric diagnosis, as well as the idea that such forms of mental illness must be chronic or recurrent.

In 2011, the committee tasked with revising the standard American diagnostic handbook of psychiatry, the *Diagnostic and Statistical Manual of Mental Disorders* (*DSM-5*), suggested that the definition of autism spectrum disorder be reworked and simplified. The reaction from the autism community in 2011, now well organized into political lobbying organizations with substantial fund-raising capacity and celebrity spokespeople, was swift and damning, seeing this medical decision as impacting the funding for autistic clients as well as excluding certain forms of autism (especially Asperger's syndrome) from coverage in the law. The psychiatrists who suggested the reforms to *DSM-5* quickly backtracked, and the diagnostic category of autism spectrum disorders was again revised.

The autists who pressured the drafting committee for *DSM-5* acted in complex ways. They demanded *more* medicalization (or at least the reversal of a trend toward demedicalization), but at the same time they were able to exhibit their political clout as an interest group. Because the drift of most disability activism is to demedicalize disability, this is a counterthrust. Neurodiversity is their cry, but they also want to preserve medical coverage and legal protections. The medical model for madness is still potent even as the disability world tries to erode its power. The autists *do* erode the power of the medical community by putting pressure on them to reverse their decision, but the result is *more* rather than less medicalization. For autists as well as others diagnosed with mental illness or neurological disorder today, adopting the medical model of madness can still confer tactical advantage for some disability groups (Martin 2007).

38

Medicalization

Sayantani DasGupta

The term "medicalization" came into popular and academic use in the 1970s and can perhaps be first traced to medical sociologist Ivan Illich's book *Limits to Medicine: Medical Nemeses* (1975). Illich used the term in his discussion of "iatrogenesis," the ways that medicine itself may make social and biological conditions worse as a result of medical intervention. In his book *The Medicalization of Society*, Peter Conrad defines medicalization as "a process by which nonmedical problems become defined and treated as medical problems, usually in terms of illness and disorders" (2007, 4).

The medicalization of disability, then, refers to how individuals with disabilities have been categorized as "sick" and placed under the jurisdiction of the medical establishment and medical professionals. This model views disability solely through the lens of impairment and is undoubtedly related to what sociologist Arthur Frank (1995) has critiqued as medicine's investment in the "restitution narrative": the belief that all conditions are "treatable" through medical intervention, which then returns the "sufferer" to the condition of "health" and "normalcy."

The historical roots of disability's medicalization can be traced to nineteenth-century shifts from feudal to capitalist economies. The mid-1800s marked a change in how bodies were commodified and classified, with productive bodies distinguished from those that were considered less productive or nonproductive. Scholars including Michel Foucault (1979) have written about the rise of prisons, asylums, hospitals, workhouses, and poorhouses at this time as ways that those bodies perceived to be unproductive and/or nonnormative were sequestered, controlled, diagnosed, and otherwise administered to by the growing medical profession.

This physical, as well as sociocultural, "othering" of individuals with disabilities was a marked difference from previous historical periods when disability and mental illness might have been seen as retribution for spiritual or moral failings, but individuals with disabilities were still living within their communities. The mid-nineteenth century to early twentieth century also marked the rise of "ugly laws" both in the United States and abroad, targeting "unsightly beggars" and legislating that individuals considered "diseased, maimed, mutilated, or in any way deformed" not "expose [themselves] to public view" (Schweik 2009, 85). If the medicalization of this period sought to render disability socially invisible, institutionalizing and otherwise removing individuals with disabilities away from the nondisabled, it simultaneously created a highly marginalized and marginalizing space for the viewing of nonnormative bodies in the form of the freak show (Adams 2001). The classification of "freak" nonetheless became a mechanism whereby people with disabilities were increasingly distanced from nondisabled society.

It is important to note here that in both the "ugly laws" and freak shows there was a purposeful conflation of disabled bodies, immigrant bodies, impoverished bodies, criminal bodies, and racialized bodies. Consider that in the 1930s, New York–born Pip and Flip, twins with disabilities including microcephaly, or unusually small heads, were billed in the Coney Island freak show as "twins from the Yucatan." Here, individuals with disabilities were rendered so distant from the recognizable that they were made to seem as if from an exotic foreign land. Medicalization participated in such conflations, as well as in eugenic initiatives against the disabled and others not only in Nazi Germany but also in England and the United States. In the early 1900s, more than 60,000 primarily disabled individuals were forcibly sterilized in the United States alone. The 1927 U.S. Supreme Court ruling of *Buck v. Bell*, written primarily by Justice Oliver Wendell Holmes Jr., upheld the legality of such forced and compulsory sterilizations of the "unfit," including individuals with mental illness and developmental disabilities, for the "protection and health of the state" (Lombardo 2008, 157).

The social model of disability arose in the post–civil rights era of the 1960s in response to such oppression and abuses stemming from medicalization. The social model distinguishes between embodied impairments (such as an individual with Down syndrome having cardiac issues for which she might require medical intervention) and socially constructed disabilities (such as the prejudice and discrimination preventing the woman with Down syndrome from accessing appropriate educational or work opportunities). As opposed to the individual, embodiment-centered model of medicalization, the social model of disability considers the identity of a social group, a community of individuals with disabilities, and how its members are impacted by social oppressions including ableism, manifesting in prejudice, a lack of accessibility, and the like. In lieu of the patient model, it advocates for a model of citizenship.

Yet, despite the activism of the disability community around the social model, the passage of the Americans with Disabilities Act (1990), and funding for programs such as those supporting independent living, the medicalization of disability is alive and well. This is clearly problematic for a majority of disability activists and disability scholars. Beyond its historical abuses, the modern-day medicalization of disability necessarily defines the individual out of context of his or her broader social group, and always in relation to the medical community. In addition, medicalization positions medicine as a social gatekeeper, forcing many individuals with disabilities to acquiesce to diagnostic categorizations to receive work-related benefits, insurance coverage, access to therapies, rehabilitation, or prosthetic and mobility-related equipment.

More recent scholarship has begun to reconsider the medical model of disability and acknowledge its potential role in disability studies. For instance, in Susan Wendell's (2001) discussion of the close relationship between chronic illness and disability, she argues that the forgotten community of the "unhealthy disabled" benefits from both the medical *and* the social model of disability. According to Wendell, the assumption that all individuals with disabilities have stable, unchanging conditions that do not require medical care silences individuals with both chronic illnesses and disabilities, many of whom, Wendell argues, are predominantly older and often female.

Antagonisms and disagreements between supporters of the social model of disability and supporters of the medical model may be difficult to reconcile. Yet, in our modern biomedical age, where people are living longer with chronic illnesses, the space between chronic illness and disability only promises to include more and more individuals. Rigorous and continued examinations of medical power and privilege are necessary. At the same time, proponents of the social model of disability must not overlook the potential of medicine to work in the service of social justice. Together, medicine and disability studies have the capacity to produce more empowering and potentially more democratic understandings of illness, care, and embodiment.

39

Minority

Jeffrey A. Brune

During the twentieth century, the term "minority" took on new meaning in the contexts of social science scholarship and civil rights campaigns. For disability activists and scholars, defining disabled people as a minority group similar to African Americans, women, and others has been a means to claim civil rights protections, define a more cohesive and empowered group identity, counter the medical model of disability, and advance the scholarship and academic legitimacy of disability studies.

In the early twentieth century, American social scientists developed new definitions of "minority," borrowing from and expanding upon European uses of the term that referred to national minorities not living in their homeland who faced group discrimination and stereotyping. Although they did not use the term explicitly, by the 1940s many social scientists applied the concept of minority to disabled people. They studied disability as a social phenomenon and compared the stigma and discrimination that disabled people faced to that which African Americans, homosexuals, and other minority groups confronted (Hahn 1988). By the early 1960s, prominent examples of this trend included works by Louis Anthony Dexter and Erving Goffman. Although they were hesitant to challenge explicitly the dominant medical model of disability, many of their conclusions regarded disability as a collective social issue rather than as merely an individual condition. However, these researchers almost always identified as nondisabled and assumed the perspective of normality when looking at issues of disability.

As civil rights campaigns gained momentum in the 1950s and 1960s, the designation of minority took on greater importance. Civil rights activism waged in the streets, in the courts, in Congress, and in state legislatures argued that oppressed minority groups deserved legal protection against discrimination. With the reassertion of the Fourteenth Amendment's equal protection clause and new civil rights legislation for specific underprivileged groups, activists for racial and gender minorities saw how important it was to gain recognition as a minority in order to claim civil rights protections.

It took time before anyone applied the term explicitly to people with disabilities, but by the 1970s some disability activists realized how useful the minority designation could be for promoting civil rights. In 1977, during the Section 504 protests aimed at forcing the federal government to implement the antidiscrimination mandate of the 1973 Rehabilitation Act, Ed Roberts called people with disabilities "one of the largest minority groups in the nation" (qtd. in Nielsen 2012, 168). For Roberts the minority model served a dual function: it explained why disabled people needed civil rights protection, and it notified politicians that people with disabilities could wield their power as an electoral block.

In the 1980s, with the emergence of disability studies as an academic field, the minority model proved equally attractive for advancing disability scholarship as for advancing civil rights. Unlike earlier social scientists, most of whom claimed a normative status either implicitly or explicitly, many scholars engaged in disability studies deliberately identified as disabled. They proclaimed their commitment to political activism as a way to advance both civil rights activism and disability scholarship, and they used the minority model explicitly. Among those who laid out the minority model of disability most clearly in the 1980s and 1990s were Harlan Hahn, John Gliedman and William Roth, Judy Heumann, Simi Linton, Paul Longmore, and Duane Stroman. Many of their works relied heavily on analogizing between disabled people and oppressed racial groups. In *The Unexpected Minority* (1980), for example, Gliedman and Roth argued that "the stigma of handicap bears many general resemblances to the stigma of race. . . . [L]ike racists, able-bodied people often confuse the results of social oppression with the effects of biology" (22).

For disability scholars, it made sense to claim similarities to the increasingly popular fields of race and gender for a number of reasons. Classifying disabled people as a minority group made it easier to borrow from the models of other, more developed fields of scholarship to advance disability studies intellectually. Longmore, who was a critical figure in the development of disability history, explained how the minority model could enhance our understanding of disabled people's history. He urged historians to "apply a minority group analysis to the historical experience of disabled people" because "when devaluation and discrimination happen to one person, it is biography, but when . . . similar experiences happened to millions, it is social history" (1985, 586). In addition to its intellectual usefulness, the minority model has also helped disability studies claim legitimacy as an academic field. Because it emphasizes similarities with race and gender, it makes it more difficult for the growing number of scholars in those fields to dismiss disability as a similarly important topic.

Another reason the minority model has been so important for disability activism and scholarship is because it provides an alternative framework that challenges the medical model of disability. The emergence of the minority model provides a basis for disabled people to understand themselves as part of a coherent and collective population with shared social goals

and political values. The umbrella category of "disability" within the minority model counters the tendency to balkanize various disability groups and discourage them from identifying with one another. It has made it easier for groups with different impairments to mobilize around a given political agenda and foster a belief in a collective "disability pride"—a concept borrowed from other minority movements. Treating disability as a collective social, cultural, and political issue rather than as a medical condition has been one of the primary accomplishments of disability rights activism and disability studies scholarship.

Not all deployments of the minority model are alike, however, and in this regard one disability group has especially stood apart. People in the United States who identify as Deaf define themselves as a linguistic minority similar to that of non-English-speaking immigrants. For this group, American Sign Language serves as their primary mode of communication as well as the basis of their identity. While there are good reasons for Deaf people to identify as a linguistic minority, unfortunately, this claim has been used to create distance from other disabled people and support the often-repeated notion that "Deaf people are not disabled." To be sure, D/deaf cultures can be more pronounced than those of other disabled peoples because of linguistic separation and other historical factors such as deaf education. However, defining Deaf identity vis-à-vis disability—as *not* disabled—reinforces the notion that other disabilities are merely individual impairments and are not social or cultural phenomena. Denying a minority identity to other disabled peoples is not only intellectually inconsistent but also harmful to disability rights activism.

While the late twentieth century witnessed the ascent of the minority model, the concept is now losing favor in disability studies as intersectionality has become the more popular model for understanding identity. Borrowing from scholars in other fields, Susan Schweik (2009) criticizes the analogical approach of the minority model—*as with* disability, *so with* race, gender, sexuality, and so forth—that tends to isolate identity issues from one another. This makes it difficult to see how identities intersect and are mutually constitutive—how, for example, disabled people who are also black and queer understand their multiple forms of identity. The minority model does not offer a way to understand how the meaning of a disability is dialectically linked to the contexts of race, class, gender, sexuality, religion, or nationality. With its emphasis on analogies, the minority model assumes a false compartmentalization of identity issues that tends to overemphasize similarities and downplay important differences. In addition, the analogizing tendency of the minority model creates a deceptive "affect of connection" between groups. It can also make likeness, rather than difference, a central justification for social equality (Schweik 2009, 142–143). While the minority model played a key role in disability rights activism and the development of disability studies, it no longer seems adequate to the task of exploring the individual and collective intersections between disability and other forms of social, cultural, political, and economic identification.

Despite scholars' increasing and well-founded objections to the minority model, paradoxically it remains a useful political tool for a civil rights movement that still struggles for recognition. This is because in the current context civil rights protections are predicated on a group's status as an oppressed minority. Increasingly this is also true in areas well beyond the United States. The UN Convention on the Rights of Persons with Disabilities (2008), for instance, designates persons with disabilities as the world's largest minority. As this illustrates, the recognition of minority status has now become a globalized precondition for receiving civil rights protections.

40
Modernity
Janet Lyon

Beginning in the sixteenth century, the same forces that gave shape to what we now term "modernity" also produced the concept of "disability." These included burgeoning bureaucratic systems for the management of expanding global trade, the presence of increasingly concentrated, heterogeneous populations, the emergence of nation-states in the global north-west, a shift from religious and extrinsic forms of authority to the open-ended pursuit of knowledge through autonomous reason, and the continuous parsing of populations. The asylums and general hospitals that opened in the seventeenth century in order to sequester impoverished invalids and defectives generally mixed together disabled populations rather randomly and always through the common denominator of poverty. But by the beginning of the long eighteenth century, disability had emerged within modernity as a differential menu of problems to be solved, or at least controlled, via bourgeois systems of charity and in conjunction with the imperatives of a rapidly diversifying field of scientific study.

Enlightenment thinking expanded scientific attention from the immutable laws of physics to the study of the dynamic qualities of organic existence, creating new fields of knowledge about life and its forms that required new systems of naming and templates of categorization. This ever-expanding activity made it nearly impossible to link together the bearers of human difference—which included deformation, debilitating illness, madness, deafness, feeblemindedness, blindness, and so forth—except through widespread practices of discrimination and exclusion. The categorical incoherence of disability posed problems for modern management on a number of fronts, not least at a basic political level. The abstract "universal subject" of modern rights-granting states was assumed to be nondisabled in body and mind, leaving unresolved the question of how to account for the actual impairments distributed throughout the populations of the state. What degrees of disability were compatible with citizenship, and how were they to be measured? Was there a value hierarchy of disability that could be mapped onto the modern political domain? Given that the optimization of life was part of the distinctly modern pursuit of "progress," what could justify the legal devaluation of some forms of disabled life?

The nineteenth century saw the amalgamation of these legal, social, and scientific concerns in a dynamic system of population regulation that Michel Foucault has termed "biopower." Modern states came to rely on the isolation and classification of individual organic systems and functions in order to synthesize newly generated bio-knowledge. Especially important for the fate of disability was the introduction of statistics as a quasi-scientific measure of human "norms" (Davis 1995). These markedly inconsistent statistical assessments operated in tandem with the demands of a burgeoning economic system dependent on industrial labor, ever-expanding systems of imperial conquest and governance, and an urgent assessment of population health. Together, these features of the new statistical science produced "the abnormal"—and its disabled bearers—as objects of study, measure, and cure or control.

Relying on such statistical norms, the newly regulated and increasingly specialized medical profession during the midcentury created subfields of illness and disability. In this emerging medical model, disability was assessed on the basis of isolated functional deviations from norms; the systemic roles played by built environments and cultural habits of norming (the primary foci of what is now known as the "social model") were almost entirely peripheral to this approach. From the fracturing perspective of medical specialization, the individual with limited or abnormal function *is* equivalent to a broken body or mind in need of repair. A well-known fictional critique of this narrow approach to impairment occurs in what is sometimes considered to be the first modern novel, Gustave Flaubert's *Madame Bovary* (1856), when an extremely competent stable hand with a clubfoot is "fixed" by a trend-driven surgeon whose botched interventions disable the boy—within a week his leg must be amputated—and condemn him to a life of unemployment and pain. Thus in the medical model emerging in the nineteenth century, abnormality moves from the periphery to the center of therapeutic attention. Around abnormality, institutions are built, and against it the optimization of life is measured.

Other historical developments associated with modernity furthered these changes. Industrial hazards and mass warfare in the nineteenth and early twentieth centuries produced continual modifications of the social and scientific meanings of disability. Take, for example, the effect of physical disability upon a key ideological construction like masculinity. During a fraught period of imperial expansion, widespread mutilation and trauma threatened British ideals of manhood. In this context, injured masculinity required that the concepts of "the cripple," "the blind," "the deaf," and the "shell-shocked" be distanced as much as possible from the prevailing stigma of disability. If physical disability continually resisted any easy fit between the ever-expanding terrain of corporeal management and the ideological demands of the nation-state, mental disability proved to be even more problematic—and therefore more pro-liferative—as a category of population assessment and as a site of political intervention. What had seemed for centuries to be a fairly stable, if ephemeral, division between the mentally capable and incapable was transformed, after about 1850, into a set of ever-shifting evaluative discourses and terms.

The Enlightenment account of man as a self-reflexive "thinking thing" slowly came to accommodate a biologized model of mind subject to quantitative investigation. Thus began in earnest the differentiations of mental disability. In England, parliamentary acts were passed that codified vague distinctions between lunatics and idiots, between amentia and dementia, between morons and imbeciles and moral imbeciles; between 1845 and 1913 (the year of the Mental Deficiency Act), more than 140 asylums were built (Lyon 2011). Population studies created a bell curve of "normalcy," according to which "above-normal" intelligence registered not as deviation but as superiority, while "below-normal" intelligence registered as pathology. In view of Darwin's influential equation of complexity with evolutionary value, the simpleton's pathology—his limited capacity for intention, will, and reason—registered as antievolutionary and antimodern; given the rising emphasis on feeblemindedness as both a product and a nemesis of modernity, we may understand it as the sine qua non of biopower and its many contradictions.

41

Narrative
David Mitchell and Sharon Snyder

In many ways "narrative" has slipped away from its common association with strictly literary modes of communication. In popular media usage, for instance, the term has become increasingly synonymous with false forms of storytelling such as "spin" and the largely unsubstantiated claims of commodity marketing. Because narrative involves the production of stories that shape our lives and help determine possibilities for creating ways of living together, the understanding of narrative plays a crucial role in how we imagine social worlds. In the field of disability studies (DS), scholars have developed a variety of models for understanding how narrative operates in the creation of disability as a socially contested category.

In the earliest forms of writing (cuneiform tablets of ancient Sumer), the presence of narratives that interpret disability as portent helps demonstrate the force that physical, cognitive, and sensory differences exert on the development of cultural systems of meaning (for support of such a claim, see the massive evidence assembled in Albrecht, Mitchell, and Snyder's *Encyclopedia of Disability* [2005], especially the volume 5 compendium subtitled *A History of Disability in Primary Sources*). Examples of disability's centrality to the establishment of early narrative forms include the Assyrian reliance upon the birth of "deformed fetuses" and "irregularly shaped calves' livers" to predict harvest cycles. Similarly an array of origin stories about the birth of disabled children details the lives of individuals who are (1) born to first parents, (2) set out to languish from exposure to hide parental shame, and (3) ultimately survive and found entire civilizations.

Foundational roles for disabled people occur throughout the history of narrative. In ancient Greece, we learn of Odysseus's admiration of blind Demodocus's lyric songs to the Phoenician courts about the cuckolding of the crook-footed god Hephaestus. In the courts of medieval Europe, individuals with developmental disabilities and people of short stature served regularly as fools or court jesters, often using their marginal status to speak "truth to power" and thereby invert the operations of the known world for their benefactors (Stiker 1999).

Disability narratives play a central role in the advent of modern subjectivities as divided rather than unitary. In Shakespeare's portrait of Richard III, for example, a hunchbacked king's body excludes him from participation in the amorous pursuits of an England at peace. The drama tells of Richard's efforts to get revenge on those who would dismiss his "spider-like" form as unsavory. Colonial and Romantic American writers rejected the overly polished, and thus dying, narrative forms of Europe by attending to the imperfections of "rough-hewn" characters. Such imperfect figures navigate a social and geographic landscape set adrift from the expectations of "polished" society.

Disability also helps anchor modernist narrative experimentation. Sherwood Anderson's multiperspectival novel, *Winesburg, Ohio* (1919), explains an authorial mind-set that recognizes physical differences as outward contortions wrought by feelings of shame regarding one's deviancy. In a parallel manner, William Faulkner's *The Sound and the Fury* (1929) imagines the subjectivity of a character with Down syndrome as a vehicle for expressing modernist sensibilities of an increasingly chaotic world whose "center cannot hold." Within such tradition-defining tales, eugenics-based beliefs about the need to lock up deviants to prevent them from polluting the nation's hereditary pool lead to state-sanctioned exclusion schemes exposed by modernist authors. The detailing of disability detainment practices helps explain the existence of the bigotry necessary to sustain dehumanizing systems such as slavery, permanent institutionalization, and coerced sterilization.

Representations of disability also played a key role in the rise of late twentieth-century racial minority group writings. In Alice Walker's novel *Meridian* (1976), Meridian Hill's sudden-onset narcolepsy becomes a metaphor to explain the haunting nature of history for civil rights–era African American reformers. Likewise, narratives of disabling bouts of depression, alcoholism, fetal alcohol syndrome, and physical scarring in Native American writings such as Louise Erdrich's *Love Medicine* (1984), Michael Dorris's *The Broken Cord* (1989), Leslie Marmon Silko's *Almanac of the Dead* (1991), and Linda Hogan's *Solar Storms* (1995) provide emblems of the trauma experienced by dispossessed peoples. Debilitating effects occur, particularly, in the wake of violence experienced by forced participation in racially divisive wars such as those in Korea and Vietnam.

This brief catalog of disability narratives provides a glimpse at the productive value disability has played in narrative history. These meanings are commonly understood among disability studies (DS) scholars as reductive, contradictory, and mutually reinforcing. Such portrayals go beyond literary sources to span professional discourses of disability that included charity, rehabilitation, medicine, public policy, and rights-based social movements. DS has produced a veritable bevy of examples wherein disability finds itself—like other minority categories—struggling to shrug off debasing narrative portraits in order to attain the status of a resistant, diversified, yet united collective. People with disabilities

(PWDs), for instance, are often relegated to what social theorists call "expendable populations" (Bauman 2004; M. Davis 2007; Mbembe 2003)—that is, they constitute membership in untouchable categories designating social detritus. Indeed, those within the zone of the socially off-limits cannot even register as the shadowy inhabitants of an economic substratum because of the compounding impact of many disqualifying forces. In this sense, disability narratives have often pushed disabled people, as Jim Carlton (2009) has written, to the "periphery of peripheries."

To a large degree, narrative analyses in DS have been shaped by questions of representation wherein subjects find their lives overcharged with meanings—both those that are imposed and those to which one experientially gravitates. Such meanings are heavily bounded by available stories of what it means to be "disabled." In his foundational essay, "Screening Stereotypes" (2003), for example, the late DS historian Paul Longmore finds myriad representations of disability in late twentieth-century media to be awash in negative portrayals of PWDs who are routinely subjected to kill-or-cure plotlines. This narrative structure, for Longmore, sets up disability as an obstacle to be overcome with hard work and moral virtuosity. The story must first subject a character to the vagaries of life with a disability only to erase it in the pat resolution of plots that dispense with the very disabilities that propelled those plots forward. Longmore argues that, in solving the discordancy of disability in this manner, audiences are let off the hook by feeling as if nothing is asked of them in stories of disabled people's social disenfranchisement. This, then, becomes the takeaway significance of disability within nearly all mainstream narrative portrayals in the vast majority of representational studies produced by DS scholars to date (Gartner and Joe 1987; Shakespeare 1994; Norden 1994; Shapiro 1994; Garland-Thomson 1997).

Furthermore, the ubiquitous presence of conventional disability narrative patterns tends to short-circuit public awareness about the social circumstances in which disability becomes enmeshed. Disability, regarded as an individual obstacle to be overcome, is effectively erased as a predicament requiring political intervention. Particularly ignored are those exclusions that have become nearly synonymous with experiences of disability, including rampant unemployment, inaccessibility to key cultural institutions of production (both physically and intellectually), homelessness and its parallel context of chronic institutionalization, and forms of segregated education.

In the emerging genre of disability life writing, such mainstream disability narratives are roundly critiqued when compared with actual disabled lives. In fact, popular plot formulas of disability are identified as contributors to key social problems. In memoirs such as Jean Stewart's *The Body's Memory* (1993), Irving Zola's *Missing Pieces* (1982), Robert Murphy's *The Body Silent* (1990), Georgina Kleege's *Sight Unseen* (1999), Nancy Mairs's *Waist High in the World* (1997), and Kenny Fries's *Body, Remember* (1997), disability leads to individual experiences of overmedicalization of some and the radical neglect of others in need of health care and rehabilitation, chronic asexualization and hypersexualization, as well as pervasive surveillance by neighborhood, state, and federal bureaucracies. Such life writing exposes the web of seemingly benign neoliberal administrative structures that often ensnare rather than support disabled people in disciplinary social relations.

The goal of DS's engagement with narrative, then, should be to find something beyond the representational predicament Tom Shakespeare describes as "dustbins for disavowal" (1994) or the claustrophobic film narrative space identified by Martin Norden as "the cinema of isolation" (1994). Narratives of disability (as well as the analysis of such narratives) can combat dehumanizing meanings and, therefore, become politically productive for those who inhabit marginalized embodiments.

As an alternative to reading disability narrative as a negative portrait, other body theorists (ourselves included) have argued for the productiveness of approaching the question of disability representation as a matter of the ubiquity of nonnormative bodies (Mitchell and Snyder 2000; McRuer 2006; Shildrick 2009). Rather than argue that disability is overused exclusively for exploitative narrative ends, the phrase "narrative prosthesis" (Mitchell and Snyder 2000) emphasizes the prevalence of divergent embodiments in literary and filmic narratives that parallels disability's commonality across human communities. Because "being disabled" involves depths of creativity and performative labor to navigate cultures organized around narrow norms of ability, mining subjective states of disability can inspire both creative practice and alternative ways of being. Through such an approach, artists and scholars alike have multiple opportunities to rehabilitate disability's cultural significance. Indeed, there is something refreshingly revelatory in this chronic presence of disability in narrative history. In keeping with the disability rights movement's productive emphasis on the value of human interdependency, narrative prosthesis turns the tables on the false and unrealizable Western ideal of personal autonomy, self-sufficiency, and independence.

In her book *The Nick of Time* (2004), Elizabeth Grosz argues that liberatory humanities-based discourses such as those made possible by feminist, queer, postcolonial, and critical race theory have lost touch with matters of material biology. Not only are bodies constructed by the social milieus in which they find themselves immersed (a point exhaustively made in humanities scholarship), but biologies, conversely, impact environments.

Following Grosz, something equivalent to the Heisenberg uncertainty principle must emerge in the analysis of disability representations. For while the magnetic poles of ability and disability created by conventional narrative interpretations determine, to a great extent, the available meanings assigned to disability, the entry of diverse embodiments inevitably changes the nature of alternative living strategies offered by nonnormative modes of being. Further, bodily differences cause disruptions in the normative flows of information and the privilege that such information typically confers. Consider the psychological impact of entering a room full of people with disabilities for someone who suddenly realizes the rarity of encountering disability in his or her daily experiences. The unfamiliar situation demands alternative ways of narrating such happenings by analyzing how social environments are engineered to disguise the commonality of biological variation in the world.

In his disability narrative, *Operation Wandering Soul* (1993), novelist Richard Powers explores the creative activity produced by a hospital ward of orphaned disabled children. As the children read the cultural myths of deformed children left by parents to die of exposure—such as in the Hindi tale of Hirochi, the leech boy—they provide an alternative ending. The leech boy sails away in his bamboo basket originally intended as a coffin, discovers the joys of traveling by water rather than encountering multiple obstacles while on land, and circumnavigates the world. The wondrous narrative of Hirochi demonstrates that disability need not be conceived as a limit to experience but instead can be an opening onto another set of worlds.

Just as Powers's disabled children recognize the importance of reimagining ancient origins stories and classic childhood fairy tales, DS narrative analyses offer opportunities to imagine other disability stories even through the inevitable limits of historical perspectives.

To engage actively with narrative histories is to realize that meaningful accommodation of diverse embodiments requires the imagining of more accessible narrative spaces—particularly those actively countering stories of social death. In doing so, they rewrite disability history by producing narrative forms for and about PWDs that contain possibilities for alternative futures.

42

Normal

Tanya Titchkosky

When we know that *norma* is the Latin word for T-square and that *normalis* means perpendicular, we know almost all that must be known about the area in which the meaning of the terms "norm" and "normal" originated. . . . A norm, or rule, is what can be used to right, to square, to straighten . . . to impose a requirement on an existence.

Georges Canguilhem, *The Normal and the Pathological* (1978), 239.

Thinking critically about disability requires exploring the normative order of the social and physical environment that—as Canguilhem suggests—straightens out the lives of disabled people, T-squaring and otherwise measuring some people's minds, bodies, senses, emotions, and comportments against the rule of normed expectations. Both in everyday life and in the human sciences, "normal" often appears as if it is a static state of affairs, and when people are said to have an unwanted condition, they may be deemed to have an abnormality. Disability studies, in contrast, has shown not only that norms change radically over time and from place to place but also that the seemingly omnipresent commitment to seek and measure the normal is in fact a rather recent historic development (Davis 1995; Garland-Thomson 1997; Stiker 1999; Finkelstein 1998). Still, the prevailing assumption in educational, health, and rehabilitative sciences, as in everyday life, is to treat norms as static and subsequently to measure how others appear to depart from them. It is this way of treating norms that socially produces a sense of normalcy as if it is an objective and universal phenomenon.

Disability studies maintains a unique relation to what counts as normal by examining "normal" as a historical and cultural production. The term, as well as the consequences of its production and its use, are artifacts of history. While group life may have always been tied to collective expectations, Lennard Davis argues that "it is possible to date the coming into consciousness in English of the idea of 'the norm' over the period 1840–1860" (1995: 24). Tracing out this development, Michel Foucault says that the sense of a normative order required that the human sciences not only make "man" (humans) an object but also make them knowable, to one another, through "norms, rules and signifying totalities" (1970, 296, 364). This normative order is today the dominant version of self-understanding within modernity. We are measured through psychometric and intelligence tests, weight and height charts, and demographic surveys, or measured in more everyday ways by, for example, showing how a child departs from age-specific norms for walking, talking, thinking, or interacting. These measures show that the power of normalcy is to convince us that measurement and comparison are reasonable and that they can be "used to right, to square, to straighten" all conflicts, differences, ideals, or values in relation to a taken-for-granted sense of normal life.

That norms are used to evaluate with reference to group expectations demonstrates that the *normal is a referential system of sense making* and not a natural or pregiven condition of existence. Using the word "normal" followed by the suffix "ity," for example, reflects the common notion of "normal" as a static thing. In contrast, disability studies' focus on the creation of normal as it is produced and applied is reflected in the word "normalcy," where the use of the suffix "cy" emphasizes action and doing. Against the backdrop of "normal," disability is ordinarily made to stand out in a stigmatized fashion. This stigmatizing action is conveyed by "abnormal," where the prefix "ab" means "away from." "The 'problem,'" Davis writes, "is not the person with disabilities; the problem is the way that normalcy is constructed to create the 'problem' of the disabled person" (1995, 24). "Normal," therefore, is a position from which people deem other people to be lacking, different, dysfunctional, deformed, impaired, inadequate, invalid.

That "normal" can be understood as a vantage point is reflected in Rosemarie Garland-Thomson's development of the term "normate," which she describes as "the constructed identity of those who, by way of the bodily configurations and cultural capital they assume, can step into a position of authority and wield the power it grants them" (1997, 8). An ordinary practice in the production of normalcy is to make it noticeable to the normative order that one has noticed that the other departs from normality—"What are you, crazy?" or "I don't mean to pry, but have you always been disabled?" or "I would kill myself, if it happened to me."

Disability studies has responded to the norming of all of existence by the sciences (Canguilhem 1978; Foucault 1970; Stiker 1999) by critically attending to the "production" and "validation" of the normal (cf. Darke 1998, 183; Goodley, Hughes, and Davis 2012; Snyder, Brueggeman and Garland-Thomson 2002), the "ideology of normality" (Finkelstein 1998, 30), and the "hegemony of normativism" (cf. Corker and Shakespeare 2002, 14; Davis 1995). This work shows us how the "normal" is enforced, imitated, enacted; taught and bought; sold and recycled; enhanced, longed for, and resisted. It documents how normalcy's standards and measurements contribute to racist, sexist, and other forms of human diminishment that position some humans on the edges of belonging.

Disability studies also shows how the "normal" is never static but changes from group to group, over time, and from place to place. For instance, most people will live at least part of their lives with disability. Yet, despite this statistical probability, disability generally remains an unacknowledged feature within social structures and forms of interaction (see McRuer 2006, 30; Titchkosky 2011, 30). As a result, disability is treated as an exceptional state of being. "Normal," thus, does not describe what the majority is or does; rather, it represents what a given population is expected to be and to do. This means that appearing as normal takes *work* or, as Harvey Sacks puts it, each of us has "as one's job, as one's constant preoccupation, [the] doing of 'being ordinary'" (1984, 414). To "become normal," then, is to *manage the appearance of any departure* from the expected as an unwanted difference; to "act normally" or "to pass" means to be perceived by others *as moving squarely* within the realm of the expected; to "be normal" is *to do* what needs to be done to be taken as the expected. Thus, "abnormal" is not an objective departure from the norm; it is what is produced when a perceived difference is taken as an affront to ordinary group expectations. The social process of perceiving "undesired differences" is what Goffman studied as stigma (1963, 5, 137).

By exploring the constructed nature of normalcy—and rejecting the notion that normality is "just there"—disability studies is uniquely positioned to examine the power of normalcy to exclude and to stigmatize. But, as Rod Michalko reminds us, "One of the most 'abnormal' things about being 'normal' is attending to its production" (2002, 82), and thus the importance of examining the way that role obligations are used to conform to, resist and even re-create the normal. Still, scholars, artists, and activists have shown us that even as we are subjected to the daily demands to structure our perception of self and other in normalized ways, we can nonetheless crip, queer, and otherwise question the modern demand that all group expectations can and need to be normed (Titchkosky and Michalko 2009).

But queering and cripping normalcy can also entail questioning whether the system of reference that is the normalcy orientation is the only way to take group expectations and human difference into account. Every departure from normalcy can easily today be rerouted to a new normal that can put a lid on imagination. There are, after all, "normal" ways to be disabled, to become disabled, to act as a disabled person, or even to do disability studies. For example, in inclusive design, as well as in some aspects of inclusive or special education, it is sometimes said that it is "normal to be different." Medical sciences and corporate culture have made selective use of this rescripting of the language of normalcy, as in a recent Tylenol advertisement's demand to "get back to normal, whatever your normal is." Following disruption, trauma, injury, or illness, we are told to accept a "new normal." Navigating these shifting meanings of "normal" implies reconceiving expectations about how to live as embodied beings. While resistance to dominant conceptions of normal experiences of embodied existence has been central to disability studies, there is no agreement on how best to resist. The work of disability studies will need to continue to consider whether and how forms of resistance and conceptions of "new normals" might enhance our lives together or continue to T-square life to those powers that already organize the exclusive character of everyday existence.

43

Pain

Martha Stoddard Holmes

Pain's associations with disability as it is experienced, imagined, and beheld are multiple and long-standing. People with disabilities have habitually been imagined as "suffering from" impairment and "afflicted by" disability, the diction suggesting both physical and psychic pain. The nuances and complex consequences of this conceptualization of disability are dynamic throughout various time periods. Pain has its etymological roots in words from Indo-European, ancient Greek, and classical Latin signifiying penality (such as Latin *poena*), punishment, and revenge (i.e., ancient Greek ποινή or blood money). In the fourth century, words for pain acquired the meanings of suffering and affliction, in effect shifting the focus from the purpose of pain to the experience of pain (*Oxford English Dictionary*).

Pain is regularly theorized as an experience that isolates and individualizes. The difficulty of empathizing with another's pain can become hostility toward the person in pain. Adam Smith's *Theory of Moral Sentiments* (1759) articulates such a social dynamic by arguing that "though our brother is upon the rack, as long as we ourselves are at our ease, our senses will never inform us of what he suffers." Sophocles's play *Philoctetes* (ca. 409 BCE) is a touchstone for Smith as well as for later works characterizing disability, such as George Eliot's *The Mill on the Floss* (1860). The ancient Greek play dramatizes the failure of empathy in regard to bodies in extreme pain. A war hero in the Trojan army, Philoctetes

is accidentally bitten by a snake and develops a festering, painful, odorous wound that causes him to cry out. Odysseus leads his men to abandon Philoctetes on an island not simply because he is hurt but because his inability to manage his disablement and pain amounts to a failure of the unwritten social contract between those who are ill (or in pain) and those who are well.

Focusing on the individual body in pain compounds an existing tendency to view disability itself as an individual misfortune rather than a social and political identity, and pain as private suffering rather than a socially produced condition. Such a perspective both undermines the validity and importance of experiences of pain and disability and may conceal the social and physical environments that generate or exacerbate suffering, just as a camera's tight close-up of a weeping woman in a wheelchair may exclude from the frame an inaccessible movie theater, college classroom, or government office she has attempted to enter. Although the woman's suffering is caused by an ableist environment, the close-up excludes these data to suggest that pain itself defines her identity and condition.

A particularly important issue for disability studies is, as Tobin Siebers (2008a) argues, how to acknowledge the experience of pain that may accompany disability without reinforcing the assumption that disability necessarily entails pain and without presuming that pain defines the boundary between lives worth living and those that are unsupportably miserable. The assumption of disability as a state of intolerable pain underpins some arguments for disabled people's right to assisted suicide as well as physicians' right to withhold as "futile" life-sustaining treatment to disabled infants and disabled people of all ages. Some disability studies scholars and activists have noted the irony of public support for "disabled people who seek death" rather than for "disabled people who seek jobs, personal assistance services, and equal access to their community" (Gill 2010, 31; see also Longmore 2003).

Generally, such thresholds are defined by people who are able-bodied and economically privileged, and who accordingly may lack wide, diverse, and daily experience in living with disability and its potential pain. For example, legislation about assisted suicide has had a critical and even fatal impact on disabled people's lives. Such decisions are based on erroneous assumptions about the level of physical pain and suffering inherent in disability, as opposed to the psychic and/or physical pain generated by a lack of social support services and self-determination. Carol Gill argues that disabled people's experiences make them experts in the very issues articulated as constituting quality of life. However, they are rarely consulted as a resource in debates about assisted suicide. She also notes that pain "has not figured prominently in actual requests for assisted suicide" (2010, 37), given the ability of doctors to alleviate almost all pain. Pain, then, displaces and covers for the treatable problem of lack of services, lack of access, and removal of self-determination.

Ironically, while arguments for assisted suicide often rest on the equation of disability with unbearable suffering, pain is also understood to be extremely difficult to communicate. These difficulties hinge in part on the polysemy of language. The McGill-Melzak Pain Questionnaire, developed in the 1970s, is composed of sets of words derived from the descriptions of patients as a way to bridge the gap between having pain, hearing of pain, and treating pain. In the twenty-first century, however, clinical settings are now more likely to offer the Wong-Baker Faces Pain Scale or to otherwise ask the sufferer to evaluate pain numerically using a scale of 1 to 10, where 10 is the most intense. Because the assessment of pain, sometimes called the fifth vital sign, depends largely on self-report, however, the confidence gap between having pain and hearing of pain persists. As Elaine Scarry argues, "to have pain is to have certainty; to hear of pain is to have doubt" (1985, 13). The resulting mix of pity and doubt often directed at pain parallels similarly ambivalent attitudes toward disability. Scarry's emphasis on the divide between those experiencing pain and those witnessing it is tied to a more general tendency among the able-bodied to regard people with disabilities either as existing in a state of abject dependence or as exaggerating their disabilities in order to leech social resources that they do not deserve (see Schweik 2009; also see entry on "Invisibility"). In such a context, people with disabilities are sometimes forced to exaggerate pain simply to receive reasonable and necessary accommodations. For example, the popular television series *House* relies on a current cultural narrative of disability, pain, and suspicion. Physician Geoffrey House has a mobility impairment caused by a muscular infarction that generates chronic severe pain. However, in characterizing him as a Vicodin addict who self-medicates for primarily psychic pain, the show reinforces the narrative of disability as misery while concurrently suggesting that his pain is self-generated. Rather than representing "chronic pain," *House* narrates "addiction" and leads viewers to equate the two.

Despite the representational and political complexities of pain in relation to disability, theorizations of embodiment that bypass the reality of bodies in pain are neither realistic in attending to the pain experiences of many people with disabilities nor effective in promoting social justice (see Siebers 2008a).

44

Passing

Ellen Samuels

In historical and colloquial usage, "passing" was originally understood as a form of imposture in which members of a marginalized group presented themselves as members of a dominant group. African Americans passing for white, for example, or Jews passing for gentiles, were attempting to achieve the appearance of equality or to neutralize the stigma of those racialized and religious identities. Passing, as a cultural practice, has also signified in the arenas of gender and sexuality, with men passing as women, women passing as men, transgender people passing as their chosen gender, and gay or lesbian people passing as heterosexual. Comparatively little attention, however, has been given to the phenomenon of individuals passing as either disabled or nondisabled.

Indeed, the *Oxford English Dictionary* definition for "passing" addresses ethnicity, religion, and sex as the categories through which an individual might pass for something he or she presumably is not. Yet the slipperiness of that syntax—passing *through* as well as *for* identity categories—suggests that on some level all people acquire their identities through acts of passing, an insight that has been fruitfully explored in relation to race, ethnicity, gender, and sex (Ginsberg 1996). Judith Butler (1990) has defined gender as a kind of performance, a series of imitations that harkens back to an original that never existed. In her account, all social actors, not only those with nonnormative or transgressive gender identities, engage in both deliberate and unconscious gender passing. Butler argues, for instance, that the forms of self-presentation that people develop in order to successfully persuade others that they are normative members of their gender are forms of passing that make visible the hidden processes by which biological males and females learn to pass culturally as men and women.

Extending this analysis of passing to the topic of disability requires us to think about disability identity as a kind of performance, an imitation without an original (McRuer 2006). While disability is often conceived as both obviously and immediately legible on the body, most disabilities become perceptible only according to context and circumstance (Montgomery 2001). Even an individual with extraordinary bodily difference could pass as nondisabled while chatting online, for example, while a person with a learning difference such as dyslexia could not. Thus, some scholars have argued that "performed" disability identities are frequently displayed in the visual field (Davis 1995; Garland-Thomson 1997); others point out that disability identification also makes use of speech acts such as impairment narratives (i.e., the story one tells about how one "became" disabled) and forms of medical certification (Brune and Wilson 2013; Siebers 2004).

Such interpretations complicate the dominant perception that those who attempt to pass as nondisabled are merely yearning to assimilate or are seeking the social privileges conferred by the absence of visible impairment. But while passing as nondisabled may serve to minimize stigma and avoid a range of intrusive and unwelcome encounters, it is also true that people who pass as nondisabled may face greater difficulties in accessing needed rights and resources that tend to be predicated upon the assumption of obvious (and largely visible) forms of disability. While visible disability is often described as evoking a stare of enfreakment, nonvisibly disabled people who refuse to pass are confronted with the stare of disbelief. Both responses fix the disabled person in a diagnostic and objectifying gaze.

Yet passing can also be experienced as empowering in a liberatory rather than assimilationist sense. Indeed, for some, passing can serve as a force of transgression and mobility: "Passing forces reconsideration of the cultural logic that the physical body is the site of identic intelligibility" (Ginsberg 1996, 4). Transgender people, for instance, often celebrate passing in their chosen gender identity as a sign of social recognition of their true selves—which means, ironically, that they are passing for who they actually are. However, when such passing is perceived as driven by material or social benefit— such as when a woman passes for a man in order to earn higher wages or for physical safety—it is often viewed with suspicion. Similarly, passing as disabled can be understood as attempting to manipulate the system, just as passing as nondisabled can be understood as materially driven by the desire to avoid stigma.

People without visible impairments who claim a disabled identity are routinely challenged, ridiculed, and disbelieved, not only because of the assumption that true disability is clearly visible but also because disability is perceived as a highly undesirable identity that no one would claim if he or she were capable of passing as nondisabled. While sexual orientation is historically understood as nonvisible, and thus a narrative structure of "coming out" exists to enable queer subjects to claim their identity aloud or signal it through clothing or jewelry, no such discourses or rituals exist in relation to identities assumed to be transparently visible on the body, such as race and disability. The concern over the ethics of imposture becomes most vexed in the cases of those who do not pass deliberately but rather by default—those whose bodies and behavior do not signal their internal or "true" identities so that they are presumed to be something they are not (Walker 2001).

Suspicions of disability imposture, and in particular disability fraud, intensified in the mid-nineteenth century with the emergence of greater socioeconomic support structures for people with disabilities in the United States. A range of literary and filmic representations, such as Thomas Edison's film *The Fake Beggar* (1898), reflected growing social anxiety about the presence of beggars in urban areas faking disabilities, and entitlement systems such as welfare protection for the disabled, elderly, and other perceived vulnerable populations evolved with elaborate and costly mechanisms to distinguish real from false disability (Schweik 2009). Indeed, cultural representations of individual disability "fakers" far exceed the documented existence of such impostures, suggesting that such attitudes toward passing emerged less from material crisis than from the ontological dissonance produced by the overwhelming social and economic investment in disability as a visible and obvious condition.

More vexing than the question of disability fakers, however, is the increasingly vocal presence of individuals who desire to alter their bodies to become disabled through deliberate physical acts of amputation or paralysis. These individuals, sometimes called "wannabes," "pretenders," or "transabled," include both those who simulate impairment and those who produce impairment (Stevens 2011). Transabled claims of disability identity offer a profound challenge to the field of disability studies, which often seeks to distance "authentic" experiences of disability from "inauthentic" passing individuals while maintaining tolerance for disability as a desirable and worthy state of being. Ironically, it is frequently people with nonvisible disabilities, having long contended with suspicion and disbelief regarding their disability status, who react most strongly to the idea of a nondisabled person passing as disabled. The phenomenon of passing thus highlights the complex negotiations that take place among bodies, perceptions, and social values, and forces a reconsideration of the ongoing performative and contingent nature of disability as a marker of identity.

45

Performance
Petra Kuppers

You get up in the morning and go about your routine. The neighbor across the street stands at the window and watches you reaching down from your wheelchair with your grabbing tool to pick up the paper.

Your social worker comes for her annual visit, and you crip up: your limp is more pronounced as you open the door for her, you are not even thinking about it, but you somehow seem to modulate how you reach across the table when you sit down to review your service hours.

You need your psych meds, and the insurance company will not cover the prescription you researched long and hard on the survivor message boards online. So you work to emphasize side effects, using your sophisticated understanding of the working of various medications to influence your doctor to argue for what you know you need.

These three episodes are all disability performances: the involuntary ones we all engage in when our disabilities become visible or experiential to a mainstream that considers our variations different enough to be remarkable; the semiconscious alternative experience of one's embodiment when under pressure; and the conscious and artful manipulation of one's narrative of a disabled self, a performance of selfhood in politicized storytelling.

Now consider these next three events.

At the public library, people are organizing a stim-in. You are part of a group of autistic self-advocates, and you are protesting the patronizing and eugenic rhetoric of an autism charity by sitting together with your colleagues and stimming, engaging in baroque and complex bodily scripts, together, in public, hands loud and proud.

At a disability pride parade, a choir of people with cognitive differences sings for an audience spread out on a big lawn, some with their wheelchairs, some rocking back and forth, some speaking animatedly to each other with their hands when they are not watching the sign language interpreter.

In a concert hall, a tender duet takes place on stage: a man slips his manual wheelchair onto its side, and a bipedal woman dives onto the spinning wheel, now horizontal to the ground, and they touch and part in complex patterns with the movement of the metal wheel.

In these three disability performances, the action moves out from the individual and toward communal action, and a staged performance becomes a way of presenting disability in public.

Performers work with scripts. The first set of performances I described rewrite and examine the scripts of roles in the performances of everyday life (Goffman 1973). In the second set of performances, improvisation scores or set choreographies are the scripts that shape art-framed events. In different ways, these staged performances in public all subvert some expected scripts (about disability, gender, race, class, the nature of public art making, the disciplines of specific art forms) and leave others untouched. Making choices about one's intervention is part of what an artful and conscientious disability performance practitioner does, and thinking through the implications and enmeshments of these choices with the scripts of the wider cultural world is the work of the disability performance critic.

From these different ways of thinking through performance and disability, a range of topics and methodological issues arise. Are ways of being, acting, performing disability historically specific, and do these ways change over time? Are there particular styles to being disabled in particular cultures, particular and specific ways of performing one's identity or role as a disabled person? What is the range of scripts that make up intelligible disability performances in political arenas, in everyday life, and in art-framed events? If some artists use performance to subvert mainstream ideas of what disability signifies, can a similar strategy help political activists? This last question often revolves around the problem that destabilizing performances of the meaning of "disability" can, in some perspectives, undermine efforts to create powerful positive images of disabled people. Is choice, and the evasion of roles, itself an ableist construct?

Within the more narrowly defined framework of performance as art-framed behavior, other issues central to the literature include the place of cripping up in contemporary culture, that is, nondisabled people playing disabled parts; the training of disabled actors and dancers; the ethics of disability performance work, and its ways of thinking through access; the ways mainstream theater and dance can retrofit their notions of performance as well as their physical spaces and ways of working to be more widely accessible; the development and maintenance of reproducible movement techniques, such as crutch work, wheelchair tricks, and particular aesthetic modes of American Sign Language; the development of disability equivalents of color-blind casting; the relationship between professional and grassroots practice, and the development of genres specific to disability arts; whether or not there is something like a disability arts ghetto, and what that term might mean or imply; and the integration or segregation of different kinds of disabilities in stage performances. Wider aesthetic issues include how disability performance practice is influenced by the histories of the freak show, by cultural fascination with the grotesque, by eugenic discourses, by the kind of audience engagements characterized by sentimentality, and by notions of virtuosity and its space in modernist and postmodernist practice.

Many countries have thriving disability performance scenes, festivals, and artists. American dance and performance artists associated with the movement include AXIS Dance Company, Neil Marcus, Bruce Curtis, Cleveland Dancing Wheels, Dance>Detour, Sins Invalid, Frank Moore, Bill Shannon, Lynn Manning, Tekki Lomnicki, the Flying Words Project, Terry Galloway, the DisAbility Project in St. Louis, the Olimpias Disability Culture Projects, the National Theatre for the Deaf, and Deaf West. In the United Kingdom, companies and artists include CandoCo Dance Company, Blue Eyed Soul, Aaron Williamson, Mat Fraser, Liz Carr, Judy McNamara, Kaite O'Reilly, Yinka Shonibare, and the Graeae Theatre Company. Restless Dance and Back to Back Theatre operate in Australia; Different Light Theatre Company and Touch Compass Dance Company in New Zealand/ Aotearoa; Taihen in Japan; Theatre Hora in Switzerland; Gerda Koenig and Raimund Hoghe in Germany. Within this list of names and companies, many differences provide nuance and texture: some of these people operate at the grassroots level, using open workshops and community performance methods to foster disability culture and social change. Some of the artists are openly disabled but see themselves aligned with mainstream art frameworks. Yet others operate specifically at the site of intersection, analyzing and dramatizing queer, class, or race issues with a focus on disability's difference.

Many countries have arts funding streams and TV programs specifically dedicated to disability arts, seeing the field as an important part of multicultural public programming. In all, the international scene is thriving. Likewise, academic analysis and sponsorship of disabled people's performance work is an area of growth. A range of academic arts organizations began regular disability performance panels, workshops, and performances in the 1990s. In the United States in particular, many disability performance practitioners are artist-scholars who find employment in academia. Many of them are involved in thinking through issues of embodiment, enmindment, interdependence, empowerment, and alternative knowledge production through the specific lens that disabled life can provide.

How to live artfully; how to move nimbly through discursive fields, tipping past stereotype traps; ducking the diagnostic, medical, and charitable gaze: these are the kinds of guerrilla skills most disabled people learn in a disabling world. Art-based performance can pick up on these skills, enhance them, and use them to disseminate pride, critique, power, and the beauty of vulnerability and to engage in improvisation on the edge of control. Finding ways to think about living agency while wielding our bodyminds to signal to each other and the world: that is the nexus of disability and performance.

46

Prosthetics
Katherine Ott

Prosthetics fall within the broad category of assistive devices that people use to support what they want to do. Assistive devices, in general, enhance such capacities as mobility and agility, sensory apprehension, communication, and cognitive action. But the field of prosthetics, in particular, refers to those artificial body parts, devices, and materials that are integrated into the body's daily routines. Because "prosthetics," as a term, encompasses the way people select hardware, undergo procedures, and understand the results, there is no one immutable definition for it.

Prosthetics runs the range of detachable, wearable, implanted, or integrated body parts and may be functional, cosmetic, decorative, or hidden. It covers a wide range of components: from familiar designs such as peg legs, split-hook hands, and myoelectric limbs that yoke nerve signals from remaining muscles, to artificial skin, replaced hip joints, eyeglasses, hearing aids, strap-on penises, and reconstructed bones. Some prosthetics use sensory feedback, thought control, or neuronal elements to move limbs, process speech, or simulate vision. Implant engineering, by contrast, repairs the body from the inside out through integration of artificial tissue.

For most of history, prosthetics was a do-it-yourself enterprise and continues to be so in many parts of the world (Putti 1930). Because each human body and its prosthetic need are unique, each device is customized. The person takes possession of the device through alteration, decoration, daily use, and further fitting with accessories such as shoes, makeup, stump socks, gloves, and attachment methods. Society mobilizes to study the problem and provide solutions when historical events—most often wars, natural disasters, and the application of new technologies to human endeavors such as work, transportation, sports, and entertainment—create large numbers of people in need of prosthetics.

The object most commonly associated with the word in medical and popular literature is the lower limb prosthetic (Ott, Serlin, and Mihm 2002). The 1851 Great Exhibition, held in London's Hyde Park, brought attention to these objects as makers displayed the first modern prosthetics as consumer goods. During the U.S. Civil War, battlefield tactics and the weapons used produced injuries and infections that resulted in a high rate of amputation. A ball of soft lead made a ragged entry and shattered bone. Battlefield conditions, inadequately trained surgeons, and no understanding of asepsis resulted in necrosis, gangrene, and amputation. The surgical outcome often produced a painful stump, despite new flap techniques.

In the last half of the nineteenth century, a proliferation of injured people—civil war veterans, industrial workers, and those hurt in railroad, trolley, auto, and other accidents—fueled change in medical procedures and design of devices. Middle-class consumers embraced the aesthetics of lifelike designs instead of peg legs and eye patches (Herschbach 1997). The popularity of social Darwinism further increased the stigma of having a body that might use a prosthesis, and municipalities began to outlaw begging, a common livelihood for such people. Yet, veterans often preferred the valorous empty sleeve or pant leg to an awkward and heavy commercial device, even though after 1870 every honorably discharged Union soldier of the Civil War was entitled to a modern limb.

World War I brought widespread attention to veterans in Europe, the Soviet Union, and the United States who had suffered amputation on the battlefield and became wearers of prosthetic limbs as part of their transition to civilian life and the postwar industrial workforce (Panchasi 1995). The Great War also brought attention to the emerging surgical specialty of facial reconstruction and, consequently, facial prostheses, which gained relevance through the work of Anna Coleman Ladd and others. The most significant advances in prosthetics and rehabilitation began with World War II (Sauerborn 1998; Ott 2005). Not only were so many soldiers wounded, but many more survived their injuries. In 1945, the U.S. surgeon general requested that the National Academy of Sciences initiate a research program related to rehabilitation of the injured. This project generated the field of biomechanics and understanding of body forces. As a result, prosthetics began to be imagined differently, using robotics, ergonomics, kinesiology (movement), and human engineering (Serlin 2004). By the 1950s, professionals working in prosthetics and orthotics needed board certification. Government-funded research during wartime or related to war's consequences has continued to generate innovations in prosthetics. For example, a contemporary soldier injured by shrapnel from an improvised explosive device ripping through an exposed extremity will likely learn to use an Otto Bock "Utah" limb with a microprocessing chip that reads the environmental interface hundreds of times a second to facilitate motion—a user no longer "swings" the leg.

Medicine, science, and engineering have regularly deployed prosthetics to "fix" bodies perceived as having deficits, such as skeletal "deficiencies," including those born without various bones or those with atypical bodies resulting from medical treatment, such as infants born in the late 1950s with physical anomalies after their mothers took the drug Thalidomide. The advent of microsurgery, skin grafting, burn treatment, medications, and a range of medical techniques influenced both survival and the nature of the outcome for people who use prosthetic devices. For example, metal and wood were good for limb but not for facial designs. Rubber, latex, vulcanite, and plastics were appropriate for facial appliances and as components of more complicated limb designs. Acrylic resins, introduced in the 1930s, silicones in the 1960s, and hydroxyapatite in the 1980s have enabled implanted and integrated devices to take shape.

Because the contexts in which prosthetics may occur are so varied, the disciplines that engage with and discuss them are equally varied. Where technology is understood as a medium for breaking boundaries, pushing into the next frontier, and creating a new body-machine interface, the prosthesis-as-metaphor is especially rich. In the popular imagination, prosthetics has a rich visual, political, and material vocabulary. Historians, looking at prosthetics, examine macro forces that brought them into being such as war, industrialization, medicine, accident and injury, and materials science, as well as individual and community experience. Product designers deal with aesthetics of the hardware (Pullin 2009). Rehabilitation focuses on the process of incorporation of the artificial part into one's mechanical and psychic sense of self. In sociology, psychology, and anthropology, a prosthesis can function as a social symbol and a political allegory for one's self. As metaphor and metonymy, the concept of the prosthetic may compensate for an injury, serve as a symbol of devotion to country, provide an object of sexual fetish, or act as an anodyne for grief and mourning (Wills 1995; Mitchell and Snyder 2001). A prosthetic can serve as an index of modernity, manhood, or malevolence—or sometimes all three.

In disability studies, prosthetics is not typically the stuff of performance art or Hollywood special effects makeup. Yet scientists, designers, engineers, and journalists have come to rely on these metaphors and narratives of inspiration in framing analyses of prosthetics. As interpreted by journalists who cover this technology, as well as science fiction writers, filmmakers, video gamers, and graphic artists, prosthetics turns a person into a cyborg or bionic human. Such cultural producers commonly approach the subject based upon technological potential, while the actual disabled body plays only a minor role. For example, when the media feature wounded soldiers as recipients of prosthetics, the practical utility of the device is often secondary to its status as an example of bionic technology. ("Bionics" describes both the application of biological principles to engineering and design and the replacement of biological entities with electronic and mechanical components.) Discourse about cyborgs began in earnest with Donna Haraway's "Cyborg Manifesto" (1991; originally published in 1985) which offered a feminist critique of the military-industrial character of the cyborg, a hybrid term announcing the integration of the cybernetic and the organic. For Haraway, the cyborg consciously transcends human material limits and collapses the boundaries between machine and organism. The romance of the cyborg in the popular imagination is exemplified by a disabled or typically abled body that can become super-abled when engineered with superpowers that enhance human potential.

The political development of a disability rights movement in the twentieth century has gradually altered the cultural environment in which designers, engineers, and medical practitioners work. As disability became understood as a civil rights issue, the inclusion of users as authorities gained prominence. Consumer and creator input brought the split-hook hand, the Flex-Foot

and sprint leg, and countless changes in medical practice. This is because while biomechanical invention has expanded the functionality of the human form, it has also raised significant ethical and political issues, such as using a device to "pass" as nondisabled, or for what age or demographic group a particular device is appropriate, or whether the benefits of an appliance are sufficient to be subsidized by insurance. Other debates focus on the implications of runners who use prosthetic devices in athletic competitions, or whether cochlear implants foster cultural genocide, or what it means to be disabled, and who should pay the costs for artificial hearts.

These arguments go beyond those about replacements or technological interventions. For example, for many people with disabilities, acquiring and using a prosthetic limb is most often a strategy for creating access or restoring function rather than for enhancement. According to the U.S. Centers for Disease Control and Prevention, of the approximately 65,000 amputations performed each year in the United States, some 82 percent are of lower extremities and the result of vascular deficiencies such as occur with diabetes. Thus, presenting prosthetics as a superhuman or transcendent technology eclipses the everyday needs of those who use such technologies.

A critical and interdisciplinary approach to prosthetics, such as that offered by disability studies, leads to a more complex and nuanced comprehension of the human body and the role of culture, politics, and engineering in defining capacity. Unlike rehabilitation medicine or engineering science, disability studies asks questions about the role of prosthetic technology not only in relation to design and function but also in relation to disability rights, political autonomy, and cultural citizenship. Indeed, much critical disability studies scholarship examines the enduring relationship between prosthetic technologies and histories of capitalism, empire, and the military-industrial complex. The use of a prosthetic is thus not a mark of deficiency or postmodern transcendence but rather an important dimension of human experience that demands thoughtful and empathic analysis.

47

Queer
Tim Dean

Historically, the term "queer" was a stigmatizing label that often included disabled people in its purview. A century ago, for instance, someone with a missing limb or a cognitive impairment might be called "queer." In recent decades, sexual minorities have reclaimed "queer" as a badge of pride and a mark of resistance to regimes of the normal, mirroring the embrace of terms like "crip" and the capaciousness of the term "disability" itself. These are all political, highly contested terms that refuse essentializing meanings. In the late 1980s and early 1990s, the activist group Queer Nation's chant "We're here, we're queer, get used to it" was historically concurrent with the disability rights activist slogan "Not dead yet."

What the field of queer studies shares most fundamentally with disability studies is a critique of the effects of normalization on embodiment, desire, and access. "Queer" opposes not heterosexuality but *heteronormativity*—the often unspoken assumption that heterosexuality provides the framework through which everything makes sense. Before Michael Warner invented the term "heteronormativity" in the early 1990s, scholars had been working with a notion of "compulsory heterosexuality" coined by the lesbian feminist writer Adrienne Rich (1983). Disability theorist Robert McRuer picked up Rich's account two decades later in order to argue that compulsory heterosexuality depends upon compulsory able-bodiedness, since heteronormativity assumes first and foremost that sexual subjects must be able-bodied, healthy, and therefore "normal." Indeed, able-bodiedness appears to be even more compulsory than heterosexuality because the latter requires the former. Normal sex—as opposed to its deviant or perverse forms—requires a normal body. Articulating disability theory with queer theory, McRuer (2006) thus developed a "crip theory" in which a critique of sexual normalization goes hand in hand with a critique of ableist assumptions about embodiment.

Critiques of normalization have a substantial history in the fields of both disability studies and queer studies. Indeed, those critiques generated their own critical terminology in their respective areas of humanities scholarship during the 1990s. In addition to Warner's coinage of "heteronormativity," Rosemarie Garland-Thomson deployed the concept of the "normate" in her influential book *Extraordinary Bodies* to designate "the social figure through which people can represent themselves as definitive human beings" (1997, 8). Similarly, Lennard Davis's *Enforcing Normalcy* (1995) described the cultural processes that perpetuate exclusionary corporeal norms and ideals. As with Warner's critique of heteronormativity, the central claim of this area of scholarship is that, beyond examining the bodily conditions or the physical environments that produce disability, disability studies should also examine those less tangible but profoundly distorted social expectations that presume what bodies should look like and be able to do.

Queer approaches to thinking about disability and sexuality argue that neither the human body nor its capacities are biologically determined; rather, both disability and sexuality are constituted via sociocultural processes of normalization. Sociologist Erving Goffman's *Stigma* (1963), for instance, influenced both disability studies and queer studies, in part because Goffman routinely refers to "cripples" and "homosexuals" in the same breath, as parallel examples of stigmatized identities. What remains crucial in Goffman's account is his insight that everyone falls short of identity norms; we are all potentially vulnerable to the injurious effects of social stigma. In other words, normalization does not exclusively bolster the interests of the so-called normal, since it also puts them at risk. Insofar as "queer" and "disabled" designate contingent identities, anyone can be queered or become disabled by failing to live up to particular norms or ideals.

The influential philosopher Michel Foucault broadens the scope of Goffman's sociological analysis by showing that power in modern society is exerted less through the channels of regulation and prohibition than through those of normalization and rehabilitation. Foucault's critique of normalization derives, in part, from the work of French medical historian Georges Canguilhem, whose study *The Normal and the Pathological* (1978) demonstrated that illness is routinely yet erroneously understood in terms of its departure from biophysical norms. Canguilhem's point was that significant variations from what is statistically normal for a population need not imply pathology. Only when mathematical norms get conflated with evaluative norms do such variations indicate sickness. This distinction between statistical and evaluative norms, which has been indispensable for the strand of queer theory developed by Warner, is also highly relevant for disability studies. In both queer theory and disability theory, the demystification of social categories as well as medical metrics helps to highlight the ways in which illness, health, and normality are constructed.

Nowhere have social and medical norms intersected so powerfully as with the phenomenon of AIDS. As literary scholar Ellis Hanson has contended, "Queer theory itself may be said to have begun as disability studies, sparked as it was by activist energies around the AIDS crisis" (2011, 113). Queer politics grew out of the AIDS activism of the late 1980s, largely in order to insist that AIDS is not a disease of identity—that is, a disease pertaining only to pathologized social groups such as gay men or IV drug users. Among its many effects, the AIDS epidemic fostered a coalitional politics that cut across established lines of sexual, racial, and disabled identity, resulting in a specifically queer politics.

Disability studies may have catalyzed the origins of what scholars now think of as queer studies. But it is only once the two have been explicitly articulated relative to one another that the extent of their connection becomes clear. The connection enables literary scholar Anna Mollow to suggest that sex itself, in its effects on coherent selfhood, may be regarded as disabling. Drawing on a psychoanalytic strand of queer theory associated with Leo Bersani, Mollow argues that "disability" and "sex" represent "two names for the same self-rupturing force" (2012, 287). Here the connection between queer and disability stems not from social processes of normalization but from the impact of sexual intensity on bodily coherence. Mollow's challenging hypothesis points toward a possible future for queer theory and disability studies by rethinking the extent of their mutual interdependence.

48

Race
Nirmala Erevelles

Race and disability, two significant categories of difference that shape the social, have often been conceptualized as analogous to each other. Disability has often been described as being "like race" and race as being "like disability" in attempts to shift the experience of disability from the debilitating conceptual space of individual pathology to a broader social recognition of disabled people as members of a political minority. Thus, for example, Rosemarie Garland-Thomson (1997) describes disability as a "form of ethnicity" (6), while Lennard Davis (1995) maps similarities between the disabled body and "the body marked as differently pigmented" (80). Foregrounding this analogous relationship between race and disability has helped propel the disability rights movement and disability studies scholarship forward into an alternative space of empowering possibility.

In the field of critical race studies, however, there are few echoes of a similar reciprocity with regard to disability. The act of correlating race and disability is often fraught with violent and oppressive overtones. For example, the historian Douglas Baynton (2001) has noted that "non-white races were routinely connected to people with disabilities . . . [and] depicted as evolutionary laggards or throwbacks" (36) to justify discrimination based on embodied difference from a mythical norm. Literary theorist Hortense Spillers (1987) documents the unimaginable brutality of such discrimination when she describes how the representational and physical violence meted out to the black captive body during the Middle Passage and slavery enabled the slave's body to become a site where the battered flesh (disability) was transformed into the prime commodity of exchange in a violent conflation of profit and pleasure (Erevelles 2011).

These oppressive overtones continued to echo from within the Enlightenment discourses of the early eighteenth century and much of the nineteenth century, where philosophers like Hume and Kant utilized the analogy between race and disability to distinguish among "different breeds of men." Buttressed by an emerging science that proposed linkages between human anatomy and human capability (and, later, for Freud, the notion that "anatomy is destiny"), the racist practice of eugenic sterilization or selective breeding was institutionalized (Mitchell and Snyder 2003). Eugenic science sought to stem the threat of degeneration by controlling the reproduction of those designated as "feebleminded," which was fueled in part by the social and economic upheavals caused by industrialization. By the early twentieth century, the concept of feeblemindedness came to operate as an umbrella term that linked ethnicity, poverty, and gendered and racialized conceptions of immorality together as "the signifier of tainted whiteness" (Stubblefield 2007, 162). The fear of degeneracy associated with a "tainted whiteness" extended not only to Jewish Americans, African Americans, Puerto Ricans, Mexican Americans, Asian Americans, and American Indian women but also to lower-class white women based on their assumed shared "biological" inferiority and their reproductive incapacity to bear children that would assimilate into mainstream white society.

Mitchell and Snyder (2003) argue that it is necessary to recognize eugenics as a transatlantic cultural exchange—what they call the "eugenic Atlantic"—to mark how the discourse of disability was deployed throughout the European colonial diaspora. In this context, the concept of disability justified oppressive social, political, cultural, and economic policies based on the argument that racial difference and class inequalities represented pathological defects otherwise known as "disability." These ideologies of disability enabled European expansionists to justify the conquest of racialized others while simultaneously retrieving "an unspoiled, pre-modern version of an ever more complex western self" (848). With its commitment to a doctrine of human purity, eugenic science continued to erase the "histories, bodies, [and]/or cultures" (Jarman 2006, 149–150) of despised Others, as manifested in "protective" practices like genocide, forced sterilizations, rigid miscegenation laws, and residential segregation in ghettos, barrios, reservations, and state institutions like prisons and asylums.

In an ironic twist, the very same pathologized bodies made to disappear from polite society via regulatory or eugenic practices were rendered highly visible as "freaks" and transformed into spectacles for popular consumption and economic profit (James and Wu 2006; Adams 2001; Garland-Thomson 1997). For instance, the public's morbid fascination with the sexualized bodies of Saartjie Baartman, the South African woman known as the "Hottentot Venus," or other racialized freaks such as Ota Benga, and Hiram and Barney Davis, "the Wild Men of Borneo," was proof of the brutal conflation of race and disability. Such racial freaks were collectively represented to the public as the unbearable physical excesses that had to be shed to confer entry into the realm of normalcy (Adams 2001). Thus, for example, both scientists and policy makers involved in the "eugenic Atlantic" and proprietors and showmen involved in the freak show circuit presumed that it was the "natural" deviance of disability ascribed to the racialized body that constituted it as either the despised Other or the profitable freak. In both cases, science and entertainment referenced "'race' as the social locus of ascribed insufficiency while leaving disability as the default category of 'real' human incapacity" (Mitchell and Snyder 2003, 851).

Given this history, it has been difficult for critical race scholars to conceptually engage with the category of disability beyond the simplistic and problematic assertion that there is an analogous relationship between race and disability. Claiming that "race is like disability" or that "disability is like race" does nothing to engage the complex ways in which race and disability are imbricated in the construction of the pathological Other. For example, when disability is invoked in critical discourses of race, it usually suffers from what Chris Ewart (2010) has described as *dis*appropriation. Here disability is used "to affirm (an often subordinate) voice to elucidate agency and figurative empathy for other oppressed and exploited populations" (152). Used in this context, critical race scholars, such as Stuart Hall, have described the life experiences of a racialized subject as "crippling" and "deforming." In doing so, they fail to recognize that, rather than rejecting oppressive biological criteria, they unwittingly reaffirm an imagined biological wholeness (normativity) that was instrumental in the propagation of the same oppressive ideologies they were seeking to dismantle in the first place (Erevelles 2011). They inadvertently deploy disability as a master trope of disqualification that one should escape rather than embrace.

Rather than treating the analogous relationship between race and disability as prosthetic metaphor and/or nuanced intervention, it may be necessary to engage the historical contexts and structural conditions within which the identity categories of race and disability intersect. For example, special education classes became the spaces where African American and Latino students were ghettoized even after the *Brown v. Board of Education* legislation, which was supposed to make segregation on the basis of race in education unacceptable (Connor and Ferri 2005; Artiles 2011). But in recognizing the conjunction of race and disability rather than highlighting only one or the other, race and disability become clearly interdependent as disabled subjectivities are racialized and racialized subjects are disabled simultaneously. Blanchett, Klingner, and Harry (2009) have illustrated how the politics of race, class, and disability intersect when students of color in low-income, high-poverty schools "become" mildly mentally retarded and emotionally disturbed. Even when compensatory services are available, white privilege and institutional racism obstruct access to these services. Additionally, these students of color find themselves in the most segregated and punitive spaces in the public school system—social conditions that often extend into their adult lives via the school-to-prison pipeline (Erevelles 2011). Thus, in the historical context of *Brown v. Board of Education*, the oppressive practices of white supremacy and pedagogical ableism were mutually constitutive.

Social conditions of poverty also contribute to racialized subjects "becoming" disabled. The incidence of physical and mental illness in people of color communities, for instance, differs drastically from that of their white counterparts. According to the Centers for Disease Control and Prevention, African American children are disproportionately more likely to suffer from exposure to lead and toxic waste, well-known causes of developmental delays, because they are disproportionately more likely to live in old and run-down housing with lead pipes and peeling lead paint near hazardous waste sites (Stubblefield 2009; Erevelles 2011). Furthermore, people of color, especially African Americans, are less likely to be diagnosed with depression or prescribed medication when they report symptoms to a doctor, and are also institutionalized involuntarily more often, in part because racial stereotypes affect psychiatrists' assessments of their "dangerousness" (Mollow 2006, 74; Metzl 2011). Extending beyond the local context of the United States, in neocolonial and postcolonial contexts, war and intra-ethnic strife create actual physical disabilities as well as trauma in societies where there are few economic, social, and emotional supports. Race drastically transforms the life experience of becoming disabled and living with disability in both historical and contemporary contexts.

While it may be politically expedient for disability studies scholars to argue that disability is the most universal of human conditions because almost anyone can become disabled (Garland-Thomson 1997), there is often an implicit assumption that the acquisition of a disabled identity always occurs outside historical context. But rather than conceiving of "disability" and "race" as interchangeable tropes in order to foreground the ubiquity of oppression, the categories of race/ethnicity and disability might be better invoked to demonstrate how they constitute one another through social, political, economic, and cultural practices that have kept seemingly different groups of people in strikingly similar marginalized positions (James and Wu 2006; Erevelles 2011). Thus, more robust and complex analyses of race and disability are necessary for us to move beyond the initial conceptual space of analogy.

49

Rehabilitation

Gary L. Albrecht

"Rehabilitation" refers to a process, or a set of related processes, that enables persons with disabilities to interact with their environments and maintain optimal physical, sensory, intellectual, psychological, and social function levels. In common usage, rehabilitation provides persons with disabilities the tools they need to attain independence and self-determination (World Health Organization and the World Bank 2011, 96). While the intent of this definition is straightforward, rehabilitation is a contested concept because major actors in the rehabilitation field employ different perspectives, values, and explanatory models in addressing disability and how to respond to it (Shakespeare 2006a). For some, disability is defined by the medical model—that is, based on a medically identified impairment resident in the individual that can be objectively assessed and is amenable to therapies. According to this perspective, disability is an individual characteristic, medically defined and properly subject to therapeutic interventions. In this tradition, the diagnosis, proposed treatment plan, and rehabilitation process are controlled and performed by medically trained rehabilitation professionals working in hospitals, in-patient rehabilitation units, and outpatient clinics.

A revolution in thinking occurred during the 1970s when disabled people put forward the social model, which argued that disability is not a characteristic confined to an individual. Rather, disability is a condition imposed on individuals due to existing social and physical barriers in their environment—such as physical obstacles to mobility and job discrimination—which prevent them from exercising the full extent of their potential independence. Thus, the focus moved from rehabilitating the individual as a private entity to transforming the expectations and structures of the society and the community as a whole. This resulted in legislation, architectural design changes, and social programs to improve the lives of disabled people by making their environments more welcoming.

In addition, some disabled rights activists objected that external observers and health care professionals were not qualified to judge the particular character of a given person's disability and his or her perceived needs and limitations, given the specious nature of some of the measurement instruments employed to assess individual limitations. For example, some individuals reported that although members of the general public regarded them as disabled, they did not see themselves as disabled and did not identify as such (Albrecht and Devlieger 1999). Empowered by new legislation that emerged from the disability and human rights movements, many disabled people argued that they should be fully and actively involved in the decision making about and responses to their disability. (As the slogan went, "Nothing about us without us" [Charlton 1998].) This includes sharing in decisions about how to use social and financial support services available to them through insurance and/or social welfare entitlements. In this newly liberating era, the older medical model of disability and the rehabilitation sciences that undergirded it seemed more paternalistic and controlling than ever.

There are numerous advantages to including and empowering disabled people in how they define and participate in their own rehabilitation process. People who are given a sense of control over their futures are more likely to become knowledgeable about their conditions, benefits, and paths to independence and therefore to make better-informed decisions. They are also more likely to be more active and integrated within their families and communities. A step in this direction is to ask disabled people what changes in their lives they deem to be the most essential and how they envision achieving these improvements on limited family, state, and community budgets.

Another step forward is to move the bulk of rehabilitation efforts from hospitals and clinics into the world where disabled people live and encourage more interactive rehabilitation programs. The community-based rehabilitation (CBR) movement is gaining force worldwide in countries of all levels of development by involving local leaders in efforts to enhance the quality of life for disabled people and their families. This initiative aims to develop and operate local community-based programs, often assisted by government agencies, nongovernmental organizations (NGOs), and institutions like the Robert Wood Johnson, Gates, and Ford Foundations, to deliver basic health care and to provide assistive technology like low-cost wheelchairs, educational and job opportunities, social services, and residential assistance. These programs are designed to integrate disabled people into their communities and enhance their quality of lives. In the United States, the World Institute on Disability and the independent living movement have been major movers in opening up opportunities for disabled people and integrating them more closely into local communities. In the United Kingdom, disabled people are more visible and active in their communities because of the increased availability of personal mobility devices like electric scooters. On a global scale, the World Health Organization has been a promoter of CBR by organizing rehabilitation in local communities, educating local and national leaders on how to set up such programs, and publishing a set of guidelines on how to do this work (World Health Organization 2010). The World Bank has contributed to this movement by recognizing that disability is a major issue in developing economies.

In the 1980s, a further development was the insistence that disability is not an "abnormal" or "deviant" condition but part of the normal human experience and should be seen in terms of a range of differences. The argument is that societies are enriched by being exposed to and recognizing diversity in demographics, place of origin, religious and cultural beliefs, and physical and social capacities. In considering these sea changes in the disability world, thoughtful observers began to reconceptualize disability as the result of interaction between impaired persons and their environment. These forces, taken in concert, have radically affected disability concepts and theory and subsequently altered the design of rehabilitation interventions on the societal level.

At the same time, there have been equally fundamental changes in rehabilitation occurring within health care settings. Medical rehabilitation is now seen as a set of health care interventions that are best delivered by multidisciplinary teams, involving disabled people and their families in the process, monitored across time, and outcome-oriented. On a conceptual level, attention is given to the human rights of disabled people and the cost, access, and quality of the rehabilitation services delivered. Change agents argue: if you want to change an individual's or an organization's behavior, modify the criteria for evaluation and make the results public. In the case of medical rehabilitation, significant strides have been made in assessing the activity and performance of individuals who have received interventions and care over time and of health care professional groups and institutions that deliver rehabilitation services. The development and widespread implementation of the Functional Index Measure (FIM), which measures basic activities of daily living such as eating, dressing, and locomotion based on physical and cognitive functioning, is a case in point (Granger 2011). The FIM is used globally by clinicians in rehabilitation settings to assess an individual's progress, by institutions to improve care outcomes among their consumers, and by health care payers to judge whether good value for money is being achieved. This is part of a larger movement of outcomes research that clinicians, researchers, and policy makers use to evaluate performance in health care and management circles. According to this viewpoint, individuals, institutions, and professionals should be evaluated on how they behave and what they produce for a given price.

In addition to these conceptual changes in rehabilitation strategies, considerable advances have been made in the technology and practice of rehabilitation, including, but also ranging beyond, the traditional disciples of physical, occupational, cognitive, and speech therapies. Advances in surgery, neurology, pharmacology, and genetics, as well as lessons learned about the timing and intensity of interventions, team building, and integration of services, have all significantly improved rehabilitation care (Frontera 2010). Recent scientific evidence has further pointed to diet, nutrition, exercise, social engagement in the community, architectural modifications to the home and public spaces, and use of assistive technology as essential ingredients of maximizing a disabled person's independence. Such recent developments as serious exercise and nutrition programs for disabled people, exoskeletons to assist people with spinal cord injuries and strokes to walk, redesigned bathrooms, kitchens, ramps, public transportation, accommodations in the workplace, adaptations to cars and vans, and centers for independent living all allow disabled people to participate more fully in society.

REHABILITATION   GARY L. ALBRECHT

"Smart houses" are being constructed and studied that use handheld, voice-activated computer devices to adjust the temperature, lock and unlock doors, control light and electricity, turn appliances on and off, summon help if needed, and remind users of appointments or medication schedules. In the past, most rehabilitation interventions have focused on the individual, but these more recent efforts convey attention to the physical and social environments where disabled people live, the barriers they encounter, and the activities that allow them to participate in society. This conforms to the new understanding of disability as a result of the interaction between individuals and their environments. While all of these possibilities hold enormous promise, the reality lags behind the ideal. A limited number of disabled people have access to and fully utilize these technologies. The gap between ideal and reality is a problem of resources, values, and social policy. Priorities have to be set and decisions made about the treatment of disabled people in aging societies in which most people will experience some form of disability before they die (National Institute of Medicine 2012).

50

Representation
Michael Bérubé

The word "representation" has a double valence for disability studies, which consists of an intensification of its double valence in the English language more generally. "Representation" speaks to both political and aesthetic concerns; it suggests an image that stands in for and points toward a thing (in the *Oxford English Dictionary*, "an image, likeness, or reproduction in some manner of a thing; a material image or figure; a reproduction in some material or tangible form; in later use, a drawing or painting"), or a mechanism by which one person or group of people is empowered to stand in for and express the wishes of another person or group (in the *OED*, "the fact of standing for, or in place of, some other thing or person, esp. with a right or authority to act on their account"). There are other, more narrowly legal senses of representation, as when one makes a material representation of a fact or a state of affairs; but these are not as relevant to the project of disability studies as are the political and aesthetic senses, except with regard to the question of guardianship, which I will address briefly later.

In the political realm, the importance of "representation" for the understanding of disability can be gauged by the American disability rights slogan "Nothing about us without us." The slogan calls attention to, and seeks to redress, the fact that social policies and speech acts concerning people with disabilities have historically been carried out by people without disabilities, whether benevolently or maliciously. People with disabilities have long been deemed unable to represent themselves as political actors, either because their physical infirmities ostensibly rendered them unable to contribute to and/or discuss the common good or because they were ostensibly intellectually incapable of understanding the common good, or indeed of understanding their own interests. They were therefore considered to be unable to meet the criteria for self-representation as citizens of modern democratic nations (i.e., nations with representative governments). This determination held even for the Deaf, who were, by the end of the nineteenth century in the United States, considered to be a threat to national unity insofar as they spoke sign language rather than English. For people with mental illness or mental retardation, the determination of their incapacity for self-representation provided the rationale for warehousing them in institutions whose conditions ranged from merely isolating to unspeakably foul.

In his essay "Disability and the Justification of Inequality in American History" (2001), Douglas Baynton demonstrates that this logic of disability applied also to women and African Americans, who were denied the rights of citizenship on the grounds that their gender or their race disabled them. By a pernicious logic, then, women and African Americans were compelled to demonstrate that they met certain performance criteria for self-representation, that in fact they were not disabled, thereby confirming the dominant social conviction that disability constituted legitimate grounds for exclusion (as it did for millions of aspiring immigrants).

As Anita Silvers (2002) has shown, this understanding of disability has subtended a great deal of American law and jurisprudence; it accounts for, among other things, the fact that disability was excluded from the Civil Rights Act of 1964. There, the logic was that gender, race, and status as an ethnic or religious minority were accidents of birth or matters of private belief, but that disability was constitutively disqualifying. The Americans with Disabilities Act was passed in 1990 in order to extend the rights of citizenship to people with disabilities, and it was amended in 2008 in response to increasingly narrow judicial readings of the act. The disability rights movement, which originated with Ed Roberts and the Rolling Quads at the University of California at Berkeley in the mid-1960s, was inspired by the civil rights movement and was centrally concerned with the political self-representation of people with disabilities. But the roots of the reasoning behind the denial of representation to people with disabilities go back deep into Western political theory, to the origins of social contract theory in the eighteenth century.

As Eva Feder Kittay (1999) and Martha Nussbaum (2006) have argued, social contract theorists from John Locke to John Rawls have consistently sets aside or discounted the representation of people with intellectual disabilities. In Locke, the parties to the social contract are imagined as "free, equal, and independent," contracting for mutual benefit; in Rawls, similarly, "the fundamental problem of social justice arises between those who are full and active and morally conscientious participants in society, and directly or indirectly associated together throughout a complete life" (1980, 546). The performance criterion established here clearly excludes those who are not full, active, and morally conscientious participants in society and requires that they be represented by surrogates or guardians who are. "Representation" thus takes on its more narrow legal meanings in such instances, where people with intellectual disabilities are considered in the terms Karl Marx applied to the smallholding peasants of nineteenth-century France: they cannot represent themselves; therefore, they must be represented. This occlusion of people with intellectual disabilities from the democratic order that would seem most likely to embrace them can be found in various contemporary theories of democracy as well, including Amy Gutmann and Dennis Thompson's (2004) idea of deliberative democracy and Nancy Fraser and Axel Honneth's (2003) conception of participatory parity, neither of which set a place at the table for accommodation for people with disabilities who are deemed unable to deliberate or participate at a requisite level.

Disability studies, as the academic outgrowth of the disability rights movement, tends to emphasize the self-representation of people with disabilities in the aesthetic sense as well as the political. This aesthetic emphasis arises partly from the conviction that traditional forms of artistic representation of disability, and people with disabilities, have led to severe misunderstandings of disability as well as literally and allegorically demeaning depictions of people with disabilities. "Allegorically" demeaning depictions are those such as Shakespeare's version of Richard III, which imputes to the king a viciousness explicitly caused by a physical disability that the historical Richard did not actually have. Physical disability is thus represented not only as repellent in itself but as the source of broader and far more repellent personality traits. Similarly, blindness is often rendered—both in literature and in ordinary language—as something more and other than a visual impairment. It also can be taken as the index of a more pervasive moral or intellectual blindness, as in Richard Wright's depiction of Mrs. Dalton in his novel *Native Son* (1940); as Bigger's attorney, Max, puts it: "And to Mrs. Dalton, I say: 'Your philanthropy was as tragically blind as your sightless eyes!'"

Accordingly, disability studies in the humanities has devoted itself to critiquing such representations of disability, just as second-wave feminism, in the 1970s, developed a line of critique Toril Moi (1985) would later call "images of women criticism." The drawbacks of this mode of critique are numerous, insofar as it relies on a naively realist theory of mimesis (representations should be accurate reflections of the world) and a naively moralistic scale of evaluation (in which "positive" representations are better than "negative" ones). Moreover, "images of disability" criticism can sometimes entail a version of "media effects" theory, in which negative representations are claimed to have deleterious social consequences. For instance, Carol Poore writes of "the grave consequences these widely accepted negative images had and still have for the lives of people with disabilities" (2002, 261). Despite its limitations, however, "images of disability" criticism, like its "images of women" predecessor, is right to suggest that vicious, inaccurate representations of certain classes of human beings not only can bring about but may also originate in stigmatizing and unjust social realities. Just as the "virgin/whore" dichotomy and the ideology of "separate spheres" were (and remain) important aspects of the social organization of gender, the idea that people with physical disabilities are angry and embittered, and the idea that people with intellectual disabilities are incapable of understanding, empathy, or self-reflection, speak to the social organization of disability—regardless of whether or not those social arrangements and injustices are literally caused by vicious, inaccurate representations. In the groundbreaking work of Martin Norden and Rosemarie Garland-Thomson, for example, long-standing patterns of representing disability are understood as collectively creating a "cinema of isolation" (Norden 1994) or visual modes of the wondrous, the sentimental, the exotic, and the realistic (Garland-Thomson 2002)—though it is notable that for Garland-Thomson, the "realistic" is not only the most mimetically accurate but also the least stigmatizing mode of representation.

The difference between the theory of representation underlying "images of disability" criticism and "images of women" criticism, however, is an important one: disability, unlike gender, is almost always taken *as a sign of something else*. The analysis of representation in disability studies, therefore, must necessarily go beyond evaluations of "negative" and "positive" images, insofar as disability nearly always signifies something other than itself. Disability is either a metaphor for character more generally (as when one is blind to injustice or deaf to the cries of the oppressed) or the source of character traits, as in the case of Richard III; it is only rarely simply a thing in itself, a cleft lip and palate or an instance of achondroplasia with no other semiotic function or implications. In that sense, disability is *necessarily representational*—in the Christian tradition, for instance, a sign of God's wrath (in the case of leprosy) or God's grace (as in the case of epilepsy).

More complexly still, disability as representation can serve a dizzying array of functions in narrative film and literature. Ato Quayson (2007) has enumerated nine such functions, in what he calls "a typology of disability": disability as null set and/or moral test (as in *A Christmas Carol*, *The Sound and the Fury*, or the film *There's Something about Mary*); disability as the interface with otherness (race, class, sexuality, and social identity, as in *As Good as It Gets*—see McRuer [2002]); disability as articulation of disjuncture between thematic and narrative vectors (as in Disney's *Finding Nemo*); disability as moral deficit/evil; disability as epiphany (as in *To Kill a Mockingbird*); disability as signifier of ritual insight (as in the case of Tiresias); disability as inarticulable and enigmatic tragic insight (as in *One Hundred Years of Solitude*); disability as hermeneutical impasse (as in *The English Patient*); and disability as normality (as in memoirs and autobiographies, according to Quayson; this category roughly corresponds to Garland-Thomson's "realistic" mode of visual representation). To these can be added at least two more: disability as exceptionality/superability (as in fantasy and science fiction narratives such as *Dumbo*, *Happy Feet*, *Total Recall*, and the *X-Men* series) and disability as motive (for individual characters or for entire narratives, or both, as in the Oedipus cycle).

On rare occasions, however, disability is presented simply as disability, and not as a sign of something other than itself. In an unpublished paper titled "When the Saints Come Crippin' In," Alice Sheppard argues that whereas Christian writers of the first millennium typically understood disability as a sign of one's moral state or as an occasion for charity and/or miraculous cure, Old Norse epics present disability simply as itself: as a war wound with no greater semiotic significance, or as cleft lip and palate signifying nothing other than cleft lip and palate. A more contemporary example can be found in *Moby-Dick*, which may be of more interest to disability studies insofar as Captain Ahab, like Shakespeare's Richard III, is often adduced as an example of a character deformed by disability: Ahab is led to megalomania and madness by the loss of his leg to the white whale. But as James Berger (2004) has pointed out, Melville's text contains a countervailing example, that of Captain Boomer of the *Samuel Enderby*, who has lost an arm to Moby-Dick and wants nothing more to do with him: "He's welcome to the arm he has, since I can't help it, and didn't know him then; but not to another one. No more White Whales for me; I've lowered for him once, and that has satisfied me." For Captain Boomer, then (and, at least in this instance, for Melville), a lost arm is nothing more than a lost arm. Sometimes the disabled cigar is just a disabled cigar.

The exception, however, may (here as elsewhere) prove the rule: *representation* is of central interest to disability studies not only for the analysis of specific representations of disability but also for the broader analysis of what specific disabilities have been taken to represent. Disability studies critiques of representation, whether in the political or the aesthetic sense, thus provide a powerful rationale for reinterpreting ways of seeing—and, indeed, modalities of perception and representation more generally, even for those who cannot read or see.

51

Reproduction
Adrienne Asch

The field of disability studies already contributes to the understanding of reproduction and disability and can further enrich thinking on this topic. Whether scholars and policy makers focus on children who will be born with disabilities, or on the less commonly discussed area of people with disabilities becoming genetic or rearing parents, the basic questions raised by reproduction concern quality-of-life issues for the child and family, and the effects on the larger society. When a child is born with a disability, concerns focus on the impact of the disability upon the child her- or himself, the impact of living with such a child on the life of the (assumed-to-be-nondisabled) parents and siblings, and the consequences of childhood disability for the educational, social service, and health care systems. Scholars and policy makers who consider the person with a disability as a parent question whether he or she will transmit a genetic condition to a child, the outcome for a nondisabled child raised by a parent with a disability, and the effects on society of families that include people with disabilities.

In the late nineteenth century and early twentieth century, long before biologists knew a great deal about the mechanisms of heredity, a number of U.S. scientists and intellectuals promoted the idea that the nation could be improved by limiting or preventing the births of people expected to be noncontributing members of society because they were ill, disabled, or morally degenerate (Paul 1998). Although these ideas were eventually criticized by those who opposed the racial and ethnic overtones of pre–World War II eugenic laws and practices, even voluntary ones (Duster 1990), there was very little explicit protest about disability bias. Until the advent of scholarship and activism based on a social model of disability, few clinicians and bioethicists ever questioned the wisdom of using technologies to prevent bringing children with disabilities into the world.

Beginning in the early 1980s, disability scholars and activists in North America, Europe, and Australia began to mount various critiques of the practice of routine testing of fetuses (and later embryos) in order to screen out or select against future people with disabilities (Fine and Asch 1982; Finger 1984; Saxton 1984; Shakespeare 1995; Bérubé 1996; Newell 1999; Asch and Wasserman 2005; Asch and Barlevy 2012). Although not all authors articulated their critiques in identical terms, three main points surface in many of these critiques. First, even if all prospective parents tested embryos and fetuses to ensure that only those free from detectable disabilities came to term, society would never eliminate the vast majority of disabling conditions. In order to promote the goals of equality and inclusion promised by the Americans with Disabilities Act (1990) or the UN Convention on the Rights of Persons with Disabilities (2008), nations would still need to remove barriers that now prevent people with disabilities from achieving these espoused goals. Second, despite existing discrimination, people with disabilities and their families can and do flourish. As public spaces, institutions, and attitudes become more inclusive, many of the hardships associated with disability will decrease. Much of the argument against bringing children with disabilities into the family and into the world arises from serious misunderstandings of the effects of disability on people's lives, informed by the assumption that disability leads to a diminished quality of life for the individual and the family.

The third point of the critique is addressed to prospective parents as well as policy makers and health professionals. Disability is only one of a person's many characteristics, and prospective parents need to recognize that a child with a disability has a host of other attributes that will be much like those of children without disabilities and will permit parents to reap rewards akin to those of the parents of nondisabled children. The information given to prospective parents about a future child's disability needs to be put into the context of the parents' hopes for and expectations of family life. That information must include specifics about how children with any given condition negotiate school, play, and family and social life. With richer and more comprehensive information about family life that includes a child with a disability, prospective parents may be better able to envision welcoming a child with a disability into their lives.

This disability-equality view—unlike the "sanctity-of-life" arguments with which it is erroneously equated—respects the idea that some people may not wish to become parents of any child at any time, or at a particular time in their lives. However, it asks prospective parents, as well as the professionals who advise them, and the society in which they all live, to imagine whether they can be open to raising a child with a host of characteristics that could include disabling traits. According to the Prenatally and Postnatally Diagnosed Conditions Awareness Act of 2008, if, after receiving thorough information about a possible disability in an embryo or fetus, prospective parents conclude that they are unwilling or unable to raise a child with that characteristic, they should be able to make whatever reproductive choice they wish. Although contemporary reproductive testing differs from the early state-sponsored eugenics in that it is not officially coercive, practitioners may pressure prospective parents into feeling they have only one legitimate choice. According to the disability critique, practitioners should respect both the choice not to go forward if a likely disability will result and the choice to continue with implanting an embryo or maintaining a pregnancy when a disabling trait has been diagnosed. True reproductive choice requires both information about life with a range of characteristics and the respect of the professionals and the larger society for any well-thought-out choice prospective parents might make.

Much of the professional attention given to family and disability has gone into avoiding the births of children who would have disabilities, and thus the scholarly discussions of reproduction and disability from within disability studies have centered largely on rethinking the prenatal context. But a growing body of literature from people with disabilities who are themselves parents of children with and without disabilities, along with a body of law and social science literature, is beginning to examine the lives of disabled parents and their children.

Although no academic or societal consensus exists on the essentials for adequate parenting (LaFollette 2010), it has not been uncommon for adoption agencies, social service workers, or doctors to discourage people with a wide range of disabling conditions from undertaking child rearing (Mathews 1992; Mutcherson 2009). To the extent that people (especially women) with disabilities were perceived as helpless and incapable of caring for themselves, much less anyone else, women and men whose disabilities occurred before the age of typical child rearing were discouraged from becoming biological or rearing parents. The cultural messages were that they would harm future children either by passing on a genetic condition or by burdening children with a parent or parents who would be incapable of providing typical child care.

Fortunately, academic and autobiographical literature from within disability studies supports the contention that disability in and of itself need not preclude rewarding experiences for parent or child (Thurman 1985; Preston 1994; Jacobson 1999; Wates and Rowen 1999; Blind Parents Interest Group of the National Federation of the Blind 2012; National Public Radio 2013). Just as reproductive choice should mean respecting the decisions of women and men to raise or not to raise a child based on their goals for family life, it should also mean respect and support for the choice of people with disabilities to enjoy what many others without disabilities take to be one of the primary goods of life: the opportunity to nurture a future generation.

Disability studies scholars can advance the understanding of reproduction and disability through empirical research, philosophical and policy analysis, and examinations and thoughtful accounts of the lives of people with disabilities and their families. Also important is attention to the ways that cultural views, institutional practices, law, medicine, and science shape the context in which parents raise their children and in which children develop.

Much more remains to be learned about reproduction and disability from the experiences of children and adults who grow up in families where someone has a disability. Future scholarship must consider such questions as the following: What are the psychological, economic, and social circumstances that thwart or promote the well being of children born with disabilities in today's society, or that thwart or promote children raised in homes where one or both parents may have a disability? What information do prospective parents seek from prenatal testing, and what do they get? How does use of prenatal diagnosis and selective termination influence people's subsequent parenting experience? How can law, cultural change, or technological change facilitate the lives of families in which a child or parent has a disability?

52

Rights

Maya Sabatello

The concept of rights is central to disability studies: it reflects the clearest recognition of persons with disabilities as subjects under the law who are empowered to demand, on an equal basis with others, what they are entitled to as an integral part of the human race. This understanding marks a stark shift—and a crucial development—from the historical conceptualization of persons with disabilities as objects who lack reason and ability to make decisions, and hence who cannot be bearers of rights.

Rights are the fundamental normative principles of freedom or entitlement stipulating what one is allowed to perform or is owed by others. Rights exist in both national and international law, and they form the basis of an increasingly accepted international language that addresses issues of dignity, needs, and justice. In modern times, individuals are assumed to possess rights simply by virtue of being human. These rights are inalienable and universal. They apply equally to all across the world, and they cannot be withheld or withdrawn by states, governments, or private actors. Nonetheless, persons with disabilities have been historically excluded from "rights talk." With the growing influence of an international disability rights movement, efforts to remedy this wrong have in recent decades gained traction, culminating in the UN Convention on the Rights of Persons with Disabilities (CRPD), ratified in 2008.

The idea of human rights is ancient, and related principles of fairness, justice, and humanity exist in most societies and cultures. The concept of human rights protection, however, is believed to have emerged during the seventeenth and eighteenth centuries by Enlightenment-era philosophers who utilized the idea of natural law—that the authority of God or nature superseded government law—to bolster political struggles against absolutism. John Locke's theory of natural rights, for example, conferred under the social contract reflected an important shift in emphasis from the centrality of states and society to the individual, who could now make claims against the government.

The atrocities committed in World War II, such as the Nazis' systematic persecution and execution of persons with disabilities masquerading as a public health policy, formed the springboard for the modern concept of human rights. Subsequently, fervent calls were made to establish international norms that recognize the inalienable rights of individuals, especially the right to life and to dignity, while curtailing state power and preventing the recurrence of such events. Accordingly, the United Nations Charter (1945) stipulates the promotion and protection of human rights among the organization's main purposes, allowing also the later adoption of legally binding human rights treaties.

These developments have had only a limited impact on the lives of persons with disabilities. One reason for this is that disability rights claims are often seen as positive rights. Negative rights, such as voting and political participation, are assumed to require noninterference on the part of the state, and as such they allegedly impose no burden or cost. Conversely, positive rights focus on welfare (e.g., education, health, work) and are assumed to require extensive governmental action. Because disability rights often involve a request for special treatment and accommodation, they are commonly viewed as falling within the scope of positive rights and, hence, as expensive and unreasonably burdensome for states to implement.

Critics have challenged the accuracy of the division between negative and positive rights, arguing that it is impossible to seriously consider the right to life—a stipulated civil and political right—independent of freedom from hunger and the right to provide for oneself, which are economic, social, and cultural rights. They counter the charge by arguing that implementing civil and political rights is also costly and that the benefits of an inclusive society surpass the expense. For example, the loss of wages, income taxes, and public assistance expenses due to the exclusion of persons with disabilities cost far more than accommodating them in the workplace. The human costs of exclusion—the denial of financial independence, and the right to participate in and to play a responsible and productive role in society—should also be considered.

Another reason is that basing disability claims for justice merely in terms of legal rights, without a concept of moral rights, is inadequate. Legal positivists such as Austin and H. L. A. Hart hold that rights exist only in connection with a governmental legal system, when the rules of that system prescribe the right and the right is enforceable. Such an understanding of rights has only limited application in the disability context. As critical race theorists and feminists have argued, the analysis and adjudication of legal rights aim at maintaining the interests of wealthy and powerful elites—whereas persons with disabilities are commonly among the poorest and most vulnerable minorities. Given that most countries in the world do not have disability rights laws, successful disability rights rely on natural law and moral rights claims that supersede and are independent of governmental law.

Moreover, for some subgroups of persons with disabilities to be recognized as separate minorities, an acceptance of some notion of group, rather than only individualized, rights is essential. Traditional Western liberal theory assumes that rights are private, individualized, and autonomous, whereas group rights focus on collectives that have shared interests and aim at protecting cultures, ways of life and practices that are presumably not sufficiently protected by the assertion of individual interests. In the context of disability rights, this debate is rooted in the call to recognize a *group*'s political identity, pride, and sense of self-determination. The Deaf community in the United States may be the most vocal group in this regard; however, persons with mental disabilities (Mad Pride), dwarfism (Little People of America), and autism (autism rights movement), as well as indigenous people with disabilities have also demanded group recognition. To be sure, the notion of group rights does not necessarily conflict with the political theory of liberal democracies—in fact, group rights are central to the strands of multiculturalism and identity politics that have been promoted within those political systems (Taylor 1994). However, the concept of group rights raises acute debates about the potential subjugation of individual freedoms and rights to the interests of the communities.

Prevailing theories about the function and justification of rights make it all the more difficult to justify disability rights claims—especially those of the most severely disabled people. Their proponents hold that to be regarded as a "rights holder," one must have agency and rationality. This understanding is exclusionary, however, as persons with disabilities are often viewed as objects, and persons with cognitive and mental disabilities are viewed as especially lacking the qualifications for personhood. Holding persons with disabilities to the universally unrealistic test of autonomous rationality, conventional theories of rights fail to consider the interdependency of all human beings. For example, some states ban persons with mental and cognitive disabilities from voting on the basis that a disabled person's political position may be influenced or coerced by others. This argument ignores the fact that political campaigns, by their very nature, aim at persuading individuals toward one political stance over another. From a disability perspective, then, an essential alternative would be a model that seeks to further the rights holder's interests.

Disability activists developed the minority group model in response to the exclusion of people with disabilities from classic liberal versions of rights (Barnes 1991; Oliver 1990). This model was highly influential in the development of various non–legally binding human rights instruments on national and international levels, such as UN declarations and resolutions. Because it assumes that equality is achieved if the law treats all persons alike, it neglects the fact that individuals and groups are not identically situated, and thus lack equal opportunities. Indeed, some persons with disabilities are subject to multiple or aggravated forms of discrimination on the basis of race, color, sex, or other status.

Successive attempts to justify disability rights have been based on the concepts of human needs and dignity. Key to these efforts is the so-called capability approach (CA) developed by Amartya Sen and significantly expanded by Martha Nussbaum. This theory claims that the freedom to achieve well-being is of primary moral importance. It should be understood in terms of people's capabilities: the substantive freedoms or practical opportunities achieved via a combination of internal capabilities and a suitable economic, social, and political environment. This theory also recognizes the interrelationship between the two generations of rights: civil and political, as well as economic, social, and cultural rights. Notwithstanding criticism of Nussbaum's approach for being exclusive of persons with severe intellectual disabilities, the CA has been increasingly applied by activists, scholars, and international bodies such as the World Bank for the advancement of disability rights.

The CRPD provides a comprehensive instrument to address disability rights by maintaining the intrinsic value and equality of all human beings. It takes a social and relational approach to disability, combining the two generations of rights with the right to development. The rights enshrined in the CRPD have innovative features tailored to a disability perspective, such as stipulating lack of reasonable accommodation as discrimination; accessibility; and endorsing legal capacity and supportive decision making, as well as the right to live independently and to be included in the community. The development and providence of information, communication, and assistive technologies are also tied into the entire scope of human rights. The CRPD also establishes the notion of so-called inclusive development, which charges states with including persons with disabilities in the development, implementation, and monitoring of programs in their regard.

However, challenges do persist. Some states still do not recognize persons with disabilities as full rights holders. There has been no explicit requirement that states abolish special education. And disagreement remains over the implications of selective reproduction, genetics, euthanasia, and eugenics for the furtherance of disability rights. How these will be resolved—and how the other enumerated rights are to be fully implemented—is yet to be seen.

53

Senses

Kathryn Linn Geurts

The "senses" often are treated by science, medicine, and humanistic scholarship as a phenomenon affecting distinct individual bodies, but much contemporary scholarship has revolutionized how we think about the senses. For the past few decades, at approximately the same time that disability studies has developed as an academic discipline and professional field, the "anthropology of the senses" has grown in importance and has contributed to the emergence of the interdisciplinary field known as sensory studies (Bull et al. 2006). New work in sensory anthropology challenges not only the five senses model but also the notion that the experience of sensing is individualized and distinct. For example, while the term "senses" typically connotes the five modalities of hearing, taste, touch, smell, and sight, our capacities for sensory experience are not confined to these discrete channels. Humans actually possess and rely on far more than five senses. This becomes more clear when we acknowledge both exteroreceptors and interoreceptors—the former being organs that process olfaction, gustation, aurality, tactility, and visuality, and the latter referring to processes such as the vestibular system, kinesthesia, and proprioception (Geurts 2002). In addition, human sensory experience is even more complex if we are willing to include phenomena such as pheromone receptivity or a biosonar capacity called "echolocation." Any and all of these biological systems, however, can become impaired. For this reason, there is an obvious yet often neglected relationship between thinking about the senses and human experiences of disability (blindness and deafness being exceptions, since medicine has traditionally classified these conditions as "sensory impairments").

In the past few decades, sensorial anthropologists have argued for the sociality of sensations and the inter-subjective dimension of sensory processes and experience. As David Howes, one of the pioneers of sensory studies, puts it: "To a greater or lesser extent, every domain of sensory experience, from the sight of a work of art to the scent of perfume to the savor of dinner, is a field of cultural elaboration. Every domain of sensory experience is also an arena for structuring social roles and interactions. We learn social divisions, distinctions of gender, class and race, through our senses" (2003, xi). Still, the phenomenology of the senses has not been, generally speaking, as thoroughly engaged by scholars in disability studies as it might be.

Some senses have, by necessity, been used in auto-biographical and narrative writing in relation to disability; accounts of "blindness" and "deafness" as well as forms of mobility impairment or neurocognitive difference always draw on the senses to establish traction. For example, Helen Keller organized her auto-biographical account *The World I Live In* (1908) around classic sensory modalities. She described how her "seeing hand" guided her through the material world and how those tactile views could, in turn, stimulate her mind and imagination. With olfaction so vital to her experience, she reflected on why smell had been relegated to a "fallen angel." In many ways Keller deployed sense-based analogies to stress how she was more like her readers than they might think: "I understand how scarlet can differ from crimson because I know that the smell of an orange is not the smell of a grapefruit" (1908, 105). Jacques Lusseyran's *And There Was Light* (1963) recounts his first twenty years, including an accident in a schoolyard that transformed his limited eyesight into blindness. As a small child he held colored crayons and blocks in his hands, bringing them close to his eyes, to experience "light." He could identify various buildings throughout town by their smells—a perceptual experience undoubtedly shared with sighted people, though their awareness of it may not be as keen as Lusseyran's. Denying that blindness is even an impairment, Lusseyran asserts, "The only way to be completely cured" of blindness "is never to treat it as a difference, a reason for separation, an infirmity. . . . The cure is to immerse oneself again and without delay in a life that is as real and difficult as the lives of others" (36).

The sensorially rich narrative accounts of Keller, Lusseyran, and others help readers to understand that despite their impairments, these disabled individuals continue to share with all humans the spirit and consciousness that mark our species. Jean-Dominique Bauby's autobiography *The Diving Bell and the Butterfly* (1997), for example, sensuously depicts his experience with locked-in syndrome: he had no ability to speak and virtually no capacity to move, he was deaf in one ear, and he had both a numb zone and an area with some feeling on his face. Humanity often deems a person in this state to be a "vegetable," but Bauby's autobiography reveals that despite his locked-in syndrome, he continued to experience intense pleasure through conjuring up vibrant sensory imagery.

Yet the sensory autobiography approach to disabled experience has some inherent limitations. It has been referred to by some as auto/somatography and characterized as a genre of writing "devoted to exploring bodily experience" and to depicting "lives distinctively shaped by anomalous bodies or unusual somatic conditions" (Couser 2009, 164). Although the writing or the prose in these works is often lyrically descriptive and sensual, for some scholars such "autopathographies" often seem to hew too closely to the medical model of disability's understanding of the body rather than to that of the social model.

Furthermore, disability studies has intentionally downplayed attention to the senses because of its commitment to advancing the social model of disability. As Mitchell and Snyder have argued, disability studies "strategically neglected the question of the experience of disabled embodiment in order to disassociate disability from its mooring in medical cultures and institutions" (2001, 368). Detailing the sensory experiences of anomalous/monstrous bodies arguably was a form of exoticizing and fetishizing, or else putting a microscope to disabled people's sensory-affective experiences for the voyeuristic use of the audience. From such a position one could conclude that disability is an individual experience that does not require social action and structural change. Mitchell and Snyder further argue that "since disabled bodies had endured such a history of debilitating classifications, disability studies purposely refrained from formulating the embodied experiences of disabled people. This neglect was willful and strategic: it explicitly sought to leave an overanalyzed entity mercifully alone" (374). For decades, therefore, disability studies actively discouraged a phenomenological or sensory approach, favoring instead political accounts that focused on social exclusion.

Some feminist theorists within disability studies have consistently critiqued this avoidance of sensory/ embodied elements (e.g., Shildrick and Price 1998). In "Sensing Disability," Marian Corker argued that ignoring sensibility perpetuates "masculinist notions of presence, visibility, material 'reality,' and identity as 'given'" (2001, 39). Corker's powerful "critique of ontological imperialism" suggests that even disability studies has promoted an understanding of "being" that reifies bifurcation, ocularcentrism, and stable or fixed realities. The masculinist "givenness" that she points to underlies the way that our understandings of presence, visibility, material reality, and identity deny mutability, fluidity, and transience—all of which come to the fore when we focus on the senses and sensory practices. "Sensibility" by necessity is premised on the understanding that biological difference and sociocultural difference are mutually constitutive so that one's body and one's sociocultural surroundings change continuously (36). Feminist scholars in general rejected pathological constructions of the female body, as well as overdetermined notions of the female or feminine. But when it came to eliding sensation, Corker argued that the "dis-abling of sensibility effects a closure on valuable, insightful, and imaginative ways, *sensed* ways of being and knowing that can make collective expressions of disability more responsive and responsible" (42).

As the sensual revolution in scholarship has spread, disability studies has responded by fusing poetics and politics and attending simultaneously to sensory practices and social critique. For instance, in *Too Late to Die Young* (2005), Harriet McBryde Johnson broaches hardhitting topics such as disability legislation, selective infanticide of disabled infants, and muscular dystrophy telethon fraud even while acknowledging the importance of sensory perception and human sensuousness. Michael Schillmeier's *Rethinking Disability: Bodies, Senses, and Things* (2010) exemplifies the potential to explore and theorize how sensory practices can enable and/or disable. He shows how close study of the relations among bodies, minds, senses, and things is necessary for a deeper understanding of "the social" and the ways in which "inclusive differences highlight the connection between human and non-human relations that make up the different enabling and/or disabling scenarios of societal realties" (167). These are exciting critical moves, for they demonstrate that sensory studies and disability studies can stimulate growth through cross-fertilization. A disability studies perspective is vital for sensory studies to stay grounded in the difficult political reality of diverse human bodies consistently experiencing exclusion in social organization across the globe. And sensory studies can encourage scholarship in disability studies to continue pushing human sensuousness—in all its myriad forms—as a critical research agenda.

54

Sex

Margrit Shildrick

There can be few practices in everyday life that arouse such strong responses—both positive and negative—as sex. For all its joyous and pleasurable connotations, sex always has the capacity to make people feel uncomfortable, even ashamed. Nowhere is this more evident than in the conjunction of disability and sexuality. Even in the twenty-first century, there is still a widespread public perception that people with disabilities are either asexual or, the complete opposite, sexually out of control and requiring management. Either pole leads to damaging consequences not just for disabled people themselves but, arguably, for "normal" nondisabled society at large, which remains unable to acknowledge diversity fully and locked into rigid and conventional models of what sex consists.

What, then, is meant by that seemingly simple term "sex"? For many, sex begins and ends with one's own relationship to sexual practice, itself a fraught area of inquiry. In its most basic form, sex is taken to be an innate biological attribute that enables human beings to reproduce themselves over time. Sex is also usually taken to encompass issues of self-identity, self-esteem, interdependence, and social relations, all of which are typically gathered under the rubric of sexuality. Religions of all cultures have played a major part in propagating restricted views of sexuality, and historically have set strict parameters around the contexts in which sex, as a practice, should occur. Sex is, for example, usually highly gendered. Heterosexual sex is the approved form;

it involves just two adults (male: active and female: passive); intercourse is understood as the proper medium; and its primary purpose is not pleasure but the propagation of children.

Clearly, the traditionally dominant model of sex is for many people a historical relic. Nevertheless, it continues to exert a real force on prevailing attitudes and values, even in the most developed Western societies. The presumptive link between sex and reproduction is particularly pernicious with regard to disability. Even when the biological urge to procreate *is* acknowledged among those whose embodiment differs from the norm, the overriding response is that people with disabilities should not be entitled to sexual relations for fear that they will pass on congenital abnormalities. Even with knowledge of the worst eugenic excesses of the last century, the question of sterilization—usually in relation to cognitively disabled young women—still crops up with some regularity. Social policies that concern people with disabilities continue to see sex as a problem to be managed. Sex education for young people with disabilities is rarely provided, while institutions, group homes, and families often seek to limit expressions of disabled youths' sexuality to something more like friendship.

Yet disabled people, like everyone else, understand their own sexualities in multiple different ways, which do not easily fit within convenient models of social management. There is, of course, sometimes a real need to protect disabled people from sexual exploitation, particularly where power relations are in evidence. But regulation is not always the right answer. Would it not be better to provide targeted sex education that maximizes and supports opportunities for personal choices and exploration rather than trying to channel sexual feelings into "safe" asexual outlets or to silence them altogether? In *The Sexual Politics of Disability*, Shakespeare, Gillespie-Sells, and Davies (1996) gave a variety of disabled people the opportunity to talk about sexual needs and desires that far exceeded prevailing myths of sexual indifference. As their title implies, the book demonstrated—much as feminism and gay liberation had done in previous decades—that talking about disabled sexuality is about more than just recognizing and voicing individual sexual practices. The large-scale empirical project by Nosek et al. (2001) into the sexuality of physically disabled women also brings to attention both the magnitude of sexual experience and the degree to which it is thwarted, while Russell Shuttleworth's (2002) research with men with cerebral palsy does the same for male sexuality.

Why has the topic of sex within disability rights activism and disability studies taken so long to arrive alongside other more widely acknowledged political and disciplinary concerns? If those who count themselves as nondisabled have largely disavowed the conjunction of disability and sexuality, experiencing what can only be regarded as the "yuck factor" when faced with the realities of sexual desire in all of their anomalous forms, then we might conclude that it is because sexuality is always a site of deep-seated anxieties about normative forms of embodied being (Shildrick 2009). We should not be surprised, then, if people with disabilities exhibit many of the same conventional negative feelings toward sex. Indeed, though scarcely acknowledged, many physically disabled people hold dismissive views of the sexuality of those with cognitive and developmental disabilities. Beyond a shared entanglement in the sociocultural imaginary, however, the influence of the medical model of disability has dominated discussions of disabled sexuality, leading to measures as varied as eugenic sterilization and the well-meaning but controlling machinations of social workers.

For many, the emergence of the social model of disability in the early 1990s was a huge advance over the existing medical model, which blatantly pathologized disabled people's bodies even in the absence of what could be called disease or ill health. The social model focused on countering discriminatory law and policy by identifying the social and political obstacles routinely experienced by people with bodily or cognitive impairments. Over the past few decades, rapid improvements—at least in the Global North—in access to jobs, housing, leisure activities, and education have led to positive outcomes for people with disabilities. The downside, however, is the relative neglect of issues relating to disabled embodiment and subjectivity. The practical, affective, and emotional dimensions of living with a disability, not least in the arena of all things pertaining to sex, were until quite recently given little voice. The dominant discourse surrounding legislation and rights for people with disabilities has to an appreciable extent drowned out any adequate consideration of more nebulous issues. It is true that the demand for sexual citizenship is gaining momentum in activist contexts; yet such demands often reduce sexuality to that which can be measured, categorized, and, one could argue, domesticated (Shildrick 2013). As Gayle Rubin (1984) pointed out in her essay on the "charmed circle" of normative heterosexuality, gaining entrance to the citizenship club fails to challenge the normative organization of sexual matters.

Far more progressive, and often radical, understandings of disability and sex have encouraged scholars and activists to confront questions of embodiment and, more specifically, the circulation of desire. In conventional, and certainly psychoanalytic terms, desire—for nondisabled and disabled people alike—is always a response to a lack that, ultimately, is never satisfied. For Deleuze and Guattari (1987), bodies are never whole, singular, and autonomous but are simply part of extensive assemblages that include not simply human beings but animal and mechanistic components of all kinds. According to this Deleuzian model, desire is not centered on sexual practice between autonomous bodies but between those disparate elements without fixing on any particular sexual aim (e.g., reproduction) or sexual object (e.g., the penis or vagina). Desire, then, figures both "a network of flows, energies and capacities that are always open to transformation [that] cannot be determined in advance" (Shildrick 2009, 132) and a move away from unsatisfied internal drives to the positivity of mutual becomings.

The implications of such a Deleuzian model of sexuality for people with disabilities is considerable, given that embodied desire enacts all sorts of differential couplings, with no single privileged form. The reliance of many disabled people on assistive or prosthetic devices, for instance, or the support of other human bodies, to facilitate sexual encounters becomes thus unremarkable. Embodiment no longer implies separate and self-contained entities but operates intercorporeally on a "plane that is as hospitable to disabled people as it is to any others" (Shildrick 2009, 140). In the terrain of assemblages, corporeal difference loses its normative significance. At the same time, desire itself—pleasure, danger, uncertainty, joy—takes on multiple different forms and possibilities that can be regarded as much the province of disabled people as they are for the nondisabled majority.

Such new ways of imagining the relationship between disability and sex are far from mainstream, and are often alien to those struggling against the legacies of eugenics or the common prejudices that equate disability with sexual dysfunction. But they are rapidly gaining ground among disability theorists, such as Gibson (2006), Goodley and Lawthom (2011), Shildrick (2004, 2009), and others who have similarly made linkages between disability and queer theory. Many people with disabilities do, of course, identify as nonheterosexual and face similar difficulties to other LGBT people, but the term "queer" goes much further in being explicitly defined against all forms of normativity, not just sexual norms (see especially McRuer 2006). As Serlin notes, it is a matter of "demystifying the cultural and political roots of terms like *normal* and *healthy* and *whole* at the same time [as seeking] to destigmatize the conceptual differences implied by those terms" (2006, 159). Far from thinking about the conjunction of disability and sexuality as a site of fear and voyeuristic fascination for mainstream society, or else something to be monitored and controlled, sex in this expanded mode of desire celebrates the as yet unrealized potentials of all anomalous embodiment. Opening up the meanings of sex and sexuality for disabled people entails rethinking the whole nexus with respect to us all.

55

Sexuality

Robert McRuer

The history of the keyword "sexuality" is inextricably interwoven with the history of a range of other disability keywords, including "freakish," "innocent," and—most important—"normal" and "abnormal." As philosopher Michel Foucault has demonstrated, for the past few centuries, we have inhabited a culture of "normalization" that categorizes individuals and populations, marking certain bodies (for instance, those understood as disabled, ill, or lacking) *and* certain desires (for instance, those understood as perverse, queer, or mad) as "abnormal." Systems of surveillance, control, intervention, incarceration, correction, or "cure"— what Foucault (2003) would describe as "technologies of normalization" administered by authorities assumed to possess "expert opinion"—emerged in the eighteenth century and intensified over the course of the nineteenth to facilitate this categorization. Sexuality was one of the most distinct areas of social life to succumb to these systems of control and cure.

In the first volume of his book *The History of Sexuality* (1978), Foucault argued that a widespread belief emerged by the late nineteenth century that sexuality was simply "repressed" and in need of "liberation." *The History of Sexuality* worked to challenge this truism and illuminate the ways in which the contours of "sexuality" were clearly visible *within* a history of normalization (rather than beyond, in some imagined future when "repression" would have supposedly withered away). Foucault thus excavated how "sexuality"

experienced an "incitement to discourse": far from being (simply) repressed, in other words, sexuality was endlessly talked about, managed, pathologized, and (often) "corrected."

Although disability is not one of Foucault's topics in *The History of Sexuality*, his discussion of sexuality as a product of endless discourse could also be true of "ability." Through what Foucault understood as a "proliferation of discourses," "ability" and "disability," like "sexuality," materialized as supposedly knowable entities. The emergence and naturalization of these discourses positioned sexuality and ability not only as culturally and historically specific modes of experience but also as cross-temporal and in some cases even universal components of what it means to be a human being. The naturalization of sexuality and ability both privileged and linked what eventually came to be understood as "able-bodiedness" and "heterosexuality" (McRuer 2002). For instance, professional psychologists and sexologists (most notoriously, Richard von Krafft-Ebing and his study *Psychopathia Sexualis* [1886]) pathologized homosexuality and other perversions, linking them to a wide array of physical and mental impairments or disabilities.

Since the 1970s, historians of sexuality such as John D'Emilio (1983) have more specifically demonstrated the ways in which the processes of putting sexuality into discourse produced a binary system of understanding human sexuality that ultimately privileged "heterosexuality" and subordinated "homosexuality" and other so-called perversions. The sexualities known as "heterosexual" and "homosexual," then, are not somehow timeless and natural but socially constructed or "invented" (Katz 1990). In his influential essay "Capitalism and Gay Identity" (1983), D'Emilio tied this invention of sexuality to the history of industrial capitalism, arguing that as work (for men and some women) became increasingly associated with a "public" space outside the home, a homosexual or gay identity became available to certain people who discovered each other in "homosexual" locations (bars, clubs, bathhouses) that emerged throughout the West. The home, meanwhile, was no longer understood primarily as a space where inhabitants worked together for survival but rather as an ideological (private and newly "heterosexual") space where one could expect to find happiness and respite from the public world of work. This new heterosexual space was also arguably able-bodied as well, as "disability" was purged from the home (McRuer 2006). Rates of institutionalization (removal from private home spaces) skyrocketed by more than 1500 percent, for instance, between 1870 and 1915, particularly marking those deemed "feebleminded" as in need of relocation, regulation, containment, and control (Trent 1994).

D'Emilio's history fleshed out what Foucault himself famously insisted: that discourses of homosexuality materialized a "new species" of person. This new "species" was increasingly regulated by the state over the course of the late nineteenth century and into the twentieth century (Canaday 2009). Heterosexuality, in turn, solidified as the identity of the normal and *healthy* dominant group, and "heterosexuals" began to understand themselves as such. This period of increasing state control, as the institutionalization of the "feebleminded" and others suggests, was characterized by extreme intervention and regulation around disability as well (Longmore and Umansky 2001). The parallel control of disability suggests that disability in its modern form always has been implicitly, if not explicitly, integrated into the complex discursive emergence of "sexuality" in the West. Among the many ways the histories of sexuality and disability are intermeshed, we might highlight at least three. First, like "homosexuals" more generally, disabled people were subject to pathologization and normalization.

"Abnormal" sexuality, for instance, was understood to be the cause of, or at least be related to, illness and disability, such that "abnormal" embodiment was often understood to be accompanied by "abnormal" desires and (consequently) an "abnormal" sexuality. A long-standing belief that certain disabled people have "excessive" sexual desires and thus an excessive sexuality emerges from this linkage.

The generally accepted (and often causally created) link between these two perceived forms of pathological excess entailed at times excessively cruel and permanently damaging forms of "rehabilitation," such as shock therapy, sterilization, or castration. In 1927, for instance, the U.S. Supreme Court famously ruled that Carrie Buck, who had been deemed "feebleminded" and institutionalized for "incorrigible" and "promiscuous" behavior and who became pregnant after being raped, must be compulsorily sterilized. "Three generations of imbeciles is enough," Chief Justice Oliver Wendell Holmes declared for the court's majority opinion, reflecting the belief that both disability and perversion could be transmitted to future generations (Trent 1994). The early twentieth-century notion that disabled people's sexuality is excessive also can be traced in numerous cultural sites—from the freak show, where visitors might be titillated by exhibits representing both bodily difference and excessive sexuality, to literary representations such as William Faulkner's *The Sound and the Fury* (1929), in which a cognitively disabled figure, Benjy, is castrated because he is perceived to be dangerous.

During the twentieth century, a second intertwining of sexuality and disability has also emerged: not of pathological excess but of the seemingly paradoxical notion that disabled people are outside of the system of sexuality altogether. Disabled people often have been discursively constructed as incapable of having sexual desires or a sexual identity, due to their supposed "innocence."

The distinction between "excessive" and "innocent" often drew upon caricatures of race and class, as poor or working-class people (such as Carrie Buck) or people of color more likely were understood as excessive and dangerous than their white, middle-class, disabled counterparts. Still, the line between innocent and excessive was often very thin, and a given disabled figure (such as Faulkner's Benjy) could quickly cross from one side to the other.

A third intertwining of sexuality and disability can be identified in the form of disabled people's complex positioning in new systems of sexual and disabled identities. These newer, more generative understandings of the relationship between disability and sexuality have allowed, at times, for the development of alternate forms of sexual experience and subjectivity that were potentially outside of the increasingly rigidified heterosexual/homosexual binary. Historian David Serlin (2012), for example, recounts how some mid-twentieth-century sexologists, working with and interviewing disabled women about their bodies and pleasures, were confounded by forms of intimacy, touch, and autoeroticism that did not fit neatly into emerging understandings of sexuality or sexual identity. Exclusion from normality or a presumption that one could not be part of the heterosexual/homosexual system, in other words, sometimes allowed for disabled pleasures and disabled ways of knowing that were not reducible to dominant systems of heterosexuality that were dependent on able-bodied definitions of sexual norms.

These three distinct though overlapping components in a disabled history of sexuality have become legible in late twentieth-century and early twenty-first-century deployments of "sexuality," particularly by and around activists in the disability rights movement. As disabled people began to speak or sign back to the systems that historically had contained them, they deliberately confronted ideas of excessive, innocent, or alternative sexuality. This entailed at times asserting that disabled people, too, did not have excessive or unusual but "normal" (and heterosexual) sexualities. In the United States, for instance, many activists strategically challenged federal marriage penalties that would cut off benefits such as Supplemental Security Income (SSI) for disabled people who married. Activists also argued for "liberation" from "repressive" ideas, thereby repudiating the widespread notion that disabled people's sexuality was innocent or nonexistent (Shakespeare, Gillespie-Sells, and Davies 1996). Disabled activists also worked with and through theories of disability to discover or invent new (and often queer) pleasures and sexualities. Many writers, performers, artists, and activists in disability culture as it has flourished in the early twenty-first century represent the possibilities inherent in this third intertwining area of sexuality and disability. They include Mark O'Brien, Loree Erickson, Terry Galloway, Mat Fraser, Eli Clare, Greg Walloch, and Bethany Stevens, the last of whom is a self-proclaimed "uppity crip scholar activist and sexologist." Using this language, Stevens joins other disabled activists and artists who are self-consciously appropriating and resignifying terms from the oppressive history of sexology. Mark O'Brien's poetry and creative nonfiction, perhaps especially his essay "On Seeing a Sex Surrogate" (1990; the basis for the film *The Sessions* [2012]), mark a particular turning point toward this third strategy.

In 1992, Anne Finger asserted, "Sexuality is often the source of our deepest oppression; it is also often the source of our deepest pain. It's easier for us to talk about—and formulate strategies for changing—discrimination in employment, education, and housing than to talk about our exclusion from sexuality and reproduction" (9). Finger's assertion—which might serve as a gloss to all three strategies for responding to the disabled history of sexuality—had become well known and had traveled through a range of locations in both disability rights and disability studies, as the twenty-first century began (Siebers 2008b; McRuer and Mollow 2012). Sexuality does indeed remain, two decades later, a "source of oppression" for disabled people, but it has also become a profoundly productive site for invention, experimentation, and transformation.

56

Space
Rob Imrie

A fundamental part of people's existence is their emplacement in space and their relationships with objects that are geographically located at different points or places. Space is one of the major axioms of being and of life itself. It is where we are located, the places where we live and move around, and the multiple relationships that take shape among them. Space is characterized by the primacy of what Paterson and Hughes (1999, 607) describe as "non-impaired carnality," or the projection of the body-normal as the embodiment of those without impairment. Wherever one goes, one is reminded of the absolutism of the nonimpaired body and the crafting of space as places that are not easily accessible to, or usable by, people with different types of impairment. For example, from the design of steps into public buildings that prevent wheelchair access, to the absence of legible signage that may prevent ease of way finding, the construction of space is characterized by an inequality of provision. This is a world that Tony Fry aptly describes as "surrounded by things designed to function in ways that go unquestioned and absolutely taken for granted" (2009, 29).

For David Harvey, paraphrasing Raymond Williams (1985, 88), space is "one of the most complicated words in our language" (2006, 270). Although it has diverse meanings, it is most commonly defined with reference to three types: absolute space, relative space, and relational space. Writing in 1689, Isaac Newton regarded absolute space as "without relation to anything external . . . always similar and immovable" (Newton and Motte 1934, 6). For example, objects, such as buildings, have such qualities by occupying a specific terrain and are bounded by a fixed and delimited, usually legal, territory. Buildings also can be considered as part of relative space, positioned, geographically, in relation to other objects that they depend upon to function as a living environment. For instance, a care facility's functioning is part of a space of flows, of goods, employees, and residents, all of which emanate from different multiple points or locations. The care facility is also an example of a relational space in which what happens there is (inter)related with events occurring in other places, such as legal rules passed by national and supranational governments that specify minimum standards of service.

However space is defined, it is intrinsic to human existence, and for Newton the fundamental element of space as place is that "part of space which a body takes up" (Newton and Motte 1934, 6; also see Merleau-Ponty 1962). The human body is always emplaced, and its placement is conditioned, in part, by the social content and context of a place. Thus, the impaired body has, historically, been constructed as not normal, unsightly, and "out of place" in everyday environments. Where one was permitted to exist was resolved by recourse to spatial regulation, or placing certain categories of people, such as those with learning difficulties, in spaces of incarceration that, at their extreme, were asylums, special schools, prisons, and other places of confinement. For instance, following the passage of the 1913 Mental Incapacity Act, 40,000 people in Britain, categorized as "feebleminded" and "morally defective," were locked away in institutions (see Brignell 2010). Such places served as absolute spaces or physical containers designed to segregate populations on the basis of bodily differences. They reflect what de Certeau (1984, 117) refers to when he calls a space "a practiced place," where

understanding the body, according to biological and physiological characteristics, shapes the creation and maintenance of spaces of demarcation and exclusion as "natural."

Such shaping is part of the purposive production of space, by architects, designers, and others involved in the design and emplacement of objects in space (see Imrie 1996). Their actions are part of a broader, structural value system that fails to engage with, or respond to, the complexities of corporeal form and performance. It is one that devalues "not normal" bodies, a devaluation reflected in disabled people's difficulties in seeking to overcome the frictions of distance or the spaces between different places. As a result, many disabled people often have difficulty navigating what de Certeau (1984) describes as the "intersection of mobile elements" and the "ensemble of movement" that are intrinsic to spatial experiences. For instance, moving between places brings disabled people into conflict with disabling design and frictions that routinely exclude them from interfacing with the world around them in ways that they would choose. The examples of this are manifold and include bus timetables that rarely provide information in forms accessible to vision-impaired people, and steps into shops and other public buildings and commercial buildings that may prevent wheelchair users from undertaking or completing a journey.

In both instances, the design of space, and the objects emplaced within it, has the potential to influence life opportunities. Deaf people, for example, describe space as perpetuating the hegemony of aurality—sonic places created for, and by, hearing people. Space is suffused with sound, and spatial legibility is defined, in part, by the primacy of auricular values and the interplay between place and the hearing body. By contrast, vision-impaired people are subjected to definitions of space as "that which is seen," where the (re)production of place is premised on visuality. Here, the primacy of ocular values, as evidenced in the shaping of space by visual cues, signs, and symbols, disregards those without sight or the means to make sense of seeing-sensory spaces. In both cases, the lack of attentiveness to the interrelationships between (their) bodily sensing and spatial perception draws attention to issues of social justice, and the less-than-equal opportunities afforded to disabled people in accessing, and moving in and across, space. In other words, the construction of place is entwined with the status of disabled people as citizens and the exercise of their citizenship. Their access and attendant rights to full and equal participation in society require, arguably, a spatial politics, a deliberate politicization of the processes shaping the uneven (re)production of space.

Modern disability history may be characterized, in large part, by people seeking to contest spatial inequality and the unjust nature of the social production of space. For instance, the American disability rights organization American Disabled for Accessible Public Transit (ADAPT) spent much of the 1980s campaigning, with some success, for bus lifts for wheelchair users. In the United Kingdom, vision-impaired people are, at the time of writing, challenging urban design practices that seek to create shared streets, or places where all users, including motor vehicle drivers and pedestrians, share the same spaces (see Imrie 2012). For vision-impaired people, such spaces are tantamount to the loss of safe pavement environments and the creation of a new layer of spatial inequality that will lead, potentially, to their involuntary withdrawal from such places. Here, disabling design values intercede with corporeal realities, and future research about space and disability may be to deploy, analytically, the notion of "rights to the city" (see Lefebvre 1991). These rights challenge conventional liberal citizenship and its failure to recognize

the illiberal nature of spatial practices. They are also the basis for campaigning for disabled people's rights to spatial equality to be enshrined in a politics of participation. For many disability rights activists, these are nonnegotiable prerequisites for shaping the right to access, occupy, and use space.

57

Stigma

Heather Love

Stigma is part of the complex of factors that transform impairment into disability. The term refers to the disapproval and disadvantage that attach to people who are seen as different; its repercussions can be far-reaching. Stigma affects employment, social recognition, educational opportunities, friendship and sex, housing, and freedom from violence. *Stigma* in Greek means to prick or to puncture, and the word originally referred to a sharp instrument used to brand or cut slaves or criminals. The fact that stigma is still closely associated with visible forms of difference—leprosy, needle tracks, missing limbs, and obesity, for instance—recalls this history, as does the fact that it retains associations of moral disgrace. Today, the term is more abstract and more general and refers to social forms of stigma—to the discredit or dishonor that attaches to a wide range of human variation.

Stigma's associations with enslavement lasted through the nineteenth century, when the term described the brands and marks used to identify and to punish enslaved people in the United States, and it also connoted a moral taint or sign of disgrace. Along with these associations of infamy, the term is linked via the Christian tradition to the idea of grace. Stigmas (or stigmata) refer to the spontaneously bleeding wounds of saints, understood to imitate the wounds of Christ.

Since the late nineteenth century, stigma has been more stably correlated to pathology and to *kinds* of people rather than to individuals. Paralleling the large-scale processes of normalization and the management of populations that Michel Foucault has identified with Western modernity, stigma gradually lost its punitive and religious connotation; instead, it was associated with medical pathology and social groups deemed inferior as a result of poverty, racial and ethnic difference, occupational status, gender and sexual nonnormativity, and many forms of cognitive and physical difference. For scholars of disability, the rise of statistics in the nineteenth century was essential in shifting views of the visibly different from wonder to deviation from the norm (Davis 1995; Garland-Thomson 1997). The emergence of a "normal body" is instrumental in shifting stigma from individuals to broader, more systematic forms of oppression.

Human difference and its regulation have long been an object of study, but the modern concept of stigma emerges around the same time as the discipline of sociology, where it played an important role in Émile Durkheim's (1895) account of social deviance. Durkheim understood deviance as relative, the product of the sorting processes internal to communities, and as an effect of asymmetrical power relations. His understanding of deviance was crucial to the development of labeling theory, which argues that deviant behavior is not inherently pathological but is categorized by society as aberrant. During the twentieth century, stigma was understood as a sign of deviance, and it continues to play an important role today in sociology as well as in anthropology, legal studies, psychology, education, ethnic studies, and the medical humanities.

Stigma is crucial to the emergence of disability studies as a field and to the definition of disability itself. The Americans with Disabilities Act (ADA) of 1990 recognizes the importance of social opprobrium to determining who will qualify for benefits. In defining disability, the law covers not only those with impairments but also those who "are regarded as having such an impairment" (Section 12102 [3]); the authors of the ADA have deemed that the discrimination attending physical and mental impairment is disabling even in the absence of such conditions. The American Medical Association's *Guides to the Evaluation of Permanent Impairment* (2007) also incorporates stigma. Stigma is central to its criteria for compensation and accommodation, which judge facial differences as some of the most disabling impairments. How the effect of social stigma might be quantified, for instance, in cases of employment and other forms of discrimination, remains a pressing legal and political question.

The sociologist Erving Goffman developed the most influential account of stigma in his classic study *Stigma: Notes on the Management of Spoiled Identity* (1963). Although he was not solely concerned with disability, Goffman has been influential in disability studies. His account of the maintenance of social norms through the rituals of everyday life and his emphasis on the discrediting effects of stigma have set the terms for contemporary discussions of stigma in relation to disability and beyond. Goffman defines stigma as a break with expectations for "normal" appearance or behavior that results in the denigration of the stigmatized person. His definition emphasizes copresence and perception. He is less concerned with the inherent trait or the nature of the behavior than he is with the societal perception of the "stranger" who appears "different from others." Like Durkheim, Goffman understands stigma as a dynamic social situation where fitness is defined in the context of the community rather than in absolute terms. As his description of the stigmatized person as "bad, dangerous, and weak" implies, Goffman is blunt in representing the effects of stigmatization, and he does not offer a positive account of difference. His writing highlights a paradox

of scholarship on stigma: in describing the conditions of stigmatization, one risks repeating them, making a spectacle of the denigrated object.

Goffman identifies three categories of stigma: "abominations of the body," his term for physical "deformities"; "blemishes of individual character," which refers to moral transgressions such as homosexuality; and, finally, "the tribal stigma of race, nation, and religion" (1963, 4). Of these three categories, the last gets the least attention: race, ethnicity, nationality, and religion appear fairly rarely in his examples, in part because his definition of stigma turns on an individual out of place rather than the fate of an oppressed group. The rise of the disability rights movement over the past half-century has shifted the understanding of mental and bodily difference from an individual to a group phenomenon.

Moral taints are of interest to Goffman because of the way such faults discredit the entire person. While many of his examples seem dated, his analysis of blemishes of character remains relevant. The stigma attached to sexual or social deviance such as HIV infection or drug addiction is powerful, all the more so because, as Goffman argues, stigmatized people may internalize rather than contest the norms by which they are judged inferior.

Visible disability (or "abominations of the body") furnishes key examples for Goffman because of his emphasis on live scenes of interaction. Lennard Davis (1995) has argued that appearance is one of the main modalities by which disability is constructed. Rosemarie Garland-Thomson (2009, 44) considers the social dynamics and effects of staring, tracing the power of the starer over the staree. Public scenes of staring produce conditions of vulnerability for people with visible differences; however, under usual conditions not only the staree but also the starer is exposed to view. As the title of the edited collection *Staring Back* implies, people with disabilities are not the passive objects of stigmatization but rather engage in a range of strategies for resisting, refusing, and reversing stigma.

Although stigma is primarily associated with forms of difference that are readily visible, nonvisible and transient forms of stigma have equally powerful effects. Invisible disabilities such as forms of cognitive and affective difference, epilepsy, and vocal impairment raise important questions about disclosure, secrecy, and information management. Goffman and others have analyzed the acts of passing that stigmatized persons engage in on a temporary or permanent basis. While passing might shield an individual from certain forms of denigration or abuse, lack of recognition can also have negative consequences. In an essay on the complexity of passing, Tobin Siebers (2008a) argues for the significance of "disability as masquerade," or the performative acts people with disabilities engage in to minimize or exaggerate impairments in order to gain control over self-representation, as well as access to accommodations.

Such control is always tenuous, since the attribution of stigma is volatile. As work on the experience of the parents, children, and siblings of people with disabilities has shown, stigma is contagious. To be seen in the company of someone who is visibly different is to be understood as different oneself. In addition, stigmatized traits or behaviors can amplify each other, as Susan Schweik (2009) demonstrates in her study of the "ugly laws" in the late nineteenth- and early twentieth-century United States. These laws legislated against the public appearance of beggars and people with disabilities, categorizing both as "eyesores" and confounding them with each other. Once a person is stigmatized, other qualities tend to be interpreted through the lens of this trait; even relatively minor differences can have

major and snowballing consequences in the life of an individual.

Writing on stigma invariably raises questions about the constitution of social norms. In a memorable moment from the end of *Stigma*, Goffman quips, "In an important sense there is only one complete unblushing male in America: a young, married, white, urban, northern, heterosexual Protestant father of college education, fully employed, of good complexion, weight, and height, and a recent record in sports" (1963, 128). Disability studies scholars have followed Goffman in interrogating the category of the "able-bodied" or "nondisabled" in order to undermine the self-evident distinction between the normal and the pathological.

This view is valuable because it suggests that stigma is not essentially linked to particular traits or behavior, nor is it permanently fixed to individuals or groups. A person who is stigmatized in one context may be seen as unexceptional in another; once-stigmatized behavior or traits may become acceptable or even enforced as new norms down the line. According to this view, stigma is a system, a way of sorting persons into categories of normal and deviant along the lines of preexisting social hierarchies. Still, there are drawbacks to this universalizing account. It tends to underestimate the extent to which stigma attaches to individuals who are visibly marked as different. In order to understand stigma's role in the construction of disability, we must recognize its status not just as a universal experience of difference but also as a concrete force in the lives of particular individuals.

The disability rights movement has been instrumental in transforming the meaning and public perception of the stigma associated with disability. Collective redefinitions of what counts as normal and the standards for ethical treatment of those perceived as different are crucial. Nonetheless, stigma remains a powerful and unpredictable force in the lives of many, and it shapes the way individuals and groups can expect to navigate the social world. In the concrete effects of stigma, we see the afterlife of its origins as both a punishment and a technique of identification. Stigma is sticky, and it has the power to confer identity; it is general, but it attaches to particular individuals; once one is marked with stigma, it may be difficult to escape its hold.

58

Technology
Mara Mills

The definition of technology has been the subject of considerable philosophical debate. Technology was a relatively denigrated topic in Western philosophy until the early modern period, as a result of the unfavorable distinctions—dating to ancient Greece—between *techne* (craft knowledge) and *epistēmē* (theory or science). "Technology" most commonly refers to manufactured things: artifacts, handiwork, devices, and machinery (Kline 1985, 215). The term "biotechnology," coined in the twentieth century, refers to the manufacture or gainful modification of organisms, tissues, and life processes. Examples of biotechnology range from plant breeding to genetic engineering. Some scholars broaden the category of technology to include technics: technical skills, methods, and routines. More broadly still, others consider technologies to be "sociotechnical systems of use," defined by Stephen Kline as "combinations of hardware and people" brought into being "to accomplish tasks that humans cannot perform without such systems—to extend human capacities" (1985, 216). Until recently, technology has been the subject of forceful critique rather than sustained analysis in the field of disability studies. According to the social model of disability, the lack of access to technological systems, especially those required for the performance of citizenship—from workplace architecture to municipal infrastructure to telecommunications networks—is a principal source of disability.

The notion of technology as an "extension" of generalized "human capacities" has given rise to speculation about the intrinsic relationship of technology to disability. Some scholars have projected the body's natural inadequacy or impairment as the grounds for technical innovation. Arnold Gehlen, for instance, a right-wing German philosopher, surveyed European history of technology from the eighteenth through the twentieth century and concluded, "The necessity for technology derives from man's organ deficiencies" (2003, 213). Disability theorists have offered less universalizing accounts of impairment as a source of invention. Tobin Siebers contends that sensory disabilities effect new communicative practices: "The disabled body changes the process of representation itself. . . . blind hands envision the faces of old acquaintances. Deaf eyes listen to public television. . . . different bodies require and create new modes of representation" (2008a, 54). Similarly, in the field of Deaf studies, hearing loss is reframed as deaf gain to signal the linguistic and cultural benefits of deafness (Bauman and Murray 2009, 3). Exclusion can be a source of innovation, as a device or technical system is transformed by the imperative to accommodate disability. For example, talking books and text-to-speech scanning machines for people with "print disabilities" have spurred the widespread development of new reading formats.

Other theorists instead emphasize the "disabling" effects of modern technology. Disablement is a frequent trope for critics of mechanization and automation—the supplementation and replacement of human activities by machines. Many of these critics have noted that the founders of scientific management, specifically Henry Ford and Frank and Lillian Gilbreth, integrated disabled workers onto assembly lines. The "breaking down" of human motion into its components, the substitution of apparatus for some of these micro-motions, and the

proximity of people with disabilities to other laborers lead these commentators to claim, syllogistically, that "everyone is disabled" by industrialization. The rehabilitation of people with disabilities—their accommodation into the workplace—is thus problematically deployed to warn of the injuries that result from rationalized, repetitive factory work. This formulation overlooks the social context of efficiency and statistical reasoning that encompassed all bodies in the early twentieth century. "Disability" was marked as a distinct problem—a scalar difference from other human "limitations." More often than not, the incorporation of "human factors" into design gave rise to standardization technologies for statistically average users, excluding those with disabilities.

Postmodern theorists issue similar warnings about the pathological effects of digital, networked technology on embodiment and perception. Perhaps most dramatically, Paul Virilio describes the "plugged-in" users of computers and telecommunications as "terminal citizens," catastrophically "handicapped" by isolation, immobility, and suspicious equipment (1997, 20–21). Most scholars assume, however, that technology exhibits a "double logic," with additive and subtractive effects. Marshall McLuhan (1994, 42) famously proposed that electronic media at once extend and "auto-amputate" human faculties, the latter occurring through overuse or atrophy. S. Lochlann Jain cautions that "it is usually not the same body that is simultaneously extended and wounded" (1999, 36). An extension for one person might come at another's expense, as when certain users are excluded from a technical system, or a test subject does not benefit from the risks she has taken.

Disability theorists have critiqued the academic fields of science and technology studies and media studies for routinely exploiting disability as metaphor and exemplar in wide-ranging theories of prosthesis, the cyborg, and posthumanism. As David Mitchell and Sharon Snyder argue, "disability underwrites the cultural studies of technology writ large" (1997, 8). In such scholarship, disabled figures betoken technological dystopia, the exaggerated effects of new media on human bodies and relations, or the perfunctory celebration of hybridity and difference. Representations of disability in texts and audiovisual media do not simply reflect broader patterns of discourse, however. They create new symbolic associations, disseminate terminology, transmit affect, and discipline practices of looking. Thus historians Katherine Ott, Stephen Mihm, and David Serlin (2002) have called for more work on the everyday contexts of prosthesis, as ballast for the term's metaphoric proliferation. Alison Kafer similarly recommends "bringing a disability consciousness to the cyborg, attending to the specific benefits and dangers it harbors for disabled people. This shift requires an acknowledgment that human/machine interfaces are not always beneficial or pleasurable; an awareness that many disabled people lack access to the cybertechnologies so highly praised in cyborg writing; an accounting for the ways in which cybertechnologies rely on disabling labor practices across the globe; and a realization that not all disabled people are interested in technological cures or fixes" (2013, 118). Media activists and disability theorists alike have urged critical attention to the prevailing "visual rhetorics" of disability in photography and film, as well as the ways these rhetorics might be subverted or supplemented (Garland-Thomson 2001).

The category of "assistive technology" is likewise contentious within disability studies. John M. Williams, a disability journalist who has used various communication aids for stuttering, is widely credited with coining the phrase in 1982. In fact, "assistive" apparatus began to be discussed in such domains as occupational therapy, medicine, and education following World War II. In the United States, the 1988 Technology-Related Assistance Act for Individuals with Disabilities (the "Tech Act"), provided an influential definition of assistive technology, which was taken up in subsequent legislation such as the U.S. Assistive Technology Act of 1998, the Americans with Disabilities Act, the Telecommunications Act, and the Individuals with Disabilities Education Act. The 1988 act is based on a circular logic that defines assistive technology as any technology gainfully used by a person with a disability: "The term 'assistive technology device' means any item, piece of equipment, or product system, whether acquired commercially, modified, or customized, that is used to increase, maintain, or improve functional capabilities of individuals with disabilities." Katherine Ott points out that the phrasing is also redundant: "Since all useful technology is assistive, it is peculiar that we stipulate that some devices are assistive while others need no qualification. Besides serving to stigmatize and segregate a benign and inanimate entity—a device or appliance—the term 'assistive technology' also needlessly complicates understanding of the devices so designated" (Ott 2002, 21). Richard Ladner further argues that the term "assistive" "has the ring of paternalism, a view that people with disabilities need lots of extra help, are dependent and are not capable human beings" (2010, 26). The phrase advances a technological fix that is unconcerned with education, community support, or social change.

The umbrella category of assistive technology includes medical products such as prosthetics, which "replace" human anatomy or function, and orthotics, which "support" anatomy. The category includes items sold on the consumer and medical markets as well as those made by hand. Mobility, sensory, instructional, and "daily living" devices such as shoehorns become "aids" when used by people with disabilities, as do communication technologies such as speech synthesizers and smartphones. From pillboxes to screen readers, many assistive technologies are designed to accompany or provide access to other technologies. "Adaptive technology" is a synonym for "assistive"; however, it can also refer to equipment—especially computer-related—that is explicitly designed for people with disabilities. While these distinctions have a legal and financial rationale, many "adaptive" items simply repurpose the same components found in "mainstream" technologies, as is the case with hearing aid amplifiers and other electroacoustic devices. Some "assistive" technologies, such as curb cuts, are shared between different user groups.

What these technologies "assist" is sometimes questionable. They may be designed for "compensation" or extension, augmented or alternative communication. They may promise to facilitate independence but instead require new patterns of dependence upon biomedicine. Biomedical technologies might themselves be "disabling" through the establishment of norms and diagnostic categories, segregating or stigmatizing regulatory practices, and unwanted therapies or "adverse effects." These technologies may be at once rehabilitative and painful. They may become "stigma symbols," or they may serve purely cosmetic purposes to accommodate popular discomfort with difference. They draw attention to otherwise "invisible" disabilities, as in the case of the hearing aid or the white cane. They may exhibit a medical aesthetic that compounds disability. They might assist some users while "enforcing normalcy" for others. Cochlear implants, for instance, offer a partial and atypical mode of hearing, while at the same time threatening a minority linguistic culture.

According to Martha Scherer, "use" itself is a complex activity. Assistive technologies have high rates of abandonment, "noncompliance," and nonuse (2002, 2). Sally Wyatt has identified four general categories of nonuser: resisters (those who choose never to use a technology), rejectors (who stop using a technology voluntarily), the expelled (who stop using a technology involuntarily), and the excluded (those without access for social or technical reasons). In terms of use, Wyatt (2005, 76) notes that it may be forced, reluctant, or partial. Relationships to technology, moreover, are generally far more intimate than implied by the term "user", or by the related term, "wearer." Identity formation can occur through technological use, as exemplified by self-advocacy groups for "cochlear implant users." Group affiliation also results from technical exclusion, as with the category of "print disability," which unites disparate individuals who cannot read printed materials. Finally, access to assistive devices is always stratified; the devices are not equally available or affordable to those who might benefit from them.

Some scholars of disability and technology have urged universal or inclusive design to render the special category of assistive technology unnecessary. Given that true universality is unachievable, Graham Pullin suggests "resonant design," which attracts small subgroups of disabled and nondisabled users based on coincident needs. Voice-enabled smartphones, for example, are at once "hands-free" and "eyes-free" (2009, 93). Other possibilities include "critical design" (or "design for debate"), which aims to raise questions and unsettle established assumptions about disability, and "interrogative design," which protests or provokes strong interventions into ableist structures. Regardless, all work on technology risks assimilating what Tobin Siebers calls the "ideology of ability" (2008a, 7). Technology theory exhibits a ruling preoccupation with development and capacity. It emphasizes invention over the vagaries of use; moreover, it tends to neglect the piecemeal, the homemade, the low-tech, and the long-lasting.

59

Trauma

James Berger

One might assume that disability studies and trauma studies would be intimately intertwined, since both examine physical and psychological impairments. Disability studies and some directions in trauma studies are deeply concerned with the social contexts and consequences of impairments. Owing to methodological and ideological differences, however, there has been little contact between the two fields until very recently.

Approaches to trauma can be divided broadly into two categories: the medical-clinical and the cultural-historical. Medical-clinical definitions are concerned typically with an individual's response to some overwhelming stress or injury—an accident, for instance, or an event of war, or a physical or sexual assault—that produces a sense of helplessness or extreme disorientation. Due to the powerful and intrusive nature of the psychological stress or physical assault, an individual may find him- or herself unable either to address its memory directly or to be freed from that memory. Thus, she or he experiences extreme anxiety, flashbacks to the event, and nightmares, and has difficulty resuming a satisfactory experience of family or work. The emphasis here is on individual diagnosis and treatment. Clinicians, therapists, and researchers recognize that social and institutional forces—misogyny, poverty, war—contribute to traumatic experiences, and that community resources may contribute to helping the subject of trauma. But by and large most experiences of trauma, as exemplified in

the diagnosis of post-traumatic stress disorder, are understood as subjective and deeply individualized.

The medical-clinical approach to trauma clashes in some inevitable ways with the work of disability studies, as adherents to the social model of disability regard the medical view of individual pathology with suspicion. Disability, in this view, is not an intrinsic or acquired feature of an individual but a product of social barriers—both material and ideological—that restrict and stigmatize him or her. For many disability theorists, trauma studies' exclusive focus on the individual is misguided. The social model also rejects the notion that to be disabled is thereby, or concomitantly, to be traumatized. Indeed, traumatic experience itself is not of central concern, for disability studies is generally less concerned with how a physical or mental impairment was acquired—whether through illness, accident, crime, or war—than with the social response to the impairment. This disregard of social factors in the causation of physical and mental impairments is beginning to change, as seen in recent work by Davidson (2008), McRuer (2006), and Erevelles (2011).

Disability studies would seem to have more affinity with a cultural-historical approach to trauma, which largely derives from work in psychoanalysis. That this affinity has not been pursued is a function of different attitudes toward central notions of psychoanalysis: the unconscious and the symptom. Trauma studies assumes that all subjects act at least in part upon motives not immediately accessible to them. And it assumes that these unconsciously motivated acts or behaviors must be understood as symptoms—as symbolic somatic or social expressions of motives, fears, or desires, that are too painful, threatening, or overwhelming to be acknowledged directly and consciously. Disability studies, in contrast, does not view the subjectivity of the disabled as shaped by unconscious factors, although it does show how ableist ideology draws on unacknowledged anxieties (of, for instance, vulnerability and mortality; Garland-Thomson 1997; Mitchell and Snyder 2001).

This distinction has political as well as theoretical dimensions. Disability studies insists on establishing (politically) and substantiating (theoretically) the autonomy of the disabled subject and is wary of any methodology suggesting that dependence, vulnerability, ambivalence, or lack of transparent relation between motive and act may be characteristic of subjectivity. Trauma studies, conversely, takes these qualities as axiomatic of subjectivity, for trauma fundamentally compromises autonomy.

Another difference between studies of disability and trauma concerns the politics of representation. Disability studies has been wary of metaphor, which it regards as a way of appropriating disability for purposes not consonant with the interests of the disabled. As Tobin Siebers writes, "Disability has provided the public imagination with one of its most powerful symbols . . . but it always symbolizes something other than itself" (2008b, 48). Or, as Michael Davidson puts it, "Metaphoric treatments of impairment seldom confront the material conditions of actual disabled persons, permitting dominant social norms to be written on the body of a person who is politely asked to step offstage once the metaphoric exchange is made" (2008, 1). Mitchell and Snyder's theory of narrative prosthesis—that "crutch upon which literary narratives lean for their representative power, disruptive potential, and analytical insight" (2001, 490)—casts metaphor as aesthetically parasitic and politically wounding. Such critiques rely upon an Aristotelian conception of metaphor, in which the metaphoric term is a substitute for some other term. Trauma studies regards metaphor quite differently. The language of trauma arises from a moment of obliteration. The traumatic event is not remembered. It disrupts previous ways of thinking and feeling. There is literally no language for the event of trauma. Thus, the language used in relation to trauma—as narrative, descriptive, evaluative-—is necessarily metaphoric, but in a very different sense from that imagined by disability studies scholars. It cannot be an Aristotelian metaphorics of substitution because there is no original literal, true thing or word that the metaphor would replace. The metaphor here stands in the place of a radical loss of terminology and thus becomes a category not of substitution but of catachresis—the word created in a place where no adequate term exists.

Thus, one could argue that the significant distinction between the two fields is the status of the event, since unlike disability studies, trauma theory is tied irrevocably to the actuality and force of the traumatic event, however obscure and unreachable. The present, for individual and social subjects, is a landscape of symptoms. The task of analysis is to interpret these symptoms and, through them, work back to the event; and then to construct a new symbolic arrangement that will lessen the event's traumatic impact and allow the subject to live with more freedom. Trauma theory presumes an event that wounds so profoundly as to obscure the nature and cause of the wound (see Caruth 1996; LaCapra 2000; Zizek 1989). Disability theory, as I have pointed out, is mostly unconcerned with issues of loss, wounding, mourning, healing, and all those conditions that follow from an event experienced as traumatic. And yet this lack of concern seems evidence of a psychic rigidity, a refusal to admit to vulnerability and loss, that in disability theory is projected onto the ableist order. If the capacity to be wounded, disrupted, or traumatized is present in normative society—and it clearly is—it must be acknowledged among the disabled as well. Conversely, one might argue that trauma theory is too much invested in the problematics of loss, mourning, and the ineffable. And in doing so, trauma theory lacks the political force that is so valuable in disability theory. If disability theory is marked by an inability to mourn, trauma theory may be marked by an inability to stop mourning (Berger 2004).

Some recent work in disability studies begins to bridge the divide between disability and trauma. McRuer (2006) and Davidson (2008) have examined social etiologies of disability, particularly war and systemic poverty, that seem akin to trauma. Morrison and Casper (2012), in a joint essay, combine clinical observation and sociological analysis to produce what they call "critical trauma studies," in which both disabilities and posttraumatic effects are linked to historical causes. Finally, Siebers (2010) has written specifically on trauma, following on Berger's question (2004) as to why there has been a disciplinary divide between the two fields. Siebers discusses the prevalence of disabled bodies in modern and contemporary artistic products that he designates as "trauma art." Disability, for Siebers, is central to any modern consideration of trauma, as trauma is central to the culture at large.

If such inquiries are to be pursued and genuine relations between the two disciples established, disability scholars will become more open in acknowledging what Shakespeare (2006a) calls the "predicament" of disability—which may include pain and traumatic etiologies and aftermaths. And scholars of trauma will become more wary of the elegiac tone that has often characterized the field and will develop a stronger, more immediate sense of the politics of historical-cultural traumas.

60

Visuality
Georgina Kleege

It was Thomas Carlyle who coined the noun "visuality" as well as the verb "visualize" in 1841, to refer to qualities related to making mental images of abstract ideas, such as heroism. In recent decades, visuality has become a keyword in the field of visual culture studies and has taken on additional nuances of meaning. Hal Foster's edited volume *Vision and Visuality* (1998) put forward the notion that "vision" should refer to the biological functions of the eye and the human visual system, while "visuality" should refer to cultural practices and values related to vision. This suggests a parallel with the social model of disability, which posits a continuum between impairment (the physical, sensory, or mental features of an individual body that are deemed disabling) and disability (the social practices that can hinder or prevent the cultural participation of individuals with such impairments). Both vision and visuality have been central concerns for disability studies scholarship.

A good deal of disability studies scholarship has focused attention on the visuality of disability in cultural practices where disabled bodies are displayed and visually represented. A persistent theme in this work is a counterpoint between the desire to see disability framed in culturally appropriate ways and to banish unsightly versions of disability from view. Disability historians have documented and analyzed disability visuality in various institutional settings. For example, as schools for the blind and deaf were founded first in Europe and later in North America in the eighteenth and nineteenth centuries, it was a common practice to host open house exhibitions where the general public would observe the pupils demonstrating the educational and vocational benefits of their training. While the goal of these exhibitions was to raise public awareness about the educational capacities of disabled people and to encourage public support of the institutions, these practices can be compared to the popular entertainment of the freak show, where people with anomalous embodiments were displayed in ways that made them appear wondrous, exotic, or subhuman (Garland-Thomson 1996; Adams 2001). The commodification and institutional control of disability visuality was reinforced by antimendicancy ordinances, known as the "ugly laws," which sought to cleanse public spaces of the unsightliness of disabled bodies (Schweik 2009). Although the twentieth century saw a decline in some of these practices, charitable organizations seeking to cure or prevent various disabling conditions continue to display disabled bodies in posters and telethons in ways meant to inspire pity and promote donations. As if to respond to this long history of visual practices, late twentieth-century disability rights activists staged protests to make the general public visually aware of barriers in the built environment that limit disabled access to public spaces and transportation. For instance, in a 1990 event that has come to be known as the Capitol Crawl, protesters got out of their wheelchairs to haul themselves up the steps of the U.S. Capitol while legislators inside debated the passage of the Americans with Disabilities Act.

While disabled people in the industrialized world today enjoy greater rights and protections, disability scholarship has also analyzed disability visuality in terms of subtler social interactions among individuals. Many disabled people feel overlooked and underrepresented by the culture at large, but they also frequently find themselves stared at in public. As indicated by the title of the anthology *Staring Back: The Disability Experience from the Inside Out* (1997), edited by Kenny Fries, many disabled autobiographers, poets, and fiction writers frame narratives around these encounters. The confrontational tone of much of this writing defies the expectation that disabled people should be passive recipients of public scrutiny—seen but not heard. Disability scholarship has defined the stare as a social interaction that is markedly different from a look, glance, or gaze for the way it can designate the otherness of the disabled body (Garland-Thomson 2009).

Disability studies scholars have also analyzed the vision/visuality dichotomy through an exploration of people with visual impairments. In the long history of philosophical debate over the role of vision in the formation of human consciousness, blindness has served as a point of reference for discussions about normative epistemology and ontology. Disability studies has questioned the ways blindness is represented in these discussions. Typically blindness is imagined to be total and congenital—the polar opposite of sightedness, which is understood to be not only utterly unimpaired but also the only modality to access true knowledge about the world. Disability studies scholars have challenged the notion of blindness as a single, monolithic lived experience, pointing out the ways that blindness is culturally constructed. In the industrialized world, standard measurements are used to determine if an individual's eyesight is sufficiently impaired to prevent culturally significant activities such as reading print or driving a car. The designation of legal blindness makes an individual eligible for state-supported educational and rehabilitation services in countries where such services are funded. Many individuals who are considered to be legally blind, however, may retain enough vision to perform visual tasks that do not rate as culturally important, such as the ability to detect color, motion, or form, while others may retain visual memories from earlier periods in life when their sight was unimpaired. For this reason, scholars and activists debate the merits of different terminologies. Some prefer the word "blind" to refer to all levels of impairment deemed to be outside the norm; others use the plural, "blindnesses," to highlight the awareness that there is a range of visual experiences. Because the word "blind" is so often used figuratively to mean ignorant, prejudiced, or oblivious, some scholars insist on terms such as "visually impaired," or "people with vision impairments" or "people with visual disabilities."

Disability visuality also encompasses notions of visibility and invisibility—qualities in an individual's embodiment or physical behavior through which impairment is visually manifest. The international symbol for disability access—the stick figure in a wheelchair on a blue background—has come under criticism from disability activists and scholars for this reason. The symbol can be critiqued for suggesting a disability hierarchy in which people using wheelchairs are held to be the most deserving of public accommodation, whereas people using other assistive devices such as canes, crutches, walkers, hearing aids, or assistive speech or screen-reading technologies are somehow less disabled. The symbol not only sets up a hierarchy with notions of greater legitimacy or need among some individuals over others but also emphasizes visual markers of impairment. People with invisible impairments often are excluded from the general public's collective imagination of disability. Thus these individuals feel doubly stigmatized because they must disclose impairments that are not visually apparent and therefore rouse suspicions about the authenticity of their claim. Disability scholars who study invisible disabilities further complicate the understanding of the social model by shifting focus from barriers

in the built environment to entrenched ideas about normative social behavior. Their analysis suggests that a truly inclusive classroom requires a reassessment of expectations about student attendance, participation, and communication, while the inclusive workplace must be constructed around redefinitions of productivity and collegiality (Wendell 1996; Price 2011).

Disability studies scholars have scrutinized disability visuality in films, television, and documentaries, pointing out the ways in which camera angles, image framing, lighting, and other visual effects reinforce stereotypical narratives of people with disabilities as pitiable or frightening (Norden 1994). In recent decades, a growing number of internationally recognized disabled visual and performance artists have offered alternate images of disability in their work. For instance, Riva Lehrer's (1997) portraits of disability activists and artists invite viewers to engage with the subjects in ways that emphasize their complexity and humanity. Katharine Sherwood uses angiograms of her own brain taken after the stroke that left her paralyzed on one side and combines them with other references to medical images in abstract compositions whose thickly painted surfaces suggest the resilience and frailty of human embodiment (Maclay 1999).

Because disability visuality is culturally constructed, it is likely that future scholars will take all these facets of analysis to different historical periods and cultural locations. There will also be opportunities to examine new and emerging visual media and technologies through a disability studies perspective. Producers of films, television shows, art exhibits, and websites will soon be required to provide access to people with visual disabilities, through such practices as audio description, tactile drawings and diagrams, and global positioning devices, and we can expect that disability scholars will critique how these standards are implemented.

61

Vulnerability

Ani B. Satz

All living beings are vulnerable throughout their life span to the effects of biology and environment, such as disease, natural disaster, and war. Vulnerability is thus a shared and constant state among living beings (Fineman 2008, 2010) that cuts across social, geographic, and species boundaries (Satz 2009). The all-encompassing nature of vulnerability, however, is often overlooked. Vulnerability frequently is discussed in social science, public health, and other disciplines in terms of particular characteristics of individuals that render them members of "vulnerable populations." Women, children, racial minorities, prisoners, elderly persons, and individuals with disabilities all have been viewed as members of vulnerable populations because they may be subject to exploitation, discrimination, or other harm. This perspective confuses vulnerability—which all living beings share—with the fact that some individuals may (or may not) experience vulnerability more acutely than others.

The potential for disability, like vulnerability, is an inescapable aspect of the human condition (Satz 2008, 2010). All individuals are vulnerable to disability; if an individual becomes disabled, her vulnerability to disability is realized (Satz 2008, 2010). The experiences of disability and vulnerability, however, are unique to each individual. (Fineman 2008, 2010; Satz 2008, 2010). Some individuals may be more resilient based on biological factors, material supports, favorable environments, willpower, or other resources available to them.

Similarly, individuals with the same disabling condition may view themselves as differently impaired (or perhaps even as without impairment), depending on personal experience with impairment and the environments in which it is experienced.

Viewing only some individuals as vulnerable or as part of "vulnerable populations" casts a negative light on the concept of vulnerability, including vulnerability to disability. It separates those who are viewed as vulnerable from those who are not, associating weakness with vulnerability and invoking pity or concern for those who are part of a vulnerable population. This is perhaps why disability activists and lawmakers resist discussing physical and mental impairment in terms of vulnerability, stressing independence for individuals with disabilities rather than interdependence among all individuals due to universal vulnerability. Yet recognizing universal vulnerability is a step toward creating substantive equality and empowerment for individuals with disabilities. It requires that social and legal structures address disadvantage associated with deeply rooted barriers to accessing the civic and social realms and eliminates the stigma associated with viewing individuals with disabilities as a vulnerable population.

Vulnerability to disability has a number of implications for disability policy and law, particularly the civil rights approach of Western nations (Satz 2008, 2010). The Americans with Disabilities Act (ADA) of 1990 and parallel state statutes guard against disability discrimination in the workplace, in places of public accommodation (like stores and universities), on transportation, and with respect to public services as a matter of formal equality, rather than addressing structural inequalities and stigmas. Further, while it is illegal to prevent access to legally protected environments and services, only small adjustments, if any, would be required to facilitate access (Bagenstos 2004a, discussing the "access/

content" distinction, whereby individuals with disabilities have access to the same benefits as individuals who are not disabled, though the content of the benefits is not altered to meet the needs of individuals with disabilities). An otherwise qualified employee, for example, is entitled to reasonable accommodation to access her physical work space and to complete workplace tasks but not to access work more generally. Transportation to work and assistance completing vital household tasks in order to get to work—such as meal preparation, laundry, and dressing—are not covered accommodations. Additionally, systemic discrimination in promotion or retention and the lack of legal protections for workers with disabilities who are viewed as less productive than workers without disabilities also are not addressed. Similar limitations exist beyond the workplace. For example, under the ADA only "key (transportation) stations" need to be accessible, and no public buildings and services are required to make "fundamental alterations" or otherwise endure an "undue burden" to accommodate individuals with disabilities.

Meanwhile, civil rights protections apply only to those individuals who qualify as disabled under law. Individuals with impairments that limit functioning but do not rise to the legally recognized level of impairment for disability protections are not covered. No matter how expansive the definition of disability, some individuals with impairments will be excluded. Further, individuals who are vulnerable to impairment due to changes in their environment, or who are not yet strongly symptomatic for disabling illness, are not protected. Last, legally required accommodations are not subject to judicial scrutiny so long as they are reasonable, meaning they may fail to promote the most effective or preferred manner of functioning for an individual (Satz 2006).

Universal vulnerability to disability suggests that social and legal institutions must have a unified, comprehensive approach, rather than a selective (vulnerable populations) response to disability. On a macro level, this might take the form of universal programs for transportation, work, and health care. More universal approaches have in fact been embraced throughout history, including everything from Medicare for all elderly persons to the Great Society programs to international human rights instruments such as the Universal Declaration of Human Rights and the UN Convention on the Rights of Persons with Disabilities. On a micro level, universal design of discrete physical spaces and services, such as classroom education, may facilitate more meaningful access for individuals with impairments regardless of whether they rise to the legally recognized definition of disability.

62

Work

Sarah F. Rose

"Nor has any man who is crippled a right to be idle," thundered social worker George Mangold at an industrial accident conference in 1922 (67). While he inaccurately characterized most cripples as idle, Mangold nevertheless captured the long-standing role of work and productivity in defining "disability." In many cultures, disability has been characterized as the inability to do productive labor, a charge that has limited the citizenship and social standing of people with disabilities. Sailors on slave ships tossed disabled captives overboard; after the Civil War, impoverished Americans with visible impairments found themselves barred from begging in public and, in some cases, banned altogether from streets. But disability has also long been central to working life—a phenomenon that underscores the profound importance of incorporating class and economic perspectives more broadly into disability studies.

In many historical eras and regions, the threat and reality of disabling injuries have been a "normal" aspect of the everyday work experience. Until quite recently (and still today in more dangerous economic sectors), the notion that a mature worker could have an intact, unscarred body was fanciful. Indeed, the bodies of slaves, sailors, oil workers, coal miners, hotel maids, and other laborers have long borne witness to labor's toll. Slaves' scarred backs, sailors' bowlegs, oil workers' missing fingers, coal miners' shortened breath, and maids' back pains all testify to the near inescapability of disabling injuries. For many, such as an early Ford Motor Company worker who recalled his punch press crew losing "an average of sixteen fingers a month," the possibility of acquiring a work-related impairment was simply "part of the job."

Workplace dangers, however, have not always been distributed equally across communities. Racial and gender stereotypes have influenced employers' visions of the ideal workforce and served to justify unsafe conditions. In the 1930s, for instance, the Union Carbide and Carbon Corporation recruited migrant African American workers to drill a tunnel through deadly silica rock. Knowing nothing about the dangers and working without protection, laborers began dying within weeks from the lung disease silicosis. The company argued that "Negroes didn't know how to care for themselves" and refused to compensate their families. Likewise, maquiladora (export-oriented) factories on the U.S.-Mexico border have preferentially hired women, believing them better suited to electronic assembly work. These relatively high-paid and "clean" indoor jobs, however, also expose women to hazardous chemical fumes.

Disability has often been equated with the inability to do productive work, but rarely has this assumption reflected the lived experiences of people with disabilities. The staff of the 1915 Survey of Cleveland Cripples, for example, was astonished to find many individuals who were self-supporting: "The lives of unknown cripples are much more normal than supposed" (qtd. in Nielsen 2012, 128). Indeed, a man who had lost his right arm owned a saloon, and another amputee became the city's examiner of engineers.

In both the industrial and the postindustrial eras, disabled people developed strategies that have allowed them to enter—or remain—in the workforce. Deaf people discovered welcoming occupational niches: printing presses in the United States, and hair styling, sewing, and carpentry in Japan. Others turned to self-employment, such as an elderly Philadelphian who opened a newsstand in the 1920s after a laundry mangle mutilated her hand. Others have contributed to their household's economy by performing uncompensated "care work" at home: tending to young, disabled, or elderly relatives.

Some employers, too, pioneered innovative approaches to include disabled workers in the labor force. Between the 1910s and 1940s, Henry Ford hired tens of thousands of elderly and disabled workers, including people with complete blindness, epilepsy, shell shock, and missing limbs, and paid them full wages. Unlike most employers, Ford viewed people with disabilities as a potential source of efficiency. He recognized their intense desire to work and analyzed his factories to determine the positions best suited to his workers' diverse bodies. Wartime labor shortages have also led employers to willingly hire workers with disabilities; during World War II, hundreds of thousands of disabled Britons and Americans found full-time employment.

Working-class communities, moreover, rarely stigmatized what we might today classify as "disabilities"; rather, bodily variations have been understood as the result of poverty. American novelist Harry Crews, for instance, described his childhood fascination with the Sears catalog: "All the people in its pages were perfect. Nearly everybody I knew [in rural Georgia in the 1930s and 1940s] had something missing, a finger cut off, a toe split, an ear half-chewed away, an eye clouded with blindness from a glancing fence staple" (1995, 58). This is true in global perspective as well. In many Botswanan villages, for instance, disabilities among migrant miners, meatpackers, coal miners, and railroad workers were so common in the late nineteenth century and early twentieth century that diverse bodily configurations and varying levels of productivity became "normal."

As industrialization intensified, however, employers became increasingly unwilling to hire workers with disabilities—a shift that had grave economic consequences for both disabled people and their families during the twentieth century. Enamored with the efficiency movement, employers demanded workers with intact, interchangeable bodies. Making matters worse, the workmen's compensation laws passed in many countries between the 1880s and the 1910s reinforced employers' views of people with disabilities as potential liabilities and led them to begin screening out workers with disabilities. At times, labor unions supported these exclusionary policies. By the 1930s, such practices had spread as far afield as Botswana, where mine owners' strict medical examinations barred men with relatively minor impairments such as clubbed feet, nearsightedness, deafness, or epilepsy. Restricted to ill-paid work such as herding others' cattle, few could fully support a family. In Great Britain, in turn, more than half of people with disabilities lived in poverty by the 1960s, versus a quarter of the able-bodied population. As of 2013, disabled people in the United States were five times more likely than able-bodied people to be unemployed and were disproportionally likely to be employed part-time.

Certain types of disabled people's labors, moreover, have frequently not been recognized or compensated as proper work. Starting in the nineteenth century, inmates of idiot schools, mental hospitals, and other asylums contributed untold numbers of hours of cleaning, farming, cooking, sewing, and caring for other inmates. Defined as rehabilitative training that would aid reintegration into the mainstream community, such labor rarely led to release. Nor were inmates paid for their work, although their labors helped to defray asylums' expenses. Beginning in the late nineteenth century, sheltered workshops such as Goodwill Industries began to offer employment to disabled people who could not easily find regular work; such work, however, did not offer a living wage. Workshops in the United States, Canada, and Great Britain have typically taught unmarketable skills such as mat making, doll repair, or clock assembly. Furthermore, in the Fair Labor Standards Act of 1938, Congress exempted some sheltered workshops from paying the minimum wage. As of 2011, 426,000 workers with disabilities worked for wages as low as 41 cents per hour.

Lack of opportunities for paid employment has also limited or circumscribed disabled people's access to citizenship and social standing, especially in countries without a robust social welfare system. Starting in 1882, immigrants to the United States had to prove that they would not become a public charge—a category in which immigration officials automatically placed people with disabilities, even if they had job offers and a history of self-support. Rehabilitators, moreover, often characterized people with disabilities as unproductive citizens, ignoring systemic prejudice on the labor market. Goodwill Industries' founder described his work as salvaging "human waste" thrown on an "industrial scrap heap"; training would restore "good citizenship." Moreover, means-tested benefit programs such as Supplemental Security Income offer access to Medicaid but typically limit recipients' incomes to the poverty level. Effectively, recipients with significant health issues cannot work more than a few hours a week without jeopardizing their health care. Famously, the late disability historian and rights activist Paul Longmore publicly burned his first book in 1988 to protest these work disincentives (Longmore 2003); receiving even a few hundred dollars in royalties would have cost him his ventilator and in-home assistance.

Recognizing the importance of work to social standing, disability rights activists have long fought to gain access to the mainstream labor market. Deaf associations led a successful two-year campaign to overturn the U.S. Civil Service's 1906 ban on deaf and mute employees, while in the 1930s, the League of the Physically Handicapped staged sit-ins in New York and Washington, DC, to gain entrance to New Deal job programs. Despite labor unions' complex legacy regarding disability, radical unions in Argentina advocated and won minimum hiring quotas for disabled employees. And, in the 1940s and 1950s, American labor unions joined forces with—and funded—the broad-based American Federation of the Physically Handicapped, pressing the federal government to address disability as an issue of economic security.

Government initiatives to integrate people with disabilities into the mainstream workforce have had mixed success. Veterans, and disabled veterans in particular, have played a central role in these initiatives due to the implicit privileging of those disabled by war over those with congenital disabilities. Weimar Germany's pioneering Law of the Severely Disabled (1920), for instance, mandated that employers hire and retain disabled veterans, ensuring that even those with severe impairments had work during the Great Depression. Voluntary initiatives, however, such as Britain's mid-twentieth-century quota system and the U.S. "National Employ the Handicapped Week," had little effect. The Rehabilitation Act of 1973, the Americans with Disabilities Act (ADA) of 1990, and the ADA Amendments Act of 2009, however, have enabled disabled workers to request reasonable accommodations for their work environments and to file discrimination claims when those requests are not met. Judicial hostility and the failure to address employers' prejudice, however, have blunted the impact of these laws. Indeed, while other provisions of the ADA have greatly increased the public presence of disabled people, unemployment rates have barely budged. Likewise, while the UN's Year of the Disabled in 1981 and International Decade of the Disabled (1983–1993) raised awareness and led many countries to improve public accessibility, disabled people continue to face extraordinarily high rates of unemployment as of the early twenty-first century, reaching as high as 90 percent in Argentina and Bulgaria.

WORK   SARAH F. ROSE

Works Cited

Ackerman, Felicia. "Assisted Suicide, Terminal Illness, Severe Disability, and the Double Standard." In *Physician-Assisted Suicide: Expanding the Debate*, edited by Margaret Pabst Battin, Rosamond Rhodes, and Francis Silver, 149–163. New York: Routledge, 1998.

Adams, Rachel. *Sideshow USA: Freaks and the American Cultural Imagination*. Chicago: University of Chicago Press, 2001.

Agamben, Giorgio. *The Open: Man and Animal*. Translated by Kevin Attell. Stanford, CA: Stanford University Press, 2004.

Agar, Nicholas. *Liberal Eugenics: In Defence of Human Enhancement*. Boston: Blackwell, 2004

Akhtar, Nameera, and Morton Ann Gernsbacher. "Joint Attention and Vocabulary Development: A Critical Look." *Language and Linguistic Compass* 1 (2007): 195–207.

Alaimo, Stacy, and Susan Hekman. "Introduction: Emerging Models of Materiality in Feminist Theory." In *Material Feminisms*, edited by Stacy Alimo and Susan Hekman, 1–22. Bloomington: Indiana University Press, 2008.

Albrecht, Gary, and Patrick Devlieger. "The Disability Paradox: High Quality of Life against All Odds." *Social Science and Medicine* 48 (1999): 977–988.

Albrecht, Gary, David Mitchell, and Sharon Snyder. *The Encyclopedia of Disability*. Vol. 5, *A History of Disability in Primary Sources*. Thousand Oaks, CA: Sage, 2005.

Aldrich, Mark. *Safety First: Technology, Labor, and Business in the Building of American Work Safety, 1870–1939*. Baltimore: Johns Hopkins University Press, 1997.

American Medical Association. *Guides to the Evaluation of Permanent Impairment*. 6th ed. Chicago: American Medical Association, 2007.

American National Standard Specifications for Making Buildings and Facilities Accessible to, and Usable by, the Physically Handicapped. ANSI A117.1-116. New York: American National Standards Institute, 1961.

Amundson, Ron. "Quality of Life, Disability, and Hedonic Psychology." *Journal for the Theory of Social Behavior* 40 (2010): 374–392.

Anolik, Ruth Bienstock. "Introduction: Diagnosing Demons: Creating and Disabling the Discourse of Difference in the Gothic Text." In *Demons of the Body and Mind: Essays on Disability in Gothic Literature*, edited by Ruth Bienstock Anolik, 1–20. Jefferson, NC: McFarland, 2010.

Antonetta, Susanne. "Dis." *Seneca Review* 39, no. 1, and 40, no. 2 (2009–2010): 68–74.

Arneil, Barbara. "Disability, Self Image and Modern Political Theory." *Political Theory* 37 (2009): 218–242.

Arnold, Matthew. "The Scholar-Gypsy." In *The Norton Anthology of Poetry*, edited by Margaret Ferguson, Mary Jo Salter, and Jon Stallworthy, 1089–1094. 5th ed. New York: Norton, 2004.

Artiles, Alfredo J. "Towards an Interdisciplinary Understanding of Educational Equity and Difference: The Case of the Racialization of Ability." *Educational Researcher* 40 (2011): 431–445.

Artiles, Alfredo J., Elizabeth B. Kozleski, and Federico R. Waitoller. *Inclusive Education: Examining Equity on Five Continents*. Cambridge, MA: Harvard Education Press, 2011.

Asch, Adrienne. "Disability, Bioethics, and Human Rights." In *Handbook of Disability Studies*, edited by Gary L. Albrecht, Katherine D. Seelman, and Michael Bury, 297–326. Thousand Oaks, CA: Sage, 2001.

———. "Disability, Equality and Prenatal Testing: Contradictory or Compatible?" *Florida State University Law Review* 30 (2003): 315–342.

———. "Genetics and Employment: More Disability Discrimination." In *The Human Genome Project and the Future of Health Care*, edited by Thomas H. Murray, Mark A. Rothstein, and Robert F. Murray Jr., 158–172. Bloomington: Indiana University Press, 1996.

———. "Why I Haven't Changed My Mind about Prenatal Diagnosis: Reflections and Refinements." In *Prenatal Testing and Disability Rights*, edited by Erik Parens and Adrienne Asch, 234–260. Washington, DC: Georgetown University Press, 2007.

Asch, Adrienne, and Dorit Barlevy. "Disability and Genetics: A Disability Critique of Prenatal Testing and Pre-implantation Genetic Diagnosis." *Encyclopedia of the Life Sciences* (2012). http://dx.doi.org/10.1002/9780470015902.a0005212.pub2.

Asch, Adrienne, and David Wasserman. "Where Is the Sin in Synecdoche? Prenatal Testing and the Parent-Child Relationship." In *Quality of Life and Human Difference: Genetic Testing, Health Care, and Disability*, edited by David Wasserman, Jerome Bickenbach, and Robert Wachbroit, 176–216. New York: Cambridge University Press, 2005.

Auslander, Philip, and Carrie Sandahl. *Bodies in Commotion: Disability and Performance*. Ann Arbor: University of Michigan Press, 2004.

Bacon, Francis. *Essays or Counsels, Civil and Moral*. Whitefish, MT: Kessinger, 2010.

Bagenstos, Samuel R. "The Future of Disability Law." *Yale Law Journal* 114 (2004a): 1–84.

———. "Has the Americans with Disabilities Act Reduced Employment for People with Disabilities?" *Berkeley Journal of Employment and Labor Law* 25 (2004b): 527–564.

———. "'Rational Discrimination': Accommodation, and the Politics of (Disability) Civil Rights." *Virginia Law Review* 89 (2003): 825–923.

Baggs, Amanda. "In My Language." Online video. January 14, 2007. Accessed September 17, 2014. https://www.youtube.com/watch?v=JnylM1hI2jc.

Bakhurst, David, and Carol Padden. "The Mescheryakov Experiment: Soviet Work on the Education of Blind-Deaf Children." *Learning and Instruction* 1 (1991): 201–215.

Baldwin, James. "Freaks and the Ideal of American Manhood. In *Collected Essays*, edited by Toni Morrison, 814–829. New York: Library of America, 1998.

Baltes, Margret M. "Dependency in Old Age: Gains and Losses." *Current Directions in Psychological Science* 4 (1995): 14–19.

Banta, Martha. *Taylored Lives: Narrative Productions in the Age of Taylor, Veblen, and Ford*. Chicago: University of Chicago Press, 1995.

Barasch, Moshe. *Blindness: The History of a Mental Image in Western Thought*. New York: Routledge, 2001.

Barnartt, Sharon N., and Richard Scotch. *Disability Protests: Contentious Politics 1970–1999*. Washington, DC: Gallaudet University Press, 2001.

Barnes, Colin. *Disabled People in Britain and Discrimination: A Case for Anti-discrimination Legislation*. London: Hurst in Association with the British Council of Organisations of Disabled People, 1991.

Barnes, Colin, and Geof Mercer. *Exploring Disability: A Sociological Introduction*. Cambridge, UK: Polity Press, 2010.

Barton, Len. *Disability and Dependency*. London: Falmer Press, 1989.

Batavia, Andrew I. "Disability and Physician-Assisted Suicide." *New England Journal of Medicine* 336 (1997): 1671–1673.

Bauby, Jean-Dominique. *The Diving Bell and the Butterfly: A Memoir of Life in Death*. New York: Vintage, 1997.

Bauman, H-Dirksen L. "Getting Out of Line: Toward a Visual and Cinematic Poetics of ASL." In *Signing the Body Poetic: Essays on American Sign Language Literature*, edited by H-Dirksen L. Bauman, Jennifer L. Nelson, and Heidi M. Rose, 95–117. Berkeley: University of California Press, 2006.

———. *Open Your Eyes: Deaf Studies Talking*. Minneapolis: University of Minnesota Press, 2008.

———. Review of "A Mighty Change: An Anthology of Deaf American Writing 1816–1864." *Sign Language Studies* 2 (2002): 452.

Bauman, H-Dirksen L., and Joseph J. Murray. "Reframing: From Hearing Loss to Deaf Gain." *Deaf Studies Digital Journal* 1 (2009): 1–10.

Bauman, Zygmunt. *Wasted Lives: Modernity and Its Outcasts*. London: Polity Press, 2004.

Baynton, Douglas C. "Disability and the Justification of Inequality in American History." In *The New Disability History: American Perspectives*, edited by Paul K. Longmore and Lauri Umansky, 33–57. New York: NYU Press, 2001.

———. *Forbidden Signs: American Culture and the Campaign against Sign Language*. Chicago: University of Chicago Press, 1996.

———. "A Silent Exile on This Earth." In *The Disability Studies Reader*, edited by Lennard J. Davis, 33–48. New York: Routledge, 2006a.

———. "'These Pushful Days': Time and Disability in the Age of Eugenics." *Health and History* 13, no. 2 (2011): 43–64.

———. "'The Undesirability of Admitting Deaf Mutes': American Immigration Policy and Deaf Immigrants, 1882–1924." *Sign Language Studies* 6 (2006b): 391–415.

Beckett, Angharad E. *Citizenship and Vulnerability: Disability and Issues of Social and Political Engagement. Basingstoke*, UK: Macmillan, 2006. Angharad E. Basingstoke, UK: Macmillan, 2006.

Benhabib, Seyla. *Situating the Self: Gender, Community, and Postmodernism in Contemporary Ethics*. New York: Routledge, 1992.

Beredjick, Camille. "DSM-V to Rename Gender Identity Disorder 'Gender Dysphoria.'" *Advocate.com*, July 23, 2012. Accessed September 17, 2014. http://www.advocate.com/politics/transgender/2012/07/23/dsm-replaces-gender-identity-disorder-gender-dysphoria.

Berger, James. *After the End: Representations of Post-apocalypse*. Minneapolis: University of Minnesota Press, 1999.

———. "Trauma without Disability, Disability without Trauma: A Disciplinary Divide." *Journal of Advanced Composition* 24 (2004). 563–582.

Berlin, Isaiah. "Two Concepts of Liberty" (1958). In *Four Essays on Liberty*, 118–172. Oxford: Oxford University Press, 1969.

Bérubé, Michael. "Citizenship and Disability." *Dissent* 50 (2003): 52–57.

———. "Equality, Freedom, and/or Justice for All: A Response to Martha Nussbaum." *Metaphilosophy* 40 (2009): 352–365.

———. *Life as We Know It: A Father, a Family, and an Exceptional Child*. New York: Pantheon, 1996.

Bigelow, Anne. "The Development of Joint Attention in Blind Infants." *Development and Psychopathology* 15 (2003): 259–275.

Blanchett, Wanda J., Janette K. Klingner, and Beth Harry. "The Intersection of Race, Language, Culture, and Disability: Implications in Urban Contexts." *Urban Education* 39 (2009): 389–409.

Blatt, Burton, and Fred Kaplan. *Christmas in Purgatory: A Photographic Essay on Mental Retardation*. Syracuse, NY: Human Policy Press, 1974.

Blind Parents Interest Group of the National Federation of the Blind. *Parenting without Sight: What Attorneys and Social Workers Should Know about Blindness*. Baltimore: National Center for the Blind, 2012.

Blume, Harvey. "Neurodiversity." *Atlantic*, September 30, 1998. Accessed August 20, 2014. http://www.theatlantic.com/magazine/archive/1998/09/neurodiversity/305909/.

Bogdan, Robert. *Freak Show: Presenting Human Oddities for Amusement and Profit*. Chicago: University of Chicago Press, 1990.

Bois, Yve-Alain, and Rosalind E. Krauss. *Formless: A User's Guide*. New York: Zone Books, 1997.

Boorse, Christopher. "On the Distinction between Disease and Illness." *Philosophy and Public Affairs* 5 (1975): 49–68.

Borsay, Anne. *Disability and Social Policy in Britain since 1750*. London: Macmillan, 2005.

Bosl, Elsbeth. "The Contergan Scandal: Media, Medicine, and Thalidomide in 1960s West Germany." In *Disability Histories*, edited by Susan Burch and Michael Rembis, 136–162. Urbana: University of Illinois Press, 2014.

Bost, Suzanne. "From Race/Sex/Etc. to Glucose, Feeding Tube, and Mourning: The Shifting Matter of Chicana Feminism." In *Material Feminisms*, edited by Stacy Alaimo and Susan Hekman, 340–372. Bloomington: Indiana University Press, 2008.

Boster, Dea. "An 'Epeleptick' Bondswoman: Fits, Slavery, and Power in the Antebellum South." *Bulletin of the History of Medicine* 83 (2009): 271–301.

Botkin, Jeffrey R. "Fetal Privacy and Confidentiality." *Hastings Center Report* 25, no. 5 (1994): 32–39.

Bourne, Randolph. "The Handicapped." In *The Radical Will: Selected Writings 1911–1918*, edited by Olaf Hansen, 73–87. Berkeley: University of California Press, 1977.

Braddock, David L., and Susan L. Parish. "An Institutional History of Disability." In *Handbook of Disability Studies*, edited by Gary L. Albrecht, Katherine D. Seelman, and Michael Bury, 11–68. Thousand Oaks, CA: Sage, 2001.

Braswell, Harold. "Can There Be a Disability Studies Theory of 'End-of-Life Autonomy'?" *Disability Studies Quarterly* 31, no. 4 (2011). http://dsq-sds.org/article/view/1704/1754.

Braungart, Michael, and William McDonough. *Cradle to Cradle: Remaking the Way We Make Things*. New York: North Point Press, 2002.

Brignell, Victoria. "When the Disabled Were Segregated." *New Statesman*, December 2010. Accessed September 17, 2014. http://www.newstatesman.com/society/2010/12/disabled-children-british.

British Council of Organisations of Disabled People (BCODP). "Comment on the Report of the Audit Commission: 'Making a Reality of Community Care.'" August 1987. Accessed October 8, 2014. http://disability-studies.leeds.ac.uk/files/library/BCODP-report-of-audit-comm.pdf.

Brönte, Charlotte. *Jane Eyre*. New York: Norton, 2001.

Brueggemann, Brenda Jo. *Deaf Subjects: Between Identities and Places*. New York: NYU Press, 2009.

———. *Lend Me Your Ear: Rhetorical Constructions of Deafness*. Washington, DC: Gallaudet University Press, 1999.

Brueggemann, Brenda Jo, Linda Feldmeier White, Patricia A. Dunn, Barbara A. Heifferon, and Johnson Cheu. "Becoming Visible: Lessons in Disability." *College Composition and Communication* 52 (2001): 368–398.

Brueggemann, Brenda Jo, and Marian E. Lupo. "Prosing the Possibilities." *Prose Studies* 27 (2005): 1–10.

Brune, Jeffrey A., and Daniel J. Wilson. *Disability and Passing: Blurring the Lines of Identity*. Philadelphia: Temple University Press, 2013.

Buchanan, Robert M. *Illusions of Equality: Deaf Americans in School and Factory, 1850–1950*. Washington, DC: Gallaudet University Press, 1999.

Bull, Michael, Paul Gilroy, David Howes, and Douglas Kahn. "Introducing Sensory Studies." *The Senses and Society* 1 (2006): 5–7.

Bulwer, John. *Chirologia: or the naturall language of the hand. Composed of the speaking motions, and discoursing gestures thereof*. London: Thomas Harper, 1644.

Burch, Susan. *Signs of Resistance: American Deaf Cultural History, 1900 to 1942*. New York: NYU Press, 2002.

———. "Transcending Revolutions: The Tsars, the Soviets and Deaf History." *Journal of Social History* 34 (2000): 393–402.

Burch, Susan, and Hannah Joyner. *Unspeakable: The Story of Junius Wilson*. Chapel Hill: University of North Carolina Press, 2007.

Burgdorf, Marcia Pearce, and Robert Burgdorf. "A History of Unequal Treatment: The Qualifications of Handicapped Persons as a 'Suspect Class' under the Equal Protection Clause." *Santa Clara Lawyer* 15 (1975): 855–910.

Burgett, Bruce, and Glenn Hendler. *Keywords for American Cultural Studies*. New York: NYU Press, 2007.

Burke, Edmund. *A Philosophical Enquiry into the Origin of Our Ideas of the Sublime and Beautiful*. Edited by J. T. Boulton. Notre Dame, IN: University of Notre Dame Press, 1968.

Burleigh, Michael. *Death and Deliverance: "Euthanasia" in Germany 1900–1945*. New York: Cambridge University Press, 1995.

Burnet, John Robertson. *Tales of the Deaf and Dumb: With Miscellaneous Poems*. Newark: B. Olds, 1835.

Butler, Judith. *Bodies That Matter: On the Discursive Limits of "Sex."* New York: Routledge, 1993.

———. *Gender Trouble: Feminism and the Subversion of Identity*. New York: Routledge, 1990.

Butler, Judith, and Elizabeth Weed. "Introduction." In *The Question of Gender: Joan Scott's Critical Feminism*, edited by Judith Butler and Elizabeth Weed, 1–8. Bloomington: Indiana University Press, 2011.

Butler, Robert N. "Age-ism: Another Form of Bigotry." *Gerontologist* 9 (1969): 243–246.

Byrd, Todd. "Deaf Space." *ASL News* 14, no. 3 (Spring 2013), 8. (Originally published in *Gallaudet Today Magazine*, Spring 2007.)

Campbell, Fiona Kumari. *Contours of Ableism: The Production of Disability and Abledness*. Basingstoke, UK: Palgrave Macmillan, 2009.

———. "Legislating Disability: Narrative Ontologies and the Government of Legal Identities." In *Foucault and the Government of Disability*, edited by Shelley Tremain, 108–130. Ann Arbor: University of Michigan Press, 2005.

Campbell, Ruth, Mairead MacSweeney, and David Waters. "Sign Language and the Brain." *Journal of Deaf Studies and Deaf Education* 13 (2008): 3–20.

Canaday, Margot. *The Straight State: Sexuality and Citizenship in Twentieth-Century America*. Princeton, NJ: Princeton University Press, 2009.

Canguilhem, Georges. *The Normal and the Pathological*. London: D. Reidel, 1978.

Carden-Coyne, Ana. *Reconstructing the Body: Classicism, Modernism and the First World War*. New York: Oxford University Press, 2009.

Carey, Allison C. *On the Margins of Citizenship: Intellectual Disability and Civil Rights in Twentieth-Century America*. Philadelphia: Temple University Press, 2009.

Carey, James. *Communication as Culture: Essays on Media and Society*. Rev. ed. New York: Routledge, 1992.

Carlson, Licia. "Cognitive Ableism and Disability Studies: Feminist Reflections on the History of Mental Retardation." *Hypatia* 16, no. 4 (2001): 124–147.

———. *The Faces of Intellectual Disability: Philosophical Reflections*. Bloomington: Indiana University Press, 2010.

Carlton, Jim. "Peripheral Everywhere." Unpublished manuscript, 2009.

Carod-Artal, Francisco Javier, and Carolina Benigna Vazquez-Cabrera. "An Anthropological Study about Epilepsy in Native Tribes from Central and South America." *Epilepsia* 48 (2007): 886–893.

Cartwright, Lisa, and David Benin. "Shame, Empathy and Looking Practices: Lessons from a Disability Studies Classroom." *Journal of Visual Culture* 5 (2006): 1–17.

Caruth, Cathy. *Unclaimed Experience: Trauma, Narrative, and History*. Baltimore: Johns Hopkins University Press, 1996.

Cassuto, Leonard. *The Inhuman Race: The Racial Grotesque in American Literature and Culture*. New York: Columbia University Press, 1997.

Charlton, James I. "Civil Rights for Disabled Americans: The Foundations of a Political Agenda." In *Images of the Disabled, Disabling Images*, edited by Alan Gartner and Tom Joe, 181–204. New York: Praeger, 1987.

———. *Nothing about Us without Us: Disability Oppression and Empowerment*. Berkeley: University of California Press, 1998.

Charon, Rita. *Narrative Medicine: Honoring the Stories of Illness*. New York: Oxford University Press, 2006.

Chivers, Sally, and Nicole Markotic. *The Problem Body: Projecting Disability on Film*. Columbus: Ohio State University Press, 2010.

"Civil Rights, Disability Rights." EveryBody: An Artifact History of Disability in America. Accessed August 19, 2014. http://everybody.si.edu/citizens/civil-rights-disability-rights.

Clare, Eli. *Exile and Pride: Disability, Queerness and Liberation*. Cambridge, MA: South End Press, 1999.

Clark, Andy, and David J. Chalmers. "The Extended Mind." *Analysis* 58 (1998): 7–19.

Clarkson, John, Roger Coleman, Simeon Keates, and Cherie Lebbon. *Inclusive Design: Design for the Whole Population*. London: Springer-Verlag. 2003.

Clough, Patricia Ticineto, ed. *The Affective Turn: Theorizing the Social*. Durham, NC: Duke University Press. 2007.

Cogdell, Christina. *Eugenic Design: Streamlining America in the 1930s*. Philadelphia: University of Pennsylvania Press, 2004.

Cole, Michael. *Cultural Psychology: A Once and Future Discipline*. Cambridge, MA: Belknap Press of Harvard University Press, 1996.

Cole, Thomas R. *The Journey of Life: A Cultural History of Aging in America*. Cambridge: Cambridge University Press, 1992.

Connor, David J., and Beth. A. Ferri. "Integration and Inclusion: A Troubling Nexus: Race, Disability, and Special Education." *Journal of African American History* 90 (2005): 107–127.

Conrad, Peter. *The Medicalization of Society: On the Transformation of Human Conditions into Treatable Disorders*. Baltimore: Johns Hopkins University Press, 2007.

Conrad, Peter, and J. W. Schneider. *Deviance and Medicalization: From Badness to Sickness*. Philadelphia: Temple University Press, 1992.

Conroy, Colette. "Active Differences: Disability and Identity beyond Postmodernism." *Contemporary Theatre Review* 18 (2008): 341–354.

Cooper, Charlotte. "Can a Fat Woman Call Herself Disabled?" *Disability and Society* 12 (1997): 31–41.

Corina, D., and J. Singleton. "Developmental Social Cognitive Neuroscience: Insights from Deafness." *Child Development* 80 (2009): 952–967.

Corker, Marian. "Sensing Disability." *Hypatia* 16, no. 4 (2001): 34–52.

Corker, Marian, and Tom Shakespeare. "Mapping the Terrain." In *Disability/Postmodernity: Embodying Disability Theory*, edited by Marian Corker and Tom Shakespeare, 1–17. London: Continuum Press, 2002.

Couser, G. Thomas. *Recovering Bodies: Illness, Disability, and Life Writing*. Madison: University of Wisconsin Press, 1997.

———. *Signifying Bodies: Disability in Contemporary Life Writing*. Ann Arbor: University of Michigan Press, 2009.

Cowan, Ruth. *Heredity and Hope: The Case for Genetic Screening*. Cambridge, MA: Harvard University Press, 2008.

Crewe, Nancy M., and Irving Kenneth Zola. *Independent Living for Physically Disabled People*. London: Jossey-Bass, 1983.

Crews, Harry. *A Childhood: The Biography of a Place*. Athens: University of Georgia Press, 1995.

"Crip." In *Random House Dictionary of American Slang*, Vol. 1, *A–G*, edited by J. E. Lighter, 522. New York: Random House, 1994.

Cvetkovich, Ann, and Ann Pellegrini. "Public Sentiments." *The Scholar and Feminist Online* 2, no. 1 (2003). http://sfonline.barnard.edu/ps/intro.htm.

Darke, Paul. "Understanding Cinematic Representations of Disability." In *The Disability Reader: Social Science Perspectives*, edited by Tom Shakespeare, 181–200. London: Cassell, 1998.

Davidson, Michael. *Concerto for the Left Hand: Disability and the Defamiliar Body*. Ann Arbor: University of Michigan Press, 2008.

Davis, Lennard J. *Bending Over Backwards: Disability, Dismodernism and Other Difficult Positions*. New York: NYU Press, 2002.

———. "Dependency and Justice." *Journal of Literary Disability* 1, no. 2 (2007): 1–4.

———. "Disability: The Next Wave or the Twilight of the Gods?" *PMLA* 120 (2005): 527–532.

———. "Dr. Johnson, Amelia, and the Discourse of Disability in the Eighteenth Century." In *"Defects": Engendering the Modern Body*, edited by Helen Deutsch and Felicity Nussbaum, 54–74. Ann Arbor: University of Michigan Press, 2000a.

———. *Enforcing Normalcy: Disability, Deafness and the Body*. London: Verso, 1995.

———. *My Sense of Silence: Memoirs of a Childhood with Deafness*. Urbana: University of Illinois Press, 2000b.

Davis, Mike. *Planet of Slums*. New York: Verso, 2007.

de Certeau, Michel. *The Practices of Everyday Life*. Berkeley: University of California Press, 1984.

De Jong, Gerben. "Defining and Implementing the Independent, Living Concept." In *Independent Living for Physically Disabled People*, edited by Nancy Crewe and Irving K. Zola, 4–27. San Francisco: Jossey-Bass, 1983.

Deleuze, Gilles, and Felix Guattari. *A Thousand Plateaus: Capitalism and Schizophrenia*. Translated by Brian Massumi. London: Continuum, 1987.

D'Emilio, John. "Capitalism and Gay Identity." In *Powers of Desire: The Politics of Sexuality*, edited by Ann Snitow, Christine Stansell, and Sharon Thompson, 100–113. New York: Monthly Review Press, 1983.

Derrida, Jacques. "Structure, Sign, and Play in the Discourse of the Human Sciences." In *Writing and Difference*, 278–293. Translated by Alan Bass. Chicago: University of Chicago Press, 1978.

Descartes, René. "Automatism of Brutes" (1648). In *The Philosophy of Descartes: In Extracts from His Writing*. New York: Henry Holt, 1892.

Deutsch, Helen. "The Body's Moments: Visible Disability, the Essay, and the Limits of Sympathy." *Prose Studies* 27 (2005a): 11–26.

———. "Bolingbroke's Laugh: Alexander Pope's *Epistle I* and the Rhetoric of Embodied Exemplarity." *Studies in the Literary Imagination* 38 (2005b): 137–161.

———. *Resemblance and Disgrace: Alexander Pope and the Deformation of Culture*. Cambridge, MA: Harvard University Press, 1996.

Dickie, Simon. *Cruelty and Laughter: Forgotten Comic Literature and the Unsentimental Eighteenth Century*. Chicago: University of Chicago Press, 2011.

Dilts, Andrew. "Incurable Blackness: Criminal Disenfranchisement, Mental Disability and the White Citizen." *Disability Studies Quarterly* 32, no. 3 (2012). http://dsq-sds.org/article/view/3268/3101.

Dolmage, Jay. "Mapping Composition: Inviting Disability in the Front Door." In *Disability and the Teaching of Writing: A Critical Sourcebook*, edited by Cynthia Lewiecki-Wilson, Brenda Jo Brueggemann, and Jay Dolmage, 14–27. Boston: Bedford/St. Martin's, 2008.

Domínguez Rubio, Fernando, and Javier Lezaun. "Technology, Legal Knowledge and Citizenship: On the Care of Locked-In Syndrome Patients." In *The Politics of Knowledge*, edited by Fernando Domíngez Rubio and Patrick Baert, 58–78. London: Routledge, 2012.

Donley, G., S. C. Hull, and B. Berkman. "Prenatal Whole Genome Sequencing: Just Because We Can, Should We?" *Hastings Center Report* 42, no. 4 (2012): 28–40.

Dowbiggin, Ian Robert. *A Concise History of Euthanasia: Life, Death, God, and Medicine*. Lanham, MD: Rowman and Littlefield, 2005.

Dreyfuss, Henry. *Designing for People*. New York: Paragraphic Books, 1955.

DuBois, W. E. B. *The Souls of Black Folk*. 1903. Mineola, NY: Dover, 1994

Durbach, Nadja. *Spectacle of Deformity: Freak Shows and Modern British Culture*. Berkeley: University of California Press, 2009.

Durkheim, Émile. *The Rules of Sociological Method and Selected Texts on Sociology and Its Method*. 1895. Edited by Steven Lukes. Translated by W. D. Halls. New York: Free Press, 1982.

Duster, Troy. *Backdoor to Eugenics*. New York: Routledge, 1990.

Dwyer, Ellen. "Epilepsy Stories, 1880–1930." In *Framing Disease: Studies in Cultural History*, edited by Charles E. Rosenberg and Jane Goldern, 248–272. New Brunswick, NJ: Rutgers University Press, 1992.

Eagleton, Terry. *The Ideology of the Aesthetic*. Oxford: Blackwell, 1990.

Edwards, R. A. R. *Words Made Flesh: Nineteenth-Century Deaf Education and the Growth of Deaf Culture*. New York: NYU Press, 2012.

Eisenberg, C. B. "Genetic Predispositions v. Present Disabilities: What Genetically Predisposed Asymptomatic Individuals Are Not Protected by the Amended ADA." *Boston University Journal of Science and Technology Law* 16 (2010): 130–155.

Eisenberg, Myron G., Cynthia Griggins, and Richard J. Duval, eds. *Disabled People as Second-Class Citizens*. New York: Springer, 1982.

Emens, Elizabeth F. "Disabling Attitudes: U.S. Disability Law and the ADA Amendments Act." In *The Disability Studies Reader*, edited by Lennard J. Davis, 42–57. 4th ed. New York: Routledge, 2013.

———. "Integrating Accommodation." *University of Pennsylvania Law Review* 156 (2008): 839–922.

Engle, David M., and Frank W. Munger. *Rights of Inclusion: Law and Identity in the Life Stories of Americans with Disabilities*. Chicago: University of Chicago Press, 2003.

Erevelles, Nirmala. *Disability and Difference in Global Contexts: Towards a Transformative Body Politic*. New York: Macmillan, 2011.

———. "In Search of the Disabled Subject." In *Embodied Rhetorics: Disability in Language and Culture*, edited by James C. Wilson and Cynthia Lewiecki-Wilson, 92–111. Carbondale: Southern Illinois University Press, 2001.

———. "Understanding Curriculum as Normalizing Text: Disability Studies Meet Curriculum Theory." *Journal of Curriculum Studies* 37 (2005): 421–439.

Erevelles, Nirmala, and Alison Kafer. "Committed Critique: An Interview with Nirmala Erevelles." In *Deaf and Disability Studies: Interdisciplinary Perspectives*, edited by Susan Burch and Alison Kafer, 204–221. Washington, DC: Gallaudet University Press, 2010.

Evans, Simon. *Community and Ageing: Maintaining Quality of Life in Housing with Care Settings*. Bristol, UK: Policy Press, 2009.

Ewart, Chris. "Terms of Disappropriation: Disability, Diaspora and Dionne Brand's 'What We All Long For.'" *Journal of Literary and Cultural Disability Studies* 4 (2010): 147–161.

Fadiman, Anne. *The Spirit Catches You and You Fall Down*. New York: Farrar, Straus and Giroux, 1998.

Fausto-Sterling, Ann. *Sexing the Body: Gender Politics and the Construction of Sexuality*. New York: Basic Books, 2000.

Ferguson, Philip. *Abandoned to Their Fate: Social Policy and Practice toward Severely Retarded People in America, 1820–1920*. Philadelphia: Temple University Press, 1994.

Fiedler, Leslie. *Freaks: Myths and Images of the Secret Self*. New York: Simon and Schuster, 1978.

Fine, Michael, and Adrienne Asch. "The Question of Disability: No Easy Answers for the Women's Movement." *Reproductive Rights Newsletter* 4, no. 3 (1982): 19–20.

Fine, Michael, and Caroline Glendinning. "Dependence, Independence or Interdependence? Revisiting the Concepts of 'Care' and 'Dependency.'" *Ageing and Society* 25 (2005): 601–621.

Fineman, Martha Albertson. *The Neutered Mother, the Sexual Family and Other Twentieth Century Tragedies*. New York: Routledge, 1995.

———. "The Vulnerable Subject: Anchoring Equality in the Human Condition." *Yale Journal of Law and Feminism* 20 (2008): 1–23.

———. "The Vulnerable Subject and the Responsive State." *Emory Law Journal* 60 (2010): 251–275.

Finger, Anne. "Claiming All of Our Bodies: Reproductive Rights and Disabilities." In *Test Tube Women: What Future for Motherhood*, edited by Rita Arditti, Renate Duelli-Klein, and Shelley Minden, 281–297. Boston: Pandora Press, 1984.

———. "Forbidden Fruit." *New Internationalist* 233 (1992): 8–10.

Finkelstein, S. Naomi. "The Only Thing You Have to Do Is Live." *GLQ* 9 (2003): 307–319.

Finkelstein, Vic. "Emancipating Disability Studies." In *The Disability Studies Reader*, edited by Tom Shakespeare, 28–49. London: Cassell Academic, 1998.

Fischer, Renate, and Harlan Lane. *Looking Back: A Reader on the History of Deaf Communities and Their Sign Languages*. Hamburg: Signum, 1993.

Fleischer, Doris Zames, and Frieda Zames. *The Disability Rights Movement: From Charity to Confrontation*. Philadelphia: Temple University Press, 2001.

Foster, Hal, ed. *Vision and Visuality*. Discussions in Contemporary Culture. New York: New Press, 1998.

Foucault, Michel. *Abnormal: Lectures at the Collège de France, 1974–1975*. Edited by Valerio Marchetti and Antonella Salomoni. Translated by Graham Burchell. New York: Picador, 2003.

———. *The Birth of the Clinic: An Archaeology of Medical Perception*. New York: Vintage, 1975.

———. *Discipline and Punish*. Translated by Alan Sheridan. New York: Vintage, 1979.

———. *History of Madness*. Edited by J. Khalfa. Translated by J. Murphy. New York: Routledge, 2006.

———. *The History of Sexuality*. Translated by Robert Hurley. New York: Vintage, 1978.

———. *Madness and Civilization: A History of Insanity in the Age of Reason*. Trans. Richard Howard. New York: Random House, 1965.

———. *The Order of Things: An Archaeology of the Human Sciences*. New York: Random House, 1970.

———. "The Politics of Health in the Eighteenth Century." In *The Foucault Reader*, edited by Paul Rabinow, 273–289. New York: Pantheon, 1984.

Fox, Ann M. "How to Crip the Undergraduate Classroom: Lessons from Performance, Pedagogy, and Possibility." *Journal of Postsecondary Education and Disability* 23 (2010): 38–47.

Francis, Leslie Pickering, and Anita Silvers. *Americans with Disabilities: Exploring the Implications of Rights for Individuals and Institutions*. New York: Routledge, 2000.

Frank, Arthur. *The Wounded Storyteller: Body, Illness, and Ethics*. Chicago: University of Chicago Press, 1995.

Fraser, Nancy, and Linda Gordon. "A Genealogy of Dependency: Tracing a Keyword of the U.S. Welfare State." *Signs* 19 (1994): 309–336.

Fraser, Nancy, and Axel Honneth. *Redistribution or Recognition? A Political-Philosophical Exchange*. London: Verso, 2003.

Friedlander, Henry. *The Origins of Nazi Genocide: From Euthanasia to the Final Solution*. Chapel Hill: University of North Carolina Press, 1995.

Fries, Kenny. *Body, Remember*. New York: Dutton, 1997.

———, ed. *Staring Back: The Disability Experience from the Inside Out*. New York: Plume, 1997.

Fromm, Erich. *The Sane Society*. New York: Holt, 1955.

Frontera, Walter. *DeLisa's Physical Medicine and Rehabilitation*. Philadelphia: Lippincott Williams and Wilkins, 2010.

Fry, Tony. *Design Futuring: Sustainability, Ethics, and New Practice*. London: Berg, 2009.

Funk, Robert. "Disability Rights: From Caste to Class in the Context of Civil Rights." In *Images of the Disabled, Disabled Images*, edited by Alan Gartner and Tom Joe, 7–30. New York: Praeger, 1987.

Gall, James. *Historical Sketch of the Origin and Progress of Literature for the Blind: and Practical Hints and Recommendations as to their Education*. Edinburgh: James Gall, 1834.

Gallese, Vittorio, and Hannah Chapelle Wojciehowski. "How Stories Make Us Feel: Toward an Embodied Narratology." *California Italian Studies* 2, no. 1 (2011). http://escholarship.org/uc/item/3jg726c2.

Galloway, Terry, Donna Nudd, and Carrie Sandahl. "Actual Lives and the Ethic of Accommodation." *Community Performance: A Reader*, edited by Petra Kuppers, 227–234. New York: Routledge, 2007.

Gamson, Joshua. *Freaks Talk Back: Tabloid Talk Shows and Sexual Nonconformity*. Chicago: University of Chicago Press, 1999.

Garland-Thomson, Rosemarie. "The Case for Conserving Disability." *Journal of Bioethical Inquiry* 9 (2012): 339–355.

———. "The Cultural Logic of Euthanasia: 'Sad Fancyings' in Herman Melville's 'Bartleby.'" *American Literature* 76 (2004): 777–806.

———. *Extraordinary Bodies: Figuring Physical Disability in American Culture and Literature*. New York: Columbia University Press, 1997.

———. "Feminist Disability Studies." *Signs* 30 (2005): 1557–1587.

———, ed. *Freakery: Cultural Spectacles of the Extraordinary Body*. New York: NYU Press, 1996.

———. "Incorporating Disability Studies into the Existing Curriculum." *Radical Teacher* 47 (1995): 15–21.

———. "Integrating Disability, Transforming Feminist Theory." In *Feminist Disability Studies*, edited by Kim Q. Hall, 13–47. Bloomington: Indiana University Press, 2011.

———. "The Politics of Staring: Visual Rhetorics of Disability in Popular Photography." In *Disability Studies: Enabling the Humanities*, edited by Brenda Brueggemann, Rosemarie Garland-Thomson, and Sharon L. Snyder, 56–75. New York: Modern Language Association, 2002.

———. "Seeing the Disabled: Visual Rhetorics of Disability in Popular Photography." In *The New Disability History: American Perspectives*, edited by Paul Longmore and Lauri Umansky, 335–374. New York: NYU Press, 2001.

———. *Staring: How We Look*. New York: Oxford University Press, 2009.

Gartner, Alan, and Tom Joe. *Images of the Disabled/Disabling Images*. New York: Praeger Press, 1987.

Gehlen, Arnold. "A Philosophical-Anthropological Perspective on Technology." In *Philosophy of Technology: The Technological Condition*, edited by Robert Scharff and Val Dusek, 213–220. Malden, MA: Wiley-Blackwell, 2003.

Geller, Jeffrey L., and Maxine Harris. *Women of the Asylum: Voices from behind the Walls, 1840–1945*. New York: Anchor, 1994.

Gerber, David A. "The 'Careers' of People Exhibited in Freak Shows: The Problem of Volition and Valorization." In *Freakery: Cultural Displays of the Extraordinary Body*, edited by Rosemarie Garland-Thomson, 38–54. New York: NYU Press, 1996.

Gerber, Elaine. "Eat, Drink and Inclusion: The Politics of Disability and Food." *Disability Studies Quarterly* 27, no. 3 (2007). http://dsq-sds.org/article/view/19/19.

Geurts, Kathryn Linn. "Consciousness as 'Feeling in the Body': A West African Theory of Embodiment, Emotion and the Making of Mind." In *Empire of the Senses*, edited by David Howes, 164–178. Oxford: Berg, 2005.

———. *Culture and the Senses: Bodily Ways of Knowing in an African Community*. Berkeley: University of California Press, 2002.

Gibson, Barbara E. "Disability, Connectivity and Transgressing the Autonomous Body." *Journal of Medical Humanities* 27 (2006): 187–196.

Gilbert, Olive, and Sojourner Truth. *Narrative of Sojourner Truth: A Northern Slave, Emancipated from Bodily Servitude by the State of New York in 1828*. Boston: privately printed, 1850.

Gill, Carol J. "Disability, Constructed Vulnerability, and Socially Conscious Palliative Care." *Journal of Palliative Care* 22 (2006): 183–189.

———. "No, We Don't Think Our Doctors Are Out to Get Us: Responding to the Straw Man Distortions of Disability Rights Arguments against Assisted Suicide." *Disability and Health Journal* 3 (2010): 31–38.

Gilman, Sander L. *The Case of Sigmund Freud: Medicine and Identity at the Fin de Siècle*. Baltimore: Johns Hopkins University Press, 1993.

———. "Fat as Disability: The Case of the Jews." *Literature and Medicine* 23 (2004): 46–60.

———. *Seeing the Insane: A Cultural History of Psychiatric Illustration*. New York: Wiley Interscience, 1982.

Ginsberg, Elaine K. *Passing and the Fictions of Identity*. Durham, NC: Duke University Press, 1996.

Gliedman, John, and William Roth. *The Unexpected Minority: Handicapped Children in America*. New York: Harcourt Brace Jovanovich, 1980.

Goffman, Erving. *Asylums: Essays on the Social Situation of Mental Patients and Other Inmates*. Garden City, NY: Anchor, 1961.

———. *The Presentation of the Self in Everyday Life*. Woodstock, NY: Overlook Press, 1973.

———. *Stigma: Notes on the Management of Spoiled Identity*. New York: Simon and Schuster, 1963.

Goodey, C. F. *History of Intelligence and "Intellectual Disability": The Shaping of Psychology in Early Modern Europe*. Burlington VT: Ashgate, 2011.

Goodley, Dan, Bill Hughes, and Lennard Davis. *Social Theories of Disability: New Developments*. Basingstoke, UK: Palgrave, 2012.

Goodley, Dan, and Rebecca Lawthom. "Disability, Deleuze and Sex." In *Deleuze and Sex*, edited by Friday Beckman, 89–105. Edinburgh: Edinburgh University Press, 2011.

———. "Epistemological Journeys in Participatory Action Research: Alliances between Community Psychology and

Disability Studies." *Disability and Society* 20 (2005): 135–152.

Goodwin, Charles. "Gesture, Aphasia, and Interaction." In *Language and Gesture*, edited by David McNeill, 84–98. New York: Cambridge University Press, 2000.

Gorman, Carma. "Educating the Eye: Body Mechanics and Streamlining in the United States, 1925–1950." *American Quarterly* 58 (2006): 839–868.

Graham, Linda J., and Roger Slee. "An Illusory Interiority: Interrogating the Discourse/s of Inclusion." *Educational Philosophy and Theory* 40 (2008): 277–293.

Granger, Carl. "Quality and Outcome Measures for Rehabilitation Programs." *Medscape Reference: Drugs, Diseases, and Procedures.* June 27, 2011. Accessed September 17, 2014. http://emedicine.medscape.com/article/317865-overview#aw2aab6b.

Griesinger, Wilhelm. "Vorwort." *Archiv für Psychiatrie* und *Nervenkrankheiten* 1 (1868): iii–viii.

Grigely, Joseph. "Stuff." Paper presented at "Blind in the Museum" conference, Berkeley Art Museum, University of California, Berkeley, March 2005.

Grinker, Roy Richard. *Unstrange Minds: Remapping the World of Autism.* New York: Basic Books, 2007.

Groce, Nora Ellen. *Everyone Here Spoke Sign Language: Hereditary Deafness on Martha's Vineyard.* Cambridge, MA: Harvard University Press, 1985.

Grosz, Elizabeth. *The Nick of Time: Politics, Evolution, and the Untimely.* Durham, NC: Duke University Press, 2004.

Gullette, Margaret Morganroth. *Aged by Culture.* Chicago: University of Chicago Press, 2004.

Gutmann, Amy, and Dennis Thompson. *Why Deliberative Democracy?* Princeton, NJ: Princeton University Press, 2004.

Hacking, Ian. "Biopower and the Avalanche of Printed Numbers." *Humanities in Social Science* 5 (1982): 279–295.

Hadley, Bree. "(Dia)logics of Difference: Disability, Performance and Spectatorship in Liz Crow's Resistance on the Plinth." *Performance Research* 17 (2011): 124–131.

Hahn, Harlan. "Can Disability Be Beautiful?" *Social Policy* 18, no. 3 (1988): 26–32.

———. "Paternalism and Public Policy." *Society* 20, no. 3 (1983): 36–46.

Hall, Kim Q. "Queer Breasted Experience." In *You've Changed: Sex Reassignment and Personal Identity*, edited by Laurie J. Shrage, 121–134. New York: Oxford University Press, 2009.

———. "Queerness, Disability, and the Vagina Monologues." *Hypatia* 20, no. 1 (2005): 99–119.

Hanson, Ellis. "The Future's Eve: Reparative Reading after Sedgwick." *South Atlantic Quarterly* 110 (2011): 101–119.

Haraway, Donna. "The Cyborg Manifesto" (1985). In *Simians, Cyborgs, and Women: The Reinvention of Nature*, 149–181. New York: Routledge, 1991.

Harmon, Kristen C. "'If There Are Greek Epics, There Should Be Deaf Epics': How Protest Became Poetry." In *Signing the Body Poetic: Essays on American Sign Language Literature*, edited by H-Dirksen L. Bauman, Jennifer L. Nelson, and Heidi M. Rose, 169–194. Berkeley: University of California Press, 2006.

Hartman, Geoffrey H. "On Traumatic Knowledge and Literary Studies." *New Literary History* 26 (1995): 537–563.

Harvey, David. "Space as a Key Word." In *David Harvey: A Critical Reader,* edited by Noel Castree and Derek Gregory, 270–294. Oxford: Basil Blackwell, 2006.

Hay, William. *Deformity: An Essay.* Edited by Kathleen James-Cavan. 1754. Victoria, BC: University of Victoria Press, 2004.

Hayes, Jeanne, and Elizabeth M. Hannold. "The Road to Empowerment: A Historical Perspective on the Medicalization of Disability." *Journal of the Health and Human Services Administration* 30 (2007): 352–377.

Hellker, Paul, and Melanie Yergeau. "Autism and Rhetoric." *College English* 73 (2011): 485–497.

Henderson, Bruce, and Noam Ostrander. *Understanding Disability Studies and Performance Studies.* London: Routledge, 2010.

Herndon, April. "Disparate But Disabled: Fat Embodiment and Disability Studies." *NWSA Journal* 14 (2002): 120–137.

Herr, Stanley S. "Reforming Disability Nondiscrimination Laws: A Comparative Perspective." *University of Michigan Journal of Law Reform* 35 (2002): 319–322.

Herschbach, Lisa. "Prosthetic Reconstructions: Making the Industry, Re-making the Body, Modeling the Nation." *History Workshop Journal* 44 (1997): 23–57.

Hickey-Moody, Anna. *Unimaginable Bodies.* Rotterdam: Sense Publishers, 2009.

Hickok, Gregory, and Ursula Bellugi. "Neural Organization of Language: Clues from Sign Language Aphasia." In *The Handbook of Psycholinguistic and Cognitive Processes,* edited by Jackie Guendouzi, Filip Loncke, and Mandy Williams, 687–708. New York: Psychology Press, 2010.

Hilde, Lindemann. *Damaged Identities: Narrative Repair.* Ithaca, NY: Cornell University Press, 2001.

Hobbes, Thomas. *Leviathan.* Edited by Richard Tuck. Cambridge: Cambridge University Press, 1991.

Hopper, Elizabeth Kaino. "It's the Attitude: Fashion Designs for Women with Disabilities." 2012. Accessed September 17, 2014. http://www.inter-disciplinary.net/wp-content/uploads/2010/10/ekhopperpaper.pdf.

Howes, David. *Sensual Relations: Engaging the Senses in Culture and Social Theory.* Ann Arbor: University of Michigan Press, 2003.

Hubbard, Ruth. "Who Should and Should Not Inhabit the World." In *The Politics of Women's Biology,* edited by Ruth Hubbard, 179–198. New Brunswick, NJ: Rutgers University Press, 1990.

Huet, Marie Hélène. *Monstrous Imagination.* Cambridge, MA: Harvard University Press, 1993.

Huff, Joyce. "Access to the Sky: Airplane Seats and Fat Bodies as Contested Spaces." In *The Fat Studies Reader,* edited by Esther Rothblum and Sondra Solovay, 176–186. New York: NYU Press, 2009.

Hughes, Bill, Rachel Russell, and Kevin Paterson. "Nothing to Be Had 'Off the Peg': Consumption, Identity and the Immobilization of Young Disabled People." *Disability and Society* 20 (2005): 3–17.

Hutchins, Edwin. *Cognition in the Wild.* Cambridge, MA: MIT Press, 1995a.

———. "How a Cockpit Remembers Its Speeds." *Cognitive Science* 19 (1995b): 265–288.

Hvistendahl, Mara. *Unnatural Selection: Choosing Boys over Girls, and the Consequences of a World Full of Men.* New York: Public Affairs, 2011.

Illich, Ivan. *Limits to Medicine: Medical Nemeses.* London: Marion Boyars, 1975.

Imrie, Rob. "'Auto-disabilities': The Case of Shared Space Environments." *Environment and Planning* A 44 (2012): 2260–2277.

———. *Disability and the City.* London: Sage, 1996.

Ingstad, Benedicte, and Susan Reynolds Whyte, eds. *Disability in Local and Global Worlds.* Berkeley: University of California Press, 2007.

Jacobson, Denise Sherer. *The Question of David: A Disabled Mother's Journey through Adoption, Family, and Life.* Berkeley: Creative Arts Book Company, 1999.

Jain, Lochlann S. "The Prosthetic Imagination: Enabling and Disabling the Prosthesis Trope." *Science, Technology, and Human Values* 24 (1999): 31–54.

James, Jennifer C. "Gwendolyn Brooks, World War II, and the Politics of Rehabilitation." In *Feminist Disability Studies,* edited by Kim Q. Hall, 136–158. Bloomington: Indiana University Press, 2011.

James, Jennifer C., and Cynthia Wu. "Editors' Introduction: Race, Ethnicity, Disability, and Literature: Intersections and Interventions." *MELUS* 36, no. 3 (2006): 3–13.

Jarman, Michelle. "Exploring the World of the Different in Leslie Marmon Silko's Almanac of the Dead." *MELUS* 31, no. 3 (2006): 147–168.

Jay, Martin. *Downcast Eyes: The Denigration of Vision in Twentieth-Century French Thought.* Berkeley: University of California Press, 1994.

Jennings, Audra. "'The Greatest Numbers . . . Will Be Wage Earners': Organized Labor and Disability Activism, 1945–1953." *Labor: Studies in the Working-Class History of the Americas* 4, no. 4 (Winter 2007): 55–82.

Jernigan, Kenneth. "Who Are We? A Definition of Blindness." *Future Reflections* 24, no. 3 (2005). Accessed October 9, 2014. http://www.nfb.org/Images/nfb/Publications/fr/fr19/fr05sitc.htm.

Johnson, Harriet McBryde. *Too Late to Die Young: Nearly True Tales from a Life.* New York: Holt, 2005.

———. "Unspeakable Conversations." *New York Times Magazine,* February 16, 2003, 50–79.

Johnston, Trevor. "W(h)ither the Deaf Community? Population, Genetics, and the Future of Australian Sign Language." *American Annals of the Deaf* 148 (2004): 358–375.

Jokinen, Markku. "The Sign Language Person: A Term to Describe Us and Our Future More Clearly?" In *Looking Forward: EUD in the 3rd Millennium: The Deaf Person in the 21st Century,* edited by Lorraine Leeson, 50–63. Surrey: Douglas McLean, 2001.

Jolls, Christine. "Antidiscrimination and Accommodation." *Harvard Law Review* 115 (2001): 642–699.

Jolls, Christine, and J. J. Prescott. "Disaggregating Employment Protection: The Case of Disability Discrimination." *Harvard Law School John M. Olin Center for Law, Economics and Business Discussion Paper Series*. No. 496. (2004). September 3, 2004. Accessed September 17, 2014. http://lsr.nellco.org/cgi/viewcontent.cgi?article=1284&context=harvard_olin.

Kafer, Alison. *Feminist, Queer, Crip*. Bloomington: Indiana University Press, 2013.

Kant, Immanuel. *The Critique of Judgment*. Edited by James Creed Meredith. Oxford: Oxford University Press, 1952.

Karlan, Pamela S., and George Rutherglen. "Disabilities, Discrimination, and Reasonable Accommodation." *Duke Law Journal* 46 (1996): 1–41.

Katz, Jonathan Ned. "The Invention of Heterosexuality." *Socialist Review* 20 (1990): 7–34.

Katz, Stephen. *Cultural Aging: Life Course, Lifestyle, and Senior Worlds*. Peterborough, ON: Broadview Press, 2005.

Keidan, Lois, and C. J. Mitchell, eds. *Access All Areas: Live Art and Disability*. London: Live Art Development Agency, 2012.

Keith, Lois. *What Happened to You? Writings by Disabled Women*. New York: New Press, 1996.

Keller, Helen. *The World I Live In*. New York: Century, 1908.

Kelly, Christine. "Wrestling with Group Identity: Disability Activism and Direct Funding." *Disability Studies Quarterly* 30, nos. 3/4 (2010). Accessed September 17, 2014. http://dsq-sds.org/article/view/1279/1307.

Kemp, Evan, Jr. "Aiding the Disabled: No Pity Please." *New York Times*, September 3, 1981. Accessed September 24, 2014. http://www.nytimes.com/1981/09/03/opinion/aiding-the-disabled-no-pity-please.html.

Kendon, Adam. "Parallels and Divergences between Warlpiri Sign Language and Spoken Warlpiri: Analyses of Signed and Spoken Discourses." *Oceania* 58 (1988): 239–254.

Kevles, Daniel J. *In the Name of Eugenics: Genetics and the Uses of Human Heredity*. New York: Knopf, 1985.

Kim, Eunjung. "Heaven for Disabled People: Nationalism and International Human Rights Imagery." *Disability and Society* 26 (2011): 93–106.

King, Kimball, and Tom Fahy. *Peering behind the Curtain: Disability, Illness and the Extraordinary Body in Contemporary Theatre*. London: Routledge, 2002.

Kirkland, Anna. "What's at Stake in Fatness as a Disability?" *Disability Studies Quarterly* 26, no. 1 (2006). http://dsq-sds.org/article/view/648/825.

Kittay, Eva Feder. "Disability, Equal Dignity and Care." *Concilium: International Journal for Theology* 105 (2003): 105–115.

———. *Love's Labor: Essays in Women, Equality and Dependency*. New York: Routledge, 1999.

———. "When Caring Is Justice and Justice of Caring: Justice and Mental Retardation." In *Public Culture*, edited by Carol A. Breckenridge and Candace Volger, 557–580. Durham, NC: Duke University Press, 2001.

Kittay, Eva Feder, and Licia Carlson, eds. *Cognitive Disability and Its Challenge to Moral Philosophy*. Malden, MA: Wiley-Blackwell, 2010a.

———. "Introduction: Rethinking Philosophical Presumptions in Light of Cognitive Disability." In *Cognitive Disability and Its Challenge to Moral Philosophy*, edited by Eva Feder Kittay and Licia Carlson, 1–25. New York: Wiley-Blackwell, 2010b.

Kleege, Georgina. "Brain Work." In *Somatic Engagement*, edited by Petra Kuppers, 47–56. Oakland, CA: ChainLinks, 2011.

———. *Sight Unseen*. New Haven, CT: Yale University Press, 1999.

Kleinman, Arthur. *The Illness Narratives: Suffering, Healing, and the Human Condition*. New York: Basic Books, 1988.

Kline, Stephen J. "What Is Technology." *Bulletin of Science, Technology and Society* 1 (1985): 215–218.

Köbsell, Swantje. "Towards Self-Determination and Equalization: A Short History of the German Disability Rights Movement." *Disability Studies Quarterly* 26, no. 2 (2006). Accessed September 17, 2014. http://dsq-sds.org/article/view/692/869.

Kochhar-Lindgren, Kanta. *Hearing Difference: The Third Ear in Experimental, Deaf, and Multicultural Theater*. Washington, DC: Gallaudet University Press, 2006.

Kohrman, Matthew. *Bodies of Difference: Experiences of Disability and Institutional Advocacy in the Making of Modern China*. Berkeley: University of California Press, 2005.

Kontos, Pia C. "'The Painterly Hand': Embodied Consciousness and Alzheimer's Disease." *Journal of Aging Studies* 17 (2003): 151–170.

Krentz, Christopher. *Writing Deafness: The Hearing Line in Nineteenth-Century American Literature*. Chapel Hill: University of North Carolina University Press, 2007.

Kudlick, Catherine J. "Disability History: Why We Need

Another 'Other.'" *American Historical Review* 108 (2003): 763–793.

Kuhse, Helga, and Peter Singer. *Bioethics: An Anthology*. Malden, MA: Blackwell, 2006.

Kuppers, Petra. *Disability and Contemporary Performance: Bodies on Edge*. New York: Routledge, 2003.

———. *Disability and Performance*. London: Haworth Press, 2001.

———. *Disability Culture and Community Performance*. London: Palgrave Macmillan, 2011.

———. *The Scar of Visibility: Medical Performances and Contemporary Art*. Minneapolis: University of Minnesota Press, 2007.

———. *Studying Disability Arts and Culture: An Introduction*. New York: Palgrave, 2014.

Kuusisto, Stephen. *Only Bread, Only Light*. Port Townsend, WA: Copper Canyon Press, 2000.

LaCapra, Dominick. *Writing History, Writing Trauma*. Baltimore: Johns Hopkins University Press, 2000.

Ladd, Paddy. *Understanding Deaf Culture: In Search of Deafhood*. Buffalo, NY: Multilingual Matters, 2003.

Ladner, Richard. "Accessible Technology and Models of Disability." In *Design and Use of Assistive Technology: Social, Technical, Ethical, and Economic Challenges*, edited by Meeko Mitsuko K. Oishi, Ian M. Mitchell, and H. F. Machiel Van der Loos, 25–33. New York: Springer, 2010.

LaFollette, Hugh. "Licensing Parents Revisited." *Journal of Applied Philosophy* 27 (2010): 327–343.

Landsman, Gail H. *Reconstructing Motherhood and Disability in the Age of "Perfect" Babies*. New York: Routledge, 2009.

Lane, Harlan. *The Deaf Experience: Classics in Language and Education*. Cambridge, MA: Harvard University Press, 1984.

———. *When the Mind Hears: A History of the Deaf*. New York: Random House, 1984.

Larson, Dale. "Unconsciously Regarded as Disabled: Implicit Bias and the Regarded-As Prong of the Americans with Disabilities Act." *UCLA Law Review* 56 (2008): 451–488.

Lavi, Shai Joshua. *The Modern Art of Dying: A History of Euthanasia in the United States*. Princeton, NJ: Princeton University Press, 2005.

LeBesco, Kathleen. *Revolting Bodies? The Struggle to Re-define Fat Identity*. Amherst: University of Massachusetts Press, 2004.

Lefebvre, Henri. *The Production of Space*. Oxford: Blackwell, 1991.

Lehrer, Riva. Personal website. 1997. http://www.rivalehrerart.com/. Accessed September 17, 2014.

Lessing, Gotthold Ephraim. "Laocoon, or On the Limits of Painting and Poetry." In *German Aesthetic and Literary Criticism: Winckelmann, Lessing, Hamann, Herder, Schiller, Goethe*, edited by H. B Nisbet, 55–134. Cambridge: Cambridge University Press, 1985.

Lewis, Victoria. *Beyond Victims and Villains: Contemporary Plays by Disabled Playwrights*. New York: Theatre Communications Group, 2006.

Lindgren, Kristin. "Bodies in Trouble: Identity, Embodiment, and Disability." In *Gendering Disability*, edited by Bonnie G. Smith and Beth Hutchison, 145–165. Piscataway, NJ: Rutgers University Press, 2004.

Linker, Beth. "On the Borderland of Medical and Disability History: A Survey of the Fields." *Bulletin of the History of Medicine* 87 (2013): 499–535.

———. *War's Waste: Rehabilitation in World War I America*. Chicago: University of Chicago Press, 2011.

Linton, Simi. *Claiming Disability: Knowledge and Identity*. New York: NYU Press, 1998.

———. *My Body Politic*. Ann Arbor: University of Michigan Press, 2005.

Livingston, Julie. *Debility and the Moral Imagination in Botswana*. Bloomington: Indiana University Press, 2005.

———. "Disgust, Bodily Aesthetics and the Ethic of Being Human in Botswana." *Africa: Journal of the International African Institute* 78 (2008): 288–307.

Locke, John. *An Essay Concerning Human Understanding*. 1690. Chicago: Encyclopaedia Britannica, 1955.

Lombardo, Paul. *Three Generations, No Imbeciles: Eugenics, The Supreme Court, and Buck v. Bell*. Baltimore: Johns Hopkins University Press, 2008.

Longmore, Paul K. "The Life of Randolph Bourne and the Need for a History of Disabled People." *Reviews in American History* 13 (1985): 581–587.

———. *Why I Burned My Book and Other Essays on Disability*. Philadelphia: Temple University Press, 2003.

Longmore, Paul K., and Lauri Umansky. *The New Disability History: American Perspectives*. New York: NYU Press, 2001.

Lund, Roger. "Laughing at Cripples: Ridicule, Deformity, and the Argument from Design." *Eighteenth-Century Studies* 39 (2005): 91–114.

Lusseyran, Jacques. *And There Was Light*. Boston: Little, Brown, 1963.

Lyon, Janet. "On the Asylum Road with Woolf and Mew." *Modernism/Modernity* 18 (2011): 551–574.

Lysias. *Oration XXIV: On the Refusal of a Pension to the Invalid, Lysias*. Translated by W. H. Lamb. Cambridge, MA: Harvard University Press, 1957.

Macdonald, Barbara. "Look Me in the Eye." In *Look Me in the Eye: Old Women, Aging and Ageism* by Barbara MacDonald, with Cynthia Rich, 25–42. San Francisco: Spinster's Ink, 1983.

MacIntyre, Alasdair. *Dependent Rational Animals: The Virtue of Dependence and the Virtue of Acknowledging Dependence*. Berkeley: University of California Press, 1997.

Maclay, Kathleen. "A Painter Reinvents Herself." *Berkeleyan*, October 13, 1999. Accessed October 8, 2014. http://berkeley.edu/news/berkeleyan/1999/1013/painter.html.

Mairs, Nancy. "On Being a Cripple." In *Plaintext: Deciphering a Woman's Life*, 9–20. Tucson: University of Arizona Press, 1986.

———. *Waist High in the World*. New York: Beacon Press, 1997.

Mangold, George B. Untitled. *Proceedings of the First National Conference, Federal Board for Vocational Education*. Washington, DC: Government Printing Office, 1922.

Mansfield, C. S. Hopfer, and T. M. Marteau. "Termination Rates after Prenatal Diagnosis of Down Syndrome, Spina Bifida, Anencephaly, and Turner and Klinefelter Syndromes: A Systematic Literature Review." *Prenatal Diagnosis* 19 (1999): 808–812.

Marschark, Marc, and Patricia E. Spencer. *The Oxford Handbook of Deaf Studies, Language, and Education*. Oxford: Oxford University Press, 2011.

Marshall, T. H. *Citizenship and Social Class*. London: Pluto, 1950.

Martin, Emily. *Bipolar Expeditions: Mania and Depression in American Culture*. Princeton, NJ: Princeton University Press, 2007.

Martineau, Harriet. "Letter to the Deaf." In *Miscellanies*, 248–249. Boston: Hilliard, Gray and Co., 1836.

Mason, Jennifer. "Personal Narratives, Relational Selves: Residential Histories in the Living and Telling." *Sociological Review* 52 (2004): 162–179.

Massumi, Brian. "The Autonomy of Affect." *Cultural Critique* 31 (September 1995): 83–110.

Mathews, J. *A Mother's Touch: The Tiffany Callo Story*. New York: Holt, 1992.

Mathur, Gaurav, and Donna Jo Napoli. *Deaf around the World: The Impact of Language*. Oxford: Oxford University Press, 2011.

Mbembe, Achilles. "Necropolitics." Translated by Libby Meintjes. *Public Culture* 15 (2003): 11–40.

McLuhan, Marshall. *Understanding Media: The Extensions of Man*. New York: McGraw-Hill, 1964. Reprint, Cambridge, MA: MIT Press, 1994.

McRuer, Robert. "As Good as It Gets: Queer Theory and Critical Disability." *GLQ* 9 (2003): 79–105.

———. "Compulsory Able-Bodiedness and Queer/Disabled Existence." In *Disability Studies: Enabling the Humanities*, edited by Sharon L. Snyder, Brenda Jo Brueggemann, and Rosemarie Garland-Thomson, 88–99. New York: Modern Language Association, 2002.

———. *Crip Theory: Cultural Signs of Queerness and Disability*. New York: NYU Press, 2006.

McRuer, Robert, and Anna Mollow, eds. *Sex and Disability*. Durham, NC: Duke University Press, 2012.

Meekosha, Helen, and Leanne Dowse. "Enabling Citizenship: Gender, Disability and Citizenship in Australia." *Feminist Review* 57 (1998): 49–70.

Meir, Irit, Wendy Sandler, Carole Padden, and Mark Aronoff. "Emerging Sign Languages." In *Oxford Handbook of Deaf Studies, Language and Education*, edited by M. Marshark and P. Spencer, 267–280. Oxford: Oxford University Press, 2010.

Merleau-Ponty, Maurice. *The Phenomenology of Perception*. London: Routledge, 1962.

Metzl, Jonathan. *The Protest Psychosis: How Schizophrenia Became a Black Disease*. Boston: Beacon Press, 2011.

Michalko, Rod. *The Difference That Disability Makes*. Philadelphia: Temple University Press, 2002.

———. *The Two in One: Walking with Smokie, Walking with Blindness*. Philadelphia: Temple University Press, 1999.

Milam, Lorenzo. *Cripple Liberation Front Marching Band Blues*. San Diego: Mho & Mho Wors, 1983.

Millard, Candice. *Destiny of a Republic: A Tale of Madness, Medicine and the Murder of a President*. New York: Doubleday, 2011.

Minow, Martha. *Making All the Differece*. Ithaca, NY: Cornell University Press, 1990.

Mintz, Susannah B. "Invisible Disability: Georgina Kleege's *Sight Unseen*." In *Feminist Disability Studies*, edited by Kim Q. Hall, 69–90. Bloomington: Indiana University Press, 2011.

Miringoff, Marque-Luisa. *The Social Costs of Genetic Welfare*. New Brunswick, NJ: Rutgers University Press, 1991.

Mitchell, David T., and Sharon Snyder. "The Eugenic Atlantic: Race, Disability, and the Making of an International Eugenic Science, 1800–1945." *Disability and Society* 18 (2003): 843–864.

———. "Introduction: Disability Studies and the Double Bind of Representation." In *The Body and Physical Difference: Discourses of Disability*, edited by David T. Mitchell and Sharon L. Snyder, 1–32. Ann Arbor: University of Michigan Press, 1997.

———. *Narrative Prosthesis: Disability and the Dependencies of Discourse*. Ann Arbor: University of Michigan Press, 2000.

———. "Re-engaging the Body: Disability Studies and the Resistance to Embodiment." *Public Culture* 13 (2001): 367–391.

Mitchell, W. J. T. "Representation." In *Critical Terms for Literary Study*, edited by Frank Lentricchia and Thomas McLaughlin, 11–22. Chicago: University of Chicago Press, 1995.

Moi, Toril. *Sexual/Textual Politics: Feminist Literary Theory*. New York: Routledge, 1985.

Mollow, Anna. "Is Sex Disability? Queer Theory and the Disability Drive." In *Sex and Disability*, edited by Robert McRuer and Anna Mollow. 285–312. Durham, NC: Duke University Press, 2012.

———. "'When Black Women Start Going on Prozac': Race, Gender, and Mental Illness in Meri Nana-Ama Danquah's *Willow Weep for Me*." *MELUS* 31, no. 3 (2006): 67–99.

Montaigne, Michel de. *The Complete Essays of Montaigne*. Translated by Donald Frame. Stanford, CA: Stanford University Press, 1981.

Montgomery, Cal. "A Hard Look at Invisible Disability." *Ragged Edge Online*, no. 2 (March 2001). http://www.ragged-edge-mag.com/0301/0301ft1.htm.

Moran, Mayo. "The Reasonable Person and the Discrimination Inquiry" In *Accommodating Cultural Diversity*, edited by Stephen Tierney, 147–166. Hampshire, UK: Ashgate, 2007.

Morris, David. *The Culture of Pain*. Berkeley: University of California Press, 1991.

Morris, Jenny. "Independent Living and Community Care: A Disempowering Framework." *Disability and Society* 19 (2004): 427–442.

———. "Rethinking Disability Policy." Speech. November 2011. Accessed May 8, 2012. YouTube.com.

Morris, Richard. *The Blickling Homilies of the Tenth Century: From the Marquis of Lothians Unique Manuscript A.D. 971*. Translated and edited by Richard Morris. London: Early English Text Society, 1880.

Morrison, Daniel R., and Monica J. Casper. "Intersections of Disability Studies and Critical Trauma Studies: A Provocation." *Disability Studies Quarterly* 32, no. 2 (2012). http://dsq-sds.org/article/view/3189.

Munt, Sally R. "Shame/Pride Dichotomies in *Queer as Folk*." *Textual Practice* 14 (2000): 531–546.

Murphy, Robert. *The Body Silent*. New York: Norton, 1990.

Mutcherson, K. "Disabling Dreams of Parenthood: The Fertility Industry, Anti-discrimination and Parents with Disabilities." *Law and Inequality: A Journal of Theory and Practice* 27 (2009): 311–364.

Myrdal, Gunnar. *An American Dilemma: The Negro Problem and Modern Democracy*. New York: Harper and Brothers, 1944.

Nakamura, Karen. *Deaf in Japan: Signing and the Politics of Identity*. Ithaca, NY: Cornell University Press, 2006.

Nancy, Jean-Luc. *Corpus*. Translated by Richard A. Rand. New York: Fordham University Press, 2008.

National Association of the Deaf. *Cochlear Implants in Children: A Position Paper of the National Association of the Deaf*. Silver Spring, MD: National Association of the Deaf, 1991.

National Institute of Medicine. *Living Well with Chronic Illness: A Call for Public Health Action*. Washington, DC: National Academies Press, 2012.

National Public Radio. "A Life Defined Not by Disability, but Love." *NPR Morning Edition*. February 8, 2013.

Newell, C. "The Social Nature of Disability, Disease, and Genetics: A Response to Gillam, Persson, Holtug, Draper and Chadwick." *Journal of Medical Ethics* 25 (1999): 172–175.

Newton, Isaac, and Andrew Motte. *Sir Isaac Newton's Mathematical Principles of National Philosophy and His System of the World*. Berkeley: University of California Press, 1934.

Nielsen, Kim. *A Disability History of the United States.* Boston: Beacon Press, 2012.

Noll, Steven, and James Trent. *Mental Retardation in America: A Historical Reader.* New York: NYU Press. 2006.

Norden, Martin F. *The Cinema of Isolation: A History of Physical Disability in the Movies.* New Brunswick, NJ: Rutgers University Press, 1994.

Nosek, Margaret, A., Carol Howland, Diana Rintala, Mary Ellen Young, and Gail Chanpong. "National Study of Women with Physical Disabilities: Final Report." *Sexuality and Disability* 19 (2001): 5–39.

Nussbaum, Martha C. *Frontiers of Justice: Disability, Nationality, Species Membership.* Cambridge, MA: Harvard University Press, 2006.

———. "'Obesity,' the Transnational Plate, and the Thin Contract." *Radical Philosophy Review* 13 (2010): 43–67.

O'Brien, Mark. "On Seeing a Sex Surrogate." *Sun Magazine* 174 (May 1990). Accessed September 20, 2014. http://thesunmagazine.org/issues/174/on_seeing_a_sex_surrogate.

O'Brien, Ruth. *Crippled Justice: The History of Modern Disability Policy in the Workplace.* Chicago: University of Chicago Press, 2001.

———. *Voices from the Edge: Narratives about the Americans with Disabilities Act.* New York: Oxford University Press, 2004.

Ó Cathain, Mairtin. "'Blind, but Not to the Hard Facts of Life': The Blind Workers' Struggle in Derry, 1928–1940." *Radical History Review* 94, no. 1 (2006): 9–21.

Oliver, Michael. "Changing the Social Relations of Research Production." *Disability, Handicap and Society* 7 (1992): 101–114.

———. "Defining Impairment and Disability: Issues at Stake." In *Exploring the Divide: Illness and Disability*, edited by Colin Barnes and Gary Mercer, 39–54. Leeds: Disability Press, 1996.

———. "Disability and Dependency: A Creation of Industrial Societies." In *Disability and Dependency*, edited by Len Barton, 6–22. London: Falmer Press, 1989.

———. *The Politics of Disablement.* London: Macmillan, 1990.

Omansky, Beth. *Borderlands of Blindness.* Boulder, CO: Lynne Rienner, 2011.

"On the Medicalization of Our Culture." *Harvard Magazine*, April 23, 2009. Accessed September 17, 2014. http://harvardmagazine.com/2009/04/medicalization-of-our-culture.

Oppenheim, Rachel. "Impairment/Impaired." In *Encyclopedia of American Disability History*, edited by Susan Burch, 2:474–475. New York: Facts on File, 2009.

Osteen, Mark. *Autism and Representation.* New York: Taylor and Francis, 2007.

O'Toole, Corbett. "The Sexist Inheritance of the Disability Movement." In *Rethinking Normalcy*, edited by Tanya Titchkosky and Rod Michalko, 289–295. Toronto: Canadian Scholar's Press, 2009.

Ott, Katherine. "Carnage Remembered: Prosthetics in the US Military since the 1860s." In *Materializing the Military*, edited by Bernard Finn and Barton Hacker, 47–64. London: Science Museum, 2005.

———. "The Sum of Its Parts: An Introduction to Modern Histories of Prosthetics." In *Artificial Parts, Practical Lives: Modern Histories of Prosthetics*, edited by Katherine Ott, David Serlin, and Stephen Mihm, 1–42. New York: NYU Press, 2002.

Ott, Katherine, David Serlin, and Stephen Mihm, eds. *Artificial Parts, Practical Lives: Modern Histories of Prosthetics.* New York: NYU Press, 2002.

Ouellette, Alicia. *Bioethics and Disability: Toward a Disability-Conscious Bioethics.* Cambridge: Cambridge University Press, 2011.

Padden, Carol, and Tom Humphries. *Inside Deaf Culture.* Cambridge, MA: Harvard University Press, 2005.

Palmeri, Jason. "Disability Studies, Cultural Analysis, and the Critical Practice of Technical Communication Pedagogy." *Technical Communication Quarterly* 15 (2006): 49–65.

Panchasi, Roxanne. "Reconstructions: Prosthetics and the Male Body in Post WWI France." *differences* 7 (1995): 109–140.

Panzarino, Connie. *The Me in the Mirror.* Seattle, WA: Seal Press, 1994.

Parens, Erik, and Adrienne Asch. "The Disability Rights Critique of Prenatal Genetic Testing: Reflections and Recommendations." In *Prenatal Testing and Disability Rights*, edited by Erik Parens and Adrienne Asch, 3–43. Washington, DC: Georgetown University Press, 2007.

Park, Melissa. "Beyond Calculus: Apple-Apple-Apple-Ike and Other Embodied Pleasures for a Child Diagnosed with

Autism in a Sensory Integration Based Clinic." *Disability Studies Quarterly* 30, no. 1 (2010). http://dsq-sds.org/article/view/1066/1232.

Paterson, Kevin, and Bill Hughes. "Disability Studies and Phenomenology: The Carnal Politics of Everyday Life." *Disability and Society* 14 (1999): 597–610.

Paul, Diane B. *Controlling Human Heredity: 1865 to the Present.* Atlantic Highlands, NJ: Humanities Press, 1998.

Paul, Diane B, and Hamish Spencer. "Did Eugenics Rest on an Elementary Mistake?" In *Thinking about Evolution: Historical, Philosophical and Political Perspectives*, edited by Rama S. Singh, Costas B. Krimbas, Diane B. Paul, and John Beatty, 103–118. Cambridge: Cambridge University Press, 2000.

Paulson, William R. *Enlightenment, Romanticism, and the Blind in France.* Princeton, NJ: Princeton University Press, 1987.

Pelka, Fred. *What We Have Done: An Oral History of the Disability Rights Movement.* Amherst: University of Massachusetts Press, 2012.

Pender, Stephen. "In the Bodyshop: Human Exhibition in Early Modern England. In *"Defects": Engendering the Modern Body*, edited by Helen Deutsch and Felicity Nussbaum, 95–126. Ann Arbor: University of Michigan Press, 2000.

Pernick, Martin S. *The Black Stork: Eugenics and the Death of "Defective" Babies in American Medicine and Motion Pictures since 1915.* New York: Oxford University Press, 1996.

Pfeiffer, David, and Karen Yoshida. "Teaching DS in Canada and the USA." *Disability and Society* 10 (1995): 475–495.

Phelan, Jo C. "Geneticization of Deviant Behavior and Consequences for Stigma: The Case of Mental Illness." *Journal of Health and Social Behavior* 46 (2005): 307–322.

Phillips, Sarah D. *Disability and Mobile Citizenship in Postsocialist Ukraine.* Bloomington: Indiana University Press, 2011.

Plann, Susan. *A Silent Minority: Deaf Education in Spain, 1550–1835.* Berkeley: University of California Press, 1997.

Poore, Carol. *Disability in Twentieth-Century German Culture.* Ann Arbor: University of Michigan Press, 2007.

———. "'No Friend of the Third Reich': Disability as the Basis for Antifascist Resistance in Arnold Zweig's *Das Beil von Wandsbek*." In *Enabling the Humanities*, edited by Sharon L. Snyder, Brenda Jo Brueggemann, and Rosemarie Garland-Thomson, 260–270. New York: Modern Language Association, 2002.

Pope, Andrew M., and Alvin R. Tarlov. *Disability in America:*

Toward a National Agenda for Prevention. Washington, DC: National Academies Press, 1991.

Porter, Roy. *Madness: A Brief History.* Oxford: Oxford University Press, 2003.

Powers, Richard. *Operation Wandering Soul.* New York: Morrow, 1993.

Preston, Paul. *Mother Father Deaf: Living between Sound and Silence.* Cambridge, MA: Harvard University Press, 1994.

Price, Margaret. *Mad at School: Rhetorics of Mental Disability and Academic Life.* Ann Arbor: University of Michigan Press, 2011.

Probyn, Elspeth. "Shaming Bodies: Dynamics of Shame and Pride." *Body and Society* 6 (2000): 13–28.

Puar, Jasbir. "Coda: The Cost of Getting Better: Suicide, Sensation, Switchpoints." *GLQ* 18 (2012): 149–158.

Pullin, Graham. *Design Meets Disability.* Cambridge, MA: MIT Press, 2009.

Punter, David. "A Foot Is What Fits the Shoe: Disability, the Gothic and Prosthesis." *Gothic Studies* 2 (2000): 39–49.

Putnam, Constance E. *Hospice or Hemlock: Searching for Heroic Compassion.* Westport, CT: Praeger, 2002.

Putti, Vittorio. *Historic Artificial Limbs.* New York: Paul Hoeber, 1930.

Quartararo, Anne T. *Deaf Identity and Social Images in Nineteenth-Century France.* Washington, DC: Gallaudet University Press, 2008.

Quayson, Ato. *Aesthetic Nervousness: Disability and the Crisis of Representation.* New York: Columbia University Press, 2007.

Quinn, Gerard. "Personhood and Legal Capacity: Perspectives on the Paradigm Shift of Article 12 CRPD." Paper presented at the Harvard Law School Project on Disability Conference. Harvard Law School, February 20, 2010.

Ralph, Michael. "'Life . . . in the Midst of Death': Notes on the Historical Relationship between Life Insurance and Disability." *Disability Studies Quarterly* 32, no. 3 (2012). Accessed October 10, 2014. http://dsq-sds.org/article/view/3267/3100.

Rancière, Jacques. *Aesthetics and Its Discontents.* Translated by Steven Corcoran. Cambridge, UK: Polity Press, 2009.

Rapp, Rayna. *Testing Women, Testing the Fetus: The Social Impact of Amniocentesis in America.* New York: Routledge, 2000.

Rapp, Rayna, and Faye D. Ginsburg. "Enabling Disability: Rewriting Kinship, Reimagining Citizenship." *Public Culture* 13 (2001): 533–556.

———. "Reverberations: Disability and the New Kinship Imaginary." *Anthropological Quarterly* 84 (2011): 379–410.

Rawls, John. "Kantian Constructivism in Moral Theory: The Dewey Lectures." *Journal of Philosophy* 77 (1980): 515–571.

Reindal, Solveig Magnus. "Independence, Dependence, Interdependence: Some Reflections on the Subject and Personal Autonomy." *Disability and Society* 14 (1999): 353–367.

Reiss, Benjamin. *The Showman and the Slave: Race, Death, and Memory in Barnum's America*. Cambridge, MA: Harvard University Press, 2001.

———. *Theaters of Madness: Insane Asylums and Nineteenth-Century American Culture*. Chicago: University of Chicago Press, 2008.

Rembis, Michael A. *Defining Deviance: Sex, Science, and Delinquent Girls, 1890–1960*. Chicago: University of Illinois Press, 2011.

Rich, Adrienne. "Compulsory Heterosexuality and Lesbian Existence." In *Powers of Desire: The Politics of Sexuality*, edited by Ann Snitow, Christine Stansell, and Sharon Thompson, 177–205. New York: Monthly Review Press, 1983.

Rivas, Lynn May. "Invisible Labors: Caring for the Independent Person." In *Global Women: Nannies, Maids and Sex Workers in the Global Economy*, edited by Barbara Ehrenreich and Arlie Russell Hochchild, 70–82. New York: Holt, 2002.

Rogers, Rebecca, and Michael Mancini. "'Requires Medication to Progress Academically': The Discursive Pathways of ADHD." In *The Myth of the Normal Curve*, edited by Curt Dudley-Marling and Alex Gurn, 87–103. New York: Peter Lang, 2010.

Rohrer, Tim. "The Body in Space: Dimensions of Embodiment." In *Body, Language and Mind*, edited by Jordan Zlatev, Tom Ziemke, Roz Frank, and Rene Dirven, 339–378. Berlin: Mouton de Gruyter, 2007.

Rose, Heidi. "The Poet in the Poem in the Performance: The Relation of Body, Self, and Text in ASL Literature." In *Signing the Body Poetic: Essays on American Sign Language Literature*, edited by H-Dirksen L. Bauman, Jennifer L. Nelson, and Heidi M. Rose, 130–146. Berkeley: University of California Press, 2006.

Rose, Nikolas. *The Politics of Life Itself: Biomedicine, Power, and Subjectivity in the Twenty-First Century*. Princeton, NJ: Princeton University Press, 2007.

Rose, Sarah F. "'Crippled' Hands: Disability in Labor and Working-Class History." *Labor: Studies in the Working-Class History of the Americas* 2 (2005): 27–54.

Rothblum, Esther, and Sondra Solovay, eds. *The Fat Studies Reader*. New York: NYU Press, 2009.

Rothfels, Nigel. "Aztecs, Aborigines, and Ape-People: Science and Freaks in Germany, 1850–1900." In *Freakery: Cultural Displays of the Extraordinary Body*, edited by Rosemarie Garland-Thomson, 158–172. New York: NYU Press, 1996.

Rothman, Sheila, and David Rothman. *The Willowbrook Wars*. Piscataway, NJ: Aldine Transaction, 2005.

Rubin, Gayle. "Thinking Sex: Notes for a Radical Theory of the Politics of Sexuality." In *Pleasure and Danger*, edited by Carole Vance, 143–178. New York: Routledge, 1984.

Russell, Emily. *Reading Embodied Citizenship: Disability, Narrative, and the Body Politic*. New Brunswick, NJ: Rutgers University Press, 2011.

Russell, Marta. *Beyond Ramps: Disability at the End of the Social Contract: A Warning from an Uppity Crip*. Monroe, ME: Common Courage Press, 1998.

Sacks, Harvey. "On Doing 'Being Ordinary.'" In *Structures of Social Action: Studies in Conversational Analysis*, edited by J. Maxell and J. Heritage, 413–430. Cambridge: Cambridge University Press, 1984.

Salamon, Gayle. *Assuming a Body: Transgender and the Rhetorics of Materiality*. New York: Columbia University Press, 2010.

Sandahl, Carrie. "Black Man, Blind Man: Disability Identity Politics and Performance." *Theatre Journal* 56 (2004): 597–602.

———. "Queering the Crip or Cripping the Queer? Intersections of Queer and Crip Identities in Solo Autobiographical Performance." *GLQ* 9 (2003): 25–56.

Sandel, Michael. *The Case against Perfection: Ethics in the Age of Genetic Engineering*. Cambridge, MA: Belknap Press of Harvard University Press, 2007.

Sandler, Wendy, and Diane Lillo-Martin. *Sign Language and Linguistic Universals*. Cambridge: Cambridge University Press, 2006.

Satz, Ani B. "Animals as Vulnerable Subjects: Beyond Interest-

Convergence, Hierarchy, and Property." *Animal Law Review* 16 (2009): 65–122.

———. "Disability, Vulnerability, and the Limits of Antidiscrimination." *Washington Law Review* 83 (2008): 513–568.

———. "A Jurisprudence of Dysfunction: On the Role of 'Normal Species Functioning' in Disability Analysis." *Yale Journal of Health Policy, Law, and Ethics* 6 (2006): 221–267.

———. "Overcoming Fragmentation in Health and Disability Law." *Emory Law Journal* 60 (2010): 277–319.

Sauerborn, Paula. "Advances in Upper Extremity Prosthetics in the United States during World War II and Early Post–World War II Era." *Journal of Facial and Somato Prosthetics* 4 (1998): 93–104.

Savarese, Emily Thornton, and Ralph James Savarese. "Autism and the Concept of Neurodiversity." *Disability Studies Quarterly* 30, no. 1 (2010a). http://dsq-sds.org/issue/view/43.

———. "'The Superior Half of Speaking': An Introduction." *Disability Studies Quarterly* 30, no. 1 (2010b). http://dsq-sds.org/article/view/1062/1230.

Savarese, Ralph James. "More Than a Thing to Ignore: An Interview with Tito Rajarshi Mukhopadhyay." *Disability Studies Quarterly* 30, no. 1 (2010). http://dsq-sds.org/article/view/1056/1235.

Saxton, Marsha. "Born and Unborn: The Implications of Reproductive Technologies for People with Disabilities." In *Test-Tube Women: What Future for Motherhood*, edited by Rita Arditti, Renate Duelli-Klein, and Shelley Minden, 298–312. Boston: Pandora Press, 1984.

Scalenghe, Sara. *The Body Different: Disability in the Arab-Islamic World, 1500–1800*. Cambridge: Cambridge University Press, 2014.

Scarry, Elaine. *The Body in Pain: The Making and Unmaking of the World*. Oxford: Oxford University Press, 1985.

Schartz, Helen A., D. J. Hendricks, and Peter Blanck. "Workplace Accommodations: Evidence Based Outcomes." *Work* 27 (2006): 345–354.

Scherer, Marcia. "The Change in Emphasis from People to Person: Introduction to the Special Issue on Assistive Technology." *Disability and Rehabilitation* 24 (2002): 1–4.

Schillmeier, Michael. *Rethinking Disability: Bodies, Senses, and Things*. New York: Routledge, 2010.

Schweik, Susan. "Lomax's Matrix: Disability, Solidarity, and the Black Power of 504." *Disability Studies Quarterly* 31, no. 1 (2011). http://dsq-sds.org/article/view/1371/1539.

———. *The Ugly Laws: Disability in Public*. New York: NYU Press, 2009.

Scotch, Richard. *From Good Will to Civil Rights: Transforming Federal Disability Policy*. Philadelphia: Temple University Press, 1984.

Scully, Jackie Leach. *Disability Bioethics: Moral Bodies, Moral Difference*. Lanham, MD: Rowman and Littlefield, 2008.

Sedgwick, Eve Kosofsky, and Adam Frank. *Shame and Its Sisters: A Silvan Tomkins Reader*. Durham, NC: Duke University Press, 1995a.

———. "Shame in the Cybernetic Fold." *Critical Inquiry* 21 (1995b): 496–522.

Semonin, Paul. "Monsters in the Marketplace: The Exhibition of Human Oddities in Early Modern England." In *Freakery: Cultural Displays of the Extraordinary Body*, edited by Rosemarie Garland-Thomson, 69–81. New York: NYU Press, 1996. 69–81.

Serlin, David. "Cripping Masculinity: Queerness and Disability in U.S. Military Culture, 1800–1945." *GLQ* 9 (2003): 149–179.

———. "Disability, Masculinity, and the Prosthetics of War, 1945–2005." In *The Prosthetic Impulse: From a Posthuman Present to a Biocultural Future*, edited by Marquard Smith and Joanne Morra, 155–183. Cambridge, MA: MIT Press, 2006.

———. *Replaceable You: Engineering the Body in Postwar America*. Chicago: University of Chicago Press, 2004.

———. "Touching Histories: Personality, Disability, and Sex in the 1930s." In *Sex and Disability*, edited by Robert McRuer and Anna Mollow, 145–162. Durham, NC: Duke University Press, 2012.

Shakespeare, Tom. "Back to the Future? New Genetics and Disabled People." *Critical Social Policy* 15 (1995): 22–35.

———. "Cultural Representations of Disabled People: Dustbins for Disavowal." *Disability and Society* 9 (1994): 283–299.

———. *Disability Rights and Wrongs*. London: Routledge, 2006a.

———. "The Social Model of Disability." In *The Disability Studies Reader*, edited by Lennard J. Davis, 197–204. New York: Routledge 2006b.

Shakespeare, Tom, Kath Gillespie-Sells, and Dominic Davies. *The Sexual Politics of Disability: Untold Desires*. London: Cassell, 1996.

Shapiro, Joseph P. "Court Debates Disabilities Act." *All Things Considered*. National Public Radio, January 12, 2004. Accessed September 16, 2014. http://www.npr.org/templates/story/story.php?storyId=1594218.

———. *No Pity: People with Disabilities Forging a New Civil Rights Movement*. New York: Times Books, 1994.

Sheppard, Alice. "When the Saints Come Crippin' In." Unpublished manuscript.

Shildrick, Margrit. *Dangerous Discourses of Disability, Subjectivity, and Sexuality*. New York: Macmillan, 2009.

———. "Queering Performativity: Disability after Deleuze." *SCAN: Journal of Media Arts Culture* 3, no. 3 (2004). Accessed September 19, 2014. http://scan.net.au.

———. "Sexual Citizenship, Governance and Disability." In *Beyond Citizenship: Feminism and the Transformation of Belonging*, edited by Sasha Roseneil, 138–159. London: Macmillan, 2013.

Shildrick, Margrit, and Janet Price. *Vital Signs: Feminist Reconfigurations of the Bio/Logical Body*. Edinburgh: Edinburgh University Press, 1998.

Shlovsky, Victor. "Art as Technique." In *Russian Formalist Criticism: Four Essays*, edited by Lee T. Lemon and Marion J. Reis, 3–24. Lincoln: University of Nebraska Press, 1965.

Shorter, Edward. *A History of Psychiatry: From the Era of the Asylum to the Age of Prozac*. New York: Wiley, 1998.

Shuttleworth, Russell. "Defusing the Adverse Context of Disability and Desirability as a Practice of the Self for Men with Cerebral Palsy." In *Disability/Postmodernism: Embodying Disability Theory*, edited by Mariam Corker and Tom Shakespeare, 112–126. London: Continuum, 2002.

Siebers, Tobin. *Disability Aesthetics*. Ann Arbor: University of Michigan Press, 2010.

———. "Disability as Masquerade." *Literature and Medicine* 23 (2004): 1–22.

———. "Disability Experience on Trial." In *Material Feminisms*, edited by Stacy Alaimo and Susan Hekman, 291–307. Bloomington: Indiana University Press, 2008a.

———. *Disability Theory*. Ann Arbor: University of Michigan Press, 2008b.

Siebold, Cathy. *The Hospice Movement: Easing Death's Pains*. New York: Twayne, 1992.

Silverman, Chloe. *Understanding Autism: Parents, Doctors, and the History of a Disorder*. Princeton, NJ: Princeton University Press, 2011.

Silvers, Anita. "Aging Fairly: Feminist and Disability Perspectives on Intergenerational Justice." In *Mother Time: Women, Aging, and Ethics*, edited by Margaret Urban Walker, 203–226. Lanham, MD: Rowman and Littlefield, 1999.

———. "A Fatal Attraction to Normalizing: Treating Disabilities as Deviations from 'Species-Typical' Functioning." In *Enhancing Human Traits*, edited by Erik Parens, 95–123. Washington, DC: Georgetown University Press, 1998.

———. "The Rights of People with Disabilities." In *The Oxford Handbook of Practical Ethics*, edited by Hugh LaFollette, 300–327. Oxford: Oxford University Press, 2002.

Silvers, Anita, David Wasserman, and Mary Mahowald. *Disability, Difference, Discrimination*. Lanham, MD: Rowman and Littlefield, 1999.

Singer, Peter. *Practical Ethics*. Cambridge: Cambridge University Press, 1993.

———. *Rethinking Life and Death: The Collapse of Our Traditional Ethics*. New York: St. Martin's, 1995.

Snyder, Sharon L., Brenda Jo Brueggeman, and Rosemarie Garland-Thomson, eds. *Disability Studies: Enabling the Humanities*. New York: Modern Language Association, 2002.

Snyder, Sharon L., and David T. Mitchell. *Cultural Locations of Disability*. Chicago: University of Chicago Press, 2006.

Solomon, Andrew. *Far from the Tree: Parents, Children, and the Search for Identity*. New York: Scribner, 2012.

Spade, Dean. "About Purportedly Gendered Body Parts." Accessed September 19, 2014. http://www.deanspade.net/wp-content/uploads/2011/02/Purportedly-Gendered-Body-Parts.pdf.

———. "Resisting Medicine, Re/modeling Gender." *Berkeley Women's Law Journal* 18 (2003): 15–37.

Spillers, Hortense J. "Mama's Baby, Papa's Maybe: An American Grammar Book." *Diacritics: A Review of Contemporary Criticism* 17 (1987): 65–81.

Stein, Michael Ashley. "Disability Human Rights." *California Law Review* 95 (2007): 75–121.

———. "The Law and Economics of Disability Accommodations." *Duke Law Journal* 53 (2003): 79–180.

Stern, Alexandra Minna. *Eugenic Nation: Faults and Frontiers of Better Breeding in Modern America*. Berkeley: University of California Press, 2005.

Stevens, Bethany. "Interrogating Transability: A Catalyst to Viewing Disability as Bodily Art." *Disability Studies Quarterly* 31, no. 4 (2011). http://dsq-sds.org/article/view/1705/1755.

Stewart, Jean. *The Body's Memory.* New York: St. Martin's, 1993.

Stiker, Henri-Jacques. *A History of Disability.* Translated by William Sayers. Ann Arbor: University of Michigan Press, 1999.

Stone, Dan. *Breeding Superman: Nietzsche, Race and Eugenics in Edwardian and Interwar Britain.* Liverpool: Liverpool University Press, 2002.

Stone, Deborah A. *The Disabled State.* Philadelphia: Temple University Press, 1984.

Stroman, Duane F. *The Awakening Minorities: The Physically Handicapped.* Washington, DC: University Press of America, 1982.

Stubblefield, Anna. "'Beyond the Pale': Tainted Whiteness, Cognitive Disability and Eugenic Sterilization." *Hypatia* 22, no. 2 (2007): 162–181.

———. "The Entanglement of Race and Cognitive Disability." *Metaphilosophy* 40 (2009): 531–551.

Suchman, Lucy A. *Plans and Situated Actions: The Problem of Human-Machine Communication.* Cambridge: Cambridge University Press, 1987.

Swain, John, and Sally French. "Towards an Affirmation Model." *Disability and Society* 15 (2000): 569–582.

Taylor, Charles. "The Politics of Recognition." In *Multiculturalism*, edited by Amy Gutman, 25–74. Princeton, NJ: Princeton University Press, 1994.

Taylor, Steven J., and Rachael Zubal-Ruggieri. "Academic Programs in Disability Studies." Paper presented at the Center on Human Policy, Law and Disability Studies. Syracuse University, July 2012.

tenBroek, Jacobus. "The Right to Live in the World: The Disabled in the Law of Torts." *California Law Review* 54 (1966): 841–919.

Thurman, S. K., ed. *Children of Handicapped Parents.* Orlando, FL: Academic Press, 1985.

Titchkosky, Tanya. *The Question of Access: Disability, Space, Meaning.* Toronto: University of Toronto Press, 2011.

Titchkosky, Tanya, and Rod Michalko. "Introduction." In *Rethinking Normalcy: A Disability Studies Reader*, edited by Tanya Titchkosky and Rod Michalko, 1–14. Toronto: Canadian Scholars/Women's Press, 2009.

Tomkins, Silvan S. *Affect, Imagery, Consciousness: The Complete Edition: Two Volumes.* New York: Springer, 2008.

Traustadottir, Ranneveig, and Kelly Johnson. *Deinstitutionalization and People with Intellectual Disabilities.* London: Jessica Kingsley, 2008.

Tremain, Shelley. "The Biopolitics of Bioethics and Disability." *Journal of Bioethical Inquiry* 5 (2008): 101–106.

———, ed. *Foucault and the Government of Disability.* Ann Arbor: University of Michigan Press, 2005.

———. "On the Government of Disability." *Social Theory and Practice* 27 (2001): 617–636.

Trent, James W. *Inventing the Feeble Mind: A History of Mental Retardation in the United States.* Berkeley: University of California Press, 1994.

Turner, Bryan S. "Contemporary Problems in the Theory of Citizenship." In *Citizenship and Social Theory*, edited by Bryan S. Turner, 1–18. London: Sage, 1993.

———. *Regulating Bodies: Essays in Medical Sociology.* London: Routledge, 1992.

The Union of the Physically Impaired against Segregation (UPIAS). *Fundamental Principles of Disability.* London: Disability Alliance, 1975.

Vade, Dylan, and Sondra Solovay. "No Apology: Shared Struggles in Fat and Transgender Law." In *The Fat Studies Reader*, edited by Esther Rothblum and Sondra Solovay, 167–175. New York: NYU Press, 2009.

Valente, Joseph. "Modernism and Cognitive Disability: A Genealogy." In *A Handbook of Modernist Studies*, edited by Jean-Michele Rabate, 379–398. Chichester, UK: Wiley, 2013.

Vance, Mary Lee. *Disabled Faculty and Staff in a Disabling Society: Multiple Identities in Higher Education.* Huntersville, NC: AHEAD, 2007.

Van Cleve, John V., and Barry A. Crouch. *A Place of Their Own: Creating the Deaf Community in America.* Washington, DC: Gallaudet University Press, 1989.

Verstraete, Pieter. "Toward a Disabled Past: Some Preliminary Thoughts about the History of Disability, Governmentality, and Experience." *Educational Philosophy and Theory* 39 (2007): 56–63.

Virilio, Paul. *Open Sky.* Translated by Julie Rose. London: Verso, 1997.

Vonnegut, Kurt. *Welcome to the Monkey House.* New York: Delacorte Press, 1968.

Vygotsky, L. *Mind in Society: The Development of Higher Psychological Processes.* Cambridge, MA: Harvard University Press, 1978.

Wade, Cheryl Marie. "Cripple Lullaby." In *The Disability Studies Reader*, edited by Lennard J. Davis, 408–409. 3rd ed. New York: Routledge, 2010.

Walker, Lisa. *Looking Like What You Are: Sexual Style, Race, and Lesbian Identity.* New York: NYU Press, 2001.

Warner, Michael. "Introduction: Fear of a Queer Planet." *Social Text* 29 (1991): 3–17.

Wasserman, David. "A Choice of Evils in Prenatal Testing." *Florida State University Law Review* 30 (2003): 295–314.

———. "Ethics of Human Enhancement and Its Relevance to Disability Rights. In *Encyclopedia of the Life Sciences.* Chichester, UK: Wiley, 2012. Accessed September 24, 2014. http://onlinelibrary.wiley.com/doi/10.1002/9780470015902.a0024135/full.

Wates, Michele, and Jade Rowen. *Bigger Than the Sky: Disabled Women on Parenting.* London: Woman's Press, 1999.

Weicht, Bernhard. "Embracing Dependency: Rethinking (In)dependence in the Discourse of Care." *Sociological Review* 58 (2010): 205–224.

Weiss, Gail. *Body Images: Embodiment as Intercorporeality.* London: Routledge, 1999.

Welfare Federation for Cleveland, Committee on Cripples. "Education and Occupations of Cripples: Juvenile and Adult." *Publications of the Red Cross Institute for Crippled and Disabled Men* 2 (1918).

Wendell, Susan. "Old Women Out of Control: Some Thoughts on Aging, Ethics, and Psychosomatic Medicine." In *Mother Time: Women, Aging, and Ethics*, edited by Margaret Urban Walker, 133–150. Lanham, MD: Rowman and Littlefield, 1999.

———. *The Rejected Body: Feminist Philosophical Reflections on Disability.* London: Routledge, 1996.

———. "Toward a Feminist Theory of Bioethics." *Hypatia* 4, no. 2 (1989): 104–124.

———. "Unhealthy Disabled: Treating Chronic Illnesses as Disabilities." *Hypatia* 16, no. 4 (2001): 17–33.

Wertsch, James V. *Voices of the Mind: A Sociocultural Approach to Mediated Action.* Cambridge, MA: Harvard University Press, 1991.

Weygand, Zina. *The Blind in French Society: From the Middle Ages to the Century of Louis Braille.* Translated by Emily-Jane Cohen. Stanford, CA: Stanford University Press, 2009.

Wheatley, Edward. "Blindness, Discipline, and Reward: Louis IX and the Foundation of the Hospice des Quinze Vingts." *Disability Studies Quarterly* 22, no. 4 (2002): 194–212.

Wilkerson, Abby. "Food and Disability Studies: Vulnerable Bodies, Eating or 'Not Eating.'" *Food, Culture and Society* 14 (2011): 17–28.

Williams, Raymond. *Keywords: A Vocabulary of Culture and Society.* Oxford: Oxford University Press, 1985.

Williams-Searle, John. "Cold Charity: Manhood, Brotherhood, and the Transformation of Disability, 1870–1900." In *The New Disability History: American Perspectives*, edited by Paul K. Longmore and Lauri Umansky, 157–186. New York: NYU Press, 2001.

Williamson, Bess. "The Right to Design: Disability and Access in the United States, 1945–1990." PhD diss., University of Delaware, 2011.

Wills, David. *Prosthesis.* Stanford, CA: Stanford University Press, 1995.

Wilson, Robert A., and Lucia Foglia. "Embodied Cognition." In *The Stanford Encyclopedia of Philosophy*, edited by Edward N. Zalta. Accessed September 17, 2014. http://plato.stanford.edu/entries/embodied-cognition/.

Winckelmann, Johann Joachim. "Painting and Sculpture of the Greeks." In *German Aesthetic and Literary Criticism: Winckelmann, Lessing, Hamann, Herder, Schiller, Goethe*, edited by H. B Nisbet, 29–54. Cambridge: Cambridge University Press, 1985.

Wolbring, Gregor. "Disabled People's Approach to Bioethics." *American Journal of Bioethics* 1 (2001): 1–2.

Wolf, Peter. "Sociocultural History of Epilepsy." In *Atlas of Epilepsies, Part 2*, edited by C. P. Panayiotopoulos, 35–43. London: Springer-Verlag, 2010.

Wolman, David. "The Truth about Autism: Scientists Reconsider What They *Think* They Know." *Wired Magazine* 16 (2008). Accessed October 10, 2014. http://archive.wired.com/medtech/health/magazine/16-03/ff_autism?currentPage=all.

Woodward, Kathleen. *Aging and Its Discontents: Freud and Other Fictions.* Bloomington: Indiana University Press, 1991.

———. "Performing Age, Performing Gender." *NWSA Journal* 18 (2006): 162–189.

World Health Organization. *Community-Based Rehabilitation Guidelines.* Geneva: World Health Organization Press, 2010.

———. *International Classification of Impairments, Disabilities, and Handicaps: A Manual of Classification Relating to the Consequences of Disease.* Geneva: World Health Organization Press, 1980.

World Health Organization and the World Bank. *World Report on Disability.* Geneva: World Health Organization Press, 2011.

Wright, David. *Deafness: An Autobiography.* London: Mandarin, 1993.

Wrigley, Owen. *The Politics of Deafness.* Washington, DC: Gallaudet University Press, 1996.

Wu, Cynthia. *Chang and Eng Reconnected: The Original Siamese Twins in American Culture.* Philadelphia: Temple University Press, 2012.

Wyatt, Sally, "Non-users Also Matter: The Construction of Non-users of the Internet." In *How Users Matter: The Co-construction of Users and Artifacts*, edited by Nelly Oudshoorn and Trevor Pinch, 67–80. Cambridge, MA: MIT Press, 2005.

Žižek, Slavoj. *The Sublime Object of Ideology.* New York: Verso, 1989.

Zola, Irving Kenneth. "The Independent Living Movement: Empowering People with Disabilities." *Australian Disability Review* 1, no. 3 (1988): 23–27.

———. *Missing Pieces.* Philadelphia: Temple University Press, 1982.

About the Contributors

Rachel Adams is Professor of English and American Studies at Columbia University. Her most recent book is *Raising Henry: A Memoir of Motherhood, Disability, and Discovery* (2013). She is also the author of *Continental Divides: Remapping the Cultures of North America* (2009) and *Sideshow U.S.A.: Freaks and the American Cultural Imagination* (2001).

Gary L. Albrecht is Extraordinary Guest Professor of Social Sciences, KU Leuven, Belgium, and Professor Emeritus of Public Health and of Disability and Human Development at the University of Illinois at Chicago. He is a Fellow of the Royal Belgium Academy of Sciences and a Fellow of the American Association for the Advancement of Science. His major books are *Cross National Rehabilitation Policies* (1981); *The Disability Business: Rehabilitation in America* (1992); *Handbook of Disability Studies* (with Katherine Seelman and Mike Bury; 2001) *Encyclopedia of Disability*, five volumes (2006); and, as general editor, *Sage Reference Series on Disability* (2013).

Jill C. Anderson is Professor of Law at the University of Connecticut. Her work has appeared in the *Yale Law Journal* and the *Harvard Law Review*.

Adrienne Asch (1946–2013) was the Edward and Robin Milstein Professor of Bioethics at Yeshiva University and Professor of Epidemiology and Population Health and Family and Social Medicine at Albert Einstein College of Medicine. She authored numerous articles and book chapters and coedited *Prenatal Testing and Disability Rights* (2000) and *The Double-Edged Helix: Social Implications of Genetics in a Diverse Society* (2002).

Douglas C. Baynton teaches History and American Sign Language at the University of Iowa. He is the author of *Forbidden Signs: American Culture and the Campaign against Sign Language* (1996) and coauthor, with Jack Gannon and Jean Bergey, of *Through Deaf Eyes: A Photographic History of an American Community* (2007).

James Berger is Senior Lecturer in American Studies and English at Yale University. He is author of *The Disarticulate: Language, Disability, and the Narratives of Modernity* (NYU Press, 2014); *After the End: Representations of Post-apocalypse* (1999); and *Prior* (2013), a book of poems. He is also editor of Helen Keller's memoir, *The Story of My Life: The Restored Edition* (2003).

Michael Bérubé is Edwin Erle Sparks Professor of Literature and Director of the Institute for the Arts and Humanities at Pennsylvania State University. He is the author of seven books to date, including *Public Access: Literary Theory and American Cultural Politics* (1994); *Life as We Know It: A Father, a Family, and an Exceptional Child* (1996); and *What's Liberal about the Liberal Arts? Classroom Politics and "Bias" in Higher Education* (2006). His most recent book, *The Left at War*, was published in 2009 by NYU Press. He is also the editor of *The Aesthetics of Cultural Studies* (2004) and, with Cary Nelson, of

Higher Education under Fire: Politics, Economics, and the Crisis of the Humanities (1995).

Harold Braswell is Assistant Professor of Health Care Ethics at Saint Louis University. His article "Can There Be a Disability Studies Theory of 'End-of-Life Autonomy'?" won the Irving K. Zola Award for Emerging Scholars in Disability Studies. He has published additional articles in the *American Journal of Bioethics Neuroscience*, the *Journal of Medical Humanities*, the *Hasting Center Report*, and *Social Science and Medicine*.

Jeffrey A. Brune is Associate Professor of History at Gallaudet University in Washington, DC. He is the coeditor, with Daniel J. Wilson, of *Blurring the Lines: Disability, Race, Gender and Passing in Modern America* (2013). He is the author of *Disability Stigma and American Political Culture* (forthcoming).

Susan Burch is Professor of American Studies and former Director of the Center for the Comparative Study of Race and Ethnicity at Middlebury College. She is the author of *Signs of Resistance: American Deaf Cultural History, 1900 to World War II* (NYU Press, 2002). She also coedited *Women and Deafness: Double Visions* (2006), with Brenda Jo Brueggemann; *Deaf and Disability Studies: Interdisciplinary Approaches*, with Alison Kafer (2010); and *Disability Histories*, with Michael Rembis (forthcoming). She and Hannah Joyner coauthored *Unspeakable: The Story of Junius Wilson* (2007). Burch served as editor in chief of the three-volume *Encyclopedia of American Disability History* (2009).

D. A. Caeton is completing a PhD in Cultural Studies at the University of California, Davis. He focuses on nineteenth-century American methods of educating blind people. In particular, he examines how

pedagogical practices and institutional arrangements were used to choreograph blind students' performances of nineteenth-century American gender roles.

Fiona Kumari Campbell is Associate Professor in Law at Griffith Law School, Griffith University, Australia, and Adjunct Professor in Disability Studies, Department of Disability Studies, Faculty of Medicine, University of Kelaniya, Ragama, Sri Lanka. Campbell is the author of *Contours of Ableism* (2009). Her work has appeared in *Rethinking Anti-Discriminatory and Anti-Oppressive Theories for Social Work Practice*, edited by C. Cocker and T. Hafford (2014); *Generation Next: Becoming Socially Enterprising*, edited by S. Chamberlain, K. Foxwell-Norton, and H. Anderson (2014); and *South Asia and Disability Studies: Redefining Boundaries and Extending Horizons,* edited by S. Rao and M. Kalyanpuram (2014).

Allison Carey is Professor of Sociology and Director of the Interdisciplinary Minor in Disability Studies at Shippensburg University. She is author of *On the Margins of Citizenship: Intellectual Disability and Civil Rights in 20th Century America* (2009). Carey is also coeditor of *Disability and Community* (2001) and *Disability Incarcerated: Disability and Imprisonment in the United States and Canada* (2014).

Licia Carlson is Associate Professor of Philosophy at Providence College. She is the author of *The Faces of Intellectual Disability: Philosophical Reflections* (2010) and coeditor of *Cognitive Disability and Its Challenge to Moral Philosophy* (2010).

Lisa Cartwright is Professor of Visual Arts and Science Studies at the University of California, San Diego, where she is also on the faculty of the Department of Communication and the Program in Critical Gender

Studies. Her most recent book is *Moral Spectatorship: Technologies of Voice and Affect in Postwar Representations of the Child* (2008). She is coauthor, with Marita Sturken, of *Practices of Looking: An Introduction to Visual Culture* (2008). She is also the author of *Screening the Body: Tracing Medicine's Visual Culture* (1995). With Paula Treichler and Constance Penley, she coedited the volume *The Visible Woman: Imaging Technologies, Gender and Science* (NYU Press, 1998).

Leonard Cassuto is Professor of English at Fordham University. He is the author or editor of seven books on American literature and culture. The most recent of these are *The Cambridge History of the American Novel* (2011), of which he was general editor, and *The Cambridge Companion to Baseball* (2011). Cassuto is the author of *Hard-Boiled Sentimentality: The Secret History of American Crime Stories* (2008).

Christina Cogdell is Associate Professor of Design and a Chancellor's Fellow at the University of California, Davis. She is the author of *Eugenic Design: Streamlining America in the 1930s* (2004) and is coeditor, with Susan Currell, of *Popular Eugenics: National Efficiency and American Mass Culture in the 1930s* (2006). Her work is included in *The Politics of Parametricism* (forthcoming); *Visual Culture and Evolution* (2012); *I Have Seen the Future: Norman Bel Geddes Designs America* (2012); and *Art, Sex, and Eugenics* (2008). She also has published articles in the journals *American Art, Boom: A Journal of California, Design and Culture, Volume, Design Issues*, and *American Quarterly*.

G. Thomas Couser retired in 2011 from Hofstra University, where he was Professor of English and founding Director of the Disability Studies Program. His books include *Recovering Bodies: Illness, Disability,*

and Life Writing (1997); *Vulnerable Subjects: Ethics and Life Writing* (2004); and *Signifying Bodies: Disability in Contemporary Life Writing* (2009). His most recent book is *Memoir: An Introduction* (2012).

Sayantani DasGupta is a faculty member in the Master's Program in Narrative Medicine at Columbia University and the Graduate Program in Health Advocacy at Sarah Lawrence College. She is also Cochair of the Columbia University Seminar in Narrative, Health and Social Justice. She is the coauthor of a book of Bengali folktales, the author of a medical memoir, and the coeditor of *Stories of Illness and Healing: Women Write Their Bodies* (2007) and the scholarly collection *Globalization and Transnational Surrogacy in India: Outsourcing Life* (2014).

Michael Davidson is Distinguished Professor of Literature at the University of California, San Diego. He is the author of *The San Francisco Renaissance: Poetics and Community at Mid-Century* (1989); *Ghostlier Demarcations: Modern Poetry and the Material Word* (1997); *Guys Like Us: Citing Masculinity in Cold War Poetics* (2003); and *Concerto for the Left Hand: Disability and the Defamiliar Body* (2008). His most recent critical book is *Outskirts of Form: Practicing Cultural Poetics* (2011). He is the editor of *The New Collected Poems of George Oppen* (2002). He is the author of six books of poetry, the most recent of which is *Bleed Through: New and Selected Poems* (2013). He is the coauthor, with Lyn Hejinian, Barrett Watten, and Ron Silliman, of *Leningrad* (1991).

Lennard J. Davis is Distinguished Professor of Arts and Sciences at the University of Illinois at Chicago in the Departments of Disability and Human Development, English, and Medical Education. He is the author of *Enforcing Normalcy: Disability, Deafness, and the Body* (1995); *Bending over Backwards: Disability, Dismodernism,* and Other Difficult Positions (NYU Press 2002); Obsession: A History (2009); and The End of Normal: Identity in a Biocultural Era (2014). He is the editor of the Disability Studies Reader, now in its fourth edition, as well as Shall I Say a Kiss: Courtship Letters of Deaf Couple, 1936–1938 (1999). He is currently working on a forthcoming book, Enabling Acts: The Americans with Disabilities Act and How the U.S.'s Largest Minority Got Its Rights.

Tim Dean is Professor of English at the University at Buffalo, State University of New York, where he is also director of the Center for the Study of Psychoanalysis and Culture. He is the author of several books, most recently Unlimited Intimacy: Reflections on the Subculture of Barebacking (2009), and coeditor of Porn Archives (2014).

Helen Deutsch is Professor of English at UCLA. She is the author of Resemblance and Disgrace: Alexander Pope and the Deformation of Culture (1996) and Loving Dr. Johnson (2005), as well as coeditor of "Defects": Engendering the Modern Body (2000) and Vital Matters: Eighteenth-Century Views of Conception, Life and Death (2012).

Elizabeth F. Emens is Isidor and Seville Sulzbacher Professor of Law at Columbia University. Her articles about disability law and theory include "Integrating Accommodation" (2008); "Intimate Discrimination: The State's Role in the Accidents of Sex and Love" (2009); and "Disabling Attitudes" (2012, reprinted in the Disability Studies Reader, 4th ed. 2013). She recently edited the volume Disability and Equality Law (2013) with Michael A. Stein.

Nirmala Erevelles is Professor of Social and Cultural Studies in Education at the University of Alabama.

She has published articles in the American Educational Research Journal, Educational Theory, Studies in Education and Philosophy, the Journal of Curriculum Studies, Teachers College Record, Disability and Society, Disability Studies Quarterly, and the Journal of Literary and Cultural Disability Studies, among others. She is the author of Disability and Difference in Global Contexts: Towards a Transformative Body Politic (2012).

D. Christopher Gabbard is Professor of English at the University of North Florida. His articles have appeared in PMLA, Studies in English Literature, Restoration, English Language Notes, and Eighteenth-Century Studies. His work has also appeared in The Madwoman and the Blindman: Jane Eyre, Discourse, Disability (2012).

Rebecca Garden is Associate Professor of Bioethics and Humanities at Upstate Medical University, where she is Director of the Health Care Ethics course and Executive Director of the Consortium for Culture and Medicine. She has published on illness, disability, narrative, and health care in journals such as New Literary History, the Journal of General Internal Medicine, Disability Studies Quarterly, and the Journal of Clinical Ethics.

Rosemarie Garland-Thomson is Professor of Women's Studies and English at Emory University, where her fields of study are disability studies, American literature and culture, feminist theory, and bioethics. She is the author of Staring: How We Look and several other books. Her current book project is Habitable Worlds: Disability, Technology, and Eugenics.

Kathryn Linn Geurts is Associate Professor of Anthropology at Hamline University. She is the author of Culture and the Senses: Bodily Ways of Knowing in an African Community (2003).

Sander L. Gilman is Distinguished Professor of the Liberal Arts and Sciences as well as Professor of Psychiatry at Emory University. A cultural and literary historian, he is the author or editor of more than eighty books, including *Obesity: The Biography* (2010); *Seeing the Insane* (1982); and the standard study *Jewish Self-Hatred* (1986). His most recent edited volume is *The Third Reich Sourcebook* (with Anson Rabinbach [2013]).

Faye Ginsburg is Founder and Codirector of the Council for the Study of Disability at New York University, where she is also David B. Kriser Professor of Anthropology and Director of the Center for Media, Culture and History. She is an award-winning author/editor of four books, all reflecting her long-standing interest in cultural activism. She is currently working with Rayna Rapp on research and writing on cultural innovation and cognitive difference.

Kim Q. Hall is Professor of Philosophy and Humanities Council Coordinator at Appalachian State University, where she is also a faculty affiliate of the Women's Studies and Sustainable Development Programs. She is editor of *Feminist Disability Studies* (2011) and coeditor, with Chris Cuomo, of *Whiteness: Feminist Philosophical Reflections* (1999). Currently, she is completing a book manuscript that advances a queer crip feminist perspective on identity and the body's materiality.

Rob Imrie is Professor of Sociology at Goldsmiths, University of London.

Eva Feder Kittay is Distinguished Professor of Philosophy and Senior Fellow, Center for Medical Humanities, Compassionate Care, and Bioethics at Stony Brook University, State University of New York. She has authored and edited several books, as well as written numerous articles, on feminist philosophy, care ethics, and disability theory. For 2014-2015, she has an NEH Fellowship and a Guggenheim Fellowship to complete her *Disabled Minds and Things That Matter: Cognitive Disability and (a Humbler) Philosophy*.

Georgina Kleege teaches creative writing and disability studies at the University of California, Berkeley. Her recent books include *Sight Unseen* (1999) and *Blind Rage: Letters to Helen Keller* (2006). She has lectured and served as consultant to art institutions around the world, including the Metropolitan Museum of Art in New York and the Tate Modern in London.

Petra Kuppers is Professor of English at the University of Michigan. Her books include *Disability and Contemporary Performance* (2003); *The Scar of Visibility: Medical Performances and Contemporary Art* (2007); *Disability Culture and Community Performance* (2011); and *Studying Disability Arts and Culture* (2014).

Kathleen LeBesco is Associate Dean for Academic Affairs at Marymount Manhattan College in New York City. She is author of *Revolting Bodies: The Struggle to Redefine Fat Identity*; coauthor of *Culinary Capital*; and coeditor, with Jana Evans Braziel, of *Bodies Out of Bounds: Fatness and Transgression*; with Peter Naccarato, of *Edible Ideologies: Representing Food and Meaning*; with Donna Jean Troka and Jean Bobby Noble, of *The Drag King Anthology*; and of several journal special issues.

Victoria Ann Lewis is Professor of Theatre Arts at the University of Redlands in southern California and was the founder and Director of the Other Voices Project at the Mark Taper Forum from 1982 to 2002. She is the editor of *Beyond Victims and Villains: Contemporary Plays by Disabled Playwrights* (2006). Her work has appeared in *The Politics of American Actor Training* (2011) and *A History of Collective Creation* (2013).

Heather Love is the R. Jean Brownlee Term Associate Professor of English at the University of Pennsylvania. She is the author of *Feeling Backward: Loss and the Politics of Queer History* (2009); the editor of a special issue of *GLQ* on Gayle Rubin ("Rethinking Sex"); and the coeditor, with Bill Albertini, Ben Lee, Mike Millner, Ken Parille, Alice Rutkowski, and Bryan Wagner, of a special issue of *New Literary History* ("Is There Life after Identity Politics?").

Janet Lyon is Associate Professor of English and Women's Studies and the Director of the Disability Studies minor at Pennsylvania State University. She is the author of *Manifestoes: Provocations of the Modern* (1999). She is currently working on books titled *The Imperfect Hostess: Sociability and the Modern* and *Idiot Child on a Fire Escape: Disability and Modernism*. Her articles have appeared in such journals as *Modernism/modernity, English Literary History, Differences*, and the *Yale Journal of Criticism*, and her chapters have appeared in many edited books. She is the coeditor of the *Journal of Modern Literature*.

Robert McRuer is Professor of English and Chair of the Department of English at the George Washington University. He is the author of *Crip Theory: Cultural Signs of Queerness and Disability* (NYU Press, 2006); *The Queer Renaissance: Contemporary American Literature and the Reinvention of Lesbian and Gay Identities* (NYU Press, 1997). With Anna Mollow, he coedited *Sex and Disability* (2012). He is completing a manuscript tentatively titled *Cripping Austerity*.

Mara Mills is an Assistant Professor of Media, Culture, and Communication at New York University. She is currently completing a book titled *On the Phone: Deafness and Communication Engineering*. Her second book project, *Print Disability and New Reading Formats*, examines the reformatting of print over the course of the past century by blind and other print disabled readers. Her work has appeared in *Social Text, differences*, the *IEEE Annals of the History of Computing*, and *The Oxford Handbook of Sound Studies*.

Susannah B. Mintz is Professor of English at Skidmore College. She is the author of *Threshold Poetics: Milton and Intersubjectivity* (2003); *Unruly Bodies: Life Writing by Women with Disabilities* (2007); *Hurt and Pain: Literature and the Suffering Body* (2014); and coeditor, with Merri Lisa Johnson, of *On the Literary Nonfiction of Nancy Mairs: A Critical Anthology* (2011). Her "memoirette," *Match Dot Comedy*, was released by Kindle Single in December 2013.

David Mitchell and Sharon Snyder are the authors of three books: *Narrative Prosthesis: Disability and the Dependencies of Discourse* (2000); *Cultural Locations of Disability* (2006); and the forthcoming *The Biopolitics of Disability: Neoliberalism, Ablenationalism, and Peripheral Embodiment*. They are also coeditors of *The Body and Physical Difference: Discourses of Disability* (1997) and have cowritten more than thirty-five refereed journal essays on various aspects of disability culture, art, and history. They are currently at work on a new edited collection tentatively titled *The Matter of Disability: Biopolitics, Materiality, Crip Affects*.

Denise M. Nepveux is an Assistant Professor of Occupational Therapy at Utica College. As a 2002 Fulbright Scholar, Dr. Nepveux documented life stories of women in Ghana's disability movement. She continues to collaborate with Ghanaian activists and anthropologist Kathryn Geurts to study changing leadership styles, organizing strategies, gender relations, and transnational funding relationships in this movement. She has published research on sexual health knowledge, identity, and access to sexuality among LGBT youth self-advocates in Ontario and engages in elder organizing efforts in Syracuse, New York.

Kim E. Nielsen is Professor of Disability Studies at the University of Toledo, where she also teaches courses in History and Women's and Gender Studies. She is the author of *A Disability History of the United States* (2012). Her other books include *Beyond the Miracle Worker: The Remarkable Life of Anne Sullivan Macy and Her Extraordinary Friendship with Helen Keller* (2009) and *The Radical Lives of Helen Keller* (NYU Press, 2004).

Katherine Ott is a curator and historian at the Smithsonian's National Museum of American History in the Division of Medicine and Science. Ott is the author or coeditor of three books: *Fevered Lives: Tuberculosis in American Culture since 1870* (1996); *Artificial Parts and Practical Lives: The Modern History of Prosthetics* (2002); and *Scrapbooks in American Life* (2006) and is completing a monograph on interpreting objects.

Carol Padden is Professor of Communication at the University of California, San Diego. With Tom Humphries, she is the coauthor of two books on culture and community of deaf people in the United States and two American Sign Language textbooks, *A Basic Course in ASL* and *Learning ASL*. Her work has been supported by the U.S. Department of Education, the Spencer Foundation, the National Science Foundation, and the National Institutes of Health. In 2010, she received a MacArthur Foundation Fellowship in recognition of creativity and innovation in her research.

Margaret Price is Associate Professor of Rhetoric/Composition at Spelman College. She is the author of *Mad at School: Rhetorics of Mental Disability and Academic Life* (2011) and has published articles, essays, stories, and poems in *Profession*; *College Composition and Communication*; the *Disability Studies Reader* (4th ed.); *Ms.* magazine; *Bitch: Feminist Response to Pop Culture*; the *Journal of Literary and Cultural Disability Studies*; *Wordgathering*; *Breath and Shadow*; and others. With Stephanie Kerschbaum, she is at work on a mixed-methods study of disability disclosure in academic contexts.

Michael Ralph is Assistant Professor in the Department of Social and Cultural Analysis at New York University. He is the author of *Forensics of Capital* (forthcoming). He has published in *Disability Studies Quarterly*, *Souls*, *Social Text*, *Public Culture*, *South Atlantic Quarterly*, the *Journal of the History of Sport*, and *Transforming Anthropology*. He is also the editor of *Transforming Anthropology*, the flagship journal of the Association of Black Anthropologists.

Rayna Rapp is Professor and Associate Chair of the Department of Anthropology at New York University. She is the author of the award-winning book *Testing Women, Testing the Fetus: The Social Impact of Amniocentesis in America* (1999) and coeditor, with Faye Ginsburg, of *Conceiving the New World Order* (1995), as well as numerous articles and reviews. Her current research with Faye Ginsberg focuses on cultural innovation in special education in New York City.

Benjamin Reiss is Professor of English at Emory University and Codirector of the Emory Disability Studies Initiative. He is the author of *The Showman and the Slave: Race, Death, and Memory in Barnum's America*

(2001) and *Theaters of Madness: Insane Asylums and Nineteenth-Century American Culture* (2008).

Julia Miele Rodas is Associate Professor of English at Bronx Community College/CUNY (City University of New York). With David Bolt and Elizabeth Donaldson, she is coeditor of *The Madwoman and the Blindman: Jane Eyre, Discourse, Disability* (2012) and of the Literary Disability Studies book series (Palgrave Macmillan). She is currently working on a book—*Autistic Disturbances*—that theorizes the role of autistic rhetoric and aesthetics in literature.

Sarah F. Rose is Assistant Professor of History at the University of Texas at Arlington, where she directs the minor in Disability Studies. Her work has appeared in *LABOR: Studies in the Working-Class History of the Americas* and in the *Journal of Policy History*. She is completing a book manuscript entitled *No Right to Be Idle: The Invention of Disability, 1850–1930*.

Maya Sabatello is a Postdoctoral Research Fellow at Columbia University's Center on Research of Ethical, Legal, and Social Implications of Psychiatric, Neurologic and Behavioral Genetics. A lawyer with a PhD in political science, she previously litigated cases of medical malpractice and has worked as a legal adviser to national and international nongovernmental organizations to promote health-related human rights. As a Permanent Representative for a nongovernmental organization at the United Nations, she participated in the drafting of the Convention on the Rights of Persons with Disabilities.

Ellen Samuels is Associate Professor of Gender and Women's Studies and English at the University of Wisconsin at Madison and the author of *Fantasies*

of Identification: Disability, Gender, Race* (NYU Press, 2014). Her work has appeared in numerous journals and anthologies, including *Signs: Journal of Women in Culture and Society, Feminist Disability Studies, GLQ, Amerasia*, and *MELUS*, and was awarded the Catherine Stimpson Prize for Outstanding Feminist Scholarship in 2011. She is currently working on a new book, *Double Meanings: Representing Conjoined Twins*.

Ralph James Savarese is Professor of English at Grinnell College and spent the 2012–2013 academic year as a neurohumanities fellow at Duke University's Institute for Brain Sciences. He is the author of some twenty-five peer-reviewed articles and essays about autism and the coeditor of three collections, including the first collection devoted to the concept of neurodiversity. He is also the author of the memoir *Reasonable People* (2007).

Ani B. Satz is Associate Professor of Law at Emory University, with faculty appointments at the Rollins School of Public Health, the Center for Ethics, and the Goizueta Business School. Her work has appeared in numerous books and peer-reviewed journals, including the *Michigan Law Review, Washington and Lee Law Review, Emory Law Journal, Yale Journal of Health Policy, Law and Ethics*, and *Washington Law Review*. Her book *Disability and Discrimination: Cases and Materials* is forthcoming. Satz served as Chair of the Association of American Law Schools' Section on Disability Law for 2009–2010 and is the current Chair of the Section on Law, Medicine and Health Care.

David Serlin is Associate Professor of Communication and Science Studies at the University of California, San Diego. He is the author or editor of several books, including *Replaceable You: Engineering the Body in*

Postwar America (2004); *Imagining Illness: Public Health and Visual Culture* (2010); and *Window Shopping with Helen Keller: Architecture and Disability in Modern Culture* (forthcoming).

Margrit Shildrick is Professor of Gender and Knowledge Production at Linköping University, Sweden, and Adjunct Professor of Critical Disability Studies at York University, Toronto. Her books include *Leaky Bodies and Boundaries: Feminism, (Bio)ethics and Postmodernism* (1997); *Embodying the Monster: Encounters with the Vulnerable Self* (2002); and *Dangerous Discourses of Disability, Sexuality and Subjectivity* (2009). Her work has appeared in several journals and edited collections, including the *Routledge Handbook of Disability Studies* (2012).

Martha Stoddard Holmes is Professor of Literature and Writing Studies at California State University, San Marcos. She is the author of *Fictions of Affliction: Physical Disability in Victorian Culture* (2004) and coeditor of *The Teacher's Body: Embodiment, Authority, and Identity in the Academy* (2003) and has published extensively on the cultural history of the body from the Victorian era to the present, including Victorian representations of disability and the public culture of cancer. She is currently working on a graphic narrative (comic) about ovarian cancer. Stoddard Holmes is Associate Editor of *Literature and Medicine*, the *Journal of Bioethical Inquiry*, the *Journal of Medical Humanities*, and the *Journal of Literary and Cultural Disability Studies*.

Tanya Titchkosky is a Professor in the Department of Humanities, Social Science and Social Justice Education in the Ontario Institute for Studies in Education at the University of Toronto. She is author of *The Question of Access: Disability, Space, Meaning* (2011); *Reading and Writing Disability Differently: The Textured Life of Embodiment* (2007); and *Disability, Self and Society* (2003); and coeditor, with Rod Michalko, of *Rethinking Normalcy: A Disability Studies Reader* (2009).

David Wasserman works at the Center for Bioethics at Yeshiva University and is a Visiting Scholar in the Department of Bioethics of the National Institutes of Health. He is the author or editor of five books and is completing a volume on debating procreation with David Benatar.

Abby Wilkerson is the author of *Diagnosis: Difference: The Moral Authority of Medicine* (1995) and *The Thin Contract: Social Justice and the Political Rhetoric of Obesity* (forthcoming). She coedited a special issue of *GLQ: A Journal of Lesbian and Gay Studies*, "Desiring Disability: Queer Theory Meets Disability Studies" (2003) with Robert McRuer. She has also published a number of articles in journals and anthologies and teaches in the University Writing Program at George Washington University.

Bess Williamson is a historian of American design and material culture. She is particularly interested in social and political concerns in design, including environmental, labor, justice, and rights issues as they shape and are shaped by spaces and things. Her current book project traces the history of design responses to disability rights from 1945 to recent times. She teaches design history at the School of the Art Institute of Chicago.

Kathleen Woodward, Lockwood Professor in the Humanities and Professor of English at the University of Washington, is director of the Simpson Center for the Humanities. She is the author of *Statistical Panic:*

Cultural Politics and Poetics of the Emotions (2009); *Aging and Its Discontents: Freud and Other Fictions* (1991); and *At Last, the Real Distinguished Thing: The Late Poems of Eliot, Pound, Stevens, and Williams* (1980). She is the editor of *Figuring Age: Women—Bodies—Generations* (1999) and *The Myths of Information: Technology and Postindustrial Culture* (1980).